The Civilization of the American Indian Series

THE TOLTEC HERITAGE

The Toltec Heritage

From the Fall of Tula to the Rise of Tenochtitlán

by Nigel Davies

University of Oklahoma Press: Norman

By Nigel Davies

The Aztecs, A History (London, 1973)
The Toltecs until the Fall of Tula (Norman, 1977)
The Toltec Heritage (Norman, 1980)

Library of Congress Cataloging in Publication Data

Davies, Nigel, 1920–
   The Toltec heritage.

   (The Civilization of the American Indian series; v. 153)
   Bibliography: p. 380
   Includes index.
   1. Toltecs.   2. Aztecs.   3. Chichimecs.   4. Indians of Mexico—History.   I. Title.   II. Series: Civilization of the American Indian series; v. 153.
F1219.D2782   972   78-21384

Contents

Illustrations

Maps

Preface

This work seeks to bridge the gap between the story of the Toltecs until the fall of Tula and the rise of Tenochtitlán, the theme of *Los Mexicas: Primeros Pasos hacia el Imperio,* which I wrote a few years ago. Edmundo O'Gorman, renowned Mexican historian, said to me on more than one occasion that *Los Mexicas: Primeros Pasos* was a sad book because it showed how little is really known and how many questions may remain forever without an answer.

Alas, certain aspects of the intervening period between the collapse of Tollan and the rise of Tenochtitlán—such as the true role of the Chichimecs—are wrapped in even greater obscurity, though I have done my best to find my way through the maze of rather garbled data. The book contains a few pieces of detailed research, such as an effort to clarify the chronology of the Culhua rulers, but I have not tried to answer every question; for instance, while I have written at some length on Chalco, no attempt was made to sort out its medley of tecpans and tlatoanis, which require a separate study. I hope the reader will bear with me if I dwell unduly on the vexing question of chronology, for without chronology, there can be no history.

This work has an additional aim; to elaborate my views on Mesoamerican motivations as a part of human history rather than as an isolated phenomenon. Sufficient information is now forthcoming, based on the work of modern scholars, to justify the effort, even if our knowledge is still exiguous by comparison with the data on, say, Rome, or even Mesopotamia. But I believe that Mesoamerican history and Mesoamerican religion can only be dimly comprehended if placed in a world context.

The more I study the written documents, the greater my conviction that not all of their precious data can be taken too literally. Like the archaeological evidence, they require close interpretation, and without this, no one can hope to reconcile the two. Moreover, Mesoamerican history is so hard to unravel that further inquiry perforce leads to altered conclusions. If my present contribution were first and foremost an exercise in consistency, it would not be worth making.

Perhaps this book, together with the previous one on the Toltecs of Tollan and a future volume on the achievement of Tenochtitlán as the resurgent Tollan will shed a little extra light on the tangled history of pre-Conquest Mexico.

In some ways I view my writings on these topics rather as a series of lectures, that for many reasons will never be delivered orally. I hope that they will nonetheless be of use to future students; and just as I have expressed my particular views, I hope that others may be encouraged to do the same and to offer alternatives to my appraisal, which is more tentative than final.

In these endeavors, I have always valued the moral support of Don Wigberto Jiménez Moreno, and in particular his tolerance in face of differences in our points of view. Once more I am indebted to Thelma Sullivan for her help over problems of Nahuatl, as well as to Antoinette Nelken, Jaqueline de Durand Forest, and Peter Schmidt, for having read parts of the manuscript.

Nigel Davies

Mexico City

THE TOLTEC HERITAGE

MAP 1

TERRITORY ATTRIBUTED TO XOLOTL BY ALVA IXTLILXÓCHITL

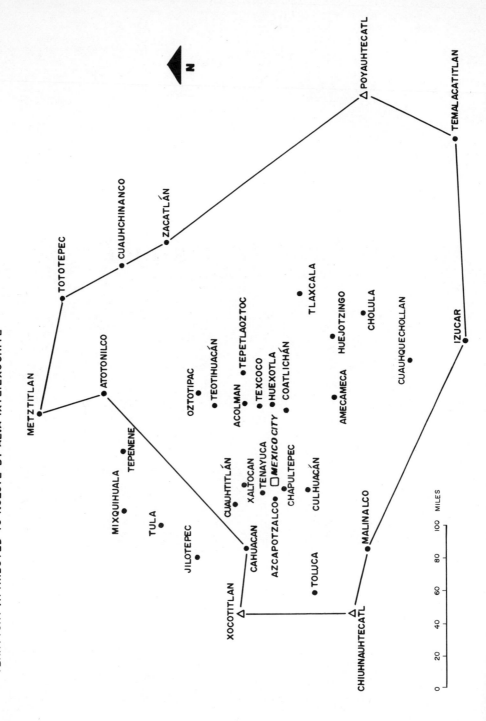

I. The Claim to Be a Toltec

The fall of Tula was both an end and a beginning. The phoenix that rises triumphant from the flames is a recurrent theme in human history. And just as Aeneas, after endless tribulations, founded a new and mightier Troy, so the Toltec diaspora led to the creation of other realms and to the ultimate triumph of Tenochtitlán, the resurgent Tollan.

The Florentine Codex relates the legend of the doom of Tollan Xicocotitlan, after Topiltzin Quetzalcoatl lost his nerve, beguiled by the agents of a malign deity, abandoned Tollan, and went to meet his destiny in Tlillan Tlapallan, the Land of the Red and the Black, or the Rising Sun, whence he originally hailed. "Thereupon he (Topiltzin) looked toward Tula, and then wept; as one sobbing he wept . . . And when he had done these things, then he went to reach the seacoast. Then he fashioned a raft of serpents. When he had arranged the raft, there he placed himself, as if it were his boat. Then he set off across the sea. No one knows how he came to arrive there at Tlapallan."[1] The source states that many of the people of Tollan followed in his wake.

The official version tells of a collapse so sudden as to match the fate of Jericho at the hands of Joshua. Succeeding generations of Calmecac students were nurtured on this tale; those last inhabitants of the great Tollan, later adopted by the Mexicas as their own fore-bears, were already enshrined in painted codices and oral recitals as beings cast in a heroic mold.

As I insisted in my earlier volume on the Toltecs, the reality was rather different. Tollan, like Rome, did not fall in a day. The Aztecs and the Incas suffered a dramatic eclipse, almost without parallel in human annals. However, as every historian knows, em-pires and kingdoms bear within them the seeds of their own destruc-tion that germinate and mature with the passage of time. Few civilizations are born "suddenly," or collapse overnight. Tollan, however, may have declined fairly swiftly, since its known lifespan as a great power embraced less than three centuries. Its whole his-tory was therefore compressed into a time interval hardly longer than Byzantium's final period of decadence, beginning with the Fourth Crusade in 1215, when the city was reduced to a shadow of its former self, and ending with the Turkish conquest in 1453.

The Gods Departed

In my first volume, I argued that, notwithstanding any implica-tions to the contrary in the *Historia Tolteca-Chichimeca,* the people who left Tollan for Cholula departed in about A.D. 1122, or over fifty years before the departure of Topiltzin Quetzalcoatl for Tlillan Tlapallan. This was more a break-away movement of dissidents than a migration of refugees from a tottering Tollan; mere fugitives could hardly have conquered Cholula and its hinterland, against the united resistance of its inhabitants.[2]

As a result of tentative and rather complex calculations, I con-cluded that Topiltzin had departed in approximately 1175, headed more probably for the Valley of Mexico than for the Maya land, whose communications with Tollan were by then likely to have been severed; Huemac, his rival, followed quickly in his wake, and in 1178 left Tollan for Chapultepec, where he perished.[3] In repeating this version of events as a basis for what follows, I am not seeking to breathe new life into a controversy in which my respected master and colleague, Professor Wigberto Jiménez Moreno, takes an opposite view. He sometimes refers to me in this context as the Devil's Advocate; in a vain attempt to range myself on the side of the angels,

I have however always accepted the parallel premise that a Topiltzin Quetzalcoatl might have been present at both the foundation and the fall of Tollan.

According to my interpretation, the decline of Tollan covered a period of some two generations—a modest interval compared with the long process of decay endured by other cultures. I refrained where possible from applying to Tollan the term "empire"; as Kirchhoff often pointed out to me, the German term *Reich* is more apt. History, in Mesoamerica as elsewhere, seldom repeats itself; nonetheless, in the archaeological and written record, the case of Tollan does run curiously parallel to that of Teotihuacán. In the case of both cities, legend describes a dramatic dispersal; several accounts survive of the inhabitants' departure from Tollan and of their arrival at their new homes, such as the Nonoalca settlement of the Tehuacán-Cozcatlán area. Only one report, however, ostensibly relates the exodus from Teotihuacán of the different peoples, including the Nahuas who went to the northwest and the Huaxtecs, their future adversaries, who dispersed in the opposite direction.

In both instances, the sources' story finds parallels in the archae-ological record. The concluding phases of Teotihuacán as a great metropolis present many problems: Bernal and others have for some time believed that an initial catastrophe occurred at the close of Teoti-huacán III, and cite as evidence the large-scale burning and destruc-tion in the Street of the Dead. René Millon only partially accepts such conclusions, and insists that Teotihuacán IV was a period of marked creativity. However, Millon agrees that Teotihuacán's popu-lation was already reduced in the Period IV; therefore, even in the most optimistic view of this phase, a process of decline had surely set in, and the city was already on the wane.

In the case of Tollan, Acosta's excavations in the main cere-monial center tell a comparable tale. He describes the city (or more precisely the sector that he explored) as razed by a great fire and then subjected to intense pillage; evidence of arson is provided by the Palacio Quemado, where adobe blocks, turned to brick by the heat of the conflagration, can still be seen. But this initial disaster did not mark the end of the ceremonial center any more than in the case of Teotihuacán: Acosta sees evidence of subsequent reoccupation by users of Aztec II pottery, located in considerable quantity *above* the

5

Tula-Mazapan level, that belonged to the apogee of Tollan. Acosta writes of new occupants who took possession and confined themselves to rudimentary repairs and reconstruction.

The University of Missouri Mission admittedly found few traces of Aztec II in certain residential zones and no evidence of outright destruction, but their findings scarcely invalidate Acosta's original thesis, based on work in the Ceremonial Center; his investigations reveal a parallel situation to that prevailing in Teotihuacán, where, in spite of apparent damage in the center of the city, life in the surrounding suburbs continued much as before. In Tollan the picture is less clear, and the period immediately following the end of Tula-Mazapan merits more detailed study.

No doubt material causes—more often related to external attack than to internal shortcomings—go far to explain the fall of Teotihuacán, Tollan, and other cities. Nonetheless, Mesoamerican communities seem to have lacked a certain fundamental stability common to those of the Old World, such as Ur or even Athens, that were so much more long-lived. In Mesoamerica, a tendency prevailed for the center of gravity to shift over the centuries. This may be in part attributed to a collapse of morale, unaccompanied by powers of recuperation and typified by the cry of despair heard in Tenochtitlán at the time of the Spanish Conquest: "The gods have departed." An aura of romance surrounds the tale of Topiltzin Quetzalcoatl and his tragic flight from Tollan that constitutes an earlier case of the gods departing; Sahagún tells us that when the wise men, the Tlamatinime, abandoned Teotihuacán, they also took the gods away with them.[4] Possibly, as Millon has suggested, the priests themselves burned the central monuments of Teotihuacán, so complete was their destruction. In such instances, if "the gods had departed," their places of worship became an empty shell, and served no further purpose.

The Diaspora

Of the earlier migration to Cholula, more will be said in a later chapter concerning the history of the Puebla-Tlaxcala Valley. As related by the *Historia Tolteca-Chichimeca,* the Nonoalcas also departed, led by Xelhua and other chiefs, and eventually reached the

Cozcatlán-Teotitlan-Tehuacan area, after settling Huaquechula, Izucar, and other places on their route. The *Anales de Tlatelolco* also relate that the Nonoalca called Timal conquered Cuauhnahuac.[5] The Nonoalca occupation of the Teotitlán region may have been only one of several Nahuatl-speaking migrations to that area: the *Relación de Papaloticpac* tells of a Cuicateca tradition to the effect that the first inhabitants of that place came from Amecameca.

In addition to the early move to Cholula and to the Nonoalca exodus, the Toltecs dispersed in many other directions. Ixtlilxóchitl mentions in this connection Xiuhcoac (situated towards the Huaxteca), Guatemala, Tehuantepec, Tototepec (on the coast of present-day Oaxaca), Tecolutla (on the Gulf Coast), and Campeche. Torquemada writes of how Quetzalcoatl sent his people to Oaxaca and all the Mixteca Baja: the *Anales de Cuauhtitlán* tell of Toltecs who went to Coixtlahuaca. Other sources also mention the Gulf Coast: for instance, the *Histoyre du Méchique* says that Quetzalcoatl himself went to Zempoala. Such reports reinforce the tentative suggestion that some kind of Toltec colony had existed on that coast, which could later have become a receiving area for Toltec fugitives, though archaeological confirmation is scanty.

But apart from those affecting the Tehuacán region, Cholula, and the Valley of Mexico, accounts of Toltec migrations should be treated with caution. Some may have been written into the record purely to reinforce claims to Toltec descent, since other peoples were ill disposed to concede to the Mexicas a monopoly in that field. Other reports perhaps derived from the presence in a given area of Nahuatl speakers, who were really the product of an earlier Pipil influx. The task of placing in any chronological context the succeeding layers of Pipil migrants is baffling and must depend upon linguistic studies, in places where the original language survives in fragmentary form.

Notwithstanding the presence of Tula-Mazapan remains in Tototepec, the coast of Oaxaca remains a doubtful receiving center for more than a handful of Toltec refugees. Swadesh pointed out that in the Nahuatl-speaking enclave of Pochutla, about 70 per cent of the words coincide with those of the more standard Nahuatl of Central Mexico; in terms of glottochronology, this percentage implies a period of separation of the people of Pochutla from the

Nahuatl mainstream of as much as fourteen centuries.[6] The reported presence of "Toltecs" in certain other areas might arise not from the use of Nahuatl but simply from a certain level of artistic refinement, since by the time of the Conquest the term "Toltec" possessed an alternative meaning, applicable to a skilled artisan rather than to a previous inhabitant of Tollan. For the latter-day Aztecs, the Toltecs were conceived as the possessors of fine jewels and the builders of beautiful houses, and the term could thus be used for the inhabitants of the Mixteca, and, in addition, to the Cholulans.

The question still therefore remains: Assuming that the population really fled from Tollan just as people nowadays might flee from a disaster area, where did they go? Ixtlilxóchitl begs the question by stating that few escaped and implies that the remainder perished.[7] This author may be perfectly right in saying that many inhabitants stayed where they were, even if they did not all succumb. Tollan was at all events repopulated, since it became a relatively important center in Late Postclassic times.[8] The Aztecs attached considerable importance to the city, and Moctezuma II was even married to a Toltec princess, later known as Doña María Miahuaxochtzin, who was the mother of Don Pedro Moctezuma, the first Conde de Moctezuma, a title that still exists today. The Tlatoani Axayácatl had also married the daughter of a previous ruler of Tula; their son, Ixtlilcuechahuac, later reigned in Tula, and it was his daughter, Miahuaxochtzin, who then married Moctezuma II. Moreover, apart from the city itself, statistics of early colonial times demonstrate that the surrounding Teotlalpan was more thickly populated in Aztec times than ever before.[9]

Notwithstanding the significance of Tula in Aztec times, our notions remain vague concerning what happened in Tollan in the key period between the end of Tula-Mazapan and the Mexica conquest two centuries later. Although Acosta found Aztec II in and around the Acropolis immediately above the Mazapan strata, information is sparse about how far the makers of this or other wares remained in occupation of the residential areas of the city in the century following the end of the great Tollan and before the Aztec conquest, that presumably caused the introduction of Aztec III, found in part but not all of the previous urban zone. Whether or not a great exodus occurred, the city's population seems to have undergone changes: from having been a predominantly Nahuatl-speaking center, Tollan by the Late Postclassic was inhabited mainly by Otomi-speakers, who still live there today. To what extent these Otomis replaced Nahuatl-speakers who had fled the city, or whether they were already there before the collapse, is still unknown.

However, even on the uncertain premise that most of the inhabitants left Tollan, the supply of fugitive Toltecs simply would not have sufficed to populate far-flung provinces throughout the length and breadth of Mesoamerica. Estimates of the population of Tollan at its apogee range from 25,000 to 60,000; even including the people of nearby centers, the total could scarcely have exceeded 100,000. Undoubtedly some Toltecs went to Cholula, while others went to Tehuacán; certain elements, including perhaps Topiltzin himself, went to join their Culhua kinsmen in the central Valley of Mexico, where numerous reports tell of Toltec settlements, not all deriving from earlier migrations. Mini-bands of exiles conceivably reached Oaxaca, though it is now considered unlikely that Tollan had been in direct contact with the principalities of that region. Caso thought that the glyph of the "Place of Rushes" in certain Mixtec codices might represent Tollan Xicocotitlan; however Elizabeth Smith has since demonstrated conclusively that these rush glyphs relate to local centers. Successive groups of Nahuatl-speakers had probably moved to the Gulf Coast because food supplies were more assured in that area; accounts survive of how even the all-conquering Aztecs were reduced to selling their children as slaves in Totonicapan during the 1450–54 famine. The cultural impact of Teotihuacán in the coastal region was strong, and Toltec influences are also visible in such places as Castillo de Teayo. Even if a move to the coast had occurred as part of the Toltec diaspora, neither archaeologists nor linguists could easily distinguish such a movement from other migrations from the Altiplano to the Gulf of Mexico.

The eagerness to assume the mantle of Tollan was not confined to the Mexicas, and peoples of remoter regions were just as ready to claim descent from a city-state endowed by legend with a vast empire and posthumously famed as a great center of art and learning. The tendency for rulers to derive authority from some ancient site, presently bereft of temporal power, is not confined to Postclassic Mesoamerica; both Charlemagne and Napoleon were crowned in

Rome and the emperors of far-off Ethiopia continued to proclaim themselves the Lion of Judah.

The Power Vacuum

Up to this point, I have briefly reviewed the immediate aftermath of the Toltec Empire. This volume, however, is mainly concerned with events in the Valley of Mexico in the longer period that followed, which runs from approximately A.D. 1200 to 1400— embracing the two centuries that divide the fall of Tollan from the rise of Tenochtitlán. By 1400, the Mexicas were already beginning to be a power in the land, making their own conquests, although campaigning under the Tepanec aegis; the defeat of Xaltocan by the Mexica-Tepanec forces in 1395 provides the first recorded instance when the Mexicas themselves acquired tributary lands from a conquered people. About this time the Tlatoani Huitzilihuitl was already waging war in Morelos, and as a result of his victories, the Mexica nobles for the first time discarded their rougher clothing and donned cotton garments.

During the first three decades of the fifteenth century, the Mexica tail began to wag the Tepanec dog, and in 1428 the process reached its climax and the takeover of the Tepanec empire was completed. I have described these events in *Los Mexicas: Primeros Pasos hacia el Imperio;* in this volume the general trends rather than detailed events of this period will be discussed.

A detailed account of the rise of the Mexica-Tepanec empire equally falls outside the scope of this book, which concerns those intermediate centuries, when a power vacuum existed in the Valley of Mexico. This era is usually called the "Period of Independent Principalities." The appellation is convenient, but may also mislead, for in ancient Mesoamerica the sharing of power by many independent city-states was (as in Ancient Greece) not a special but a normal situation. We do not know how many separate principalities existed at the time of Teotihuacán's cultural ascendancy; power in the Maya area tended to be fragmented, notwithstanding attempts by the Itzás and others to conquer mini-empires. Even in Central Mexico, political unification under a dominant power was the exception rather than the rule; the Toltec achievement in that respect was at best partial, and only the last century before the Conquest witnessed the the certain existence of an ecumenical empire, ruled by the Triple Alliance. And even this empire had to tolerate within its boundaries the presence of independent *señoríos!*

Nonetheless, the thirteenth and fourteenth centuries are an era notable for the proliferation of small centers of power, each seeking to impose tribute upon its neighbors or to free itself from the obligation to pay tribute. In attempting to present a coherent picture of a period whose jumbled history resembles a patchwork quilt, I seek to discern trends rather than to explain in detail the tangled tale of every principality. Enough data have survived on several city-states to merit a separate study of each; for instance the dynasties of Culhuacán, the early history of Texcoco, to say nothing of Chalco and its thirteen tecpans, offer ample material for future ethnohistorians. In the case of Chalco, I shall limit myself to its role in the general history of the Valley of Mexico—that tends to be underrated—and to the over-all significance of its epic struggle against the Mexica-Tepanecas; I shall not offer a refurbished version of my study of this war, to be found in my work on the early Mexicas. Equally, I shall not repeat my account of the rise of the Mexica monarchy and of the feats of the early rulers although certain problems concerning the rise of the Mexicas will receive renewed comment in the light of recent work by other investigators.

Problems of Chronology

The limited fraction of the Mesoamerican past treated by the written records presents endless problems of chronology, but my task in this volume is eased by my previous studies of chronology, that include a detailed scheme, beginning with the birth of Tezozomoc of Azcapotzalco, probably in 1340, together with a much more tentative list of dates, that run from the death of Topiltzin Quetzalcoatl in 1175 to the arrival of the Mexicas in Chapultepec in 1319.[10] The task remains of completing the circle, by filling in the short gap between the two periods; the principal surviving dates for these early decades of the fourteenth century relate to the rulers of Culhuacán; they present many problems to be discussed in Appendix A.

I feel reasonably confident of my chronology from mid-fourteenth century onwards that hinges upon the dates of the early Mexica rulers; for the Toltec and immediate post-Toltec period, I could only attempt to provide a kind of fixed framework for a period whose chronology may never be clarified in any detail. Dates from the founding of Tenochtitlán onwards can be interpreted more clearly, although it often surprises one that some historians and anthropologists are slow to accept the arguments of Caso, Kirchhoff, and Jiménez Moreno, who all insisted that those dates in the written sources only make sense if taken as belonging to a series of different year-counts. Even such a distinguished investigator as H. Nicholson is still to be counted among the doubters, though he pays me the compliment of saying that when I state the case for the use of different year-counts, my reasoning is backed by copious data.[11]

Personally, I consider that the various chronological studies prove this particular point beyond reasonable doubt. To take one simple example: we possess eight different native dates for the accession to the Tenochca throne of Acamapichtli, and eleven for his death or for the accession of his successor, Huitzilihuitl. By accepting that these belong to different native calendars and by setting out these proposed year-counts or calendars in tabular form, side by side, a coherent picture demonstrably emerges; dates that are ostensibly different can be related to the same Christian calendar year, that has a different equivalent in the various native year-counts.[12] The system used for correlating Christian and native years for Acamapichtli's accession survives the most crucial test, since it makes equal sense in interpreting the many dates both for his death, for the death of his successor, and for other key events, such as the beginning of the Tepanec war against Texcoco or the Mexica assault on Cuauhtinchan. In such calculations, discrepancies amounting to two or three years are permissible: for a variety of reasons, the native dates given by different sources seldom coincide *exactly,* and it is not even possible to say for certain whether Moctezuma II ascended his throne in 1501, 1502, or 1503. I hope one day to make a new study, exclusively devoted to calendric problems, in order to elucidate some of those finer points.

If the use of different year-counts is not accepted, there is no way of accounting for the manifold discrepancies between dates given by the historical documents—including the occurrence within a single source of several distinct dates for the same event; for instance, Chimalpain gives three different dates for the accession of Acamapichtli. Alternative explanations involve the assumption that either native chroniclers made glaring errors in copying the original material at their disposal or that these documents were themselves totally unreliable in matters of chronology. But if the chroniclers are to be regarded as so inept that they bungled the simple task of copying figures, then their general reliability is thereby reduced to zero, and their whole work might as well be consigned to the rubbish heap!

A Cautious Approach

Nevertheless, while I cannot believe that the early writers were so muddle-headed, investigators do now tend to approach the information they provide with increasing caution. The present volume depends almost entirely on the written sources, since relevant archaeological data for the Valley of Mexico and the surrounding region are limited. Ancient Tollan was not obliterated by Tula de Allende, but in the case of Texcoco, not to speak of Tenochtitlán, little has survived the ravages of time and the vestiges of past glories lie buried beneath the modern cities. Studies of pottery provide certain pointers, but are seldom decisive in making historical reconstructions. Moreover, in the fourteenth-century struggle for power within the Valley of Mexico—so confined in space, but so large in its significance—the protagonists often used the same type of pottery and even built the same kind of pyramids (viz., Tlatelolco II, that is almost a replica of Tenayuca II).

Certain investigators continue to spurn the written sources and show scant respect for evidence not directly produced by the dirt archaeologist. But as Eric Thompson aptly put it: "An ounce of documents is worth more than a peck of artifacts."[13] In theory at least, where written sources exist, they offer a more detailed and animated picture than one that is based on pure archaeology. But the Mesoamerican archaeologist can unearth no counterpart to the voluminous inscriptions that make of the Egyptian and Mesopotamian past such a living reality. By comparison, the slabs and stones of Mesoamerica convey a notion of religious beliefs and modes of living; however, for lack of intelligible texts, history—with certain exceptions—remains anonymous until the period preceding the Spanish Conquest. And some of what we know, or think we know, about the earlier civilizations depends upon deduction based on Spanish reports of the period of contact.

The dangers have often been stressed of extrapolating sixteenth-century information and using it to interpret the situation in the sixth century. The problem is self-evident; part at least of our picture of the Teotihuacán civilization is a subconscious, if not conscious, reflection of our knowledge of the Aztecs and their contemporaries. For instance, we might not even recognize Tlaloc as a rain god, judging purely from frescoes of a deity from whose hands fall drops of blood as well as water. The perils of historical deduction are even greater, and the ready assumption that, because Tenochtitlán made vast military conquests, Teotihuacán must ipso facto have done the same, is at best uncertain.

In dealing with the earlier periods, for which he is mainly dependent on the findings of archaeology, the investigator may expect that his information was free from current prejudice and that he is dealing with unvarnished reports. But in approaching the final era, when we depend not on archaeology but on sixteenth- and seventeenth-century writers, we encounter a disconcerting degree of inbuilt bias and have to face the fact that Mesoamerican sources are seldom unprejudiced in their accounts.

In this respect, some offend more than others; however, as a general rule, the documents offer the official historical version of one city-state, laying particular stress upon the claims to legitimacy of its rulers and on their success in conquering their neighbors against adverse odds. Even the *Anales de Cuauhtitlán,* that at first sight may appear to be tolerably impartial, suffers from the obligation to provide an overextended pedigree for the Cuauhtitlán dynasty; not only are the reigns attributed to the early rulers of that city unrealistically long, but in several cases their dates are made to coincide to a quite uncanny degree with contemporary monarchs who supposedly reigned in Tollan, but who were probably from Culhuacán. Therefore, if these early Cuauhtitlán rulers existed at all, as more than a mere reflection of contemporary Culhua princes, then their reigns began much later than the source implies.[14]

14

We are at least fortunate, however, to possess for Mesoamerica—unlike Peru—two distinct groups of sources, the Mexica and the Texcocan. Therefore a process of cross-checking becomes possible, though discrepancies between the different versions are often baffling. For instance, one set of reports maintains that the Mexicas defeated the Texcocans in battle after a squabble that arose following the creation of the Triple Alliance, while another emanating from Texcoco, insists that the Texcocans were victorious in the same war. Faced with such problems, ethnohistorians tend at times to be driven into two camps; the majority may retain a reasonable degree of impartiality, but some writers become the modern champions of a given cause, and will even attribute the whole Aztec achievement to the genius of Texcoco, called in this context "the Athens of America," on the basis of Ixtlilxóchitl's description of its libraries and palaces; going to the opposite extreme, others will treat that city as little more than a willing helpmate of Tenochtitlán on the road to power.

Sahagún's voluminous data are ostensibly unprejudiced, since he merely records what his informants related. But his contribution to history is a limited part of his whole work; and by what criteria can we assess the reliability of his informants, who were themselves citizens of a specific city-state and nurtured in a specific tradition and thereby disinclined to take an unbiased view of Mesoamerican history?

Another main pitfall confronting students of the Mesoamerican past is now fairly universally recognized: the investigator is presented with a picture of events mainly provided by Spaniards, or by Hispanized Indians, such as Ixtlilxóchitl, who were educated in the European tradition. The most cursory study of the works of Tezozomoc and Durán, supposedly derived from a "Crónica X," reveals that Spaniards such as Durán and Hispanicized Indians like Tezozomoc would draw almost identical conclusions from an original native source.

This shortcoming affects the study of Mesoamerican religion so essential for an understanding of its history. Though convinced that all native religious practices were the work of the devil, the friars listened attentively to descriptions of those former beliefs but often failed to put the most pertinent questions to their informers. Who

15

for instance was really the supreme god of the Aztecs, Huitzilopoch-tli or Tezcatlipoca? To what degree was Huitzilopochtli conceived a solar deity?

As a consequence, the surviving data may be likened to a magnificent series of color photographs, illustrating certain facets of pre-Columbian religion but with much more stress upon outward signs than on inner convictions. The rituals are described in elaborate detail, but comments are scant on the beliefs that inspired such ceremonies, of which they were the external manifestation. For lack of appropriate data, we may never attain a true comprehension of Mesoamerican religion. Perhaps comparative studies may one day further our understanding: the well-documented Hindu paradox of Shiva as creator and destructor or the cult of Mithraism, with its contrasting forces of light and darkness, might help us to comprehend the mystery of the many-sided Tezcatlipoca.

Subjective Thinking

In the study of Mesoamerican history and religion, a further problem arises, that often escapes comment. It might be supposed that in this scientific age, any analysis of the available data would be rigidly objective. But the historian is to some extent a prisoner of his time, and can never be wholly impartial; the writing of history, as Professor E.H. Carr puts it, is a "dialogue between the present and the past." Each age examines what has gone before and makes a different analysis, from which it extracts significant pointers, lessons, and warnings. Or as Benedetto Croce once wrote: "The practical requirements which underlie every historical judgment give to all history the character of 'contemporary history,' because, however remote in time events thus recounted may seem to be, the history of reality refers to present situations wherein those events vibrate."[15] Modern investigators of Mesoamerican sources cannot escape from this situation. Like other historians, they entertain preconceived notions, and may tend to pile their contemporary prejudices upon those inherited from Spaniards and Hispanized Indian scribes.

The monolithic and militant catholicism of Spain nowadays finds its counterpart in an all-pervading materialism, and the social and political history of Mesoamerica is liable to be subjected to such criteria. Arguments have even been advanced for abandoning the study of Mesoamerican religion, regarded in this context as a mere competing brand of "opium for the people." Notions such as class war are introduced into the equation, and the Tenochca have perforce to be portrayed as divided into opposing factions—though no one can really explain how the merchants, for instance, can be fitted into this doctrinal strait-jacket since they clearly formed a third or intermediate class. Attempts are now frequently made to interpret Mesoamerican society in terms of dogmas whose nineteenth-century inventors went out of their way to explain that their theories applied to England in that era and not to the European Middle Ages, let alone to their contemporaries, the Toltec and Aztec empires. The dividing line is narrow between scholars who view the history of Tenochtitlán as nothing but a prolonged confrontation between two hostile groups, the Pipiltin and the rest, and those popular writers who see the Spanish Conquest as the fruit of a concerted uprising of all the subject peoples against the Aztec "oppressors," though ample evidence refutes this theory. Purely materialistic attitudes display a lack of comprehension not merely of Mesoamerica, but of other civilizations of the ancient world, whose basic concepts and motivations are so remote from our own.

To illustrate this point one might reverse the situation and consider the sheer bewilderment that would have afflicted the votaries of Huitzilopochtli and Tezcatlipoca if they had suddenly been told that their destinies were no longer subject to the dictates of their familiar gods, but that they were to be governed instead by a parliamentary democracy or by a dictatorship of the proletariat. The teaching of Jesus, the victorious Man-God, whose church was the patrimony of a resplendent priest-ruler, was far less alien to native thought; however, even Christian doctrines were hard for the friars to expound, and endless misconceptions ensued, such as the adoration of the cross as a deity in its own right.

The grip of scientific materialism on the modern mind is so firm—regardless of individual political sympathies—that contemporary man can barely comprehend the mystico-religious approach to life of his own medieval forebears, let alone of their Mesoamerican counterparts. The Spaniards, notwithstanding their preconceived notions, were better equipped to understand this mystico-religious

17

native outlook. A parallel between Spanish and Aztec attitudes has often been noted; typical was Cortés himself, filled with a fervor to convert the heathens to Christ and to save them from Hell, but intent upon extracting, on their road to salvation, every ounce of gold that they possessed.

Such attitudes were not alien to the Aztecs, who conquered in the name of their gods but levied tribute on a transnational basis in exchange for the privilege of doing homage to Huitzilopochtli. Ahuitzotl immolated hordes of prisoners to honor the gods, but also believed in putting the money to work that he squeezed from the conquered lands. As Sahagún records, the Emperor would gather his tribute and then arrange that his merchants should resell part of these spoils to other conquered peoples at a handsome profit, in return for concessions to do business in their territories.[16]

Sifting the Evidence

Any modern tendencies to take a doctrinaire view are probably no more than a passing phase in Mesoamerican historical research. For in the course of a century, since the time when interest in the Mexican past became intensified, attitudes have changed continuously and rapidly. Nineteenth-century historians, such as Orozco y Berra (and even Prescott), tended to take the sources at their face value and simply related what these documents reported. Mesoamerican history was thereby reduced to its lowest common denominator and became mainly a process of counting heads. Faced with glaring discrepancies within the sources, it seemed natural to assume that if version "A" was supported by eight accounts, and version "B" occured in only five, then version "A" was correct. But such methods overlook one obvious problem: the eight reports occurring in eight separate documents may all emanate from one single source: the ratio of support for versions "A" and "B" is then no longer 8:5, but 1:5, if we accepted the uncertain premise that the five reports favoring version "B" are of independent origin.

As a counterweight to such tendencies, certain investigators then went to the opposite extreme, and simply treated the sources as mythical make-believe. Bandelier, for instance, denying reports to the contrary, treated the Aztecs as a primitive tribal society; Brinton believed that the whole story of Tollan was a mere legend. But little progress can be made in interpreting Mesoamerican documents, either by treating them as fairy tales or, alternatively, by always taking them at their word.

In the twentieth century, Mesoamerican history has been subjected to a process of critical analysis in which the work of Kirchhoff and of Jiménez Moreno is outstanding. For a brief spell Barlow made important contributions for Central Mexico, while Krickeberg and others provided major studies on a regional basis; in this respect Thompson's work on the Mayas is of major significance, as well as Caso's interpretations of the Mixtec codices.

However, while more objective approaches to Mesoamerican history have undoubtedly been made, the counting of heads has not been wholly discarded as a yardstick. To take one example, the general assumption still prevails that the Tepanecs killed Chimalpopoca, the *roi faineant* of Tenochtitlán, whom they supposedly carried off in a cage dressed in the full regalia of Huitzilopochtli: so say Durán and Tezozómoc. But Chimalpopoca was the Tepanec ruler's grandson, and a Tepanec partisan, and no evidence suggests that he changed sides or placed himself at the head of a resistance movement to Tepanec hegemony. Therefore, the latter had no motives for eliminating Chimalpopoca, and Maxtla, Tezozomoc's volatile heir, had enough trouble on his hands without any new problems created by the liquidation of a compliant Tenochca ruler, ostensibly a Tepanec puppet.

On the other hand, Chimalpopoca's attitude was calculated to provoke indignation among the more chauvinistic Mexica nobles; it was therefore natural that they should take advantage of Tepanec dissensions to stage a palace revolution that eliminated the fainthearted monarch and replace him by the staunch Itzcoatl. Chimalpopoca was the Tepanec puppet, while Itzcoatl and his supporters were the leaders of the Mexica resistance movement. But Sahagún reports that Mexica history was re-edited on the instructions of Itzcoatl, who naturally did not want to figure as a regicide and preferred to put the blame on the Tepanecs for killing his predecessor. On the basis therefore of logic, regardless of mere numbers, I prefer to believe one source, the *Anales Mexicanos,* insistent that Chimalpopoca was killed by dissident Tepanecs allied with Itzcoatl, rather than accept the orthodox version, quoted by a series of documents, to the effect that he was slain on the orders of the Tepanec ruler, Maxtla.[17]

Even where the surviving accounts coincide over a certain event or series of events, the historian cannot automatically take their version for granted. The Mexica migration is almost universally accepted as historical, on the basis of a single story cited with variations in different sources. But Van Zantwijk may be correct in thinking that much of this story derives from earlier migrations and that Mexica history is to be sought more in the Valley of Mexico than elsewhere. Good grounds may exist for supporting such a standpoint, as I shall later demonstrate. Equally, the epic of Xolotl and his Chichimecs emanates from one basic document, the Codex Xolotl, and the corresponding written version of Ixtlilxóchitl served to enhance the ancestral standing of Texcocan ruling dynasty, of which Ixtlilxóchitl was the proud descendant. In Chapters III and IV, a closer look will be taken at Xolotl as a historical personage rather than as the embodiment of a legend, and he will be seen to have acquired a fame that exceeds his real status and achievements.

Jiménez Moreno recently observed that even Sahagún was not infallible, since he depended on what his informants told him. We can never be sure that they did not sometimes follow the time-honored Indian custom of telling their interlocutor what they guessed he wanted to hear.

To cite a specific example: Sahagún lends added force to statements in other sources depicting Quetzalcoatl as a benevolent deity who shuddered at the mere thought of human sacrifice. According to parallel versions of this story, Quetzalcoatl, like his Peruvian counterpart, Viracocha, traveled through the land dressed rather as a Dominican friar, and conducted a kind of preaching tour, healing the sick and summoning the people to repentance.

But Viracocha in his original form was a sun deity, and Quetzalcoatl both as creator and god of fertility was connected with agriculture. Both were therefore typical ancient American gods, and their pitiless nature was quite alien to those Christian or European virtues with which they were credited by Spanish chroniclers. Moreover, in other passages, the same chroniclers make no secret of Quetzalcoatl's propensity for human sacrifice and even relate that, on the occasion of Ahuitzotl's famous holocaust to celebrate inauguration of the Templo Mayor, one of the four major participants in the slaughter was dressed as Quetzalcoatl.

Both in Peru and Mexico, however, alarmed by the Spanish revulsion at their religious practices, the natives hit upon the idea of whitewashing at least one of their own gods to make him respectable in the eyes of the conquerors, who even chose at times to identify themselves with these deities.

A tendency prevails among Andean scholars to subject to even closer scrutiny the reports of their historical sources, that at times seem to be dependent upon one basic version of events. Murra insists that more recently Andean ethnohistorians have made a point of systematically inquiring which source copied which. He quotes Carlos Aranibar: "It becomes necessary to transform casual reading of the chroniclers into a rigorous examination; only by a persistent analysis of the primary sources will it be possible to find a substitute for those outmoded methods of arbitrary selection of quotations and the indiscriminate accumulation of reports of questionable value."[18] By employing more rigorous criteria, Maria Rostworowski has been able to make a good case for the hypothesis that Cuzco was governed by two rulers at a time, notwithstanding the insistence of the Hispanized written documents on the presence of a single and supreme Inca.

Zuidema, in his criticism of Brundage's more orthodox version of Inca history, went so far as to question the very existence of Pachacuti, the great empire builder who combines in one person the roles played by Moctezuma I and Tlacaelel. While few Mesoamericanists would go so far as to doubt the historicity of both Moctezuma and Tlacaelel, many, including myself, agree that the role of Tlacaelel is exaggerated by certain sources, that make of him the power behind the throne during no less than four reigns.[19]

Both in Mexico and in Peru, the practice of counting heads is of scanty validity. In this volume, I shall try instead to analyze the reports, to determine which are strictly historical and which are of a more legendary nature, or, in certain cases, merely borrowed from another people or another century to add luster to a city or enhance the prestige of its dynasty. Such a procedure, where it involves the rejection of a traditional account, may appear iconoclastic, but is surely necessary if we want to know what really happened in Meso-america in the centuries before Columbus.

II. Favorite Sons

Teoculhuacán

Culhua, or Colhua, according to Seler, derives from *colli,* meaning "grandfather," and Culhuacán is "the place of those who have Grand-fathers" and hence "the place of those who have Ancestors"; therefore, by implication, Culhuacán is a city that stands for ancient traditions. The name Culhua thereby came to be associated with the Toltec urban dwellers of the Valley of Mexico as distinct from the successive waves of Tolteca-Chichimecs who poured into the region after the collapse of Tollan. The distinction is a fine one, since the Toltecs of Tollan Xicocotitlan were themselves a blend of Tolteca-Chichimecs, who had originally come from the northwest, and of Nonoalcas from the southeast. Later, notwithstanding the aura surrounding their name, Culhua blood was copiously diluted as the people of the city mingled with Acolhuas and other newcomers.

The *Memorial Breve* names the Culhuas among the original migrants into central Mesoamerica, who came out of Chicomoztoc in Toltec times; it also calls them Chichimecs.[1] Six cities were sub-ject to Culhuacán when it was Tollan's partner: Xochimilco, Cuitla-huac, Mizquic, Coyoacan, Malinalco and Ocuilan. The same source insists on the importance of Culhuacán during this era and states that a triple alliance of Tollan, Culhuacan, and Otompan ruled the Toltec Empire.

Quite apart from this much-prized connection with Tollan, and from the remoter migration from Chicomoztoc—shared by so many peoples—a more particular legend of their origins arose from links with the legendary Teoculhuacán, usually taken to mean "the Old, or Holy, Culhuacan." It could equally mean "great"; Sahagún in his prologue to Book XI states that the prefix "Teo" means something that has extreme qualities for good or bad, i.e., it has a sense of exaggeration or greatness. This city of fable had a unique place in the mythology of the new Culhuacán, even if other migrants, such as the Mexicas, also claimed to derive from Teoculhuacán; the Mexicas at times also even called themselves Teoculhuaque.[2]

The *Relación de la Genealogía* relates the legend of Culhua origins, and of their coming from a remote and venerable Teoculhuacán; the people of Culhuacán in the Valley of Mexico no longer knew where it lay. Surprisingly, however, these Culhuas, the future upholders of civilization, then lived as typical Teochichimecs, without houses, cotton, or magic rituals, gathering wild plants and hunting deer, rabbits, and birds; they dressed in skins and at times went naked.[3] This account, followed by assertions that the early Culhuas only had one wife apiece, form part of the standard description of typical Chichimecs, repeated by many sources; it was doubtless inspired by the way of life of those Chichimecs whom the Spaniards found in Zacatecas, Guanajuato, and other regions lying beyond the bounds of Mesoamerica. The account of the *Relación de la Genealogía* actually states that many Chichimecs of that kind still existed.

Accordingly, even the Culhuas, the very epitome of refinement, conformed to convention, and boasted of Teochichimec origins— that universal status symbol among the peoples of central Mesoamerica in the final pre-Conquest period.

The importance that certain sources attach to Teoculhuacán raises questions as to its true location; Kirchhoff in particular doubted that the Culhuacán of the Valley of Mexico existed at all in Toltec times and believed that Tollan's partner was the original Teoculhuacán, to be identified with San Isidro Culiacán, near to the Hill of Culiacán in the southern part of the state of Guanajuato; Aztlan and Chicomoztoc lay close by.

While I accept the consensus opinion that both Aztlan and Teo culhuacán lay to the northwest, I am ever more convinced that to search for their exact location on a modern map is an unrewarding task; if the Culhuas at the time of the Conquest did not know where Teoculhuacán lay, hopes of pinpointing its true whereabouts must today be slim. Like Tlalocán and Tamoanchan, the mythical homes or resting places of gods and men, Aztlan, Chicomoztoc, and Teoculhuacán belong partly to the realm of fable. Scholars have cogently argued at different times that Tamoanchan lay in the east, south, north, and west!

The people who shared such legends had vague notions of where these places were situated; the Aztec Emperor Moctezuma I actually tried to find out where Aztlan lay: he sent an expedition of sixty magicians, furnished with sumptuous gifts. At a location that was reputedly the birthplace of Huitzilopochtli, a demon conveniently turned them into birds. They then took wing to a remote destination, where they met the mother of Huitzilopochtli, now an ancient hag, but, they returned to Moctezuma no wiser concerning the location of Aztlan. In different epochs and for different peoples Chicomoztoc or Teoculhuacán could have different associations, and cannot therefore be pinned for all time to a single point on a map. In the *Annals of the Cakchiquels,* even Tollan was no longer a real city, but became a legendary place of origin; for the Cakchiquels, in all four Tulans existed, one in the east, one in the west, one in the sky, and one in the nether regions.[4] Tollan thus found its counterpart in a mythical Tulan, or Teotollan, a place of splendid palaces that might even be situated in the sky, just as the real Culhuacán had to have Teoculhuacán as its legendary image.

And just as Tollan Xicocotitlan inspired the story of four Tulans in the Maya land, more than one place called Teoculhuacán, or Chicomoztoc, may have once existed; but it remains hard to understand how pure nomads could have inhabited such a wondrous city as Teoculhuacán, that is now lost in the mists of time to a point where it becomes untraceable.

Moreover, in the case of Teoculhuacán, the legend of the far-distant city is only part of the story, since at least one real Teoculhuacán—or Old Culhuacán—existed in or near the Valley of Mexico. The *Historia de los Mexicanos* tells how the Mexicas, on their way

25

from Chapultepec to Culhuacán, passed through a Teoculhuacán just before they reached Coyoacan.[5] The *Memorial Breve* repeats this story and lists a Teoculhuacán on their itinerary, just before reaching Tepetocan and Huitzilopochco; the place, far from being a city of fable, was devoted to the more mundane task of producing salt.[6] The same source mentions what is apparently another Teoculhuacán, next to Acahualtzinco, near San Juan del Río in the State of Querétaro.[7]

Tollan's Partner

Both Kirchhoff and Jiménez Moreno have tended to regard the Culhuacán of the Valley of Mexico as a post-Tollan development. Certain written sources admittedly back this hypothesis; for instance, Ixtlilxóchitl states that Culhuacán came after Tollan and was the kingdom of those who were driven out of that place.[8] Other accounts of the settling of the new Culhuacán by people from Teoculhuacán can also be taken as supporting evidence. But his view presupposes that Topiltzin was the last, not the first ruler of Tollan; he was born in Culhuacán in the Valley of Mexico, and the city must therefore have existed in his time, whether that corresponds to the beginning or the end of Tollan. I regard Culhuacán as Tollan's associate as much as its successor; my conclusions, based on the archaeology of that city, have been set out in detail in another context.[9] Far from being a new creation during the latter part of the reign of Tollan Xicocotitlan, Culhuacán, if anything, preceded Tollan as an important center. In the case of the latter, some kind of small settlement may possibly have existed in late Teotihuacán times; but Culhuacán can boast of substantial Teotihuacán IV remains, in contrast to the scanty sherds of that period located around Tollan.

Moreover, Culhuacán was not an isolated outpost of Teotihuacán culture; during that city's period of predominance—I hesitate to employ the word "empire"—Azcapotzalco, Xico, and Tenayuca also flourished, and all have yielded Teotihuacán IV pottery, also found in the Coatlichán region.[10]

Culhuacán's significance during the apogee of Tollan was clearly great. Not only is Aztec I, contemporary with Tula-Mazapan, found in that site, but it was already proposed in the time of Boas and

26

Gamio that Aztec I originated there. Noguera subsequently supported this view as well as Griffin and Espejo.[11] Aztec I has also been found in Chalco, Xico, and Xochimilco, and therefore in Toltec times a thriving community of Aztec I users existed in the southern part of the Valley of Mexico, flanked to the north by people who, in Tenayuca, and even in Tenochtitlán-Tlatelolco, came to use Aztec II. Coyotlatelco, that both began and ended rather earlier than Mazapan, is more universalized, being found in Azcapotzalco, Xico, Tenayuca, Culhuacán, and Texcoco; in Culhuacán it is much less abundant than Aztec I, but has been located in substantial quantities in recent excavations in the Cerro de la Estrella, adjacent to that city.

Thus during the latter part of the Tula-Mazapan horizon, when Aztec II was current in the Tenayuca region, a kind of ceramic frontier seems to have existed, dividing the northern and southern halves of the Valley of Mexico. However, I hesitate to draw bold historical conclusions from a mere preference for one pottery design over another; too many examples could be cited of the pitfalls of such attempts. Nonetheless, the southern part of the Valley of Mexico did form in Toltec and post-Toltec times a fairly compact unit, centered round the chinampa cities of Culhuacán, Cuitlahuac, Mizquic, and Xochimilco. In Aztec conquest lists, the four cities usually figure together, coupled with the enigmatic Cuauhnahuac that Barlow regarded as a homonym in the Valley of Mexico, but that I prefer to identify with the Cuernavaca of the valley of Morelos, an area with which Culhuacán always enjoyed close relations. The chinampa cities formed a close-knit religious community. Cihuacoatl was patron deity of Culhuacán but was also worshiped in Xochimilco: Cuaxalotl, or Xantico, fire goddess of Xochimilco, seems to have been connected with Culhuacán: Quilaztli, also goddess of Xochimilco, is described as the deer of Mixcoatl, the legendary founder of Culhuacán, while Amimitl, who became the patron deity of Cuitlahuac, is described as Mixcoatl's rod.

Of greater political importance is Chimalpain's mention in the *Memorial Breve* of a triple alliance of Tollan, Culhuacán, and Otompan. I suspect that the reference to Otompan is rather figurative, and implies that an Otomi polity played an important role in the Toltec confederacy, rather than that the town of Otompan, near Teotihuacán, was itself one of three leading cities in that era.

Significant in Toltec times and thereafter is the special relationship between Culhuacán and the corner of the valley of Toluca that lies nearest to the city. The *Memorial Breve* describes Culhuacán as ruling not only its chinampa neighbors, but also the towns of Ocuilan and Malinalco. Therefore, Tollan's partner, Culhuacán, may have extended its influence, not only into Morelos, but also over part but not all of the valley of Toluca. Archaeology demonstrates that certain connections existed during the Tula-Mazapan horizon between the valley of Morelos and the valley of Toluca. Noguera remarks that Tlalhuica laquer pottery displays analogies with decorative patterns appearing in the Matlatzinca area.[12]

After the fall of Tollan, its surviving partner, Culhuacán, probably sought to maintain a hold over the valley of Morelos— important as supplier of cotton and other products of a warmer climate. The Mexicas who, as Tepanec auxiliaries, gave the coup de grâce to the shrinking power of Culhuacán, inherited this interest in the valley of Morelos, and from earliest days made incursions into that region.

Passing Glory

After the collapse of Tollan, Culhuacán's material power proved ephemeral, though its glory lived on. The city was unable to emulate Byzantium, that resisted the assaults of the barbarian for a millennium, as the Rome of the East. Culhuacán was immediately jeopardized by its partner's fall. As a repository of Toltec culture it survived, but its power base was slowly eroded.

Nauhyotl, who reportedly succeeded to the Culhua throne not long after Topiltzin's flight from Tollan, probably reigned from 1213 to 1248, or until 12 Calli or 13 Calli, dates given respectively by Ixtlilxóchitl and the Codex Xolotl for the defeat and death of this Nauhyotl at the hands of Nopaltzin, Xolotl's heir.

Their accounts of this event may be in part apocryphal. According to a consensus of the sources, Huetzin, ruler of Coatlichán, defeated Culhuacán and usurped its throne in I Calli or 2 Tochtli, the equivalent of 1253 or 1254, about five years after the death of Nauhyotzin. Only the brief reign of Cuauhtexpetlatzin separated Nauhyotzin's death from Huetzin's accession; Nopaltzin wedded

Azcaxochitl, daughter of Pochotl of Culhuacán and granddaughter of Topiltzin; Huetzin's bride was Atotoztli, daughter of Achitometl.

As will be seen in the next chapter, Nopaltzin and his successor Tlotzin are shadowy figures, and the story of Nopaltzin's blitzkrieg against Nauhyotzin of Culhuacán rather bears the stamp of a semi-legendary pre-enactment of a historical event—the conquest of Culhuacán by Huetzin, a more substantial personage; this repetition of a single occurrence in two distinct periods is quite frequent in Mesoamerican history. Doubts, moreover, persist about the origins of Nauhyotl. Ixtlilxóchitl in one context describes him as a member of the Toltec royal house, but in another passage he becomes a usurper, while the true descendant of Topiltzin Quetzalcoatl was Pochotl, also ruler of Culhuacán, whose daughter Nopaltzin married.[13] Perhaps Nauhyotl and Pochotl were the same person, though Torquemada states that Nauhyotzin was a Chichimec, of Chichimec descent, and thereby implies that he was not true Culhua-Toltec.[14]

Before various semi-barbarians invaded the Valley of Mexico, Culhuacán probably enjoyed a brief sunset of hegemony, as the surviving bastion of the former empire, in the interval before new rivals appeared upon the scene. Neither the Acolhua nor Tepanec cities were as yet of any consequence; many places in the Valley of Mexico derived from Teotihuacán times, but were now revitalized after being occupied by people described as Chichimecs. Archaeology demonstrates the antiquity of these centers, and the written evidence also confirms that Azcapotzalco, Tenayuca, Tlacopan, Coyoacán, and Coatlichán were cities that the Chichimecs took over, but did not found.[15]

In Toltec times, power was shared by Tollan, Culhuacán, and Otompan, as mentioned above. But in the period after the fall of Tollan, the Codex Vaticano-Ríos relates that control passed to a combination of Culhuacán, Tenayuca, and Xaltocan. This situation prevailed during the interim between the end of Tollan and the take-over of Culhuacán by Huetzin of Coatlichán. Xaltocan was an Otomi center, and the "Chichimecs" who occupied Tenayuca—as will later be explained in more detail—are also likely to have been part-Otomi; in effect, therefore, the report indicates a shift in the balance of power; Toltec Culhuacán was now in a minority in the new coalition,

29

though as leading cultural center of the Valley of Mexico, it still might claim an over-all primacy. In the following century, say from 1300 to 1350, Xaltocan and Tenayuca also declined, and Sahagún states that power then came to be divided among yet another triple combination of Culhuacán, Azcapotzalco, and Coatlichán. By this time, after the Acolhuas had taken over Culhuacán, its share of political power may have been as much nominal as real; its role might then be compared to that of Tlacopan, as a very junior partner within the Aztec Triple Alliance and heir to the former rulers, the Tepanecs.

The story of Nopaltzin's wolf-like descent upon the Culhua fold, reinforced by Xolotl in person, needs to be treated with a certain reserve; but in 1253 or thereabouts Huetzin of Coatlichán made himself ruler of Culhuacán, according to several sources. The *Memorial Breve* states that he ruled jointly with Nonoalcatl, whose identity remains obscure; the *Anales de Cuauhtitlán* name the latter as Huetzin's successor, not his contemporary and co-ruler. Some form of plural rule may have prevailed in Culhuacán, and thus Huetzin simply retained a reigning monarch of the traditional dynasty as co-ruler. According to the *Memorial Breve,* Huetzin was an unwelcome conqueror, and his presence was resented.[16] The source also states that he was incited to attack Culhuacán by his mother, wife of Itzmitl, first ruler of Coatlichán and the leading Acolhua monarch before Huetzin himself.

Barlow wrote of the "Chichimecization" of Culhuacán, perhaps better described as Aculhuanization. No doubt some pure Chichimec blood was infused when the city was occupied by Mixcoatl prior to the fall of Tollan, or, according to other interpretations, before Tollan's foundation. Nonetheless, I regard Mixcoatl's incursion more as sweeping conquest than as ethnic merger; on the other hand, after Huetzin's usurpation of the Culhua throne, the city remained within the Acolhua orbit for several generations. Acolhua influences thus persisted, and intermarriage would have been common between peoples who shared the same ruler and whose cities lay close to each other. Even as late as 1370, certain links between the two centers still survived, and sources differ about whether Acamapichtli, the first Tlatoani of Tenochtitlán, came from the one or the other.

The Dynasties of Culhuacán

Culhua history between Huetzin's conquest, some time after 1253, and the settlement of the Mexicas in Tizapán, after leaving Chapultepec, reveals many a blank page. This period, covering the reigns of Huetzin and his immediate successors before coxcox, will be considered later in connection with the conquests of the Acolhua dynasty. The Mexicas probably reached Culhuacán in 1319 and left in 1343 to found Tenochtitlán; but before dealing with the story of Xolotl and his followers that belongs to a previous era, it may be convenient to anticipate events and consider the story of Culhuacán up to the time when the city collapsed under the assault of the Tepanec-Mexicas, in the 1370's; a succession of Culhua rulers is named in different sources and forms a background to the history of an age that witnessed the decline of the power of Culhuacán but the survival of its prestige.

The dates of the dynasty or dynasties of Culhuacán are very difficult to establish. I first studied the question in my previous volume and sought to fix a tentative chronology for its rulers until the time of Coxcox, who occupied the throne when the Mexicas arrived in 1319. My object at the time was to work backwards and try to determine dates for the last Toltec rulers, from whom those of Culhuacán reputedly descended.

In Appendix A, I have re-examined the whole problem in greater detail; though my methods have been modified, I have come to very similar conclusions, but they still remain tentative.

An almost diabolical confusion permeates these king-lists for Culhua rulers, mainly provided by the *Anales de Cuauhtitlán* and the *Memorial Breve;* the dateless lists of Torquemada and the *Relación de la Genealogía* contribute little to a solution, because only by identifying dates can any sense be made of the names; equally, information provided by Ixtlilxóchitl occasionally offers an extra clue, but his dates are ritual, not historical, and record in most cases reigns of exactly fifty-two years.

The *Anales de Cuauhtitlán,* the *Memorial Breve,* and to a lesser extent Chimalpain's other *Relaciones,* provide a plethora of names and dates. The *Anales de Cuauhtitlán* give the accession and death of rulers both of Culhuacán and of Tollan; however, on examination

31

it becomes clear that the two lists, one for Tollan and one for Culhuacán, both starting with a Nauhyotzin, are intimately linked.
Chimalpain's *Memorial Breve* begins with a few kings of Tollan and
then offers dates for a long series of rulers of Culhuacán; but in this
case, too, the list is demonstrably not a true sequence, but a shorter
series that repeats a limited number of rulers twice, if not more. We
thus in effect have four parallel lists: the two halves of the *Anales
de Cuauhtitlan* king-list (some are in theory rulers of Tollan) and the
two halves of the Culhua king-list, given by the *Memorial Breve.*
In setting these lists side by side, in a previous context, I was able
to show their close relationship, if not identity.[17]

In addition to the earlier rulers included in the lists mentioned
above, these two sources also provide other names of subsequent
monarchs, that I have now also studied in more detail. These rulers
are even more difficult to place correctly and possess a plethora of
names, such as Cuauhtlix, Chalchiuhtlatonac, and Cuauhtlatoa,
that recall titles more than personal appellations. These later names
in each list, some of which are also repeated in Chimalpain's other
Relaciones and in Torquemada's undated list, are perplexing; they
repeat themselves but never in the same order; the dates also recur,
but are applied in almost chaotic fashion to one king in one list and
to his successor or predecessor in another. For instance, Chimalpain's
Relación gives Yohuallatlatonac as ruler of Culhuacán from 7
Tecpatl to 1 Acatl, while the *Anales de Cuauhtitlán* list Cuauhtlix
as reigning in Culhuacán from 7 Tecpatl to 1 Acatl and date his
successor, Yohuallatlatonac, from 1 Acatl to 11 Calli; but 1 Acatl
to 11 Calli are the dates of Yohuallatlatonac's successor, Tziuhtecatl,
in Chimalpain's account.

In many instances, dates that obviously apply to the same reign
vary by one or more years; for instance, in the *Anales de Cuauhtitlán*
list of rulers of Tollan, Nonoalcatl reigns as Huetzin's successor
from 9 Tochtli to 4 Acatl; but in the *Memorial Breve* series of rulers
of Culhuacán, Achitometl, described as successor to a joint rule by
Huetzin and Nonoalcatl, reigns from 10 Acatl (9 Tochtli plus 1) to
4 Acatl. As explained in Appendix A, these are obviously dates for
an identical reign (regardless of the city where the king in question
is supposed to have ruled); the differences of one or two years can
largely be discounted; even in the case of such a familiar figure as

Moctezuma II, sources give dates of 9 Calli, 10 Tochtli, and 11 Acatl for his accession.[18] For Moctezuma I, the spread of year-dates is yet wider. This phenomenon is even more noticeable where obscure kings of Culhuacán are concerned; for reasons explained in Appendix A (related to different methods of counting years), for events of a once-and-for-all nature, a series of alternative but consecutive years are apt to be given by the sources.

Bearing this in mind, I have been able to affirm and amplify my previous conclusions; certain specific reigns, with dates, can be established for rulers of Culhuacán from about A.D. 1200 until the foundation of Tenochtitlán, when the pattern changes. Having determined the chronology of such reigns, one has to deduce the name of the ruler or rulers who occupied the throne during those years. The choice is often wide; for instance, in different lists Nonoalcatzin reigns from 9 Tochtli to 4 Acatl, Achitometl from 10 Acatl to 4 Acatl, and Mazatzin from 6 Acatl to 3 Tochtli. These all refer to one reign, expressed differently.

The problem is further complicated by the possibility that Culhuacán possessed more than one ruler for at least part of the period and by the application to each monarch of several names. This in itself is hardly surprising; the biographies of European royalty of the nineteenth and early twentieth centuries fill whole paragraphs, if not pages, with the complete names and titles of a single personage, even if he or she never became a reigning monarch!

Nonetheless, the plethora of complimentary titles applied to each Culhua ruler and the difficulty of knowing his true name makes one wonder whether some ancient taboo against pronouncing the name of past kings had not survived in some form, just as it still exists today among certain African and South American tribes.

Following the two principles of grouping together linked dates, e.g. 3 Tochtli, 4 Acatl, and 5 Tecpatl, and of then seeking to establish reigns rather than rulers, I came to the following conclusions, explained more fully in Appendix A; where several near identical dates are given for one reign, the median or average date has been taken.

Reign I   5 Calli to 13 Calli
Reign II   13 Calli to 9 Tecpatl

Reign III	9 Tecpatl to 1 Calli
Reign IV	1 Calli to 9 Tochtli
Reign V	9 Tochtli to 4 Acatl
Reign VI	4 Acatl to 5 Calli
Reign VII	5 Calli to 10 Acatl

So far so good: a firm basis for such a definition lies in the fact that the dates of three rulers of the *Anales de Cuauhtitlán* list (Huetzin, Cuauhtexpetlatzin, and Nonoalcatzin) and of three rulers of the *Memorial Breve* list (Cuauhtexpetlatzin, Nonohualcatl plus Huetzin, and Achitometl) correspond precisely to reigns III, IV, and V of the above list. At first sight, therefore, everything is perfectly in order; what could be more natural than a perfect coincidence between the dates of the king-lists for Culhuacán in the two sources? Unfortunately matters are not quite so simple, for these reigns bearing identical dates occupy quite different positions in the respective lists of rulers, even when in this case (but not in others) the names of rulers to *some* extent correspond. The *Anales de Cuauhtitlán* reigns in question are for the first six rulers of Culhuacán in the immediate post-Tollan period; but the identical *Memorial Breve* reigns belong to Culhua monarchs number seven to twelve, as listed by that source.

Moreover, as set out in Appendix A, the next three Culhua kings of the *Anales de Cuauhtitlán* list, i.e. numbers seven to nine, correspond almost but not exactly to the names in the *Memorial Breve* for rulers nine to twelve; in other words, the *Anales de Cuauhtitlan* dates of rulers seven to twelve virtually repeat over again those of rulers one to six, while the *Memorial Breve* also repeats its reigns, but starts the second time not from the top of its first list, but from a point about halfway down.

Two facts emerge from this study: first, the data on Culhua kings in the *Anales de Cuauhtitlán* and in Chimalpain are clearly linked, and emanate from a common source: second, a degree of repetition is involved in both accounts and both really refer to far fewer reigns than they pretend to record.

By a process of deduction, it was possible to establish seven positive reigns, and by the same token conclude that the jumble of extra names did not correspond to separate rulers, but were a mere

34

repetition of the monarchs who governed during these seven reigns; the dates appended to these extra names seem to follow a common pattern or rhythm, except for certain mavericks that probably belong to a different year-count and that have been explained in quite a different way in Appendix A.

With so many names to choose from in each instance, it is hard to say for sure which is the key or principal name to apply to each reign. However on the basis of a consensus among sources that Nauhyotzin was an early ruler with a longish reign, and taking Coxcox as the principal ruler at the time of the Mexica captivity, while accepting reports that he was grandson of Huetzin, the names were applied as follows (the Julian calendar dates will be explained below):

Reign I	4 Tecpatl, 1204,	to	13 Calli, 1213	Chalchiuhtlatonac
Reign II	13 Calli, 1213,	to	9 Tecpatl, 1248	Nauhyotzin
Reign III	9 Tecpatl, 1248,	to	1 Calli, 1253	Cuauhtexpetlatzin
Reign IV	1 Calli, 1253,	to	7 Tecpatl, 1272	Huetzin
Reign V	7 Tecpatl, 1272,	to	4 Acatl, 1295	Nonoalcatl
Reign VI	4 Acatl, 1295,	to	5 Calli, 1309	Xihuiltemoc
Reign VII	5 Calli, 1309,	to	10 Acatl, 1327	Coxcox

The most likely Julian calendar equivalents for the native dates are given above. Again, as emphasized in Appendix A, the conclusion was reached that these numbers, not surprisingly, are related to the Culhua Texcocan year-count, (i.e., 1 Acatl is 1539 not 1519, and dates are therefore twenty years later than in the Tenochca count). I have explained the problem of the different year-counts more fully in a previous work.[19]

In this respect, a most interesting phenomenon now arises. Chimalpain's seventh *Relacíon* gives 10 Acatl for the death of Coxcox; the chronicler goes out of his way to insist that this monarch had no successor and that Culhuacán was ruled by a military government (Cuauhtlatolloc) for sixteen years until 1 Tecpatl, when Huehue Acamapichtli (possibly the uncle of Acamapichtli of Tenochtitlán) succeeded him.

For practical purposes, 10 Acatl (7 Tecpatl plus three years) may be equivalent to the 7 Tecpatl of the *Anales de Cuauhtitlán* list for the end of the same reign (number VI), and 7 Tecpatl is the year more often used for the end of this reign—see Appendix A, table C. Now Chimalpain's sixteen-year gap in the Culhua monarchy has always seemed to me to be an anomaly, since this occurred long before the collapse of Culhuacán under the flows of the Tepanec-Mexicas (the *Memorial Breve* mentions a gap of thirty-six years). At this stage in Culhua history no ostensible reason exists for a break in the king-list, and a much better explanation can be offered. In the Culhua-Texcoco count, in which these dates are probably given, 7 Tecpatl is the exact equivalent of 1 Tecpatl in the official Tenochca count, and both correspond to the year 1324.

This supposition is backed up by the mention in the *Anales de Cuauhtitlán* of 1 Tecpatl both for the death of Coxcox and for the accession of Huehue Acamapichtli, without any suggestion in this text of an interregnum between the two. The Tenocha count came to be used for the majority of dates from the accession of Acamapichtli of Tenochtitlán and of Tezozomoc onwards; in Culhuacán it was evidently used earlier, for the accession of Huehue Acamapichtli in 1 Tecpatl (the same year in the previous year cycle as that of the Tenochca tlatoani of that name). Clearly this explanation makes better sense than the inexplicable interregnum, filled by a military government, inserted into the record by Chimalpain or by the documents that he copied. Moreover, as will be seen below, Huehue Acamapichtli's death and his successors' reigns are clearly given in the Tenochca count, and his accession date was evidently also taken from a Tenochca list and not, like that of his predecessor, Coxcox, given in the Culhua-Texcocan count. The changeover from the Culhua calendar for one reign to the Tenochca for the next must automatically produce for the chronicler an *apparent* gap of twenty years in king-lists, i.e., the difference between the one and the other year-count. If King A's death is listed in the Culhua count and King B's accession belongs to the Tenochca, then an interregnum of this nature, to anyone unaware of the use of different counts, will *seem* to occur.

Most significantly, it was found that exactly the same phenomenon occurs in the list of Cuauhtitlán rulers given in the *Anales de Cuauhtitlán,* and parts of which bear an odd resemblance to the Culhua lists. Xaltemoctzin, ruler of that city, was killed in 7 Tecpatl, precisely the same date as the end of reign VII in the Culhua list. He was executed by the Tepanecs, and the source states that no king followed him for nine years, and once more insists that a military government took charge. In point of fact the gap was not nine years but more like twenty-two, since his successor Teçoçomoctli is not mentioned until 3 Tochtli (twenty-two years later in the same count), when he apparently became ruler, and was then driven out. But 3 Tochtli is 1 Tecpatl plus two years, and therefore the assumed gap, filled by a military government, is almost identical to that of the Culhua king-list, from 7 Tecpatl to 1 Tecpatl. A changeover at this point in the king-list of Cuauhtitlán from the Culhua to the Tenochca count is surely the right explanation. The matter will be explained more fully in Chapter IX; moreover, the phenomenon occurs not only in Cuauhtitlán, but also in Toltitlán; on the death of Epcoatl, *also* listed under the year 7 Tecpatl, an interregnum in that city of twenty years without any king reportedly followed![20]

The problem of changeover from other year-counts to the Tenochca, in common use at the time of the Conquest, is an obvious stumbling block in studies of Mesoamerican chronology. Therefore the fixing of a recognizable point when the change occurred, in the case of three separate peoples, is a modest step forward in the task of setting the different year-counts on a firmer footing. As will be seen in Chapter X, a change also occurred in Chalco, but at a later date.

Coxcox

Reasons for supposing that Coxcox was the principal, if not the only ruler in reign VI, during the Mexica captivity, are also given in Appendix A. Eight sources state that Coxcox was king at that time, while 4 name Achitometl, and 3 Chalchiuhtlatonac.

I formerly inclined to the view that there might have been as many as four simultaneous rulers in Culhuacán, as mentioned by the *Memorial Breve* and the *Anales de Tlatelolco,* and even depicted in the Codex Azcatitlan in the act of receiving the vanquished Mexica ruler. Further study has revealed that such names as Chalchiuhtlatonac and Cuauhitonal, while listed and even illustrated as separate monarchs, are really titles, as also, in a sense, are Coxcox and Achitometl; Techotlalatzin of Texcoco, for instance, Nezahualcoyotl's grandfather, was additionally called Coxcox.

Durán says that Culhuacán had two rulers when the Mexicas arrived: Coxcox and Achitometl; the *Historia de los Mexicanos* states that Achitometl was senior ruler, and that Chalchiuhtlatonac, was his "principal"—perhaps a kind of cihuacoatl, or leading dignitary. The *Memorial Breve,* however, states that Coxcox was the first of a series of four "kings"; in view of statements by several sources that Coxcox was the grandson of Huetzin, and that he was in turn the father of Huehue Acamapichtli, it seems clear that he was the true descendant of the Coatlichán dynasty that had taken over Culhuacán two generations before, and was therefore probably the principal or senior ruler, perhaps seconded by an Achitometl, to whom it is impossible to assign dates with any assurance; the Achitometl who succeeded Huehue Acamapichtli is another person.[21]

A rather confusing passage of Chimalpain implies that the Mexicas virtually gained control of Culhuacán during their period of refuge in Tizapán. But this is surely another of those frequent anachronisms, whereby events of, say, 1370 are confused with those of 1323—in this case because of chronological misunderstandings on the part of the chronicler; 13 Acatl, (1343 Culhua) when the Mexicas left Tizapán has probably been confused with 13 Acatl (1375 Tenochca), the date of a major attack on Culhuacán by the Tepanec-Mexicas. Ixtlilxóchitl also states that the Mexicas fought the Culhuas and scored a notable victory before they left Culhuacán.[22] But Ixtlilxóchitl mentions Acamapichtli as leading the Mexicas—another indication that some anachronism or transposition of events from one generation to another is again involved and that we are dealing with a victory over Culhuas that belongs to the 1370's or 1360's.

The Mexicas recouped their strength during their stay in Tizapán, but they can hardly have been strong enough at that stage to rout the Culhuas and impose a military government.

The role and importance of Culhuacán at the time of the Mexica captivity is hard to define. Reading between the lines, any pretences that the city was still a major power appear more as a form of lip service to Toltec traditions and culture. We are told that when the Mexicas occupied Chapultepec, their new home bordered on the lands of the Tepanecs, Acolhuas, and Culhuas; in view of the continued presence on one of the Culhua thrones of Coxcox, direct descendant of Huetzin of Coatlichan, this is a way of saying that the

Mexicas were situated on the borders of the Tepanecs and of the Acolhuas, together with their dependents, the Culhuas.

According to certain accounts, the Mexicas were expelled from Chapultepec by a combination in which the Culhuas played a leading role. However a more convincing account by Chimalpain suggests that the Chalcas or Xaltocans took the lead. Culhuacán, where the Mexica leader Huitzilihuitl was killed, was probably a convenient place for the other victors to settle the Mexicas out of harm's way; at that time they were undesirables and to accommodate them was no privilege. In Culhuacán they provoked dissension; Coxcox and Achitometl were both well disposed, but many other leading Culhuas demanded that a stronger line be taken to control such unwanted guests.[23] Mexica assistance against the Xochimilcas was a small compensation for all the trouble that they had caused.

Downfall

According to the *Anales de Cuauhtitlán,* Coxcox' son, Huehue Acamapichtli, succeeded him in 1 Tecpatl, probably the equivalent of 1324.[24] However, Ixtlilxóchitl maintains that Acamapichtli (whom he confuses with Acamapichtli of Tenochtitlán) made war on Coxcox and caused him to flee to Coatlichán, where he also ruled; the report implies that Coxcox' death marked a turning point when, after three generations of joint rule, Coatlichán and Culhuacán once more were divided; there is no suggestion that Huehue Acamapichtli or his successors ever reigned in Coatlichán.[25]

But while Culhuacán thus shook off the Acolhua yoke before succumbing to the Tepanecs and Mexicas, it never recovered its former power and no longer even controlled the neighboring Chinampas cities. In 1343 or 1344, the Culhuas had to call in the upstart Mexicas in order to subdue Xochimilco. Therefore if Culhuacán was then a member of a triple alliance that included Coatlichán and Azcapotzalco, as some sources suggest, its role in such a combination was limited. Toltec Culhuacán still commanded great respect, and more prestige was to be gained from keeping the city as an ally than in making it into a subject.

The fact that Huehue Acamapichtli was Coxcox' son and may even have seized his father's throne adds force to the contention that no interregnum ensued between the two reigns, as described by Chimalpain. It is hard to envisage Acamapichtli driving his father out of his kingdom, only to leave the throne vacant for sixteen years before assuming power; if the throne passed peacefully from father to son, the long interregnum becomes even harder to explain.

The *Anales de Cuauhtitlán* state that Achitometl, generally called Achitometl 11, killed Acamapichtli in 13 Tecpatl, probably equivalent to 1336, and usurped the throne. The *Relación de la Genealogía* also states that Acamapichtli reigned for twelve years and was the last legitimate sovereign. The word "legitimate" in this context is applied to descendants of Huetzin of Coatlichán, himself a usurper. Chimalpain gives the same date for the death of Acamapichtli and the accession of Achitometl. Both the *Anales de Cuauhtitlan* and Chimalpain state that Achitometl died in 11 Acatl; I consider, for reasons explained in Appendix A, that this is really 1371, or 9 Acatl, rather than 11 Acatl in the Tenochca count; 11 Acatl in this calendar is the equivalent of 1347. Achitometl, not Coxcox, was therefore the principal ruler of Culhuacán when the Mexica captivity ended; this accords perfectly with reports of the gruesome incident involving the flaying of that monarch's daughter, that led to the precipitate departure of the Mexicas; the episode will be discussed in connection with early Mexica history in Chapter VIII. The symbolism of the "marriage" of Achitometl's daughter to Huitzilopochtli may be symptomatic of that urge on the part of intruders, both men and gods, to wed a Culhua princess.

It could, of course, be argued that the forced departure of the Mexicas, just prior to the foundation of Tenochtitlán, led to an upheaval that brought Achitometl's reign to a premature end. However, Achitometl's death is implicitly linked by that source with the period of Tezozomoc of Azcapotzalco, and his Tenochca and Tlatelolca colleagues; at this moment, and not in 1343, a generation earlier, the Tepanec-Mexica expansion was gathering momentum and claimed Culhuacán as one of its first victims. Moreover, if Achitometl had died in 1347, an unduly long interregnum ensued before the accession of his successor, Nauhyotzin 11; the *Anales de Cuauhtitlán*'s mention of such a gap is probably just another example of a calendric adjustment being read as a hiatus in the king-list.

The *Anales de Cuauhtitlán* further state that Culhuacán literally fell apart under the weight of internal dissension on the death of Achitometl; some of the inhabitants migrated to Cuauhtitlán.[26] The source discusses at some length the civilizing effects of these migrants upon the people of Cuauhtitlán—another example of that continuous fusion between peoples of "Toltec" and "Chichimec" origins. The Culhua settlers in Texcoco in the reign of Techotlalatzin probably also migrated as a result of these disasters to their native city. These events form part of the story of Tepanec-Mexica conquests as told in Chapter IX, when it will be suggested that some assault on Culhuacán had already taken place in the early 1360's; it was not in itself decisive, but initiated the process of disintegration that was completed a few years later, after the end of Achitometl's long reign. The principal Mexica blow—under Tepanec auspices— seems to have fallen in 2 Calli (1377), when the *Anales de Cuauhtitlán* say that the Mexicas were roused to pity by the state of desolation prevailing in Culhuacán. An expedition was sent against the city and Nauhyotzin, called Nauhyotzin II, apparently a Mexica, was set upon the Culhua throne. He reigned until 12 Calli (1413), when he was killed by Tezozomoc of Azcapotzalco; Acoltzin, his successor on that ill-fated throne, was murdered by Nezahualcoyotl in 3 Tochtli (1430).

In outlining the story of Culhuacán until its downfall, nearly two centuries after its partner, Tollan Xicocotitlan, I have anticipated events before returning to the immediate post-Tollan period and to the Chichimec invasions of the Valley of Mexico. But the role of Culhuacán, as the bastion of Toltec culture in the Valley of Mexico, is fundamental to the whole history of the period that separates the Toltec from the Aztec Empire, and forms an essential background to all that follows concerning Chichimecs, Acolhuas, Tepanecs, Chalcas, and even Mexicas. These successive claimants to power sought in turn to occupy Culhua land, while their leaders wooed the daughters of its ruler.

In general terms, we have seen that while Culhuacán's real power shrank fairly swiftly after the fall of Tollan, its fame lived on; it was even coveted as ally or partner until finally absorbed by the Mexicas, who adopted the very name Culhua, to set the stamp of legitimacy on their claim to the Toltec heritage.

41

III. Back to Methuselah

The Legend

After the fall of Tollan, Culhua claims to supremacy were soon challenged, when Xolotl and his Chichimecs, like wolves upon the fold, descended upon the Valley of Mexico. The familiar version of this influx derives from the Codex Xolotl, a sixteenth-century Texcocan document, on which Fernando de Alva Ixtlilxóchitl based his detailed account of Chichimec and early Aculhua history, written in the seventeenth century; he gleaned supplementary information from the Mapa Tlotzin, and from the Mapa Quinatzin. The combination of a still extant native pictorial story, amplified in Spanish prose, is rare in the annals of Mesoamerica. For the most part, this history merely complements the codex, but, as Charles Dibble reveals in his classic commentary to the Codex Xolotl, instances arise where the Texcocan historian misread his primary source. Ixtlilxóchitl's story is retold, with additions and variations, by Veytia, an eighteenth-century writer, who also belongs to the Texcocan tradition; Torquemada, much of whose work runs parallel to Ixtlilxóchitl's text, gives a similar account of the arrival of Xolotl.

The story, rich in picturesque if apocryphal detail, can be briefly summarized. The great Xolotl gathered his six clans, who lived in the vicinity of the legendary Chicomoztoc, and set off a few years after the fall of Tollan for the heartland of Mesoamerica, where he arrived in 5 Tecpatl, or, according to the *Anales de Tlatelolco,* seven years later in 12 Acatl. For Ixtlilxóchitl, this 5 Tecpatl is the equivalent of A.D. 946 in the Julian calendar, but according to my previous calculations, Tollan probably fell in 1175, and 5 Tecpatl thus becomes 1179.

Xolotl first went to Tollan, by then a mere ruin deserted by its former inhabitants. Before reaching the city, he had visited Cuechteca-Ichocayan and Tepenene, two favorite staging points for migrants to the Valley of Mexico: the Mexicas subsequently passed through Cuechteca-Ichocayan: Tepenene also lay on the route of those Chichimecs who had left Chicomoztoc for Cholula at the behest of the Tolteca-Chichimecs, and of those other Chichimecs whom Muñoz Camargo describes as the founders of Tlaxcala.

After leaving Tollan, Xolotl first proceeded to Mizquiahuala and then himself went to Tenayuca, while detailing part of his levies to explore Chapultepec and others under his son Nopaltzin to visit Huexotla, Coatlichán, Tepetlaoztoc, Teotihuacán, Cholula, and Oztoticpac. Xolotl had also stayed in Cahuac, described by Ixtlilxóchitl as a major Toltec center, before establishing his capital in Tenayuca, another former Toltec stronghold, but now greatly enhanced in status as the foremost city of the region.

Xolotl's entry into the Valley of Mexico was reportedly unopposed. Thereafter, reluctant to rest on his laurels, he proceeded to explore and occupy the whole territory that had previously belonged to Tollan. In this task, in addition to Nopaltzin, he was seconded by six leaders—Acatomatl, Cuauhtlapal, Cozcacuauh, Mitliztac, Tecpan, and Iztaccuauhtli. The forces at his disposal are variously estimated by Ixtlilxóchitl at 3,002,000 (centzonxiquipilli, that is really the equivalent of 3,200,000), or in another context, at one million; not surprisingly, the Texcocan chronicler describes this army as the largest that ever operated before or after that date in the New World. This surmise applied equally to the Old World, since Xolotl's hordes reportedly outnumbered by one hundred to one the average force employed in the Thirty Years' War that raged in Europe in Ixtlilxóchitl's time! Xolotl's exploratory route embraced a region bounded by Poyautecatl (the Cofre de Perote), Cuauhchinanco, Tototepec,

43

Metztitlán, Atotonilco and Cahuacán: this territory he designated as Chichimecatlalli (Chichimec land). The Codex Xolotl, (and also the Mapa Tlotzin), portrays his Chichimecs as housed in caves and dressed in clothing made of skins and zacate grass. The codex depicts them as arriving in small groups, notwithstanding Ixtlilxóchitl's imaginative estimates of their numbers.

Five years later, in 10 Calli, Xolotl dispatched four other Chichimec leaders on yet more distant expeditions, in order to explore the Gulf and Pacific coastlines. They visited such places as Tecolutla and Xiuhcoac, on or near the Gulf Coast, where they reported the presence of Toltec refugees: these welcomed Xolotl's representatives and allowed them to take formal possession of the land.

Some twenty years after Xolotl's arrival, or thirteen years in another context, six more Chichimec leaders arrived and were also endowed with appropriate principalities; fearful of their ambitions, the Emperor gave them only small territories in the Tepetlaoztoc region. According to the Codex Xolotl, these six leaders came successively in 1 Calli and the five following years; 1 Calli follows nine years after 5 Tecpatl, and Ixtlilxóchitl's estimate of the interval between their arrival and that of Xolotl himself is thus marginally greater.

The sole resistance to the Chichimecs' triumphal progress occurred in 12 Calli, when Nopaltzin conquered Culhuacán, then ruled by Nauhyotzin, described by other sources as a kind of phantom Toltec king who ruled after the fall of Topiltzin. Culhuacán, having recuperated its strength and increased its population, refused to pay tribute to Xolotl, claiming that the land belonged to Nauhyotl as the rightful heir. Vengeance was swift; after a fierce battle, Nopaltzin defeated and killed the Culhua monarch. He then married Azcaxochitzin, daughter of Pochotl, the reputed son of Topiltzin, and therefore legitimate ruler of Culhuacán, who still lived near to Tollan. Achitometl, son of Pochotl, then only five years old, was restored to the vacant Culhua throne.

The year 1 Tecpatl, forty-seven years after Xolotl first established himself in the Valley of Mexico, or fifty-two years after the fall of Tollan, was marked by a significant event. From the direction of Michoacán yet three more señores arrived, who ruled over three branches *(parcialidades)* of the Acolhua nation and whom Ixtlilxóchitl describes as Michoaca-Chichimecs. Xolotl most conveniently had some spare señoríos at his disposal; accordingly, on the most important of the three, called Aculhua, leader of the Tepanecs, the Chichimec emperor bestowed Azcapotzalco as his capital; Chiconquauh, leader of the Otomís, received Xaltocan and its surrounding territory, while Tzontecomatl, described as leader of the "true" Acolhuas, became ruler of Coatlichán. Aculhua of Azcapotzalco married Cuetlachxochitzin, daughter of Xolotl, and Chiconquauhtli married another daughter, Tzihuacxochitl.

The pictorial and written sources provide copious if confusing information on genealogies. Xolotl himself had married Tomiyauh, daughter of the ruler of Tampico in the Huaxteca, who bore him two daughters. The Codex Xolotl offers no confirmation of Ixtlilxóchitl's assertion that the Nopaltzin who was Xolotl's leading lieutenant was also his son, though another Nopaltzin is depicted in that source as son of Tlotzin and therefore as Xolotl's great-grandson.

From the first Nopaltzin's marriage with the Culhua princess Azcaxochitzin, Tlotzinpochotl, his heir was born, as well as two other sons. Tlotzin in turn married the daughter of one of the rulers of Chalco, and begat a number of offspring, including Quinatzin Tlaltecatzin, a second Nopaltzin mentioned above, Tochintecuhtli, referred to as first ruler of Huexotzingo in this context, together with a daughter named Malinalxochtzin; for his male progeny, the long-lived and munificent Xolotl provided suitable principalities.

Tzontecomatl of Coatlichán, leader of the true Acolhuas, married a Chalca princess and fathered a son called Tlacotzin (or Itzmitl in other versions), who in turn married Malinalxochtzin, elder daughter of Tlotzin Pochotl. Tlacotzin's son and heir was called Huetzin, who plays a leading part in Ixtlilxóchitl's history; he later married Atotoztli, daughter of Achitometl of Culhuacán, restored to his throne by Nopaltzin. Huetzin, who was thus, according to Ixtlilxóchitl, great-grandson of Topiltzin and great-great-grandson of Xolotl—an anomaly to which we will return later—when still a youth was presented by Xolotl with the principality of Tepetlaoztoc, thereby becoming entitled to an annual quota of rabbits and hares, animal skins, and fiber mantles, a rustic tribute conforming to Chichimec custom.

On this occasion, however, trouble ensued, since the principality so lavishly donated to Huetzin was not vacant but possessed a hereditary ruler, called Yacanex, whose subjects showed no desire to exchange their native prince for an alien upstart imposed by the Chichimec emperor. They complained loudly of the oppressive rule of the usurper; a sordid struggle arose between the two claimants for the hand of Atotoztli of Culhuacán; Huetzin is actually portrayed in the Codex Xolotl conversing with her father Achitometl, whom he visited to advance his suit. However Achitometl, who owed his throne to Nopaltzin's intervention, saw clearly on which side his bread was buttered and opted for Huetzin, who duly became his son-in-law. The young Huetzin was unable to subdue his rebellious subjects, even with the assistance of those six leaders mentioned above, who had been endowed with mini-principalities, all subject to Tepetlaoztoc.

To put matters right and to enforce his will, Xolotl then called upon Tochintecuhtli, described as Señor of Huexotla, to perform a rescue operation. In 2 Acatl, the Emperor sent for this prince, and in the Codex Xolotl they can be seen conversing in Tenayuca. Tochintecuhtli thereafter went to Xaltocan to enlist the support of its ruler (Tochintecuhtli in this context is described as the son of the ruler of Cuauhacan, not of Tlotzin); he was also ordered to marry Totomiyauh, Xolotl's great-granddaughter. After his marriage he was to take possession of Huexotla and proceed to the aid of Huetzin.

Ixtlilxóchitl's account, which runs parallel to the Codex Xolotl, describes at some length the joint struggle of Tochintecuhtli and Huetzin against the "tyrant" Yacanex, who was aided and abetted by the rulers of Metztitlán and Tototepec. In these campaigns, the two allied princes were powerfully reinforced by Quinatzin, also son of Tlotzin, and hence brother of Tochintecuhtli. By this time Quinatzin had inherited the señorío of Tenayuca, but then transferred his capital to Texcoco. A more detailed account of this war against Yacanex and his confederates forms part of the early history of the Acolhuas, and will be given in Chapter V.

Having launched four generations of his descendants on successful careers of conquest, Xolotl breathed his last on 12 Tecpatl, or 112 years after he had first descended upon the Valley of Mexico, and 117 years since the collapse of Tollan.

Xolotl was succeeded as Chichimec emperor and ruler of Tena-yuca by Nopaltzin, who ruled for thirty-two years until his death in 5 Acatl; he in turn was succeeded by Tlotzin, whose reign lasted for thirty-six years. When Quinatzin, Tlotzin's heir, transferred his capital to Texcoco, he left his uncle, Techotlalatzin, in possession of Tenayuca. According to Ixtlilxóchitl, Quinatzin was the first Chichimec ruler to force his people to alter their rustic ways, to speak Nahuatl, and to become incorporated into the Mesoamerican consumer society by occupying permanent homes and wearing elaborate attire. The pictorial accounts draw a fairly sharp distinction between the primitive adornments of the pure or untainted Chichimecs of Metztitlán and Tototepec, who fought against Huetzin and Tochintecuhtli, and the dress of these neo-Mesoamericans, who wore a simplified form of the traditional clothing; however, they still bore typically Chichimec arms, the bow and arrow. In general terms, Dibble in his commentary on the Codex Xolotl sees these Chichimecs as themselves maintaining an unsophisticated mode of living, while at the same time respecting the cultivated fields and settled pattern of life of the peoples they encountered in the Valley of Mexico.

A Long Reign

The official story told by the Texcocan sources is of inestimable worth to the historian, and without their valuable aid knowledge of the period in question would be fragmentary; however, their account, summarized above, obviously poses many problems and begs many questions. Notwithstanding its merits as a source of information, the story told by Ixtlilxóchitl hardly holds together as a consistent narrative, if it is simply taken as it stands. In this respect, a difference of emphasis arises between myself, on the one hand, and Jiménez Moreno and Caso, on the other, who both tend to place a more literal interpretation on the Texcocan historical sources, even if they also express certain reserves. Caso in particular doubts whether Xolotl could have conquered so vast an empire in so short a time.[1]

After sifting the evidence, I have come to be even more skeptical than Caso. As I will later explain in detail, I suspect that if there was any Chichimec Empire, it was conquered by Tochintecuhtli

47

of Tenayuca—identified by various sources with Xolotl—in about 1250, rather than by any semi-legendary hero named Xolotl who invaded the valley of Mexico after the fall of Tula.

If a more literal interpretation is to be placed on the account of Ixtlilxochitl, the first stumbling block that we encounter is the exaggerated longevity of Xolotl himself. He supposedly died 112 years after first reaching the Valley of Mexico; moreover, at the time of his arrival he already possessed a grown-up grandson, Tlotzin, illustrated in the Mapa Tlotzin marching with his father and grandfather into the promised land. In addition, Xolotl at that time already had behind him an active career as ruler and reputedly had controlled the destinies of six kingdoms in the northwest. Therefore, on any literal interpretation of the record, he could hardly have been less than 160 years old when he died, still in full possession of his faculties and busy at his favorite pastime of distributing other peoples' lands to his heirs and vassals.

The Codex Xolotl gives 13 not 12 Tecpatl for the Emperor's death—a date that logically shortens his reign by twelve years, and leaves him to die as a mere stripling of 150. But the glyphs painted above the Lake of Texcoco in Plate III of the codex indicate clearly that 104 years had passed between the fall of Tollan and the war between Tochintecuhtli-Huetzin and Yacanex. The date of this conflict is given as 1 Tecpatl, or twelve years before the 13 Tecpatl in question. In several cases this one-digit difference occurs between Ixtlilxóchitl's dates and those of the Codex Xolotl (see Appendix A). In this appendix the problem is attributed, not to continuous errors on the part of a seemingly myopic historian—a most improbable solution—but to the use by Ixtlilxóchitl of a different year-count. Thus we also have both 13 Calli and 12 Calli dates for the slaying of Nauhyotzin of Culhuacán and even of 1 Acatl and 2 Acatl for Topiltzin's flight from Tollan.

The anomaly of Xolotl's longevity is further illustrated by his donation of Coatlichán to Huetzin, who was already a young man when the war against Yacanex started, but who in Ixtlilxóchitl's account becomes the Emperor's great-great-grandson, as the son of Malinalxochitzin, and grandson of Tlotzin. Huetzin's other grandfather was of Tzontecomatl, first ruler of Coatlichán, and virtual contemporary of Xolotl, since he reputedly arrived as an adult in the Valley of Mexico only forty-seven years after his master.

Other Contradictions

After a closer examination of our principal sources, and of brief passages in other documents, the contradictions multiply. In the first place, certain accounts question the whole notion that Xolotl arrived in the Valley of Mexico as a conqueror from outer Mesoamerica, and suggest instead that he was born and bred in cenral Mexico. Vetancurt says that he and his brother Achcautzin were sons of a Chichimec ruler named Tlamacatzin, who was already installed in Amecameca when the Toltecs dispersed.[2] Torquemada, in conformity with Ixtlilxóchitl, states that Xolotl's father was called Tlamacatzin, but affirms in addition that Tlamacatzin was the son of Moceloquichtli, who had succeeded to Tepeticpac, one of the four señoríos of Tlaxcala.[3] The *Anónimo Mexicano,* regardless of Tlamacatzin's origins, describes him as a true Chichimec, who wore no proper clothing.[4] Rather curiously, Muñoz Camargo mentions a priest, not ruler, called Achcauhtli Teopixque Tlamacazcuachcua-uhtli (Teopixque and Tlamacazqui are simply words for two categories of priests), who performed special rites for the Chichimecs of Poyauhtlán at the moment when they were engaged in a desperate struggle to storm the defenses of Tepeticpac, prior to the establishment of their capital in Tlaxcala.[5] Muñoz Camargo also associates the Chichimecs of Poyauhtlán with Amecameca, according to Vetancurt Xolotl's native city, by stating that those Chichimecs who later founded Tlaxcala visited Amecameca after they had departed from the plains of Poyauhtlan, near Texcoco.[6] The *Memorial Breve* adds to the confusion by stating that Xolotl (whom it identifies with Tochintecuhtli) became in Amaquemecan Chicomoztoc the first ruler of the Acolhuas, the people of Texcoco and Huexotla.[7] Accordingly various sources, whose accounts of these events differ in other respects, concur in identifying Xolotl, not with Michoacán and the northwest, but with Amecameca and even with the early Tlaxcala.

A baffling feature of the whole Ixtlilxóchitl–Codex Xolotl story is the presence of Xolotl, Nopaltzin, Tlotzin, and many of his original henchmen in a totally different context in the *Historia Tolteca-Chichimeca.* Apart from Xolotl himself, this source mentions the following of his Chichimec leaders: Tzontecomatl, Tecpatzin (Tecpa in Ixtlilxóchitl), Nequametl, Ueuetzin (Huetzin), Nopaltzin, Tlotzin, Mitl (Iztacmitl), Quauhtliztac (Iztacquauhtli), Tochtzin (Tochintecuhtli), and Tlamaca (Tlamacatzin). Xolotl's move into the Valley of Mexico might admittedly have coincided with the migration of those Chichimecs from the northwest, who came to the rescue of the Toltecs beleaguered in Cholula, since both incursions are ostensibly linked with the collapse of Tollan. In theory, however, the two episodes have little else in common, and I have previously proposed that the Chichimec migration to Cholula took place *before* Tollan fell, since I find it hard to conceive that the Olmeca-Xicallancas of Cholula were overthrown by a group of mere refugees, and prefer to regard the Toltec occupation of that city as a breakaway movement from Tollan at a time when the city was still fairly powerful.[8]

Although the events described both at the beginning of the Codex Xolotl and of the *Historia Tolteca-Chichimeca* could have coincided approximately in time, it is disconcerting to rediscover in such a different context so many of Xolotl's principal leaders and collaborators. Moreover, some of the same names also reappear in Muñoz Camargo's account of the movements of yet another group of Chichimecs, who founded Tlaxcala: Cozcaquauhtli (Cozcacuauh in Ixtlilxóchitl), Tetzitzmitl (Itzmitl), Tecpa (given as a place-name by Muñoz Camargo), and Quauhtzin, perhaps the equivalent of Ixtlilxóchitl's Quauhtliztac. A large proportion of Muñoz Camargo's Chichimec leaders also figure in the *Historia Tolteca-Chichimeca;* the two stories are ostensibly unrelated, though I demonstrated in my previous volume that they form two branches of a single mass movement.[9]

Xolotl and Tochintecuhtli

Confusing also at first sight is the statement in the *Memorial Breve,* twice repeated, that Xolotl is the same person as Tochintecuhtli, the confederate of Huetzin and ostensibly Xolotl's own great-

great-grandson.[10] Torquemada's assertion that a Tochintecuhtli was brother of the great emperor is a pointer in the same direction.[11] The suspicion that Tochintecuhtli and Xolotl might be one and the same person is reinforced by their marriage to wives of virtually the same name: Tomiyauh in Ixtlilxóchitl and Miahyatotocihuatzin in the *Memorial Breve.*

Ixtlilxóchitl and Chimalpain certainly appear to be writing of one and the same Tochintecuhtli rather than of two rulers of that name belonging to different periods. The names of their wives coincide in the two versions: both Tochintecuhtlis arrive in Huexotla in 1 Tecpatl: both have a son called Quiyauhtzin. In the *Memorial Breve,* another son, called Tlaçolyaotl, inherits the throne of Huexotla from Tochintecuhtli, but in Ixtlilxóchitl's account, Tochintecuhtli equally has a son called Yaotl; the *Anales de Cuauhtitlan* mention a Tlaçolyaotzin as ruler of Huexotla.[12] The *Memorial Breve* states that Xolotl-Tochintecuhtli was ruler of Tenayuca, Xolotl's capital in Ixtlilxóchitl's history.

Another monarch, apparently also identifiable with Xolotl and with Tochintecuhtli, appears in the *Anales de Tlatelolco* in the person of Tecuanitzin, equally described as ruler of Tenayuca.[13] This Tecuanitzin has a daughter called Cuetlachxochtzin, the name of one of Xolotl's two daughters, according to Ixtlilxóchitl and the Codex Xolotl: in Ixtlilxóchitl *and* in the *Anales de Tlatelolco,* a Cuetlachxochtzin marries Aculhua, ruler of Azcapotzalco. Such parallels are hard to attribute to pure chance, and Jiménez Moreno concurs with me in identifying Tecuanitzin of the *Anales de Tlatelolco* with Ixtlilxóchitl's Xolotl, though he does not necessarily accept any identification of this twin personality with Tochintecuhtli.

Tochintecuhtli is on one occasion called Tochintecuhtli Tequihuatzin by Ixtlilxóchitl, an appellation or title that obviously has a different derivation *(tequihua)* to Tecuanitzin *(tecuani)* and merely refers to his warrior status. Ixtlilxóchitl also mentions a Quauhtequihua, to whom Xolotl gave land, and twice refers to Tochintecuhtli, son of Nopaltzin, as Toxtequihuatzin, to whom he gave Zacatlán as his cabecera, "together with many lands and places."[14] Torquemada refers to "Quauhtequihua, por otro nombre Tochintecuhtli," who became ruler under Xolotl of the important province

51

of Zacatlán.[15] The Zacatlán in question may be the Zacatepec, in the valley of Toluca, that Chimalpain describes as "Zacatlán, sometimes called Zacatepec."[16]

Yet a further anomaly concerns the six leaders who arrived twenty years after Xolotl, whose names coincide exactly with the place-names of the six señoríos subject to Tepetlaoztoc and who rebelled against Huetzin when he usurped this principality, supported by Tochintecuhtli (who is sometimes himself named as ruler of Tepetlaoztoc).

If these chieftains had really arrived nearly a century before, as Ixtlilxóchitl states, their names would hardly have been preserved intact as those of six señoríos, notwithstanding a tendency in certain sources to confuse places and people. These six leaders, usually identified with Xolotl, are thus more likely to have been contemporaries of Tochintecuhtli and Huetzin, and the names reported in the Codex Xolotl are more probably those of the leaders themselves, who fought against Huetzin, and not of the señoríos.

A passage of the *Anales de Cuauhtitlan* adds force to the view that Tochintecuhtli played a Xolotl-like role. We are told that in the year 2 Tecpatl the Cuauhuaca Otomís arrived and settled in Chichimecacuicoyan, then governed by Tochintecuhtli: they remained fifteen years under his dominion and then moved on to Tlacopantonco in the Xolotl gorge of Tepotzotlán.

Tochintecuhtli was certainly an empire builder in the Mesoamerican sense of the word; he and Huetzin jointly sought to absorb other principalities in their own neighborhood and even beyond. Torquemada relates that Tochintecuhtli deprived many rulers of their kingdoms and killed some of them.[17] The *Anales de Cuauhtitlán* state that he fixed the boundaries of other señoríos.[18] In their first mention of Tochintecuhtli, they describe him ruling as a noble and a prince in Chichimecacuicoyan.[19]

Even the glyphs of Tochintecuhtli and Xolotl in the Codex Xolotl are at times easy to confuse. In Plate II, we see Xolotl in Tenayuca seated on his *icpalli* with his wife Tomiyauh behind him. His glyph is a rather nondescript version of the bald-headed dog. Nopaltzin appears just above Xolotl, fighting against Nauhyotl of Culhuacán; to the right of Nopaltzin is a figure with the same glyph, conversing with Achitometl (the newly designated ruler of Culhuacán), whom Dibble in his commentary equally identifies as Xolotl. However, in his key to the name-glyphs of Plate II, Dibble designates this same personage as Tochintecuhtli! In Plate III, we actually see a rather submissive Tochintecuhtli conversing with Xolotl, seated once more on his *icpalli* in Tenayuca: in this instance, a certain difference in color and in the form of the ears distinguishes the rabbit glyph of Tochintecuhtli from the bald-headed dog of Xolotl. Incidentally, in the Mapa Tlotzin, the Chichimec emperor's glyph is a kind of flag and he is named in the Nahuatl glossary as Amacui, not Xolotl.

Dynastic Dilemmas

Native dates contained in a story that so generously blends legend with history defy interpretation. Moreover, such dates are few and far between, and attempts to correlate in tabular form, say, the 5 Tecpatl of Xolotl's arrival and the 12 Tecpatl of his death must lead to nebulous results. Since I consider that early events of the Codex Xolotl bear dates whose consistency cannot be cross-checked, I prefer to use those later but more substantial thirteenth-century figures, Tochintecuhtli and Huetzin, as the basis of Table A, that attempts to reconcile the various genealogical and chronological anomalies.

In view of their Methuselan longevity, something is palpably wrong with the story of Xolotl and of Nopaltzin, depicted with Tlotzin, his adult heir, five years after the fall of Tollan, though he lived on for a full century after that event. Quinatzin Tlaltecatzin is described as supreme commander in the wars of A.D. 1250, and by inference as an almost bicentennial figure when he served as Acamapichtli's ally in the 1370's, though this record is beaten by Aculhua, first ruler of Azcapotzalco, actually credited by Ixtlilxóchitl with a life of two hundred years.

Huetzin is less hard to place, because of his usurpation of the throne of Culhuacán. The dates of the rulers of that city may be confusing, but, as demonstrated in Chapter II and Appendix A, concrete evidence suggests that Huetzin reigned from 1 Calli to 9 Tochtli, the probable equivalent of A.D. 1253 to 1274. His son, Acolmiztli, also became ruler of Culhuacán, and Acolmiztli's son,

Coxcox, in turn inherited the throne of that city; the latter was reigning when the Mexicas arrived in 1319, or 2 Acatl. Coxcox probably ruled from 1295 to 1327.[20]

The dates of Huetzin (and his contemporary, Tochintecuhtli) are thus definable, and their reigns form a fixed point, around which can be reconstructed the history of the period from the collapse of Tollan to the key date 1319, marking the arrival of the Mexicas in Chapultepec. At all events, such uncertainties serve to illustrate certain common problems of Mesoamerican dating (see Appendix A).

The identification of Coxcox, Huetzin's grandson, with the Mexica captivity in Culhuacán is a crucial factor, since it thereby becomes indisputable that the Tochintecuhtli-Huetzin era corresponds to the late thirteenth and cannot possibly belong to the fourteenth century. This point is fundamental in any search for the identity of those involved.

The same names, Achitometl, Coxcox, Quinatzin, and even Huetzin, crop up at fairly frequent intervals in late Mesoamerican history, and the custom prevailed of applying a bewildering variety of names to the earlier characters portrayed in Mesoamerican historical sources. (Far from dying out, the practice re-emerges in early colonial documents). Topiltzin Quetzalcoatl was also known as Nacxitl, Nacaxoch, Meconetl, and Tlacomihua; his father, Mixcoatl, is variously referred to as Mazatzin, Totepeuh, or (by Ixtlilxóchitl) Iztaccaltzin. This tendency, confusing to historians, has no obvious explanation. However, our knowledge of these leaders derives from both oral and pictorial accounts: possibly a man having one basic appellation possessed a number of different second names: these other names or titles were then applied to describe that individual in the annals of bygone centuries.

The name or title Xolotl equally seems to apply to more than one ruler: Tezozomoc of Azcapotzalco, who claimed Xolotl's original title of Chichimecatecuhtli, is twice addressed in the *Anales de Cuauhtitlan* as "O Xolotl."[21]

Taking into account such conundrums of nomenclature and other reasons previously stated, I suspect that the feats attributed to the great Xolotl immediately after the fall of Tollan are really inspired by the historical campaigns in the following century of Tochintecuhtli; even if the latter's achievements were more modest than

Xolotl's grandiose career of conquest, as described by Ixtlilxóchitl, nevertheless the triumphs attributed to Tochintecuhtli suggest that he had a better historical claim than any other ruler between the fall of Tollan and the rise of Azcapotzalco to the title of "emperor," intrinsically a European concept, though vaguely applicable in Meso-american terms to any prince who could impose his will on a series of señoríos, lying beyond his own city-state.

So far as the concept of Xolotl, the Chichimec emperor, is not embodied in the performance of Tochintecuhtli, his saga merely constitutes—as will be shown in Chapter IV—an alternative version, with a few altered names, of those other accounts presented in the *Anales de Cuauhtitlan,* Muñoz Camargo, and the *Historia Tolteca-Chichimeca* of twelfth-century Chichimec incursions, and that I have categorized as forming the Mixcoatl saga.[22]

At first sight such a premise may startle, as deleting an exciting chapter in Mesoamerican history and as questioning the validity of the colorful account, familiar to every student, of the century fol-lowing the end of Tollan's empire, bequeathed to us by venerable sources. But once it is evident that the version of those sources *cannot* be accepted at its face value without conceding active life-spans of 150 years or more, not only to Xolotl, but to Nopaltzin, to the "Gran Quinatzin," and to Aculhua of Azcapotzalco, then at least some major reconstruction of their story is inescapable, to avoid repetition of data that, unadjusted, becomes sheer nonsense. By im-plication, though in less explicit terms, other investigators have already undermined the orthodox version of events. Ixtlilxóchitl himself seeks to mitigate the muddle by making A.D. 958 into the Julian equivalent of the year 1 Tecpatl in which Tollan was de-stroyed, four years before Xolotl's arrival; this would allow ample time for Xolotl's great-great-grandson to be still reigning in 1270, though his assertions that Xolotl was then still alive confuse the record. A consensus of modern investigators favors 1168 for the fall of Tollan (I have preferred 1175). Once a late twelfth-century date is accepted for that event, the interval of time between the arrival of Xolotl in, say 1180, and the accession in Tenayuca of the more historical Tochintecuhtli in about 1250 becomes totally insufficient to allow for Xolotl's great-great-grandson to reach manhood and usurp a principality. Little scope exists for any alternative solution that would relegate the Tochintecuhtli-Huetzin era to beyond 1300. Any notion that Huetzin really belonged to the fourteenth-century would make nonsense of the documented genealogy of subsequent Culhua rulers, repeated by several sources. Moreover, the age of Tochintecuhtli-Huetzin marks the rise of the Acolhuas of Coatlichán, whereas the fourteenth century witnessed a temporary decline in Acolhua fortunes before Texcoco came to the fore under Ixtlilxóchitl, grandson of Quinatzin, who ascended the throne in 1409 or 1410.

The evidence that Xolotl is at least in part to be identified with Tochintecuhtli is supported by the insistence of the *Memorial Breve* that they were one and the same person and on Torquemada's hint that they were brothers. In Ixtlilxóchitl, the name of Xolotl's and Tochintecuhtli's wives are the same, and Chimalpain gives an equivalent name for this princess. The main spheres of action of Xolotl and of Tochintecuhtli coincide: both ruled in Tenayuca, and both were closely associated with Cuauhuacan: both, moreover, are reported as taking possession of a number of principalities; further, Xolotl and Tochintecuhtli are both partly identifiable with Tecuanitzin of Tenayuca.

Of this line of reasoning Jiménez Moreno, the foremost student of the period in question, seemingly accepts part, but not the whole. He, like Caso, sees a common identity for Tecuanitzin and Xolotl and even points to a probable similarity between their respective glyphs, but hesitates to associate this twin personality with Tochintecuhtli. However Jiménez Moreno overcomes the problem of Xolotl's alleged longevity by proposing that Ixtlilxóchitl's chronology is wrong and that Xolotl really arrived not in the 1180's but in the 1 Tecpatl that is equivalent to 1244, if taken to belong to the Texcocan-Culhua year-count. And yet this assertion, while not conceding any identity between Xolotl and Tochintecuhtli, strongly suggests that they were approximate contemporaries. The placing of Xolotl's arrival in 1244 demolishes his claim to be great-great-grandfather of Huetzin, Tochintecuhtli's partner, and calls in question the genealogical scheme presented in the traditional accounts. If Xolotl is really Tochintecuhtli's contemporary, but is *not* the same person, then what did Xolotl do, and who was he?

Nopaltzin

Apart from the problem of Xolotl himself, the true identity of Nopaltzin remains in doubt. Ixtlilxóchitl, but not the Codex Xolotl, states that Nopaltzin was son of Xolotl—an assertion that completes the Tezcocan genealogical tree and makes Xolotl appear as great-grandfather of the "Gran Quinatzin" and great-great-great-grandfather of Nezahualcoyotl. In the Codex Xolotl, Nopaltzin figures as the emperor's leading henchman and the pioneer in surveying the vast domains that submitted without a fight to the Chichimecs. After this initial burst of activity, Nopaltzin fades from view and becomes a rather shadowy figure, though his nopal cactus glyph makes him readily distinguishable from his companions. Matters are complicated by the mention by Ixtlilxóchitl and the Codex Xolotl of another Nopaltzin Cuetlachihui, son of Tlotzin and brother of Tochintecuhtli, and of Quinatzin Tlaltecatzin; this Nopaltzin is a prominent captain in the campaigns of Tochintecuhtli and Huetzin, great-grandson of the first Nopaltzin.

The original Nopaltzin reportedly inherited Xolotl's throne in 12 Tecpatl and reigned for thirty-two years until 5 Acatl (though by one of those anomalies mentioned above, thirty-two years after 12 Tecpatl is really 5 Tecpatl, not 5 Acatl). So little is told of Nopaltzin's reign that Dibble, in his commentary on the Codex Xolotl, describes it as peaceful and untroubled! Ixtlilxóchitl, perhaps in order to provide a little padding, gives an account of Nopaltzin's legislative program—distinctly reminiscent of Nezahualcoyotl's lawmaking—imposing the death penalty on anyone who made fires in mountains or fields without a government permit and decreeing that poachers would have their bows and arrows confiscated; like other Meso-american rulers, Nopaltzin outlawed the permissive society, and imposed draconian penalties for adultery, not always obeyed to the letter of the law by future Texcocan rulers such as Nezahualcoyotl!

As between Xolotl and Tochintecuhtli, a certain duplication is also evident between deeds ascribed to Nopaltzin (before he became ruler of Tenayuca) and those of Huetzin. Both monarchs occupied Culhuacán, married the daughter of the reigning prince, and became

TABLE A: *The Principal Dynasties*

(letters above names refer to the notes to Table A, pages 60 and 61, below)

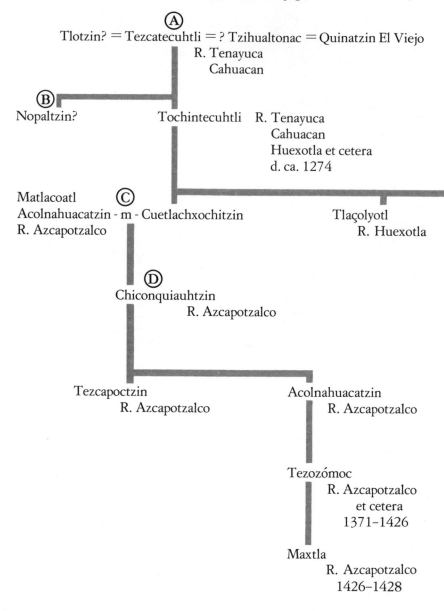

(A) Tlotzin? = Tezcatecuhtli = ? Tzihualtonac = Quinatzin El Viejo
R. Tenayuca
Cahuacan

(B) Nopaltzin?

Tochintecuhtli   R. Tenayuca
Cahuacan
Huexotla et cetera
d. ca. 1274

Matlacoatl (C)
Acolnahuacatzin - m - Cuetlachxochitzin
R. Azcapotzalco

Tlaçolyotl
R. Huexotla

(D) Chiconquiauhtzin
R. Azcapotzalco

Tezcapoctzin
R. Azcapotzalco

Acolnahuacatzin
R. Azcapotzalco

Tezozómoc
R. Azcapotzalco
et cetera
1371–1426

Maxtla
R. Azcapotzalco
1426–1428

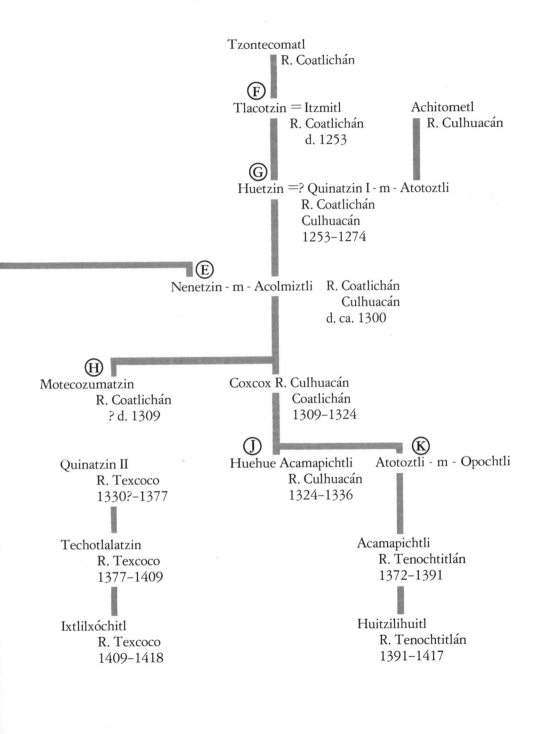

Tzontecomatl
R. Coatlichán

Ⓕ

Tlacotzin ═ Itzmitl
R. Coatlichán
d. 1253

Achitometl
R. Culhuacán

Ⓖ

Huetzin ═? Quinatzin I - m - Atotoztli
R. Coatlichán
Culhuacán
1253–1274

Ⓔ

Nenetzin - m - Acolmiztli   R. Coatlichán
Culhuacán
d. ca. 1300

Ⓗ

Motecozumatzin
R. Coatlichán
? d. 1309

Coxcox R. Culhuacán
Coatlichán
1309–1324

Ⓙ

Quinatzin II
R. Texcoco
1330?–1377

Huehue Acamapichtli
R. Culhuacán
1324–1336

Ⓚ

Atotoztli - m - Opochtli

Techotlalatzin
R. Texcoco
1377–1409

Acamapichtli
R. Tenochtitlán
1372–1391

Ixtlilxóchitl
R. Texcoco
1409–1418

Huitzilihuitl
R. Tenochtitlán
1391–1417

NOTES TO TABLE A

The letters below correspond with the letters in Table A, pages 58 and 59, above.

A. Ixtlilxóchitl names Tlotzin as father of Tochintecuhtli. The *Anales de Cuauhtitlán* give Tezcatecuhtli, but state that his real name was Quinatzin el Viejo, who was also called Tezcatecuhtli.

B. Ixtlilxóchitl and the Codex Xolotl mention a Nopaltzin as brother of Tochintecuhtli (and of Quinatzin), and as co-belligerent of Tochintecuhtli and Huetzin. The original Nopaltzin (son of Xolotl) is reported by Ixtlilxóchitl to have married Azcaxochitl, daughter of Pochotl, ruler of Culhuacán.

C. Acolnahuacatzin, according to several sources, married Cuetlachxochitzin. One princess of that name was daughter of Xolotl. The *Anales de Tlatelolco* say that Cuetlachxochitzin was daughter of Tecuanitzin of Tenayuca, i.e. probably Tochintecuhtli.

D. For dynasty of Azcapotzalco, see Chapter VI.

E. Acolmiztli, Huetzin's heir, married Nenetzin, according to the Codex Xolotl. Ixtlilxóchitl states that Quinatzin married a daughter of Tochintecuhtli. It seems more likely that his statement refers to the marriage of Nenetzin to Acolmiztli, who may also have been called Quinatzin (as was his father Huetzin).

F. Tlacotzin is reported by Ixtlilxóchitl as marrying Malinalxochitzin, sister of Tochintecuhtli. Conceivably the chronicler slipped a generation, and Malinalxochitzin is really of a generation previous to Tochintecuhtli. Malinalxochitzin is also stated to be sister of Quinatzin, perhaps Quinatzin el Viejo, one of the names of Tochinte-cuhtli's father.

G. Huetzin is son of Itzmitl, according to the Codex Xolotl, and grandson of Tzontecomatl, first señor of Coatlichán (called Tlacotzin by Ixtlilxóchitl). The *Memorial Breve* mentions Tlacoxiqui as Huetzin's father, and the *Anales de Tlatelolco* call him Tlaxinqui.

H. Ixtlilxóchitl gives alternatively Motezumatzin and Iyxuchitlanax [*sic*] as successors of Acolmiztli to the throne of Coatlichán (unlike Coxcox, this person does not seem to have reigned in Culhuacán). Coxcox is another son of Acolmiztli, who inherited the throne of Coatlichán after Motecozumatzin.

I. Ixtlilxóchitl states that Quinatzin is the son of Tlotzin, and grandson of Nopaltzin, thus making the rulers of Texcoco descend from the Chichimec "emperors." But, as explained in Chapter V, Quinatzin is really the contemporary of Acamapichtli of Tenochtitlán, who reigned two centuries after Xolotl. Techotlalatzin, Quinatzin's son, married a daughter of another Acolmiztli of Coatlichán; this Acolmiztli presumably succeeded in Coatlichán (but not in Culhuacán) after Coxcox and may have been his son; conceivably Quinatzin was a son of Motecozumatzin, since Techotlalatzin's wife (daughter of Acolmiztli) is described as his cousin.

J. For dates of Huehue Acamapichtli, see Appendix A.

K. According to various reports, Acamapichtli of Tenochtitlán was son of Opochtli and of Atotoztli, a Culhua princess. Chimalpain states that this Atotoztli was daughter of Coxcox of Culhuacán, a seemingly plausible assertion.

joint ruler (Nopaltzin married Azcaxochitl, daughter of Pochotl, while Atotoztli, daughter of Achitometl, became the bride of Huetzin); Achitometl, according to several sources, was son of Pochotl, but both appellations are very generalized, more comparable to a title, and Pochotl may be the same person as Nauhyotl or as Achitometl, his reported son, and by the same token Atotoztli may be another name for Azcaxochitl. Durán strengthens this suspicion by saying that Atotoztli was not daughter of Achitometl, but of his predecessor, named as Nauhyotl.[23] Pochotl and Nauhyotl are alternately named as successors to Topiltzin. Another Azcaxochitl is mentioned by the *Anales de Tlatelolco* as spouse of the ruler of Xaltocan. The Pochotl who ruled in Culhuacán, reportedly the son of Topiltzin and father of Nopaltzin's Azcaxochitl, is another shadowy figure; Quinatzin of Texcoco, the contemporary of Acamapichtli, was also incidentally called Quinatzin Pochotl.[24] Certain aspects of the killing of Nauhyotl by Nopaltzin are again suggestive of a semi-allegorical pre-enactment of a historical event: the Codex Xolotl version, repeated by Ixtlilxóchitl, cannot be taken at its face value, since Nauhyotl was supposedly slain in 13 Calli, seventy-three years after Xolotl and Nopaltzin, his adult son, reached the Valley of Mexico.

Moreover, according to Ixtlilxóchitl, Nauhyotl was killed by Nopaltzin in 12, not 13 Calli. But this is the year when Tezozomoc of Azcapotzalco slew a Nauhyotzin, who was then reigning in Culhuacán. With fifty-two years to choose from and about twenty alternative names for rulers of Culhuacán, the odds are very great indeed against a Nauhyotl, ruling in that place, being killed twice over on two distinct years 12 Calli, on the orders of the great king, or Chichimecatecuhtli of the period—in the one case Xolotl of Tenayuca, and in the other Tezozomoc, who also first reigned in Tenayuca.

How many Quinatzins?

In the early part of the Codex Xolotl, a personage called Quinatzin plays an outstanding and commanding role; he has a glyph resembling Xolotl's bald-headed dog, but surmounted by a flag. In the war conducted by Tochintecuhtli-Huetzin against Yacanex, this Quinatzin seems to assume Xolotl's own function and is portrayed by Ixtlilxóchitl as "emperor," dictating to Tochintecuhtli and Huetzin as subordinates. But this Quinatzin cannot be the same person as the ruler of that name who, a century later, was allied to Acamapichtli of Tenochtitlán.

Ixtlilxóchitl treats these two Quinatzins as a single person, but gives names for three of the six children of his *original* Quinatzin (who directed the campaigns of Tochintecuhtli-Huetzin), that coincide exactly with those of three of Huetzin's seven offspring. Such repetition can hardly be fortuitous, and suggests that this early Quinatzin is really the same person as Huetzin, the outstanding Acolhua ruler of a period when Texcoco, the capital of the second, or fourteenth-century Quinatzin, was of minor significance. The historical sources mention other Quinatzins: the *Anales de Cuauhtitlán* write of a "Quinatzin el Viejo," and of yet further Quinatzins who ruled not in Texcoco but in Cuauhtitlán.[25]

A Tentative Genealogy

Huetzin and Tochintecuhtli loom large in the history of their time, but their precise identity is uncertain and their genealogy can only be presented in tentative fashion by a rather arbitrary selection of data. If all the sources' anomalies and contradictions were expressed in a table, the result would be unintelligible, if not nonsensical. Table A at least attempts a plausible solution, and the supporting evidence is given in the accompanying notes.

A start may conveniently be made with Huetzin, whose ancestry is the least obscure. According to the Codex Xolotl, he is the eldest son and heir of Itzmitl, ruler of Coatlichán (also called in one context Tlacotzin and in another Tlacoxinqui); he is therefore grandson of Tzontecomatl, usually named as first señor of Coatlichán. Apart from other acquisitions, Huetzin succeeded to the principality of Coatlichán, then the leading Acolhua city. He later usurped the throne of Tepetlaoztoc, and married Atotoztli, daughter of the ruler of Culhuacán, named Achitometl. Other sources state that Huetzin usurped the throne of Cuauhtexpetlatzin, successor not of Achitometl in Culhuacán but of Nauhyotl.[26]

The *Memorial Breve* names Huetzin as becoming ruler of Culhuacán in the same year 2 Tochtli as another prince, called Nonoalcatl, who also died in the same year as Huetzin, 9 Tochtli, and who, as this account states, *may* have been the same person.[27] The *Memorial Breve* insists that Huetzin was an unwelcome usurper and that Coatlichán, not Culhuacán, was his real home; the Culhuas resisted his rule by force. The source states that Huetzin received the support of Xolotl, whom it names in another context as the double of Tochintecuhtli, Huetzin's main ally.

A plethora of contradictions obscures the origins of Tochintecuhtli, though the list of principalities associated with his name is impressive: for Ixtlilxóchitl and the Codex Xolotl he is the son of the ruler of Cahuacan and señor of Huexotla, though Ixtlilxóchitl also states that he was son of Tlotzin, Xolotl's grandson and that he was given the señorío of Zacatlán, along with many others. The *Memorial Breve* names Tochintecuhtli as ruler of Huexotla, but in the *Anales de Tlatelolco* he is the son of the ruler of Cuitlachtepec, northwest of Tenayuca, and in Torquemada he himself is ruler of that city. Torquemada, however, in another passage says that he was ruler of Cahuacan, and the *Anales de Cuauhtitlán* also mention him in connection with the "Otomís of Cahuacan," but without specifically stating that he was ruler of that place. Torquemada reports that Tochintecuhtli was son of "Millato" [*sic*], señor of Coatlichán, and in the *Anales de Cuauhtitlán* he is described as son of Tezcatecuhtli, señor of Cuauhtitlán.

Table A attempts a logical interpretation of such data, that clearly involve many homonyms. Our genealogical reconstruction faces the problem that, in Ixtlilxóchitl's account, Tochintecuhtli is son of Tlotzin and brother, not only of the second Nopaltzin, but also of the first Quinatzin Tlaltecatzin, who, as already stated, may be identical with Huetzin. In this version of the facts Huetzin and Tochintecuhtli become brothers, or even one and the same person; but most sources describe Huetzin as heir to Coatlichán, whereas Tochintecuhtli is credited with quite different origins and is variously linked with Cahuacan, Cuitlachtepec, and Tenayuca, situated on the opposite side of the Lake of Texcoco, in the northwestern part of the Valley of Mexico. However, the careers of the two princes are so interwoven, that at times the distinction between them becomes blurred, and details pertaining to the one may erroneously be applied to the other.

Ixtlilxóchitl's account serves to dramatize the feats of these two conquerors and makes great play of their major campaign against the "pure" Chichimecs of Metztitlan, Tototepec, Atotonilco, and Tulancingo, conducted in areas reportedly explored by Nopaltzin and then absorbed into Xolotl's wide domains. The introduction of the fourteenth-century king of Texcoco, Quinatzin, ally of Acamapichtli, into the equation as supreme allied commander of these thirteenth-century wars endowed him with a brilliant military career which he otherwise lacked; Ixtlilxóchitl's account of these feats is based on the Codex Xolotl, where Quinatzin is seen treating Tochintecuhtli and Huetzin, the true protagonists in these wars, as vassals.

The reconstruction offered in Table A perforce presents a different picture to the orthodox, or Ixtlilxóchitl, genealogy. For instance, Aculhua of Azcapotzalco and Tzontecomatl of Coatlichán are no longer contemporaries who pay joint homage to the venerable Xolotl; the adjusted version has to face the fact that Tzontecomatl is reportedly Huetzin's grandfather, while Aculhua is son-in-law of Huetzin's contemporary, Tochintecuhtli. This anomaly lends force to our view that early Aculhua history preceded the rise of the Tepanecs (whose ruler is so confusingly named Aculhua, alias Acolnahuacatzin) a problem that will later be examined in greater detail.

Caso makes a brave attempt at reconstruction, based on a fairly literal interpretation of the Codex Xolotl. The royal house of Coatlichán does not figure in Caso's accompanying chart, except for Huetzin, who appears in a footnote as reigning from 1129–50; this is apparently a misprint for 1229–50. Caso thus makes Huetzin the contemporary of Nopaltzin, whose reign in Tenayuca is given as from 1232–63. But the drawbacks of such a genealogy are typified by the awkward fact that, according to the very sources on which it is based, Nopaltzin is Huetzin's great-grandfather, though in Caso's table the two are contemporaries (Huetzin, according to Ixtlilxóchitl, was son of Malinalxóchitl, daughter of Nopaltzin's son, Tlotzin).[28] Tezozomoc of Azcapotzalco in the Caso version is the son of Cuetlachxóchitl, another contemporary of Nopaltzin; but Nopaltzin's reign, according to the same table, began in 1232, and Tezozomoc's ended in 1426.

A similar genealogy made by Espejo and Monzon leads to similar conclusions and does nothing to relieve the confusion implicit in any too literal interpretation of the Texcocan sources.[29] Such attempts amply illustrate the pitfalls of an all-too-ready assignment of Julian calendar dates to Mesoamerican rulers before the Aztecs; in my Table A, dates are few and tentative, and reigns can seldom be surely fixed in time without a fairly exhaustive study of the kind that I previously undertook for Tezozomoc and Acamapichtli.[30] To quote a single instance, Caso's date of 1357 for the 8 Calli in which Quinatzin of Texcoco died ends the life of this ruler well before the accession of Acamapichtli of Tenochtitlán, notwithstanding Ixtlilxóchitl's descriptions of their joint campaigns.

The insistence of the *Anales de Tlatelolco* that Tochintecuhtli spent seven years in Azcapotzalco suggests that he reigned in that city, then of very limited importance; he also controlled Cahuacan and Tenayuca, as well as Cuitlachtepec, while on the opposite side of the Lake of Texcoco he ruled in Huexotla. Huetzin, who dominated Tepetlaoztoc and Culhuacán, as well as Coatlichán, emerges as the joint founder of Acolhua power, and his triumphs made Coatlichán the leading Acolhua city for several succeeding generations; conquests ranging as far as Atotonilco and Tulancingo laid the basis for the future dominance of Texcoco, Coatlichán's successor, in that region. Accordingly, the territorial acquisitions of Huetzin-Tochintecuhtli deserve the title of "empire" in terms of the Mesoamerica of that transitional period. Out of the ample but confusing data of this period, their achievements emerge as the first tentative essay to fill the gap left by the fall of Tollan.

Such a hypothesis seeks at least to distinguish between fact and allegory, and to escape from a situation where Xolotl, a twelfth-century figure, when aged 150, instigates a thirteenth-century war in which the chief protagonist is Quinatzin, king of Texcoco in the late fourteenth century.

The Recording of History

In seeking to determine who these Chichimecs of Xolotl really were and whence they came, the question naturally arises of how the history of the period ever came to be recorded in a manner so confused, or oversimplified. Ixtlilxóchitl's written account, as Dibble makes abundantly clear, adds many extra touches to the pictorial version of the Codex Xolotl. Ixtlilxóchitl makes Nopaltzin into

Xolotl's son and then, to complete the genealogy of his ancestors, promotes Quinatzin, ruler of a single and not over-powerful city, into a great emperor, lording it over his fellow rulers.

The major embellishments to the historical record are already present in the Codex Xolotl and, to a lesser extent, in the Mapa Tlotzin. For instance, the allegorical account of the joint arrival at Xolotl's court of the three leaders, Aculhua the Tepanec, Cozcacuauh the Otomí, and Tzontecomatl the Acolhua appears in the Codex Xolotl, that gives a date of 1 Tecpatl for their coming and for the acquisition of their respective principalities. In the Codex Xolotl Quinatzin figures prominently in the wars of Tochintecuhtli and Huetzin, even if Ixtlilxóchitl further enhances his ancestor's role in those events. The codex, however, tends to depict Xolotl and Nopaltzin as explorers more than conquerors; only in rare cases, such as that of Culhuacán, are hostilities illustrated. Moreover, in the codex the Chichimecs arrived in small groups, in contrast to the hordes described by Ixtlilxóchitl.

Opinions differ as to whether Ixtlilxóchitl himself wrote the accompanying Nahuatl glossary of the codex, though an expert calligrapher might perhaps help to resolve the problem, using other available examples of this author's handwriting. It remains uncertain whether Ixtlilxóchitl was himself responsible for attributing the name or title of Xolotl to the leading personage, who bears the dog-head glyph.

How did the Codex Xolotl come into being? As Dibble explains in his introduction, the present document is a fifteenth-century copy, based on an earlier original, as also were the Mapas Tlotzin and Quinatzin. But a codex whose narrative ends a century before the Conquest was surely recorded long before 1519; it does not thereby form an unbiased record of events and had perhaps undergone a measure of re-editing, possibly at the prompting of Nezahualcoyotl, long before a copy came into the hands of his descendant, Alva Ixtlilxóchitl.

Sahagún, in a familiar passage, records how Itzcoatl "rewrote" history and suppressed certain parts of the Mexican past. But, if Itzcoatl could remold the history of his people, so also could Nezahualcoyotl, or his father, Huehue Ixtlilxóchitl. Without due embellishment, the known ancestry of the Texcocan royal house was not conspicuously glamorous, since the city had only recently risen to prominence. Nor could an unvarnished Texcocan genealogy compare with the impressive, if contrived, family tree of Itzcoatl and Moctezuma I, who at a stroke of the pen had made themselves into the heirs of Culhuacán and hence of the great Tollan and of Topiltzin Quetzalcoatl. While Ixtlilxóchitl, Nezahualcoyotl's father, was a distinguished if tragic ruler, it does not seem as if either Ixtlilxóchitl's father, Techotlalatzin, or his grandfather Quinatzin, could boast of many a glittering triumph, and the latter merely played a limited part in Acamapichtli's campaigns in the Chinampa region. The marriage of Nopaltzin to the daughter of Pochotl of Culhuacán, and grandaughter of Topiltzin, also made the Texcocan monarchs— according to Ixtlilxóchitl—descendants of Topiltzin, as well as heirs to the Chichimec Empire.

Crucial to the correct, or incorrect, interpretation of Mesoamerican history is the question of chronology, and the earlier written documents tend to present comparable shortcomings in that respect. For instance, the *Anales de Cuauhtitlán* offer far more historical data than the Codex Xolotl, but of a kind that means little without scholarly interpretation. Probably the pictorial codices were copied rather indiscriminately one from the other over the centuries and were enriched by oral tradition. Confusion over dates thus arose in earlier versions, on account of the very nature of the fifty-two year cycle, and the absence of any means of distinguishing, say, the year 5 Calli of one year cycle from another 5 Calli occurring 104 years previously. A given episode could accordingly be displaced in time by several fifty-two-year periods at a stroke of the pen by a *tlacuilo* who either did not understand the proper historical sequence, or who deliberately predated a series of events by several cycles at the behest of a master seeking greater antiquity and prestige for his own dynasty. In this respect the Texcocan sources bear witness to the efforts of the rulers of that dynasty to vie with the rulers of Tenochtitlán in the search for venerable ancestors.

In this instance, a key to this process of either confusing or adjusting the chronological record lies in the role of Quinatzin, Nezahualcoyotl's great-grandfather, whose significance was transformed by making him the hero of battles that took place one hundred years before his time. Quinatzin is made into the direct descendant of Xolotl, Nopaltzin, and Tlotzin, from whom he accordingly inherited the throne of Tenayuca. But, as will later become apparent, Quinatzin's voluntary renunciation of Tenayuca is probably apocryphal. Moreover, Table A can offer no concrete evidence that Quinatzin was ever ruler of Tenayuca, even if he descended in the female line from Tochintecuhtli, who by all accounts did govern in that city; Quinatzin was more probably a direct descendant of Huetzin of Coatlichán. Perhaps even more significant is the story of Tochintecuhtli, who seems to have been the leading empire builder in the interval between Toltec and Tepanec times, as well as an ancestor in the female line of Quinatzin; his deeds form the basis for the apocryphal narrative of another emperor who ruled several generations before him and bore the appellation of Xolotl—a name that may also have been given to Tochintecuhtli, and was later used to address Tezozomoc of Azcapotzalco. An earlier Xolotl is included in the *Historia Tolteca-Chichimeca* list of Chichimec leaders at the time of Tollan's collapse, but does not figure very prominently in that history.

As I have already insisted, it may be less pertinent to say that Tochintecuhtli *is* Xolotl (since he cannot be his own great-grandfather) than to insist that many details of the career of the great emperor (such as the occupation of Tenayuca and Cahuacan, and the expedition to the Metztitlán region), are inspired by the deeds of Tochintecuhtli more than by those of any other historic personage. In so far as Xolotl is *not* Tochintecuhtli, he becomes a rather legendary figure. The story of Xolotl is open to question on general as well as on detailed grounds, and long before I ever examined this problem more closely, I had already expressed doubts concerning the saga of a great Chichimec emperor who descended on the Valley of Mexico and assumed power after the fall of Tollan. That city may indeed have suffered a great catastrophe and collapsed, though the archaeological record tends to question any mass abandonment. In my first volume on Tollan, I stressed that any people who could ravage that center were no true nomads, surely incapable of such feats, but Toltecized former Chichimecs, who bore little resemblance to those rustic intruders depicted in the Codex Xolotl.

The historical sources do not suggest that this sudden collapse had an immediate parallel in the central part of the Valley of Mexico, and archaeology offers no evidence of such a catastrophe. On the contrary, Culhuacán is portrayed as continuing to prosper, and as even consolidating its position, to the chagrin of Xolotl; the city acted as a safe haven for refugees from Tollan, that stood alone in being suddenly stricken. And yet, notwithstanding the apparent survival of civilization outside Tollan, Xolotl is supposedly welcomed as lord and master not only by those thriving communities of the Valley of Mexico, but in territories lying far beyond its bounds—without so much as a blow being struck, except in the case of Culhuacán. The Mexicas defeated Azcapotzalco after a bitter struggle in 1428; but following this victory they were still obliged to fight hard battles in order to subdue city by city a populous region that surrendered to Xolotl without a fight.

The supposition that the politico-military fabric of Central Mexico collapsed like a house of cards at the mere approach of marauding Chichimecs—depicted in the Codex Xolotl as arriving in *small* bands—is hard for the historian to accept. Why, one may ask, did such traditional centers of population as Azcapotzalco, Xaltocan, and Coatlichán, whose foundations have been dated by the archaeologist to Toltec, and even pre-Toltec times, lie open as vacant fiefs, to be bestowed as mere parcels of real estate on favored suppliants? What had happened to their previous rulers, of whom the record remains silent, except in the case of Tepetlaoztoc, which gave Huetzin a chilly welcome. In Culhuacán, the only other known center of resistance, Xolotl and Nopaltzin, far from extirpating the previous dynasty, restored it to power.

The indiscriminate parceling out of territories to alien rulers runs counter to all Mesoamerican traditions. The Aztecs, who were quite as ruthless as any nomad intruder and better versed in ways of administering occupied territory, almost invariably treated the existing ruler as an indispensable instrument for the gathering of their tribute; after a bout of bargaining about his future liabilities, the previous señor was normally left in charge of his principality as an Aztec underling.

Cases where the Aztecs supposedly imposed direct or military rule, such as Chalco or Culhuacán, are open to challenge, since alternative sources usually list a more or less unbroken succession of rulers in such places. The Aztec Triple Alliance had inherited from

70

Tezozomoc of Azcapotzalco a highly organized system of adminis-
tration and tribute gathering. People who had scarcely emerged from
their caves, who dressed in skins and possessed no established seat of
power, might conceivably have overthrown a tottering Tollan; but
the notion is surely far-fetched that they were capable of suddenly
setting up an empire of their own, of a kind that the Aztecs succeeded only in conquering after bitter struggles. If they had imposed
tribute on a comparable scale, they would not have known what to do
with it or even how to count it. Much of what the Aztecs collected
consisted of baubles for the nobles, not of consumer goods or com-
modities for the common people. Contributions were reportedly made
to Xolotl of rabbits and deer; but it is hardly conceivable that boundless regions, stretching from the Valley of Mexico to the Gulf Coast,
should have been subdued with nothing better in view than the
accumulation of vast quantities of animal skins for the benefit of an
emperor who would don nothing finer, according to the pictorial
codices that provide the "official" version of these events.

IV. Chichimecs and Ex-Chichimecs

The Background

Chapter III has dealt mainly with the principal actors in the drama of the Chichimec invasion and its aftermath. The attempt to produce a meaningful genealogy led to the conclusion that, in several instances, either one person had become two, belonging to different eras, or, alternatively, as in Quinatzin's case, a single individual had been endowed with two distinct careers.

But even if the earliest leaders may belong to legend as well as to history, several migrations undoubtedly took place. The sources contain accounts of people called "Chichimecs," all of whom have a good deal in common; though ostensibly separate movements, their leaders surprisingly tend to share the same names. The question still remains: Aside from their achievements—or their shortcomings—who *were* these "Chichimecs" who infiltrated the Valley of Mexico in the era of Tollan's decline and fall? Plainly this southeastward movement of less advanced peoples was no single migration, but a protracted process, triggered by events more distant in time and space. As proposed in my first volume, according to data derived from the southwest of the United States and from the eastern margin of the Great Plains, the North American arid zone was expanding in all directions between the twelfth and the fifteenth centuries; this change must have disturbed the subsistence pattern of nomad Chichimecs living in the sensitive border zone between savannah and steppe climates.[1] Nearer to Mesoamerica, southern Tamaulipas also became slowly drier from about A.D. 1000 onwards.

The significance of fluctuations in climate is fundamental; Armillas in particular has demonstrated that the frontier between Mesoamerica and nomad territory in Conquest times coincided fairly exactly with the northern limits of land suitable for seasonal agriculture. The cultural disparity between neighboring groups on either side of this dividing line corresponded to the environment of their respective habitats; Armillas, however, also stresses that certain peoples defy categorization either as pure nomads or as fully sedentary peoples. "In the region that lies between the Sierra Occidental of Durango and Zacatecas and the eastern escarpment of the Altiplano, the dividing line between sedentary peoples and nomad groups corresponds in general with the contemporary limit of the arid zone; to the south of this line, prairie vegetation predominates in the plains and forest in the mountains, while to the north stretches the steppe and beyond it the desert."[2]

Probably conditions in the sixteenth century did not greatly differ from those of today, when rainfall registered by meteorological stations in the Lerma Valley, the historical frontier zone of the Kingdom of Michoacán, varies between 700 and 800 millimeters p.a., whereas in the strip of territory that stretches from Aguascalientes through the northeast of Jalisco, the Sierra of Guanajuato, and the south of Querétaro, as far as the Valle del Mezquital, the precipitation is only from 500 to 600 mm p.a.; north of this, it averages about 350 mm. The basic types of climate, according to the Köppen categorization, are Cw to the south, and BS to the north of the dividing line.

Resulting in part from this change in climate, marking the advance of the arid zone, archaeological finds bear witness to the steady erosion of the northwestern frontier of Mesoamerica, dating from early Toltec times and perceptible even in the Late Classic, when Teotihuacán influences reached as far as Chametla in Sinaloa. The situation in Zacatecas and Durango deteriorated at a relatively remote date; the Vesuvio phase of the Chalchihuites culture lasted from about A.D. 500 to 950, but after 800 the number of occupied sites declined. The great fortress of La Quemada, that blocked the way down the open valley of the Río Malpaso-Jérez, may have fallen as early as A.D. 1000.[3]

At the time when Tollan became a leading power, a wide buffer zone probably screened the city from the Teochichimecs, so hard to tame. The population of such a region would have been at least semicivilized and semi-Toltecized; however, pressures from farther north, arising out of ecological deterioration, may have forced these semi-Toltecs to move southward; the former buffer zone, long before Tollan's collapse, thereby became the domain of roaming Teochichimecs, who made no pottery and practiced little or no agriculture. This process affected areas as far south as the present state of Guanajuato.

Accordingly, the enemy stood almost at the gates of Tollan long before its collapse, and those more quiescent peoples, who had lived in the former buffer zone, had already changed their habitat. Such was the general background to the cataclysms that ensued, and the age of flux that accompanied the end of Tollan was probably heralded by a build-up of these nomad Chichimecs, whose center of gravity previously lay farther to the north, but who, already in late Teotihuacán times, began to harass the outer marches of Mesoamerica and to exert a southward pressure.

But the groups who later moved into the Valley of Mexico, and even those who dealt a mortal blow to Tollan itself, were probably not so much pure Chichimecs as Kirchhoff's former Chichimecs and Otonchichimecs, dislodged from Guanajuato, Querétaro, and perhaps the valley of Toluca, by real nomads who had come from regions lying still farther to the north.

I previously proposed that Otomís may have played a significant role in the great Tollan, an ostensibly Nahuatl-speaking polity. At all events, the Otomís were left in possession of the field as far as Tollan was concerned, and were probably also in at the kill. The peoples who then penetrated the Valley of Mexico—perhaps themselves of Otomí stock—may well have been accompanied by certain pure or Teochichimecs, such as Pames or Cascanes, whom Jiménez Moreno identifies with the Chichimecs of Xolotl.

Carrasco remarks on a general agreement among scholars that

the Chichimecs of Xolotl differed profoundly from the Otomís. I, however, diverge from this consensus, to the extent that I believe that at least some of these "Chichimecs" were Otomís. Kirchhoff insisted that they spoke Otomí, and it may be added that Carrasco himself, who sees Xolotl's followers as Pames, concurs that they probably brought Otomís in their train.[4] Moreover, he outlines certain parallels between Chichimecs and Otomís, stressing that the latter were great hunters—in the Florentine Codex they are dressed as such—and that, like the Teochichimecs, they were monogamous.[5]

Jiménez Moreno splits the difference between Carrasco and Kirchhoff by suggesting that the Chichimecs of Xolotl were Pame-Otomís.[6] He regards Sahagún's Teochichimecs as a blend of Pames, Guamares, and Cuachiles, together with peoples from southern Zacatecas. Such a combination includes some rather contrasting elements; there is surely a world of difference between, say, the Pames and the Cuachiles. The latter, at the time of the Conquest, were extremely ferocious; together with the Guamares, they were the most untamed of all the Chichimecs and fought bitter wars against the Spaniards. The Pames on the other hand had adopted certain Mesoamerican social and religious customs, while the Cuachiles' only concession to the mores of Mesoamerica was the imbibing of pulque.[7] Pame is linguistically akin to Otomí, and Soustelle lists an impressive number of words in common, more particularly related to hunting, such as "kwa" for rabbit in both tongues.[8]

The Pames provide an excellent example of the difficulties of drawing an exact dividing line between Chichimecs and Mesoamericans. Although they depended for their sustenance more on hunting and gathering than on agriculture, culturally they stood at an intermediate level between the civilized and noncivilized peoples. Not only did social stratification exist among the Pames, but they had temples, idols, and priests, and displayed other typically Mesoamerican traits. It is interesting to note, moreover, that in Pame and in the related Otomí and Matlatzinca languages the words for cultivated plants seem to contain proto-Otomí roots, indicating that the practice of agriculture dated from a distant past. This phenomenon leads Armillas to suspect that Conquest-time Pame culture was the product of an ecological deterioration and that, though they then lived in the arid zone, they preserved the norms of civilization as a relic of better times.[9] Not only did the Pames constitute a borderline case between Chichimecs and non-Chichimecs, but certain evidence suggests that the term "Chichimecs" was at times virtually interchangeable with "Otomí," and that the prime movers in the southward migration were indeed Otomís. Sahagún, for instance, writes of the "Otonchichimecas."

In the *Historia Tolteca-Chichimeca,* the Chichimecs who came to the rescue of the Toltecs in Cholula refer to themselves as Otomís (see Chapter III). Torquemada states that the Chichimecs who came to Poyauhtlán, and whom he mentions in connection with Mixcoatl, spoke Otomí. The *Historia de los Mexicanos* goes so far as to write of "the Chichimecs, whom we call Otomís."[10]

The sources concur that of the three señores who reportedly arrived in 1 Tecpatl and who became the beneficiaries of Xolotl's "donation," one, Cozcacuauh, led a group of Otomís who settled in Xaltocan; probably, according to Jiménez Moreno, these were Otomí-Mazahuas. But Jiménez Moreno has also proposed that not only the Tepanecs, but also the Acolhuas may have had Otomí antecedents;[11] he does not, however, reiterate Kirchhoff's assertion that the Chichimecs of Xolotl were Otomí-speakers.

The picture is confused, though in this context we are less concerned with the general meaning of the term "Chichimec" than with its actual significance when employed by Ixtlilxóchitl, Muñoz Camargo, and other sources in describing this particular sequence of events. Like "Toltec," "Chichimec" probably meant different things in different contexts. Indeed, Ixtlilxóchitl, when seeking to draw a distinction between "Toltecs" on the one hand and "Chichimecs" on the other, is adamant that he includes among the latter not only pure Otomís, Mazahuas, and Matlatzincas, but also Acolhuas, Tlaxcalans (i.e., those Chichimecs who refounded Tlaxcala), and even the Mexicas.[12] "Dos linajes había en esta tierra, y hay hoy día según parece en las historias; Chichimecas es el primero y el segundo tultecas; y de estos dos linajes de gentes hay muchas generaciones, que tiene cada una de ellas su lengua y modo de vivir; pero de todas ellas la mayor parte se precian y dicen que son Chichimecas de los que trajo Xolotl, y que son los meros Chichimecas, y los Acolhuas y Aztlanecas que ahora se llaman Mexicanos, Tlaxcaltecas, Tepehuas, Totonaques, Mezcas, Cuextecos, Michuaques, Otomites, Mavahuas, Matlatzincas y otras muchas naciones que se precian de este linaje. Y la segunda (i.e., los Toltecas) son Coculhuas [*sic*], Cholultecas, Miztecas, Tepanecas, Xochimilcas, Tozpanecas, Xicalancas, Chonchones, Tenimes, Cuauhtemaltecas, Texolotecas y muchas otras naciones." ("There were two types of people in this land, that still exist today, according to the various histories; Chichimec is the first, and Toltec the second; and of these two types, there are many subdivisions, each one of which possesses its own language and mode of living; but of all these, most boast that they are of the Chichimecs that Xolotl brought. The real Chichimecs [*los meros chichimecas*] are the Acul-huas, the Aztlanecas that are today called Mexicans, Tlaxcaltecans, Tepehuas, Totonacs, Mazcas, Huaxtecs, Michuaques, Otomís, Ma-zahuas, Matlatzincas, and many other nations that boast of this descent. And the second type [i.e., the Toltecs] consists of Cocul-huas [*sic*], Chololtecans, Mixtecs, Tepanecs, Xochimilcans, Toz-panecs, Xicalancas, Chonchones, Tenimes, Guatemalans, Texolo-tecs, and many other nations.")[13]

So much for Ixtlilxóchitl's definition, but, as Kirchhoff pointed out, what all the different and conflicting meanings of the term Chichimec really had in common was the association of this term with the north.[14]

Ixtlilxóchitl in a different context describes the three groups who arrived together at Xolotl's court in 1 Tecpatl as generically Acolhuas, and as coming from Michuacán; he states that they were all of Michuaque Chichimec stock, though each spoke a separate tongue.[15] In yet another passage, the same author again writes of "The three Aculhua Señores" and says that these señores *collectively* brought with them "La Nación de Otomites." He does in this in-stance draw a distinction between these new arrivals and Xolotl's own followers by stating that the newcomers worshiped idols and built temples, and again repeats the words "estos Aculhuas" to de-scribe the whole tripartite group.[16]

The so-called Chichimec invaders of the Valley of Mexico in post-Toltec times had surely become, not merely former Chichimecs, as Kirchhoff also stressed, but were in effect latter-day Tolteca-Chichimecs, i.e., people whose cultural attainments were comparable to those of the Tolteca-Chichimecs who had come long before from the northwest and, jointly with the Nonoalcas, founded Tollan.

Basically they were semi-Mesoamericanized invaders of territories inhabited by city dwellers.

A Contradiction in Terms

The appellation of Tolteca-Chichimec is a contradiction in terms: "Toltec" implies full adoption of Mesoamerican cultural traditions; "Chichimec," interpreted literally, signifies the opposite and is applicable to nomad people, not adherents of Mesoamerican civilization or votaries of Mesoamerican gods.

Perhaps the problem may be expounded by saying what is not meant by the term Chichimec (including Tolteca-Chichimec). Sahagún states: "The people to the east [of the Sierra Nevada] are not called Chichimeca; they are called Olmeca, Uixtotin, Nonoualca."[17] He adds the rather confusing assertion that the Toltecs are also called Chichimecs, writing in this context of the intermediate category, the Tolteca-Chichimecs; he also affirms that people like the Tepanecs, Acolhuas and Chalcas ranked as Chichimecs, because they had come from Chichimec territory (in the north).

The people described by Sahagún as Tolteca-Chichimecs are thus distinct from those, such as Nonoalcas, who came to Tollan from regions lying to the east of the Puebla-Tlaxcala valley, and his definition of non-Chichimecs embraces the Totonacs, Huaxtecs, and Mayas, though the term "Huaxteca-Chichimeca" is occasionally used for nomads living to the north of the Huaxteca. Ixtlilxóchitl, in the passage cited above, included Huaxtecs and Totonacs among the general grouping of Chichimecs, but he was anxious to claim that Xolotl visited and even populated the Gulf Coast, and was therefore reluctant to assign its inhabitants to a distinct category. The term Tolteca-Chichimec first pertained to the tribes who came to Tollan Xicocotitlan in earlier times, as opposed to the Nonoalcas who arrived from the southeast. But the same expression became applicable to those people who came from a northwesterly direction after the fall of Tollan. Therefore, succeeding waves of Tolteca-Chichimecs were in effect responsible both for the establishment of Tollan and for its downfall. But while Tolteca-Chichimec marks a degree of adherence to Mesoamerican culture, it does not necessarily imply a knowledge of Nahuatl. Probably the disparity between

Nonalcas from the Gulf Coast and Tolteca-Chichimecs from the northwest was less pronounced than the cultural divide that separated the Tolteca-Chichimecs from the pure Chichimec nomads, dressed in skins and shunning the practice of agriculture or the possession of fixed dwellings. The stress in the hybrid expression is surely more on "Toltec" then on "Chichimec"; the Mexicas are sometimes called "Mexica-Chichimecs," but the description lacks formal content, and the addition of the adjective "Chichimec" in this instance means little or nothing. And in a sense the term "Tolteca-Chichimec" aptly applies to the migrant Mexicas; we are told that they sowed crops and built temples, customs alien to pure Chichimecs. To some extent Tolteca-Chichimec becomes equivalent to Toltec, an appellation also subject to several interpretations.[18]

The Chichimecs, or Tolteca-Chichimecs as I prefer to call them, who penetrated to Tollan and beyond in the twelfth century are unlikely to have been of homogeneous stock; their numbers surely included disparate elements, differing in their cultural attainments and ethnic affiliations. The fate is obscure of the essentially Mesoamerican population still settled in early Postclassic times in the present-day states of Guanajuato and Querétaro, and we even ignore the true lot of the inhabitants of Tollan, despite stirring accounts of utter ruin and total destruction. By the same token, the surrounding Teotlalpan is unlikely to have been denuded of its population, even if some inhabitants sought greater security in the central Valley of Mexico, as certain sources relate. But it remains improbable that Otomís and other Mesoamericanized peoples previously living farther to the northwest of Tollan were all slaughtered by incoming Chichimecs (so peace-loving, in the Ixtlilxóchitl–Codex Xolotl account). They, together with some but not all of the inhabitants of Tollan and the surrounding Teotlalpan, probably swelled the numbers of those who entered the Valley of Mexico in the twelfth century. The distinction between Toltec refugees and Chichimec or Tolteca-Chichimec invaders, who both reportedly penetrated into that region, then becomes a fine one.

A Multitude of Sins

The Chichimecs themselves are no easier to define than the

Tolteca-Chichimecs. "Chichimec" literally covers a multitude of sins; the name itself is probably not derived, as is often suggested, from "chichi" (dog), "mecatl" (cord). The plural of such an appellation would not be "Chichimeca" but "Chichimecame." "Chichimec" probably comes notionally from the place-name Chichiman, which produces chichimecatl in the singular, and whose plural is "Chichimeca." Chichiman might mean "Place of Sucking," i.e., "Place of the Newly Born" or "Place of the Young." The Chichimecs would accordingly be the new or young people, uninitiated into the arts of civilization. However, according to Thelma Sullivan, Chichiman is more likely to derive from a noun than from a verb, and then simply means "Place of Dogs," a rendering to which it is hard to attach a precise significance.

Chichimecs are often described by Sahagún and others as Teochichimecs, i.e., true or extreme Chichimecs. Sahagún begins his description with a fairly orthodox account of such Teochichimecs; many lived far away on the grassy plains and deserts, being nomads without any home, maintaining themselves by hunting and dressing in animal skins. The chieftain dwelt in a grass hut. The same account stresses their strict monogamy and their Calvinistic abhorrence of adultery.

But the same author, still writing of Teochichimecs, adds details that present a conflicting picture. These Chichimecs are additionally described as fine stonecutters; they carried mirrors on their backs, so that, when walking in single file, each one could admire his own figure in the mirror worn by the man who preceded him; in other words, these ragged nomads wore the *tezcacuitlapilli,* that typical and traditional Mesoamerican adornment depicted in many codices. Sahagún's Teochichimecs also made objects of turquoise and were fine feather-workers; they lived a healthy outdoor life and were very long-lived. Ixtlilxóchitl evidently took his cue from Sahagún, when he credits Xolotl and his offspring with a lifespan of over 150 years. In general terms, therefore, Sahagún's description of Chichimecs is somewhat at variance with other Spanish sixteenth century accounts of those Chichimecs who, in Aztec and early Colonial times, were established not so far from the City of Mexico, occupying lands that bordered on the Otomí kingdom of Xilotepec, that acted as a buffer between what was then Chichimec territory and the Nahuatl-speaking regions to the southeast.

The designation "Chichimec" is vague, and Sahagún gives another definition when he states that it could be applied to all the peoples who used the bow and arrow. He adds that people who were not really Chichimecs were proud to use this appellation, that in practice came simply to imply the possession of manly virility, and could thus be applied to all those immigrants who reached the Valley of Mexico after enduring the harsher life of the marginal regions. As Kirchhoff again insists, while the term Toltec always referred to civilized Mesoamericans, "Chichimecs" was used both for savage food-takers, who lived in the north, and also for simpler farming peoples.[19]

After dealing with the Teochichimecs, Sahagún next describes the Otonchichimecs, or plain Otomís, as they were known at the time of the Conquest; they wore fine clothing and possessed lords and rulers; they followed such traditional Mesoamerican customs as the perforation of the lower lip in order to insert a plug of green stone. But though they were gaudy dressers, Sahagún reminds us that their cultural attainments fell short of the more refined and urbanized population of the Valley of Mexico. For instance, they showed a preference for straw huts over flat-roofed houses; in addition, they were "untrained, stupid, covetous, lazy, and shiftless." Moreover, while their diet consisted of those basic staples of maize, beans, and chile, these were supplemented by such uncouth victuals as serpents, squirrels, kangaroo rats, mice, and black beetles.[20]

Sahagún's Otomís may therefore be viewed as well advanced on the road to civilization; the difference between them and the most sophisticated urban dwellers is merely one of degree. Today in Mexico and elsewhere in Latin America, such distinctions in cultural levels survive in some form or other. Certain segments of the population, whether in town or country, live in fragile dwellings that bear little comparison with the standard accommodation of the city center, and include items in their daily fare that would have little appeal to its more favored inhabitants. Sahagún's general description of the diet of the people of Tenochtitlán lists items that recall those included on the Otomí menu. Not only his Otomís, but even

81

Sahagún's Chichimecs had risen far above the cultural level of pure nomads, having become expert in stone cutting and feather-work. Such people, whom he also describes as occasionally wearing tattered clothing, stood at a considerable remove from the real Teochichimecs—whom he briefly mentions—who dwelled in the grassy plains and deserts. When Sahagún's informers spoke of Teochichimecs, they presumably had in mind those Chichimecs, or former Chichimecs, with whom they were themselves familiar, rather than the true nomads whom they had never even seen and only knew by reputation, if at all. The people they described formed a minority class or caste who had come late into the Valley of Mexico and who at the time of the Conquest fulfilled menial tasks, just as some European countries today import laborers from outside to do work uncongenial to the local inhabitants.

Sahagún's statements have interesting implications concerning Tenochca society, that, as far as I know, have received little attention. Where, for instance, do these Chichimecs in tattered clothing fit into the social organization that is now the object of close study by modern scholars? Were the *mayeque,* who tilled the lands of the *pipiltin,* perhaps immigrant Chichimecs? Alternatively, were these Chichimecs liable for military service, and what relationship did they have with the *calpulli* organization, if any? Did they do manual work for the Tlatelolcan *calpullis* of specialized artisans? Possibly they also acted as porters, or *tlamamaque,* on the Aztec campaigns. Probably these Chichimecs, described by Sahagún's informers, became as distinct from the desert nomads as the Turkish gastarbeiter, established in the German Federal Republic, differs from the relatives whom he left behind in a remote Anatolian village. Such individuals had clearly acquired skills, as marginal members of sophisticated communities, that were unheard of in true Chichimec territories, beyond the receding bounds of Mesoamerica.

While therefore at one end of the cultural spectrum we do find pure nomad Chichimecs, not usually in contact with settled urban communities, and at the other extremity a range of peoples who are definitely non-Chichimec, the intermediate variations are numerous. Apart from Teochichimecs and Otonchichimecs, Sahagún discusses yet a third branch of the same family, the Tamine of "shooters of arrows." These also acquired a rudimentary culture, living among the Nahaus or Otomís, although they were housed in caves or gorges. They spoke a little Nahuatl, wore ragged clothing, and depended upon primitive agriculture as well as on hunting. They often attached themselves to some nobleman, to whom they paid a tribute of rabbits, deer, and serpents.[21] The text does not explain what the nobleman did with so many serpents (that he surely scorned to eat), nor, in more general terms, how such people fitted into the social organization of the Valley of Mexico as adumbrated by the sources.

Sahagún's informants draw their net so wide, and include so many disparate elements within the term Chichimec that the picture tends to be confused. Such descriptions differ markedly from other accounts, such as those of Las Casas, portraying the pure Chichimecs whose territory, in the immediate pre-Conquest period, was by no means remote from Tenochtitlán.

At the time of the Conquest most of the Querétaro region, as well as the southwest and northwest corners of Guanajuato, was occupied by Pames, and the remainder of Guanajuato by the Guachilcos. Those Chichimecs who lived near the bounds of civilization mixed at times with Otomís and other settled peoples; for instance, to the south of Ixmiquilpan lived nomad hunting Chichimecs, speaking a Chichimec tongue but interspersed among Otomís who practiced agriculture.[22] The Spaniards actually reversed the process of Chichimec advance, that preceded the establishment of the Aztec Empire, and established colonies of Otomís near the present site of Querétaro; in this region certain Otomís were already settled, including a trader called Conin or Conni, who cultivated crops and sold them to the true Chichimecs in return for animal skins.[23]

Among the most bellicose and cruel of the true Chichimecs—so far as this term has a precise validity—were the Guamares of the San Juan Valley, described as practicing a most primitive form of religion; they lived on roots cooked in ovens, as well as on game; wild tunas were their favorite fruit. They even ate maguey leaves, but did not use the fiber for clothing, preferring to go completely naked except for a kind of belt of deerskin worn by the women. According to Las Casas, this style of life was typically Chichimec.[24] So lived the unadulterated breed of Chichimecs, who possessed no technical skills except hunting, wore no finery, possessed no houses, and practiced no agriculture. Las Casas merely reports that occasionally they would cover their nakedness with tatters when parleying with the Spaniards. At other times they would decorate their bodies with red ochre or even paint them black and yellow.

A graphic description of the wretched way of life of those pure Chichimecs in northern Mexico and beyond is given by Cabeza de Vaca. For three months of the year they ate little else but tuna fruit; this they considered their time of plenty, for on this meager diet they at least did not go hungry and their bellies swelled up. For the remainder of the year nature was less bountiful, and they depended mainly upon two or three kinds of roots that were hard to find and very bitter. They occasionally killed a deer or caught a little fish; but this occurred so seldom that they even kept the fish bones, as well as those of serpents, and of these made a kind of edible powder. More often they ate spiders and ants' eggs, poisonous snakes, and even the excreta of deer.

The sources are apt to treat human sacrifice as one of the refinements of Mesoamerican civilization, unknown to the noble savage of marginal Mesoamerica. However, these Chichimecs described by Las Casas far outdid their more fastidious neighbors in brutal practices; even mothers and children taken in war were killed and scalped; adult male prisoners would be scalped first, leaving the whole crown bare, and their captors would then take out the bones of the arms and legs and sometimes even the ribs, while the victim was still alive.

Motolinía provides similar data on the simple nomad life: the Chichimecs of Michoacán went nude and had no sort of dwelling. Chichimec religion was rudimentary, and they were principally sun-worshipers, but had no idols or temples.[25]

Ixtlilxóchitl, when writing of the Chichimecs of Xolotl, is in partial accord with the above information, telling of people who dwelt in caves and whose sustenance derived from hunting and gathering. But he omits any mention of cruelty and credits them with certain more advanced customs, stating that they sometimes lived in straw huts and that their "kings and lords" (ranks surely unknown to true Chichimecs) wore skins, with cloth garments underneath, sometimes made of cotton.[26]

Reading between the lines, any peoples who moved into the Valley of Mexico after the fall of Tollan and who are often described as the Chichimecs of Xolotl were not remotely comparable to the Guamares of the San Juan Valley, as depicted by Las Casas. They seem instead to have constituted a blend in varying proportions of Sahagún's three varieties of Chichimecs; part were Teochichimecs, already somewhat Mesoamericanized, in accordance with the Sahagún account, and probably including Pames, as suggested by Jiménez Moreno, and Cascanes, though Armillas places the latter not among the nomads, but among the civilized peoples of Mesoamerica; to these were added a sprinkling of those rather nondescript Tamines— who had already climbed one rung higher on the ladder of civilization—and last but not least, a considerable contingent of Otonchichimecs. The latter, in view of their higher cultural attainments, naturally took the lead and set the tone.

Admittedly the pictorial records show people who conform closely to the true Chichimec model, even if they do not exactly fit Las Casas' description of naked savages. Invariably (perhaps in deference to Spanish susceptibilities) they are well covered with skins except when fighting. As illustrated in these documents, their process of adaptation was slow; Nopaltzin at the time of his death, as described in Plate IV of the Codex Xolotl, is already attired as a typical Mesoamerican ruler, indistinguishable from the ruler of Culhuacán, but in Plate III he still wears garments darker in hue and simpler in form, as a kind of halfway house to the adoption of the full trappings of civilization.

From Rags to Riches

But the codices, painted in post-Conquest times, can mislead as easily as any written text and should be interpreted with equal caution. By mid-fifteenth century, the rule apparently prevailed that anyone described in the broadest terms as a Chichimec must indeed be drawn as a conventional Chichimec, complete with skins and cave dwellings, and never as an Otomí or a Otonchichimec. The claim to rustic—or "Chichimec"—ancestors lent color to tales of tribal origins and satisfied a Mesoamerican yearning for a pedigree that spelled progress from rags to riches. Nowadays United States presidents—and Texas tycoons—will proclaim their humble or bucolic origins and will proudly stress that their success owes nothing

85

to inherited privilege. Such tendencies were alien to pre-industrial Europe, that sought continuity with the Roman and medieval past. The name Chichimec came to acquire an aura of romance, associated with the noblest qualities of man; in fact the Mesoamericans could justly claim to have invented the noble savage long before Jean-Jacques Rousseau. In Mesoamerica, the "rags to riches" legend almost amounted to a status symbol. Moreover, because the Toltecs derived in part from marginal Mesoamerica, would-be heirs to their legacy perforce boasted of similar origins; claimants to power in the Valley of Mexico and its vicinity would assert in unison that their forebears had emerged as tribal migrants from Chicomoztoc, though their cities were really settled in Teotihuacán times, if not before; even the Mayas had their seven caves in the vicinity of Tulán, the semi-mythical Tollan of Maya legend.

To reconcile a double claim to long occupancy of the Valley of Mexico, combined with Chichimec or Tolteca-Chichimec ancestry, the Mexicas and their neighbors would assert that they had once upon a time lived in central Mexico but had gone off into the wilds and subsequently returned. Kirchhoff tended to place a more literal interpretation on such reports, but I now view these traditions of emigration and return as belonging more to legend than to historical reality. Kirchhoff, however, had rightly stressed that the term Chichimec had a strictly northern connection, and that, because the Toltecs and Aztecs looked upon themselves as young, virile, and numerically strong, they proudly called themselves and others in the same situation "Chichimecs," but with equal pride applied to their peoples the term "Toltec," or its equivalent, "Culhua."[27] As Kirchhoff writes, the way to an understanding of the complexities of Toltec-Chichimec relations, and of the urge for civilized Indians to call themselves Chichimecs, will be open only when we have understood the principles involved and the generic reasons for the apparent contradictions.

The Codex Xolotl, the Mapa Tlotzin, and the Mapa Quinatzin clearly overemphasize the continued rusticity of the people they depict. For instance, Tochintecuhtli in Plate IV of the Codex Xolotl appears in a cave; but this monarch and his confederate Huetzin are the prototype of those more sophisticated empire-building caciques, who sought a tribute of luxury produce from conquered subjects that would have been distinctly out of place in a cave, serving as the "palace" of a ruler clad in skins. Tenayuca, the domain both of Xolotl and of Tochintecuhtli, with its elaborate pyramid, of which the early substructures probably predate this period, was no cave settlement, but an ancient Mesoamerican city.

I remain convinced that any "Chichimecs" who participated in the overthrow of Tollan Xicocotitlan and who invaded the Valley of Mexico were well led and highly organized and had little in common with, say, the Guamares of Conquest times. Doubts may persist concerning the chronology of those Chichimecs whom the *Anales de Cuauhtitlán* portray as accompanying Mixcoatl to Culhuacán; but neither they nor those other Chichimecs who went to Poyauhtlán and then founded Tlaxcala—also led originally by a Mixcoatl—were in any sense of the word true Teochichimecs. The future Tlaxcalans, according to Muñoz Camargo: "Bore as their idol Camaxtli . . . and were great worshipers of the other gods and idols, whom they venerated and adored with reverence, and whose precepts and laws they scrupulously observed."[28]

Such rites and customs were unknown to those Chichimecs whom the Spaniards invariably report as sky or star worshipers and as having no idols or temples.

The same may be said of followers of Mixcoatl, described by the *Anales de Cuauhtitlán* and the *Leyenda de los Soles*. They worshiped Itzpapalotl, a version of the traditional mother goddess, and the name of Mixcoatl himself is coupled with that veteran deity, Xiuhtecuhtli. Their religious practices are intrinsically Mesoamerican; Xiuhtecuhtli may be related to the Otomí patron deity, Otontecuhtli, but played no part in the rites of nomad Chichimecs; the god is always depicted with his face painted in the Otomí fashion. Armillas generally concurs with these views, though his interpretation of the Mixcoatl saga is very different from mine. He pointed to the cultural anomaly represented by the Chichimecs of Xolotl. As far as these and other invaders were in fact hunter-gatherers, Armillas suggests that this was not their original way of life, but a means of living that had been forced upon them when the advance of the arid zone impeded the cultivation of crops. Armillas also sees the true nomads not as the invaders of the Valley of Mexico, but as people who followed in their wake and occupied territory farther to the north: "These

waves [of migrants] . . . coming from the Bajío and from the south of
the present-day state of Guanajuato . . . certainly consisted of bands of
agriculturalists, doubtless forced to migrate by the dessication of that
region; in these movements nahua peoples participated—including
Aztecs—and Otomí groups. In their train came nomad Guamares
and Cuachichiles, who must originally have lived more to the north
and then spread to the territory that the sedentary peoples had abandoned, and where these nomads still were living at the time of the
Spanish Conquest."[29]

The saga of the great Xolotl, who descended upon the Valley of
Mexico like a wolf upon the fold, partly recalls the invasion of the
Tartars, who had swept through Asia not so long before the discovery
of America, or even the victories of the Turks, who had conquered
Hungary and stood at the very gates of the Hapsburg domains. But
such incursions, even if they influenced the thinking of Ixtlilxóchitl
and other Europeanized chroniclers, offer no true parallel. The Turks,
for instance, were no Teochichimecs: they practiced a higher religion and had already built imposing mosques in Anatolia. The Tartars of Genghis Kahn drew their sustenance from flocks and herds;
they were indeed clothed in animal skins; however, they lived not in
caves but in tents of felt, stretched over fine wattle rods, at times
furnished with looted carpets.

The Teochichimecs described by Las Casas would have been
incapable of such incredible feats of conquest, even if they had been
mounted on horses. Don Francisco de Ibarra, who saw the Zacate-
cans in 1554, insists that they lived in small groups and were unable
to adapt themselves to any form of permanent settlement; their
religion was likewise of a rudimentary nature.[30] The nomad bands
who then roamed in Michoacán surely lacked the military cohesion
to overthrow civilized policies, and could not have set up their own
principalities. The Chichimecs who fought wars of extinction against
the Spaniards, and who were virtually eliminated, were merely re-
sisting attempts to adapt their territory to settled agriculture: it
never entered their heads to copy the Spaniards and to learn to grow
crops after the manner of Xolotl's followers.

Xolotl is reported as accepting the submission of so many señoríos, and establishing his own principality of Tenayuca, together with
a kind of super-señorío, or "empire," reminiscent of the Toltecs or

Aztecs. But real Chichimecs, dwelling in caves and going naked or occasionally wearing skins could not have adapted themselves overnight to the city life of Tenayuca, nor could an "empire" have been administered from a cave. We are informed that Xolotl exacted tribute from his countless vassals, but this presupposes a political structure far beyond the capacity of his followers. The Aztec Empire was a complex entity, and required an elaborate bureaucracy for the collecting, counting, and distribution of the massive spoils received. An organization of this kind, in part inherited from the Tepanecs, took generations to perfect.

According to the orthodox version of events, few of the former rulers seem to have survived to pay tribute to Xolotl. Mysteriously, except for Nauhyotl of Culhuacán, they vanished from the scene, and their lands were left vacant, awaiting a rather capricious redistribution by the all-powerful Xolotl, who lavished them upon his own followers and on other migrant chieftains who happened to present themselves at his "court," or cave mouth.

In the history of Aztec conquests, the opposite system prevailed. Rulers, with very few exceptions, were left in charge of their domains, since they constituted the only reliable tribute-gatherers from their own people, even if they sometimes rebelled. The groups who moved into the Valley of Mexico in the twelfth and thirteenth centuries can scarcely have been empire builders on this scale, even if they managed to impose their will on certain settled communities, such as Tenayuca, Cuauhacan, and Culhuacán; even such feats imply a cultural level typified by Otomís or Otonchichimecs, who were probably accompanied by Teochichimec elements serving as auxiliaries. These post-Toltec invaders had rulers, nobles, gods, and a certain political cohesion, and adopted immediately to city life, in precise conformity with Sahagún's description of non-Chichimecs. The intruders may have been subject to Tollan, having been gradually pushed southeastward, as the boundary of Mesoamerica slowly receded. They finally came to the Valley of Mexico—as part of a movement of peoples already part-civilized, though distinct from the reported bands of fugitives towards Chapultepec, Chalco, Culhuacán, and Xico, who came from the stricken Tollan, presumably also left in possession of Otomí-speaking peoples, rather than of Teochichimecs, who shunned city life.

89

An Odd Coincidence

The historian still faces the enigma of the coincidence between so many names of the dramatis personae of the early part of the Codex Xolotl and those given in the *Historia Tolteca-Chichimeca.* The proportion of names that appear in both sources, as already given in Chapter III, is too large to be attributed to mere chance. Not only Xolotl, Nopaltzin, and Tlotzin, but a fair proportion of their leading followers are listed in the *Historia Tolteca-Chichimeca.* Mere coincidence can surely be eliminated from the equation; if this factor were present, the source would logically also include some names belonging to the rulers of Culhuacán, such as Coxcox or Achitometl, or typical Acolhua titles such as Acolmiztli, none of whom occur in the list of migrants to Cholula.

The *Historia Tolteca-Chichimeca* like the Codex Xolotl, tells a story that spans several centuries, beginning in the century of Tollan's collapse. The Chichimec leader Moquihuix led the rescue operation to Cholula, leaving Chicomoztoc twenty-nine years after his Toltec allies had left Tollan. But according to dates given in the *Historia Tolteca-Chichimeca,* he thereafter lived for a further eighty years; and if Mengin's suggested chronology is accepted, Moquihuix' military career was thus prolonged for 138 years, and he lived nearly as long as Xolotl. But, as in other instances, not excluding the case of Tezozómoc of Azcapotzalco, reports of legendary longevity are too often recorded by modern commentators without due acknowledgment that such flights of fancy call for reinterpretation of the data to produce a picture that is at least realistic. To appreciate the irrelevancy of such bicentennial reigns, one has only to consider that of the forty British monarchs between William the Conqueror and Elizabeth II, only seven reigned for more than twenty-five years.

The *Historia Tolteca-Chichimeca,* with its plethora of names and its circuitous comings and goings, makes greater sense if related, not to the movements of a single Chichimec group, but to different bands who entered the Valley of Mexico and the Puebla-Tlaxcala valley at different times. The names included in the text thereby constitute a kind of social register of successive Chichimec leaders (as well as of some non-Chichimecs), who took part in these migrations. Somewhat confusingly, Xolotl and Nopaltzin, mentioned early in this source, here figure not as Chichimecs, but as Toltecs, who had previously left Tollan and occupied Cholula in the face of Olmeca-Xicalanca opposition. Included in that same Toltec exodus was Quauhtliztac, (Iztacquauhtli in Ixtlilxóchitl, who describes him as leader of the Xaltocamecas and founder of Xaltocan). Tzontecomatl, first ruler of Coatlichán, received as a gift from Xolotl, figures prominently in the *Historia Tolteca-Chichimeca,* not as a Toltec, but as one of a select group of five Chichimec leaders who had their noses perforated (i.e., were ritually Mesoamericanized) in Chicomoztoc: he is also called Acolchichimecatl, in full accord with Ixtlilxóchitl's descriptions of him as the original Acolhua leader. Tecpatl or Tecpatzin, another leading henchman of Xolotl, also figures among these five important personages in the *Historia Tolteca-Chichimeca,* that describes him as leader of the Tlaxcalans, i.e., of the people sometimes known as the Chichimecs of Poyauhtlán, where they first settled before later founding Tlaxcala. After the perforating ceremony, the five were seated on "royal" mats, after which Quauhtliztac was worshiped as a god, and then they took part in a ritual ball game, another un-typically Chichimec pastime.

The distinction between the Toltecs of the *Historia Tolteca-Chichimeca* and their accompanying Chichimecs may be rather overdrawn. Listed among the Toltecs in this source are not only Xolotl himself, but the future founder of the Otomí stronghold of Xaltocan. The Chichimec leadership includes Tzontecomatl, also called Acolchichimeca, as well as Moquihuix. And in this account the Chichimecs alternately describe themselves as Otomís, in addition to their partaking of non-Chichimec pastimes and rituals. In Chicomoztoc, when soliciting their aid, the Cholulan Toltec delegates, Icxicouatl and Quetzalteueyac, eat maize with the Chichimecs; the latter, speaking of themselves and not of the Toltecs, then chant: "O may the Otomí, may the Otomí eat."[31] After this ceremony, they all leave Chicomoztoc, "within the mountain of Acolhuacán."

Mixcoatl and Xolotl

The *Historia Tolteca-Chichimeca,* the Codex Xolotl, the *Anales de Cuauhtitlán,* and Muñoz Camargo all describe movements of peoples into the Valley of Mexico; some migrants went to Tlaxcala

(Muñoz Camargo), some to Cholula (the *Historia Tolteca-Chichimeca)* some to Culhuacán, (the *Anales de Cuauhtitlán);* those of the Codex Xolotl, ostensibly arriving a little later, first established bases nearer to the Teotlalpan, in such places as Cahuacan, Tenayuca, Xaltocan, and Azcapotzalco and thus settled localities with a long history. Tenayuca is reported by Ixtlilxóchitl as a leading center in Toltec times, and has yielded Coyaltlatelco pottery in large quantities. Another Toltec-period ware, Aztec I, was found in Xaltocan; Teotihuacán remains were located at Portezuelo near Coatlichán, and both Teotihuacán and Coyaltlatelco sherds were found at Azcapotzalco.[32]

Ixtlilxóchitl, the Codex Xolotl, Torquemada, Vetancurt, and Veytia write of Xolotl, but mention no Mixcoatl among migrant leaders. On the other hand, Muñoz Camargo, the *Anales de Cuauhtitlán,* as well as the *Leyenda de los Soles,* the *Historia de los Mexicanos,* the *Relación de la Genealogía,* and the *Anales de Tlatelolco* write of Mixcoatl or Mixcoatl Camaxtli, but *not* of Xolotl. Surely this selective process, whereby accounts of Chichimec invasions are found in many sources, some of which mention only Xolotl, while others write of Mixcoatl but exclude Xolotl, is most significant, though caution should be exercised in drawing conclusions.

In the realm of the divine, the ties between Mixcoatl and Xolotl need no stressing. Xolotl as god of the evening star is the twin of Tlahuizcalpantecuhtli, god of the morning star. But the facial and body painting of Mixcoatl and Tlahuizcalpantecuhtli are identical, as well as their adornments, except for the headgear, and Mixcoatl is thus the virtual double of Tlahuizcalpantecuhtli, with whom Xolotl forms a pair. Xolotl is symbolically connected with Xiuhtecuhtli, god of fire, since his glyph is the fawn dog and this color is associated with fire. Moreover, for Seler, Xolotl is basically the lightning, the fire that falls from the heavens, and he appears in this guise in the Codex Borgia. According to Seler, Xolotl is not a dog, but a god with dog's head, appearing in all codices with this dog's head, but with the bodily adornments of Quetzalcoatl as god of wind, and is thus linked not only with Tlahuizcalpantecuhtli, but also directly with the original Quetzalcoatl, son of Mixcoatl.[33] Like Xolotl, Mixcoatl is linked with Xiuhtecuhtli and with fire, and the two names figure jointly in the opening paragraphs of the *Anales de Cuauhtitlán;* moreover, Xiuhtecuhtli, in common with Mixcoatl, has Otomí associations.[34] Xolotl represents the principle of duality, but Mixcoatl represents the same concept through his symbol, the two-headed deer, also fawn in color.

In Mesoamerica, the relationship of legendary heroes to the gods they represent is hard to unravel. Certain points, however, remain clear: Mixcoatl is god of hunting and the human Mixcoatl and Xolotl both lead groups of hunting Chichimecs that invaded the Valley of Mexico and then ranged far beyond. By all accounts Xolotl arrived shortly after the fall of Tollan, while Mixcoatl and his supporters are also associated with the closing phase of the city. Mixcoatl, in certain narratives, conquered Culhuacán, and in others led the Chichimecs to Poyauhtlán, and then faded from the picture. But most significantly, Torquemada writes of a group who came to the "Plains of Poyauhtlán" where they mingled with other Chichimecs led not by Mixcoatl, as in Muñoz Camargo, but by Xolotl.[35]

Of equal significance is the assertion by the *Historia Tolteca-Chichimeca* and by Muñoz Camargo that the same Chichimec groups visited both Poyauhtlán and Amecameca. For it will be recalled from Chapter III that the *Memorial Breve* describes Xolotl as ruler of Amecameca, while Vetancurt states that his father, Tlamacatzin, ruled in that city, which he associates with Xolotl and his brother Achcautzin. And yet, according to Muñoz Camargo, Achcautzin was a leader in Poyauhtlán of those Chichimecs who had been brought there by Mixcoatl; Torquemada, however, associates Xolotl, not Mixcoatl, with Moceloquichtli, one of the rulers of Tlaxcala, founded by the Chichimecs of Poyauhtlán. These Poyauhtecas thus provide vital clues, if no absolute proof, of some connection between Xolotl and Mixcoatl. Torquemada even states that some of this particular group of Chichimecs were led by Xolotl, while for Muñoz Camargo their chief was called Mixcoatl, but who was assisted by Achcautzin, described in other contexts as Xolotl's brother. Attention has already been drawn in Chapter III to the recurrence of no less than four of Xolotl's Chichimec leaders in Muñoz Camargo's account of Mixcoatl's Chichimecs of Poyauhtlán. In Muñoz Camargo's story, Mixcoatl becomes Chichimecatecuhtli, the title habitually employed by Xolotl and his successors; Xolotl's daughter is called Cuetlachxochtzin, whereas in the *Leyenda de los Soles* Cuetlachcihuatl is described as the elder sister of Mixcoatl. The two names are interchangeable or at least easily confused: Ixtlil-xóchitl in one context names Cuetlachcihuatzin as daughter of Tezozómoc of Azcapotzalco and in another calls her Cuetlachxochitl.

Motolinía and Mendieta refer to Iztac Mixcoatl as Acolnahua-catzin, while the *Anales de Tlatelolco* gives the same title to Tecuan-itzin, ruler of Tenayuca, whose identity with Xolotl is accepted by Caso and Jiménez Moreno as well as by me. According to the *Anales de Tlatelolco,* when the Acolhuas left Chicomoztoc, they were led by Mazatl, but Ixtlilxóchitl calls Xolotl Aculhuatecuhtli, i.e., leader of the Acolhuas. Thus both Mazatl and Xolotl are leaders of the Acolhuas; but Mazatl in this context is surely the equivalent of Mix-coatl, since in the *Anales de Cuauhtitlán,* the Chichimec leader Mixcoatl is sometimes called Mazatzin. Sahagún incidentally lists a Mazatzin as predecessor of Tochintecuhtli in Huexotla. Odd parallels therefore arise between the two Chichimec heroes, though to insist on a total identity would be to oversimplify the situation, since in theory at least, Mixcoatl preceded Xolotl. Aside from the parallels between their followers' names, Xolotl and Mixcoatl did play comparable roles and led peoples whose cultural attainments and religious practices were similar and who invaded the Valley of Mexico and adjacent regions during the period of Tollan's decline and fall. They were quick to imitate the people with whom they came into contact, and both Mixcoatl and Xolotl's son, Nopaltzin, married Culhua princesses. The two heroes bore the names of gods that form a pair; as humans they might equally be paired, as two semilegendary beings, cast in the same historical role as leaders of invasions of Otonchichimecs or Teochichimecs.

The Order of Their Coming

The human Xolotl, like Mixcoatl, is an imposing but rather shadowy figure, and the surviving data imply that the post-Tollan movement of people into the Valley of Mexico was a long-drawn-out affair, involving many groups and many leaders. Ixtlilxóchitl's version is quite plain: Xolotl and his Chichimecs came first, followed a generation later by Acolhuas, Otomís, and Tepanecs; but this rather oversimplified account is contradicted by other sources. The *Historia Tolteca-Chichimeca* hints that the Xaltocan Otomís, or at least

94

their leader, arrived before any of the Chichimecs, and perhaps before the fall of Tollan; the Acolhuas, or Acolchichimecs, under the guidance of Tzontecomatl, were not late-comers, but formed part of this earliest recorded Chichimec migration. Muñoz Camargo also reverses Ixtlilxóchitl's order of events, and reports that his Chichimecs (under Mixcoatl) came to seek out the Acolhuas and Tepanecs, who were therefore already in the Valley of Mexico, together with the Culhuas and Olmeca Xicallancas. The same historian describes their eagerness to learn Nahuatl, a language "soft and lovable," in contrast to other "rude and rough tongues"; they spoke it after their own fashion (rather as the English learned French under their Norman masters).[36]

These different peoples sought to adopt the same culture and certain distinctions between them thereby became blurred; the task of analyzing their ethnic origins is made harder by this process of adaptation to common norms.

The subsequent history of the region centers upon the reported late-comers, the Tepanecs and the Acolhuas; more than one source suggests that of these the Acolhuas came first, together with the Xaltocamecas, while others insist that the three groups came simultaneously. I tend to regard the Acolhuas as among the earliest arrivals, and they probably had become thoroughly Mesoamericanized by the time of Tzontecomatl's grandson, Huetzin, in mid-thirteenth century. If the assertion is accepted that Tzontecomatl was indeed Huetzin's grandfather, then his active life would have coincided with the end of the twelfth and the beginning of the thirteenth centuries, or about a generation after the fall of Tollan.

The Otomí origins of the Xaltocamecas are not in doubt, and the Tepanecs have long been viewed by Carrasco and others as of partly Otomí-Matlatzinca derivation. Genuine distinctions between the Chichimecs of Xolotl and the Acolhuas and the Otomís of Xaltocan are hard to draw; Ixtlilxóchitl actually states that the Acolhuas, Tepanecs, and Xaltocamecas came together from Michoacán, and were all of the same "nation" of Chichimec Michuaque. Therefore, all were at times designated as Chichimecs. The basic difference between the Otomís of Xaltocan, the Acolhuas, and the Tepanecs was surely that the Xaltocamecas continued to speak Otomí; when Ixtlilxóchitl says that they spoke the strangest language of the three groups, he is surely inferring that the other two spoke Nahuatl rather than, say, Pame, which would have seemed still stranger to him, not more familiar.

Like any other invaders, probably the Acolchichimecs led by Tzontecomatl originally also spoke Otomí, though by the time of his grandson, Huetzin, they were already becoming Nahuatized, and thus began to qualify as non-Chichimecs. The sharp contrast between Chichimec and Otomí origins was more probably inserted later into the record, owing in part to the traditional aspiration towards a "rags to riches" pedigree, and the resultant tendency to claim Chichimec antecedents. Some sources tend to overuse the term Chichimec, which served as a convenient generalization for all non-Toltecs, and therefore included Otomís. Even the urbane Tezozómoc did not call himself Tepanecatecuhtli, but Chichimecatecuhtli, usurping this title from the unfortunate Huehue Ixtlilxóchitl of Texcoco. Much of what Xolotl and Nopaltzin designated as Chichimecatlalli (Chichimec land), including Metztitlán, Atotonilco, and Cahuacan, is really Otomí land to this day, and also formed part of the Tepanec Empire.

The distinction between former Chichimecs—one might almost call them pseudo Chichimecs—and the Acolhuas is a fine one, and the belief that the Acolhuas arrived after the Chichimecs is probably mistaken. Xolotl himself, par excellence Chichimec, is sometimes described as an Acolhua, and even Ixtlilxóchitl writes of "Xolotl Acolhua."

The Xolotl Concept

Where the immediate aftermath of Tollan's collapse is concerned, history and legend are interwoven and the archaeological record is obscure. For the succeeding century firmer conclusions may be drawn, and in Chapter III it was related how, between about 1240 and 1270, Tochintecuhtli carved out for himself a mini-empire jointly with Huetzin. Though such conquests were more modest in scope than the gains that tradition accords to Xolotl, they included Tepetlaoztoc, Huexotla, Coatlichán, Tenayuca, Cahuacan, and the radius of military action was extended to the Metztitlán-Atotonilco area. Tochintecuhtli and Huetzin are variously reported as devouring other señoríos, or as reordering their bounds. While Huetzin also

took Culhuacán, Tochintecuhtli appears to have taken over Tenayuca, where a ruler named as Tecuanitzin may be identified both
with Xolotl and with Tochintecuhtli himself. If Xolotl's claims of
conquests are accepted as exaggerated and his chronology is confused,
few distinctions remain between his performance and that of his
alleged great-great-grandson, Tochintecuhtli, even if it cannot be
stated in precise terms that they are one and the same person.

Ixtlilxóchitl and the Codex Xolotl appear to combine twelfth-
century legend with thirteenth-century history, to confect a long line
of glamorous ancestors whose achievements add luster to the more
limited attainments of Nezahualcoyotl's more immediate forebears.
These Chichimec super-ancestors were unsubstantial if imposing
figures, even if Teochichimecs as well as Otomís are to be included
among the invaders of the Valley of Mexico. But about one hundred
years after these movements began, in the person of Tochintecuhtli
a kind of Xolotl did arise. Though there were Chichimec invaders,
there were strictly speaking no Chichimecs of Xolotl; for so far as
Xolotl is *not* Tochintecuhtli, his story runs parallel to the Mixcoatl
saga, aptly refurbished to provide an imperial ancestry for the kings
of Texcoco, the would-be equals of the Tlatoanis of Tenochtitlán.
Aztlan plays an important part in the story of the Mexicas, more as
a concept than as a definable locality. Equally Xolotl looms large in
the annals of Texcoco, but his precise identity as a historical personage is elusive, though he represents the concept of imperial authority
and imperial lineage. Tenayuca may indeed have been an important
city in the immediate post-Tollan period and have had rulers of some
status before Tochintecuhtli's time. Any such prince, however, who
then presided over Tenayuca and its ceremonial center, whether or
not he was called Xolotl, was more probably an Otomí or a Matlatzinca, rather than a Pame Chichimec.

Tollan was first and foremost a concept, transferable from one
metropolis to another; equally Aztlan and Chicomoztoc are concepts
as much as places. By the same token Xolotl, a name or title that
lends itself to more than one interpretation, is more to be related to
a concept than a single individual.

Wall of Serpents, Tenayuca pyramid. *Photograph by Sonya de la Rozière*

Detail from Wall of Serpents. *Photograph by Sonya de la Rozière*

Detail of Pyramid Tlatelolco II. *Photograph by Sonya de la Rozière*

Pyramid Tlatelolco II with later superimpositions in foreground and Church of Santiago in background. *Photograph by Sonya de la Rozière*

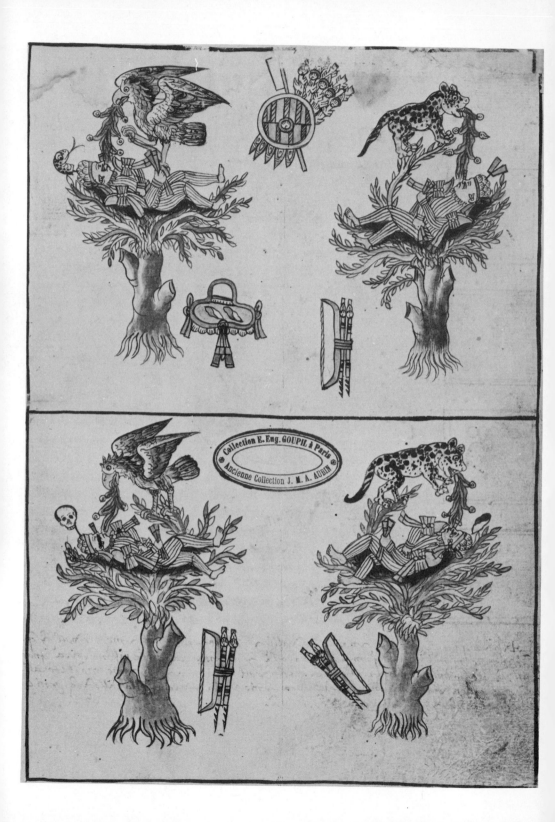

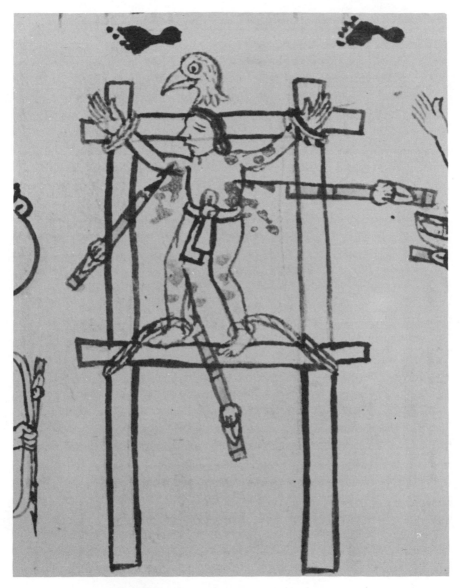

Chichimec arrow sacrifice to god of hunting. *Historia Tolteca-Chichimeca,* folio 32V. *Courtesy Bibliothèque Nationale, Paris*

(Facing page) Eagles and tigers "feed" the four Chichimec leaders before they leave Chicomoztoc. *Historia Tolteca-Chichimeca,* folio 20R. *Courtesy Bibliothèque Nationale, Paris*

Deer shot by Chichimec. *Mapa Quinatzin. Courtesy Bibliothèque Nationale, Paris*

(Facing page) Toltec leaders perform nose perforation ceremony on Chichimecs before they leave Chicomoztoc. *Historia Tolteca-Chichimeca,* folio 21R. *Courtesy Bibliothèque Nationale, Paris*

The leaders of the Tepanecs, Acolhuas, and Otomís arrive at Xolotl's court. Codex Xolotl, plate II. *Courtesy Bibliothèque Nationale, Paris*

Chiconcuaua, the Otomí leader, confers with Nopaltzin above glyph of
Xaltocan. Codex Xolotl, plate II. *Courtesy Bibliothèque Nationale, Paris*

Tochintecuhtli confers with Xolotl, seated in his cave. Codex Xolotl, plate III. *Courtesy Bibliothèque Nationale, Paris*

Achitometl, ruler of Culhuacán, beside glyph of Culhuacán. Codex Xolotl, plate III. *Courtesy Bibliothèque Nationale, Paris*

(Upper) The taking of the oath as ruler of Texcoco by Ixtlilxóchitl, seated second from right with his son Nezahualcoyotl behind him. Codex Xolotl, plate VII.

(Lower) Death of Ixtlilxóchitl. Codex Xolotl, plate VII. *Courtesy Bibliothèque Nationale, Paris*

Nezahualcoyotl on the Hill of Cuauhyacac after his father's death. Codex Xolotl, plate VII. *Courtesy Bibliothèque Nationale, Paris*

Quinatzin of Texcoco receives the Tlaillotlaque. *Mapa Quinatzin. Courtesy Bibliothèque Nationale, Paris*

Vessel from the transitional
period, Tula to Tenayuca.

Bowl, transitional Aztec II
to Aztec III style.

Plate with unusual
Aztec III design.

All courtesy Museo Nacional, Mexico City

V. The Early Acolhuas

Acolhuas and Chichimecs

According to the accepted tradition, the Chichimecs poured into the Valley of Mexico after the fall of Tollan, followed about a generation later by the Tepanecs and Acolhuas, accompanied by those Otomís who occupied Xaltocan.

In the previous chapter, the Acolhuas were seen as far from being late arrivals, but as an integral part of the original post-Toltec migrant waves that were generally designated as Chichimecs but included in reality several distinct elements. Of these intruders, some were already called Acolhua, or soon thereafter adopted the name, while another tribe ultimately came to be known as Tepanecs. Of these Acolhuas most but not all settled to the east of the Lake of Texcoco, while the proto-Tepanecs made their home to the west of the lagoon; both became gradually Nahuatized.

According to Pomar, *acolli* means "shoulder," and the Acolhuas were therefore people who possessed strong shoulders, implying, in an indirect sense, rustic or Chichimec origins, as pertaining to a stocky physique.[1] Motolinía writes of a man called Acolhuatl, a Chichimec so named because he tied a leather strap to Quetzalcoatl at the point where the arm meets the shoulder. Alternatively, Acolhua could simply mean a non-Colhua, or a non-Toltec; in support of such an etymology, Thelma Sullivan points out that to judge from the modern *Vocabulario Mexicano de Tetelcingo, Morelos,* Acolhua could be taken as meaning either "the Place of People with Shoulders" or "the Place of People without grandfathers," in the form of a play on words so common in Nahuatl.[2]

In surviving documents, "Acolhuacan" (Place of Acolhuas) tends to be identified with Texcoco, the leading Acolhua center in Aztec times. In contrast to this tendency, Tepanohuayan more often applies to Azcapotzalco, the pre-Aztec capital of the Tepanecs, than to Tlacopan, though in one instance the *Anales de Cuauhtitlán* mention "Texcoco de Acolhuacan and Tlacopan de Tepanohuayan."[3] "Acolhuacan" was previously appled to other Acolhua cities, more particularly to Coatlichán, described by Chimalpain as "Coatlichán Acolhuacan."[4] In another context the same writer simultaneously names Huexotla and Texcoco as Acolhuacan.[5] To confuse matters further, the *Crónica Mexicayotl* and the Aubin Codex report that the itinerant Mexicas passed Acalhuacan, situated between Ecatepec and Tolpetlac, i.e., due south of Xaltocan; this is far removed from the land later inhabited by the Acolhuas, but Acalhuacan, if this is the correct rendering, has a quite different derivation and means "Place of People Who Possessed Canoes."[6] Nonetheless, the *Memorial Breve* does mention a Coatlichán situated near Ecatepec, and the Codex Boturini and other sources describe an Acolman as lying on the Mexica route between Tula and Cempoala. If, as I suggest, the Acolhuas were among the earlier post-Toltec migrants into the Valley of Mexico, it is conceivable that they first sojourned in the northern part of the Valley of Mexico before reaching their final homeland; in roving from one place to another before settling, they would have merely followed the procedure later adopted by the Mexicas, Tlaxcalans, and other migrant tribes.

Though Acolhua and Colhua have contrasting derivations, the names are occasionally confused. Torquemada writes of "the Acolhuaques who are of the city of Culhuacan and the surrounding territory."[7] Pomar states that when the Acolhuas learned Nahuatl, they became Culhuas.[8] This tendency may be due, not to any superficial similarity between the terms, but to the subsequent control of Culhuacán and of Coatlichán, the Acolhua capital, by the same dynasty, and to the Nahuatization, or Culhuanization, of the Acolhuas.

Indications have already been cited that the Acolhuas were less distinct from other Chichimecs than Ixtlilxóchitl implies: even this author, it may be recalled, wrote of "Xolotl Acolhua"; Xolotl in other sources is described as first king of the Acolhuas, or as Acolhuatecuhtli; Tecuanitzin of Tenayuca, Xolotl's alter ego, is also called Acolnahuacatzin. The Codex Santa Cecilia Acatitlan mentions a Xoloc, father of Nopaltzin and señor of Acolnahuacan. Moreover, Quinatzin of Texcoco, repeatedly described as heir of Xolotl's empire and of his capital, Tenayuca, proclaimed himself Acolhuatecuhtli rather than Chichimecatecuhtli, the usual title of Xolotl and Nopaltzin.

Additional pointers associate the terms "Acolhua" and "Chichimec" and cast doubt upon a separate identity for the Acolhuas as distinct from the other invaders, more loosely termed "Chichimec." Tzontecomatl, usually described as first ruler of Coatlichán, and as grandfather of Tochintecuhtli, is called "Acolchichimecatl" in the *Historia Tolteca-Chichimeca,* and arrives with the first Chichimecs.[9] The same source writes of "the Acolhuas, the enemies of the Toltecs," thereby associating them with those Chichimecs who overran the Toltec domain and crushed the Toltecs of Culhuacán.[10] Torquemada writes that Nauhyotzin of Culhuacán was a Chichimec and consequently "de los Aculhuas."[11] Pomar states that Acolhuacan was so named "in memory of the Chichimecs, its first settlers."[12] The *Anales de Tlatelolco* describe the original Acolhuas as led by Mazatzin, alternative name given by the *Anales de Cuauhtitlán* for Mixcoatl, the great Chichimec invader who is also called Mixcoamazatzin.

A further indication that the Acolhuas arrived as early as any other Chichimecs is provided by Muñoz Camargo, when he tells how the Chichimecs who founded Tlaxcala and who had previously settled in Poyauhtlán, decided to move on rather than remain in the Poyauhtlán region "among the Acolhuas."[13] The *Memorial Breve* also hints that the Acolhuas were an integral part of the original influx rather than late arrivals; the source lists eight ethnic divisions of the Teoculhuaques (the people from the Teoculhuacán-

Chicomoztoc region) as Huexotzingans, Chalcas, Xochimilcas, Cuit-lahuacas, Malinalcas, Chichimecas, Tepanecas, Matlatzincas; the Acolhuas are conspicuous by their absence, though the translators, Lehmann and Kutscher, infer, probably correctly, that Acolhua in this context is the equivalent of Chichimec; the omission of the Acolhuas from a list that includes, among others, the Tepanecs, is otherwise hard to explain. A passage from the *Historia Tolteca-Chichimeca* states: "They [the Chichimecs] left Chicomoztoc, [coming] from inside the hill of Acolhuacan."[14] This surely implies that the name Acolhuacan, the Place of the Acolhuas, was initially also the Place of the Chichimecs and of all migrants from marginal Mesoamerica before it was applied to a specific region within the Valley of Mexico. That the mention of Acolhuacan in this context is a mere mistake is unlikely, since Clavijero also puts Acolhuacan on a par with Chicomoztoc, by referring to Teoaculhuacán as the place of origin of the three señores of legendary fame who came to pay homage to Xolotl. In one passage of Ixtlilxóchitl, all three rulers are described as belonging to "the Acolhua nation, the most cultured and civilized of those that occupied this land after the Toltecs."[15]

Clavijero, a historian who had access to sources of information now lost, insists upon the generic nature of the term Acolhua and its close interconnection with Chichimec. He writes: "The two nations continued to mingle [the Acolhuas and Chichimecs] to the point of forming one single people, that was called after the noblest of its two components, and assumed the name Acolhua, while the principality was called Acolhuacan."[16] The historian goes on to describe how the term Chichimec was further applied only to marginal groups who refused to adopt agriculture and returned to the mountains northwest of the Valley of Mexico, preferring to live without leaders and without law. He states that these people, mixed with Otomís, occupied a large territory and gave the Spaniards much trouble after the Conquest.

A distinction between Chichimecs and Acolhuas might none-theless remain, if it could be shown that they came from different places. But Ixtlilxóchitl specifically states that Xolotl, in addition to the Tepanecs and Acolhuas, came from Michoacán. Sahagún refers to Michoacán as Chichimec territory, and at the time of the Conquest, both Chichimecs and Otomís were to be found in that region.

117

Ixtlilxóchitl also writes of the original leaders of the Tepanecs, Xaltocamecas, and "true" Acolhuas as "the Three Acolhua lords," again using Acolhua as a generic expression.[17]

Like "Toltec," "Acolhua" may have meant different things at different times. Beginning as a generalized term for certain Chichimec groups coming from Chicomoztoc or "Acolhuacan," it later came to be applied more strictly to people who had settled in the Coatlichán-Texcoco region. And even in their final home, the Acolhuas were not a very close-knit people and at times displayed a marked lack of cohesion. Quinatzin was plagued by disloyalty among his subjects; during his grandson's struggle against Tezozomoc in 1414, few Acolhua principalities remained loyal, and some even profited from Texcoco's misfortunes. When the victorious Tepanec monarch carved up the Texcocan domains, Coatlichán and Acolman were eager to obtain their share.[18]

Even Ixtlilxóchitl, who insists upon their late arrival upon the scene, describes these Acolhuas as not unlike the other Chichimecs who preceded them; they only differed in that they wore clothing, possessed gods, and built temples.[19] This distinction is more apparent than real, for if the Tepanecs and Acolhuas indeed came forty-seven years later, Xolotl and his followers had surely by then been civilized to a point where gods and temples were taken for granted, after living in the ancient city of Tenayuca for so long.

Nopaltzin, moreover, can hardly have remained a mere sky worshiper after marrying his Culhua princess. Ixtlilxóchitl himself lays stress on the process of educating the Chichimecs. Therefore, if the Acolhuas arrived a half-century later, they would have encountered Chichimecs already as advanced as themselves on the road to civilization.

To balance Ixtlilxóchitl's assertion that the Acolhuas came *after* the Chichimecs, it could equally well be argued that they came *before,* in view of Muñoz Camargo's assertion, already cited, that the Chichimecs came to Poyauhtlán "in pursuit of the Culhuas and Tepanecas and Aculhuaques." I hesitate, however, to accept this order of events, any more than that of Ixtlilxóchitl, and prefer to regard Acolhuas as part of the original movement of Otomí-speakers, accompanied by Pame and other Teochichimecs.[20] Jiménez Moreno, also hesitant in accepting Ixtlilxóchitl's version at its face value, thinks that the Tepanecs came first, though I tend to view the Acolhuas as among the earliest arrivals. Possibly they came from Michoacán, as Ixtlilxóchitl states, though this remains uncertain; the Tepanecs have certain associations with the Valley of Toluca, and the notion that Tepanecs and Acolhuas arrived together and then rose to power simultaneously oversimplifies the issue. As I shall explain in detail in the following chapter, the Tepanecs emerge more as the successors and conquerors of the Acolhuas, who then staged a successful comeback, supported by the military muscle of the Mexicas.

Otomís and Acolhuas

Pointers to some association—and at times almost an identity—between the terms Acolhua and Chichimec are numerous. But in Chapter IV it was already implied that if the Chichimecs of Xolotl were at least part Otomí, then the distinction between Otomí and Chichimec also at times became blurred.

In addition to connecting links between Chichimecs and Acolhuas cited above and between Chichimecs and Otomís, adumbrated in Chapter IV, certain evidence ties the Acolhuas themselves more directly to the Otomís. The *Histoyre du Mechique* describes Nezahualcoyotl as "Ce dict seigneur de Texcuq du costé des Otomís."[21] Otompan ("the Place of Otomis") is described by Ixtlilxóchitl as an Acolhua city.[22] The first Tepanec ruler is generally known as Acolhua or Acolnahuacatzin; but the Tepanecs had Oto-Manguue associations, as will be demonstrated later. Mixcoatl, a leading deity among the Acolhuas, was also worshiped by the Otomís. Tochintecuhtli, linked in the *Anales de Cuauhtitlán* with the Otomís of Cahuacan, was described by the *Memorial Breve* as the first Acolhua ruler, and was the ancestor through the female line of many generations of Acolhua princes.

The First Acolhua Expansion

I accordingly view the Acolhuas as forming part of the original migration into the Valley of Mexico; alternatively, the term is first used in a more collective sense to describe specific groups of invaders who also possessed another name. Under Tzontecomatl, grandfather of Tochintecuhtli, and ruler of Coatlichán about a generation after Tollan's collapse, the Acolhuas assumed their final identity as inhabitants of the cities lying to the east of the Lake of Texcoco.

Few details survive of the reigns of Tzontecomatl and of his son Tlotzin. This semi-legendary past precedes the empire-building achievement of Tochintecuhtli and Huetzin, that form a prelude to the known history of the Acolhuas and of the whole Valley of Mexico in the Late Postclassic era. Information on these achievements is confused and contradictory. The Ixtlilxóchitl–Codex Xolotl version is as follows: Xolotl still clung to the reins of power about 110 years after he had first entered Central Mexico, accompanied by his adult son Nopaltzin and adult grandson Tlotzin. As already mentioned in Chapter III, he had sent for Tochintecuhtli, son of the ruler of Cahuacan, and ordered him to proceed first to Xaltocan, and there marry Tomiyauh (also the name of Xolotl's own spouse); this Tomiyauh was Xolotl's great-granddaughter and daughter of the ruler of Xaltocan.

Having been duly married, Tochintecuhtli was then to proceed to Huexotla, in order to reinforce Huetzin, the embattled señor of Coatlichán, and capture or kill Huetzin's rival, Yacanex, Huexotla's original ruler. Huetzin, Tlotzin's grandson, was Xolotl's great-great-grandson, and was still a young man at the time; he had been ordered by Xolotl to marry Atototzin, daughter of Achitometl, ruler of Culhuacán.

After the victory of Xolotl's minions, Yacanex took refuge in Panuco, while Tochintecuhtli became ruler of Huexotla. At the time of this conflict, Aculhua, ruler of Azcapotzalco, was also waging war on Cozcacuauh, described as señor both of Tepotzotlán and of Chalco; Cozcacuauh, according to Ixtlilxóchitl, had been one of Xolotl's original companions when he first invaded the Valley of Mexico. But Ixtlilxóchitl describes these battles as occurring 117 years after the destruction of the Toltecs, or 112 years after Xolotl's original takeover.

After brief mention of the seemingly calm and uneventful reigns of Nopaltzin and his son Tlotzin as rulers of the Chichimec Empire, Ixtlilxóchitl then records that Quinatzin, Tlotzin's successor, transferred his capital to Texcoco, formerly founded by Nopaltzin; Quinatzin left his uncle, Tenancacaltzin, bastard son of Nopaltzin, as ruler of Tenayuca.

In the first Ixtlilxóchitl–Codex Xolotl account of the wars of Tochintecuhtli, Quinatzin is already presented as a leading co-belligerent. But when Ixtlilxóchitl later deals more specifically with Quinatzin's reign, the story of this campaign is repeated once more; in this second account, Quinatzin, not Tochintecuhtli or Huetzin, becomes the main combatant.[23]

According to this alternative version by the same author, Yacanex, leading an army that contained contingents from Metztitlán, Tototepec, and Tepepulco, besieged Texcoco. Quinatzin put Tochintecuhtli, in this context described as his subordinate, in charge of one-fourth part of his total forces; Tochintecuhtli's brother, another Nopaltzin, led a second contingent, while Huetzin commanded the third, and Quinatzin himself the fourth. After an epic struggle, the "tyrant" was crushed by Quinatzin and his army, and his levies were mostly slaughtered by Quinatzin's men. Huetzin, Nopaltzin, and Tochintecuhtli also won notable victories, and all the surviving rebels, including, surprisingly, Quinatzin's own sons, were sent to the province of Tlaxcala and Huexotzingo, to be kept under the watchful eye of the friendly princes of those señoríos. Quinatzin's enemies are described by Ixtlilxóchitl and depicted in the Codex Xolotl as true Chichimecs, dressed only in skins, while his supporters are portrayed as already half-Toltecized.

In Ixtlilxóchitl's *Relaciones,* further details are added to the account given in his *Historia.* Huetzin's father is here called Itzmitl, not Tlacotzin; Torquemada rather confusingly writes of Iztacmitl as ruler of Tepeaca and father of a Nopaltzin.[24] Tochintecuhtli in one context is described as ruler of Cuauhtitlán and in another as ruler Huexotla; he is told to go to Xaltocan, as in the *Historia,* but thereafter to proceed to Coatlichán, not Huexotla, in order to help Huetzin. The joint wars of "El Gran Quinatzin" are again described and of his "Electors," Tochintecuhtli and Huetzin, who in this instance advance as far as Tulancingo and secure the submission of this province to Quinatzin.

In Torquemada's parallel description of these events, certain variations occur: Xolotl duly sent for Tochintecuhtli, ruler of the province of Cuauhuacán, and dispatched him on an important errand to Xaltocan (marriage is not mentioned). But after fulfilling his mission, Tochintecuhtli then returned not to Xolotl's presence, as ordered by the Emperor in this version of events, but to Coatlichán, against his master's orders. Xolotl therefore deprived him of his principality of Cuauhuacán and forbade him to return there, on pain of death; he was instead exiled to Tepetlaoztoc. Undaunted by his humiliation, he thereafter campaigned on behalf of Huetzin and Quinatzin. Torquemada asserts that Tochintecuhtli deprived many rulers of their señoríos and even killed some.[25]

So far so good. At first sight this narrative may strike the reader as forming a single if exciting page in the history of the Valley of Mexico. But from certain observations already made in Chapter III, it may be seen that while Mesoamerican history can be exciting, it is never simple.

Ixtlilxóchitl leaves his reader in no doubt about the historical Quinatzin's true chronology by stating that he assumed his throne in the year of the foundation of Tenochtitlán.[26] In another context, Quinatzin is described as a contemporary of Coxcox, ruler of Culhuacán during the Mexica captivity in that place (i.e., just prior to the foundation of Tenochtitlán). Ixtlilxóchitl further mentions that towards the end of his reign, Quinatzin helped to quell a rebellion in cities subject to the Mexicas, Cuitlahuac and Mizquic, and that they probably were first conquered between 1378 and 1380.

In unamended form, Ixtlilxóchitl's narrative makes apparent sense only to those unversed in the chronology of the period in question. As already explained, the campaign of Tochintecuhtli and Huetzin against Yacanex took place in about 1270 (Coxcox of Culhuacán who was ruling in 1319 was Huetzin's grandson). This conflict reportedly arose through the machinations of a Methuselan Xolotl—though the resulting battles were fought under the supreme command of "El Gran Quinatzin," whose later triumphs belong to the age of Acamapichtli, who ascended the Tenochca throne in 1371.

Quinatzin, still alive in the 1370's, and Xolotl, already a grandfather in the 1170's, are cast in the same role vis-à-vis Tochintecuhtli and Huetzin, who serve as underlings to two Chichimec "emperors," first Xolotl and then Quinatzin (Ixtlilxóchitl, taking his cue from the Holy Roman Empire, calls them Quinatzin's "electors"). At the beginning Xolotl gives the orders, and later "El Gran Quinatzin" takes over.

Such a confusing picture can be understood only if events belonging to three distinct periods, or centuries, are first separated, in order to make sense of each. The first period of Acolhua history runs approximately from the time of Tzontecomatl of Coatlichán, beginning in, say, A.D. 1200, and ends with the conquests of his grandson Huetzin in about 1270. Any historical Xolotl lived about one hundred years before Huetzin, while Quinatzin reigned one hundred years after this monarch, and neither could have shared his triumphs.

The second Acolhua period covers about a century and a half from Huetzin's death until the reign of Huehue Ixtlilxóchitl of Texcoco, who died defeated in 1417.[27] During the initial part of this second phase, Huetzin's successors, Acolmiztli and Coxcox, clung the power in Culhuacán, and their capital, Coatlichán, retained its place as leading Acolhua city. By Quinatzin's time however, in mid-fourteenth century, Texcoco assumed the mantle of Coatlichán; this change, far from increasing Acolhua power, led initially to a collapse when Quinatzin's grandson, Huehue Ixtlilxóchitl, was routed and killed by Tezozómoc of Azcapotzalco.

For a few years Texcoco lay prostrate at Tezozómoc's feet, before the beginning of the third period, marked by the Acolhua revival under Nezahualcoyotl, who astutely joined forces with the Mexicas to defeat the Tepanecs in 1428. This revival of Acolhua power in effect ended before the Conquest with the death of Nezahualpilli in 1515; after this Texcoco became a prey to internal strife, and its ruler was completely overshadowed by the might of the Tenochca *tlatoani.*

The Codex Xolotl, with Ixtlilxóchitl's added refinements, enhances the glory of Texcoco and its dynasty by crediting Quinatzin of Texcoco with participation in wars fought a full century before he grew to manhood; not only does Quinatzin himself thereby gain stature, but the pre-Conquest history of Texcoco—in reality fairly short—acquires a greater depth in time. Just as Tochintecuhtli-Tecuanitzin of Tenayuca inspired the story of an earlier Xolotl, so Quinatzin is made to share the victories of his ancestor Huetzin that far outshone those of the real Quinatzin, whose achievements were constructive rather than dramatic. In ancient Mexico history tended to be presented in terms of black and white, good and bad, hero and villain, with few intermediate stages between the two opposites. The idea of sifting the evidence to attempt to produce an impartial version is a European concept commencing with Herodotus. In many countries today, history is a mere instrument for the creation of a national conscience rather than a search for truth. The Mexicas and the Texcocans adopted the same criteria, and it would be surprising if their respective versions of events did tally.

I have already suggested that the most plausible solution is to identify the early Quinatzin with Huetzin. Quinatzin in this context becomes more title than name, as in the case of Acolhua, Acolmiztli, and even Coxcox. But if "Quinatzin el Viejo" or "El Gran Quinatzin" is the same person as Huetzin, he is also apt to be confused with Tlacotzin, Tochintecuhtli's father; it is even arguable that this Quinatzin is really Tochintecuhtli, not Huetzin, since the *Anales de Cuauhtitlán* refer to Quinatzin el Viejo as ruler of Cuauhtitlán, and Tochintecuhtli is also at times described as ruler of the city.

After divorcing the historical Quinatzin of Texcoco from the period of Tochintecuhtli-Huetzin, where he does not belong, what remains of the story of these early Acolhua rulers, and what did they achieve?

We have already seen that Tochintecuhtli absorbed many señoríos, of which the most important are Cahuacan, Tenayuca, and Huexotla. Equally his fellow conqueror, Huetzin, began his career as ruler of Tepetlaoztoc, and acquired Coatlichán, as well as Culhuacán. The radius of action of the two confederate rulers was wide, and included the Atotonilco-Metztitlán-Tulancingo region. The Acolhuas had perhaps already played a significant role under Tzontemoc, but in Huetzin's reign their achievements take a more positive shape, and the process of Nahuatization, that distinguished the Acolhuas from certain other Otonchichimecs, probably began with the occupation of Culhuacán.

As depicted in the codices, the Acolhuas then still dressed in skins, though their attire is distinguishable from the pure Chichimecs of Metztitlán. They were already becoming Mesoamericanized, and any notion that they still preserved a nomad way of life, first adopting agriculture under Quinatzin of Texcoco a century later, must be treated as apocryphal. The daughter of Tochintecuhtli, Nenetzin, married Acolmiztli, son of Huetzin, and the two rulers thus became the joint progenitors of the future Coatlichán and Texcocan dynasties. Their empire seems to have been based on a kind of dual alliance, and embraced a territory that stretched from Cahuacan, on the borders of the Valley of Toluca, as far as Atotonilco, and Tulancingo, reportedly also conquered.

The Acolhua Dynasty

Sahagún gives the following list of the Huexotla dynasty, (though the *Memorial Breve* describes Tochintecuhtli as the first, not the second, Acolhua ruler):

> Mazatzintecuhtli, who reigned 70 years
> Tochintecuhtli   38 years
> Ayotzintecuhtli   4 years
> Quatlauicetecuhtli   55 years
> Totomochtzin   52 years
> Yaotzintecuhtli   53 years

Unfortunately no such list survives for Coatlichán, but Huetzin's son and heir is generally reported to have been called Acolmiztli, also a rather generalized name, more equivalent to a title. According to Ixtlilxóchitl, Acolmiztli, or Acolmiztli I as I prefer to call him, had four children including Coxcox, who inherited the throne of Culhuacán; Mozxomatzin, who also became ruler of Coatlichán; and a daughter, Tochquentzin, who married Techotlalatzin of Texcoco. In reality Techotlalatzin, son of Quinatzin and contemporary of Huitzilihuitl, second *tlatoani* of Tenochtitlán, probably reigned from 1377 until 1409, and cannot have married the sister of the Coxcox who was ruler of Culhuacán at the time of the Mexica captivity, beginning in 1319; Techotlalatzin surely married the daughter of a subsequent Acolmiztli.[28]

The picture is as usual confused, since in another context Ixtlilxóchitl names Mozxomatzin as son, not brother of Coxcox.[29] He also states that Mozxomatzin conquered Culhuacán, where Coxcox reigned.[30] Possibly Coxcox and Mozxomatzin are the same person. Coxcox, moreover, is another name that recurs so frequently that it almost amounts to a title, qualified by a second or alternative appellation.

The *Memorial Breve* states that Quinatzin was the fourth ruler to occupy the throne of Texcoco; taking Huetzin as the first historical ruler of that city, Huetzin's son Acolmiztli thereby becomes the second, Mozxomatzin the third, and Quinatzin the fourth. The first three monarchs were primarily rulers of Coatlichán, of which Texcoco was then no more than a dependency, and Quinatzin was thus the first really independent Texcocan monarch; with his additional claim to the throne of Tenayuca, I will deal later.

We are told nothing of the activities of those intermediate rulers between Huetzin and the later Quinatzin, or Quinatzin II. Ixtlilxóchitl mentions briefly wars between Acolmiztli of Coatlichán and an unnamed ruler of Tenayuca. Quinatzin reigned until 8 Calli, probably 1377; it is more difficult to give an equivalent Christian year for the 1 Tochtli in which he ascended the throne, though he is reported to have reigned 60 years. Assuming that Huetzin died in 1274, 107 years (1274 to 1381) is a relatively long time span for only three reigns. The possibility therefore exists that an additional reign intervened and that Quinatzin belonged to the fourth, not the third, generation after Huetzin, probably his namesake as well as forebear.

The Early Texcoco

Whilst for at least a century Coatlichán remained the Acolhua capital, Huexotla also played an important role. Its rulers could justly claim that they were the political heirs of the Coatlichán dynasty, and Jiménez Moreno sees Huexotla as enjoying a brief hegemony after the decline of Coatlichán; however, lacking evidence to the contrary, I tend to regard their reign of glory as more or less contemporary.

As I have made abundantly clear, the history of Texcoco is hopelessly confused by the idolizing of Quinatzin, its first known independent ruler, and by crediting him with the conquests of the first Acolhua Empire a century before his reign, that marked the outset of the second Acolhua period.

By virtue of this spurious antiquity conceded to Quinatzin, his true place in history is obscured, and his genealogy confused. His reported descent from the "emperors" of Tenayuca appears apocryphal; at all events, he cannot, as Ixtlilxóchitl maintains, have been the son of Tlotzin, already depicted as an adult in the Mapa Tlotzin when the Chichimecs reached the Valley of Mexico, nearly two-hundred years before Quinatzin's death, 1377.

Quinatzin is surely more likely to have been the son of Mozxomatzin of Coatlichán; or if, as suggested above, a fourth reign intervened between Huetzin and Quinatzin, then Quinatzin becomes the grandson of Mozxomatzin, or possibly of his brother Coxcox.

Ixtlilxóchitl's story of the Quinatzin who was contemporary of Huetzin and Tochintecuhtli is followed by his second Quinatzin narrative that describes this ruler's support of the Mexicas, not long after the foundation of Tenochtitlán in 1345. We are first told that the Mexicas, after the establishment of their two cities, went secretly to Quinatzin and asked him to provide them with suitable rulers. The Texcocan monarch politely declined the honor, insisting that Aculhua of Azcapotzalco was their rightful lord. According to other sources, the Tlatelolcans in fact opted for a Tepanec prince, while Acamapichtli of Tenochtitlán did have certain Acolhua associations, since his mother descended from the dynasty that had controlled both Culhuacán and Coatlichán.

Ixtlilxóchitl then relates how Quinatzin campaigned on behalf of the Mexica rulers, some twenty years after the foundation of Tenochtitlán.[31] A kind of joint offensive was launched: Quinatzin attacked Cuitlahuac, that was already a Mexica tributary; he then helped to occupy Mizquic, where the Mexicas met strong resistance (Mizquic at that time reportedly paid tribute to Chalco Atenco). Ixtlilxóchitl also credits Quinatzin with a more ambitious campaign against the Tlahuicas and lists Huaxtepec among his objectives.[32]

Texcocan participation in these wars perhaps offers a foretaste of the future Tenochtitlán-Texcoco axis. The Mexicas, campaigning under the aegis of the Tepanecs, had made of the Chinampa cities of Culhuacán, Mizquic, and Xochimilco their first conquest, according to Mexica sources. Cuauhnahuac also figures in the conquest lists of the first ruler, and I incline to think that this was indeed the Cuauhnahuac of the valley of Morelos, rather than a homonym situated in the Valley of Mexico, as suggested by Barlow. The reported submission of Mizquic to Chalco Atenco is interesting; that city may have been a major bone of contention at the outset of the epic struggle between Chalcas and Mexicas that began in 1372 and ended only with the overthrow of Chalco by Moctezuma I in 1465.

The early history of Texcoco is obscure. Teotihuacán remains have been found in the vicinity; Ixtlilxóchitl nonetheless insists that the city was "founded" by Nopaltzin, though in another passage he states that it had existed in Toltec times. According to the same author, Quinatzin left Tenayuca in charge of his uncle, Tenancacaltzin; the latter was then attacked by the Mexicas, acting under the orders of Aculhua of Azcapotzalco. But Tenayuca by this time had surely gravitated into the Tepanec orbit and Ixtlilxóchitl also relates that Aculhua gave Tenayuca to his heir, Tezozomoc, who became ruler of that city a few years before succeeding to the throne of Azcapotzalco.

Quinatzin's predecessors, described also as Chichimec emperors, had apparently maintained Tenayuca as an Acolhua foothold west of the Lake of Texcoco, but at some point were driven out by the growing power of the Tepanecs, using the Mexicas as auxiliaries, and henceforth confined to the opposite side of the lagoon. Ixtlilxóchitl's account hints that Quinatzin's renunciation of Tenayuca was not altogether voluntary, and I suspect that the Acolhua control over Tenayuca had really been loosened well before Quinatzin's time. The Tepanecs' appetite for conquest, however, had scarcely been sated by this acquisition, and they soon began to think in terms of a more ambitious penetration into the Acolhua heartland. It is significant that the investiture of Quinatzin as Aculhuatecuhtli took place in Azcapotzalco.[33]

Quinatzin—or Quinatzin II, as I prefer to call him—clearly enhanced the importance of Texcoco, perhaps little more than a village before his time, and his reign heralded the city's position of hegemony among the Acolhuas. While Quinatzin's achievements hardly measure up to those of his forebear, Huetzin, he at least attained a place of honor in the hierarchy of local rulers, in whose intrigues and battles he played an effective if limited part. Where the Acolhuas are concerned, he stepped into a power vacuum left by the decline of Coatlichán.

The history of Texcoco is suggestive of Acolhua links with the Otomís. After his defeat of Texcoco under Quinatzin's grandson, the victorious ruler of Azcapotzalco sent a captain to make a proclamation in "Chichimec and Toltec"; "Chichimec" may be taken to signify Otomí, since by that time the Texcocans are not likely to have spoken, say, Pame. If we accept Ixtlilxóchitl's version, Texcoco first became fully Nahuatized in the reign of Quinatzin's son and successor, Techotlalatzin. We are told how the Toltecs had tried to teach Quinatzin their rites, but that he frustrated their efforts; he appears in the Mapa Quinatzin dressed in skins and seated on a mat, while his successor clothed as a Toltec sits on a throne.

Quinatzin, of whose other deeds little is known, died in 8 Calli (1381); Ixtlilxóchitl says that he was then 112 years old; not to be outdone, Acolhua of Azcapotzalco died in 7 Acatl at the age of 200.

The Migrants

The process of Nahuatization in Texcoco was advanced by a series of migrants who arrived during the reigns of Quinatzin and Techotlalatzin.

Under Quinatzin, people known as Tlaillotlaques and Chimalpanecas came from the Mixteca, and in the Mapa Quinatzin are welcomed by a rather pastoral Quinatzin, seated on his mat. Ixtlilxóchitl stresses that the two groups were highly civilized and spoke "the language of the Toltecs"; they were masters of the art of painting historical codices.[34] This infusion of new blood clearly served as a cultural tonic and helped to make the Texcoco of Nezahualcoyotl and of Nezahualpilli "the Athens of America."

Under Techotlalatzin, these groups were followed by a second and yet more significant influx, consisting of fugitives expelled from Culhuacán by Coxcox, the part-Acolhua ruler of that city. According to Ixtlilxóchitl and the Mapa Tlotzin, they were divided into four contingents: Mexicas, Huitznahuas, Culhuas, and Tepanecs. Some settled in Texcoco, while the remainder went to other cities.[35]

Significantly, Ixtlilxóchitl reports that they bore many idols,

129

particularly those of Huitzilopochtli and Tláloc, and states that Techotlalatzin, in his resolve to Toltecize Texcoco, allowed them to practice the rites of those deities, proscribed by his father, Quinatzin. In another context, the same author says that the newcomers were worshipers of Tezcatlipoca.[36]

The Mapa Quinatzin also depicts the migrants as more Toltec than Chichimec by showing them as bearing not only their gods, but seeds of maize and beans. Ixtlilxóchitl credits them with distant origins, and states that Culhuacán was a provisional abode, before they moved on to Texcoco. He mentions that Culhuacán was then dominated by the Mexicas—a development confirmed by other sources, which state that the Mexicas made their early conquests as Tepanec confederates in the reign of Huitzilihuitl, who was Techotlalatzin's approximate contemporary.

The striking parallels between the institutions of Texcoco and Tenochtitlán may date from this migration, that brought in its train worshipers of Huitzilopochtli and Tezcatlipoca. The Acolhuas of Coatlichán and Huexotla were surely part-Nahuatized long before Quinatzin, and the act of bringing seeds is more symbolic than real, since it is inconceivable that Huetzin's first Acolhua empire lacked agriculture and depended solely upon hunting and gathering. The process of Nahuatization was probably completed rather than initiated under Quinatzin's son, at a time when Texcoco was already the leading Acolhua city. The introduction of Huitzilopochtli as well as Tezcatlipoca and Tláloc suggests that this process was one of Mexicanization as much as of Toltecization—as far as the two can be distinguished.

The ethnic composition of the new settlers remains obscure, and it is hard to see why authentic Mexicas should have emigrated at this time to Texcoco. Tenochtitlán was already the rising star in the Mesoamerican firmament; the back-breaking task of completing the chinampas on the two islands was by then under way, and the Mexicas needed every available man to work and fight on their behalf in order to enhance the status of their burgeoning city. Conceivably Tezozomoc, foreseeing the growing status of Texcoco, sought to infiltrate selected Mexica and Tepanec elements into the city. Alternatively the Tepanecs in question may not have been true Tepanecs at all, but other Otomís, perhaps from Xaltocan, then undergoing pressure from Azcapotzalco. The main contingent surely consisted of Culhuas and Huitznahuas—also to be identified with Culhuacán. That city was then declining, if not disintegrating, under the assaults of the Mexicas and Tepanecs.[37] The *Anales de Cuauhtitlán* refer to a diaspora of Culhuas at this time, others of whom went to Cuauhtitlán. Accordingly, the influx into Texcoco more probably consisted of fugitive Culhuas, perhaps accompanied by Mexicas who then occupied Culhuacán and who introduced into Texcoco the worship of Huitzilopochtli. This process of Mexicanization ultimately led to a situation where the two peoples possessed a culture that was strikingly similar if not identical. By the time of the Conquest, Tezcatlipoca had his temple in Texcoco in the Huitznahuac barrio, exactly as in Tenochtitlán; both cities had temples jointly dedicated to Huitzilopochtli and Tlaloc, and the rulers of Texcoco were buried in the robes of Huitzilopochtli. Texcoco also had its Cihuacoatl, though his office was more religious than political; its armies were commanded, as in Tenochtitlán, by a Tlacochcalcatl.

Techotlalatzin

Notwithstanding references to "El Gran Techotlalatzin," additional information about his achievements is scarce. As in the case of Quinatzin, little is known except for sundry mention of campaigns that also involved the Mexicas. News of a rather minor incident survives, arising from the Mexica-Tepanec war against Xaltocan. After that city had been crushed and its lands expropriated, the ruler, Tzompantzin, fled towards Texcoco—yet a further hint of Texcoco's Otomí connections. However, the defeated monarch received a cool welcome from Techotlalatzin, who blandly asserted that his friend Tezozomoc had acted under provocation, and Tzompantzin was forced to seek remoter refuge among his Otomí kinsmen in Metztitlán. However certain fugitives from Xaltocan were granted lands in the Otumba region, thus adding yet another element to the population of the Texcocan domain. This episode, suggestive of Techotlalatzin's urge to appease Tezozomoc, implies that the early Texcoco was in no position to defy Azcapotzalco, and this situation only changed in Techotlalatzin's successor Huehue Ixtlilxóchitl, who flung down the gauntlet to the imperious Tepanec.

Techotlalatzin married a daughter of Acolmiztli, señor of Coatlichán, obviously a second or third ruler of that name and a descendant of that other Acolmiztli, son of Huetzin, who ascended the throne of Coatlichán a century earlier. The later Acolmiztli is mentioned in other sources as a contemporary of Tlacateotl, second ruler of Tlatelolco.[38] Equally, any Coxcox who instigated the above-mentioned migration from Culhuacán to Texcoco cannot be the same Coxcox who received the Mexicas in Culhuacán in 1319.

Like Acolmiztli and Achitometl, the name Coxcox constantly crops up in the annals of this period; a Coxcox is mentioned by Ixtlilxóchitl as regent in Texcoco during the minority of Nezahualcoyotl, after the death of his father.[39] The *Anales de Cuauhtitlán* mention a further Coxcox as father-in-law of Chalchiuhtlatonac, fifth son of Tezozomoc.[40]

A whole series of Achitometls seem to have reigned in Culhuacán; and in addition to earlier rulers of Coatlichán called Acolmiztli, the sources mention four further Acolmiztlis: one is brother of Nezahualcoyotl; another is eldest son of Tlacateotl of Tlatelolco; a third is sixth señor of Toltitlán; and a fourth is señor of Atenchicalcán. Quinatzin is another generalized name used by a number of individuals. The *Anales de Cuauhtitlán* tell of a whole dynasty of successive Quinatzins in Cuauhtitlán.[41] The same source equates "Quinatzin el Viejo" to Tlacotzin by stating that he was the father of Tochintecuhtli. Quinatzin is additionally called Tlaltecatzin by Ixtlilxóchitl and others; the *Memorial Breve* mentions Quinatzin Pochotl Tlaltecatzin, ruler of Texcoco Acolhuacan.[42] Pochotl figures in certain accounts as the son of Topiltzin Quetzalcoatl and Tlotzin is also called Tlotzin Pochotl by Ixtlilxóchitl. The ruling dynasties of Chalco Atenco, Teyacuac Chalcohuatenco, and Chiapaxina could all boast of a Pochotl at different moments in their respective histories.[43] This duplication of names such as Achitometl, Coxcox, Acolmiztli, Quinatzin, and Pochotl, coupled with a duplication of dates, recurring in like form in each fifty-two-year cycle, magnifies the perplexities of Mesoamerican history. Faced with identical names for several rulers and identical dates taken from several year cycles or even from several calendars, the task of unraveling the course of events at times defies the efforts of the ethnohistorian. One bearer of the title Coxcox, Achitometl, Nauhyotzin, or Quinatzin is readily taken for another; the years, say, 5 Calli or 8 Tochtli of several successive year cycles are then confused, and history is telescoped in a process whereby two, three, or even four homonymous rulers become a single personage, endowed with a life of incommensurate length.

Techotlalatzin died in the same year as Cuacuapitzahuac of Tlatelolco (1409, or 8 Calli in the Tenochca count), after a reign that probably lasted thirty-two years, rather than the 104 years mentioned by Alva Ixtlilxóchitl.[44] He was succeeded by his son Huehue Ixtlilxóchitl, during whose reign Acolhua power suffered a temporary eclipse at the hands of the greedy Tezozomoc; the story of this Ixtlilxóchitl and of the early years of Nezahualcoyotl belong to a later period in Acolhua history, that will be reviewed in a subsequent chapter. During the reigns of Quinatzin and Techotlalatzin, Texcoco became the leader among the Acolhua cities, following the decline of Coatlichán. But Mexica-Tepanec influences were quick to make themselves felt, and the Mexica-Tepanec conquest ensued in the time of Techotlalatzin's son, Huehue Ixtlilxóchitl. The true genius of Texcoco only came to fruition after the scales had been reversed, and the Tepanecs overthrown. Even then, it flourished as Tenochtitlán's main ally rather than as a great power in its own right.

VI. The Dark Secret

Origins

Walter Lehmann wrote in 1933 of the "dark secret" of Tepanec origins. The mystery is far from being solved, and even the origin of the name Tepanec remains in doubt. For Seler, Tepanecatl means "Those of the Stone", i.e., "those who live on the field of lava (pedregal)" (that flowed into the Valley of Mexico from the peak of Ajusco).[1]

But, notwithstanding the stone that figures in the Tepanec glyph, the name is sometimes thought to have derived from Tecpanecatl, meaning "palace people." Supporters of this interpretation may point to the general use by Alvarado Tezozómoc of the term Tecpaneca, not Tepaneca. However Tepanecatl, not Tecpanecatl, was the more general usage at the time of the Conquest; Ixtlilxóchitl, Durán, Torquemada, and Chimalpain write exclusively of Tepanecas, not Tecpanecas. Moreover, the term Tepanohuayan figures in several documents, including the *Anales de Cuauhtitlán,* Chimalpain's *Relaciones,* and the *Anales de Tlatelolco.* Oddly enough, as Thelma Sullivan has pointed out to me, Tepanecatl and Tepanohuayan have no etymological connection, since Tepanohuayan derives from the impersonal form of *pano,* which is *panoa* and means "to cross over."

This thought is perhaps suggestive of yet further remote derivations of the term Tepanec.

At all events, Tepanohuayan is unquestionably used for the territory or city of the leading Tepanec power at a given moment; for instance, the *Anales de Cuauhtitlán,* writing of the time before the Aztec victory over Azcapotzalco, refer five times to that city as Tepanohuayan, but only once use the name to designate Tlacopan, in connection with the period when it had become the leading Tepanec city. The *Memorial Breve* associates Azcapotzalco with Tepanohuayan and also writes of Azcapotzalco Tepanecapan.

The *Anales de Tlatelolco* mention Tecpanecas as well as Tepanecas, as if the two terms were interchangeable, and meant the same thing.[2] However, beside a single reference to Tecpanecatl, Tepanecatl occurs ten times in this document, and Tepanohuayan once. Muñoz Camargo employs Tecpanecatl, but in a different sense. Xicalan, the Chichimec leader, is called Tecpanecatl, and a Tecpanecatl Cocotzin is also mentioned.[3] No particular reason exists to identify these two people with Tepanecs, and Tecpanecatl in this usage appears to be a title or proper name, not an ethnic designation. Equally, Torquemada, who invariably writes of Tepanecs, mentions two individuals, who are called Tecpanecatl, but who are not ostensibly Tepanecs. Durán goes so far as to draw a distinction between the two forms; in a list of honors conferred by Moctezuma I, the title Tecpanecatl is given to Citlacoatzin, and that of Tepanecatl Teuctli to Xiconoc.[4] A personage called Tecpa figures in the *Historia Tolteca-Chichimeca* as a Chichimec leader and is also mentioned by Torquemada and Vetancurt as a principal follower of Xolotl.

Nonetheless, the ease with which Tecpanecatl and Tepanecatl could become confused in speech, if not in glyph, is illustrated by the title of Atempanecatl (Lord of the Water). The *Anales de Cuauhtitlán* tell of an Atempanecatl, who came to Cuauhtitlán from Culhuacán, and also says that Huemac, as last ruler of Tollan, bore the title Atecpanecatl (Atempanecatl is, of course, the correct version). The *Memorial Breve* and other sources refer to Tlacaelel as Atenpanecatl, and a personage of that name also appears in the *Historia Tolteca-Chichimeca.* However, the same name or title is corrupted in the *Relación de la Genealogía* to become Atepanecate (the name of Mixcoatl's rebellious brother-in-law) and the *Leyenda de los Soles* and the *Origen de los Mexicanos* use the version Apanecatl. A lurking suspicion therefore remains that the Tepanecas were once upon a time Tecpanecas, to judge by what we know of their history; the notion that they were civilized or palace people has more meaning than a mere association with stones. Evidence for such a supposition is admittedly hard to find, and even if they *were* called Tecpanecas, the subsequent usage of Tepanecas is current in the surviving records.

In the previous chapter, a certain affinity between Tepanecs and Acolhuas was noted. A tradition exists that the two peoples reputedly arrived in the Valley of Mexico together, and "Acolhua" is quite often employed as a generic term for several migrant groups, including both the "true" Acolhuas and the Tepanecs; in like manner, the distinction between "Chichimec" and "Acolhua" was also seen to be not very clear cut.

The conclusion might therefore be drawn that the Tepanecs were just another Chichimec tribe. And indeed, the *Relación de la Genealogía* states that "Chichimecs" founded, not only Coatlichán, but the leading Tepanec centers of Azcapotzalco, Tlacopan, and Coyoacan.[5] The source stresses the point by asserting that Tezozomoc of Azcapotzalco was a Chichimec, who was also called a Tepanec ("llamado por otro nombre Tepaneca").[6] But such statements lack any clear significance, since "Chichimec" was an all-embracing term, applicable at times to non-nomads as well as to nomads, and was even used to describe the Mexicas of Tenochtitlán.

The *Anales de Cuauhtitlán* report the arrival of certain Tepanecs, "Who are now called Toltitlantlaca" in the year 7 Tecpatl, but no valid clues exist for determining the equivalent to this date in our calendar.

The Tepanecs are listed by several documents among the tribes who emerged from Chicomoztoc, and who are variously mentioned as being five, six, or seven in number. Durán writes of six groups, Xochimilcas, Chalcas, Tepanecs, Culhuas, Tlalhuicas, and Tlaxcaltecas.[7] Chimalpain gives the same list, to which he adds the Teotenancas and Amecamecas, who went to Chalco.[8] The *Anales de Tlatelolco* describe the migrants from Chicomoztoc as Azcapotzalcas (i.e., Tepanecs), Acolhuas, Huexotzincas, Colhuas, Cuitlahuacas, Mizquicas, Cuauhnahuas, Coixcas, Malinalcas, and Matlatzincas.[9]

The Codex Azcatitlán says that the tribes that came from Teoculhuacán were the Matlatzincas, Tepanecs, Chichimecs, Malinalcas,
Cuitlahuacas, Xochimilcas, Chalcas, and Huexotzincas. Sahagún
mentions Michuaques, Tepanecs, Acolhuas, Chalcas, Huexotzincas,
and Tlaxcaltecs as departing successively from Chicomoztoc.[10]

Such reports tell little of when the Tepanecs arrived or what
happened thereafter. According to Ixtlilxóchitl's more detailed account, the Tepanecs came from Michoacán, together with the Acolhuas and the Otomís who settled in Xaltocan, forty-seven years after
the coming of Xolotl and fifty-two years after the fall of Tollan.
Although he at times describes all three groups as Acolhuas, he
more often distinguishes between them, and emphasizes this difference by calling the group led by Tzontecomatl as the "true" Acolhuas.
The same writer goes on to state that the true Acolhuas were the most
important of the three, and further insists that each spoke a different
language.[11] The Otomí Xaltocamecas are described as the most
"remote" of the migrant bodies and as speaking a "strange" tongue.

Sahagún in one passage makes a parallel distinction between the
Tepanecs and the non-Nahua Acolhuas. After the various peoples
had gone to make offerings at Chicomoztoc, the Toltecs departed
first, and the Michoaque were the next to leave. They were followed
by the Tepanecs: "Niman ic oalocoaque in Naoatlaca, in Tepaneca"
("then the Nahuas, the Tepanecs departed").[12] Sahagún goes on to
state that the Acolhuas left afterwards, and were not called Nahuas.

Moreover, while Ixtlilxóchitl in one context writes jointly of the
Tepanecs and Acolhuas, in another he makes a positive distinction
between the two: in a passage already quoted in Chapter IV, he lists
the Acolhuas and even Mexicas among the peoples generally described
as "Chichimecs," while placing the Tepanecs, along with the Cholulans, Culhuas, and Mixtecs, among the non-Chichimec Toltecs.

Other sources link the Tepanecs with the Culhuas, or alternatively with the Mexicas, who came to adopt the Culhuas as their ancestors. Chimalpain writes of "Azcapotzalco Mexicapan," because
so many Mexicas settled there.[13] The *Anales de Cuauhtitlán* writes
of the "Tepanecs of Culhuacán" and also of "The Culhuas of Asca-
patzalco." The *Historia de los Mexicanos* mentions "Those of Tacuba
and Culhuacán and Azcapotzalco, who were called Tepanecs," thereby
putting the Culhuas and Tepanecs into the same category.[14] The same

source says that the Tepanec ruler, Tezozómoc, was a "Mexicano."[15] Torquemada also writes of "Tepaneca Mexicano."[16] Muñoz Camargo mentions "Culhuas y Tepaneca Mexicanos."[17] The Tepanecs were grouped together with Culhuas, Huitznahuas, and Mexicas in Ixtlil-xóchitl's account of the four elements who made a joint migration to Texcoco during the reign of Techotlalatzin. Moreover, they shared certain Culhua-Mexica institutions and traditions; also according to Ixtlilxóchitl, the office of Cihuacoatl existed in Azcapotzalco, and Tezozómoc says that one of the original Mexica barrios in Aztlan was called Tlacatecpan.

The Otomí Connection

A considerable body of evidence points in quite another direction, however, and hints that the Tepanecs were connected not so much with Nahuas and Toltecs as with the Otomí-Mazahua-Matlatzinca ethnic family. Carrasco in his important work on the Otomís sets out this evidence, linking the Tepanecs in particular with the Matlatzincas. In the proceedings of the Holy Office against certain Indians of Azcapotzalco, Tlamatzincatl is mentioned as a Tepanec god. But, as his very name implies, and as Torquemada confirms, Tlamatzincatl is a Matlatzinca deity. According to the *Historia de los Mexicanos,* the god of the Tepanecs was Ocotecuhtli, or Otontecuhtli, lord of the Otomís.[18]

Cervantes de Salazar states that in Tlacopan, another Tepanec center, Matlatzinca and Mazahua were spoken, in addition to Nahuatl. Durán provides another clue by reporting that the god Xocotl and the feast of Xocotecuhtli held a special significance for the Tepanecs of Coyoacan. Motolinía mentions the importance of Xocotl-huetzi for the people of Coyoacan, Tlacopan, and Azcapotzalco; these rites are intimately connected with Otontecuhtli, and, as Seler writes, Xocotl *is* Otontecuhtli.[19]

Soustelle concurs with Carrasco and sees the Tepanecs as connected with the linguistic family of the Otomí-Mazahua-Matlatzinca. Martínez Marín shares the same view and also insists that the Tepanecs came from the valley of Toluca, where they had previously lived in association with Matlatzincas.[20] Walter Lehmann supports this view, that he was among the first to voice: he sees the people of Azcapotzalco as of partly Acolhua stock, but says that Tezozómoc himself was of Matlatzinca descent, though he offers no specific evidence for the statement. Jiménez Moreno steers an intermediate course, crediting the Tepanecs both with Toltec and with Matlatzinca connections.

Carrasco's detailed case for linking Tepanecs and Matlatzincas rests mainly but not solely on religious parallels; he also calls attention to a passage in the *Anales de Cuauhtitlán* in which the Tepanecs are described as using the sling and as worshiping Cuecuex, whereas their enemies used the bow and arrow and were votaries of Mixcoatl (revered both by Otomís and by Chichimecs). But, like Xocotl, Cuecuex is at least in part to be identified with Otontecuhtli under another name; Sahagún's "Song of Otontecuhtli" contains the words: "Nitepanecatli aya Cuecuex" ("I am the Tepanec, the Cuecuex"). In the *Relación de Temazcaltepec,* Otontecuhtli, god of the Matlatzincas who lived in that place, is also named Cuecuex.[21] And Cuecuex, like so many Mesoamerican deities, has human counterparts: Durán writes how Maxtla, Tezozómoc's successor as ruler of Azcapotzalco, conferred with Cuecuex, depicted as an intimate counselor of the king. Tezozómoc goes even further and refers to the two leaders, Maxtlaton and Cuecuex, almost as if they were joint rulers.[22]

Carrasco makes a convincing case for Tepanec-Matlatzinca associations, and other evidence points in the same direction. In particular, one might note a general orientation of the Tepanec Empire towards the valley of Toluca, much of which is included in the territorial claims of Tlacopan, as listed in the *Memorial de los Pueblos.* However, before one jumps to any conclusion that the Tepanecs came in a single body from the region of Toluca, the reverse side of the medal has also to be kept in view.

By the same token, the *Anales de Cuauhtitlán* draw a distinction between the Tepanecs who (like the Matlatzincas) worshiped Cuecuex, i.e., Otontecuhtli, and other tribes who are followers of Mixcoatl. But, according to passages of Torquemada already cited, the Otomís, par excellence the votaries of Otontecuhtli, also venerated Mixcoatl, and therefore distinctions between the followers of Mixcoatl and Otontecuhtli-Cuecuex lose some of their validity.

Mesoamerican gods delight in defying neat definitions and resist attempts to file them into tidy pigeonholes as deities that perform a particular function or belong to a specific clan. Accordingly, tribal gods are not always a sure guide to tribal origins.

To illustrate this point, let us suppose that two ethnic groups of patently distinct origins are votaries of God A and God B; let us also suppose that a third group, whose provenance we ignore, worships God C. Now if God C can be identified in some way with God A, then presumably the first group that follows God A and the third group that follows God C are in some way related. This contention is logical, but nonetheless falls apart if God A is also shown to share many facets of God B; the same argument cannot be applied in this case, since the origins of the adherents of God A and God B are demonstrably distinct.

The origins of Otontecuhtli, together with Cuecuex, Matlat-zincatl, and Xocotl are complex, since these gods of ostensibly less developed peoples are linked with the oldest of Mesoamerican gods, Xiuhtecuhtli, and hence with those champions of traditional Meso-american values, the Chinampa cities of the Valley of Mexico, whose origins are clearly different. As Soustelle points out, Xiuhtecuhtli, as well as Xantico, fire god of Xochimilco, always had his face painted in the Otomí manner; the first day of the feast of Xocohuetzi is dedicated to a celebration in honor of Xiuhtecuhtli. The *Historia de los Mexicanos* also associates Otontecuhtli with fire, stating that the Tepanecs worshiped Otontecuhtli, who actually personified the fire, and that for this reason they burned their captives alive.[23]

Equally, Mixcoatl, far from being Otontecuhtli's opposite, is also closely linked with Xantico. Mixcoatl's association with the deer (in certain instances the two-headed deer) connects him not only with hunting but with fire, and Seler in particular identified this two-headed deer with Xantico.[24] The true significance of the two-headed deer is rather obscure, though other specimens exist, not ostensibly connected with Mixcoatl: in the Codex Borbonicus, Oxomoco and Cipactonal, the primeval human couple, are surmounted by a double deer-head. Quilaztli, also deity of Xochimilco, is called "the Deer of Mixcoatl." This goddess adds to the confusion by being part deer and part bird, since she descends from the sky, perches in a tree, and is also described as being dressed in feathers.[25]

Therefore we find ourselves back precisely at our point of departure, and Kirchhoff's remark may again be recalled: having been taught that black is black and white is white, we are disconcerted to find that white is the complement of black, not its opposite. The Tepanecs are followers of Otontecuhtli-Cuecuex, and thereby appear to be distinct both from the invading Chichimecs who followed Mixcoatl and from the traditional Chinampa peotles, who worship Xantico, or the mother goddess, under a variety of names. But after closer study, such fine distinctions between old gods and new, between gods of primitive and civilized peoples, or between those of one valley and of another lose much of their validity. Each deity shares many traits with his supposed opposites, and in particular the gods of the valley of Toluca have much in common with those of the Chinampas, and at times appear as almost the same deity wearing a different hat and bearing a different name. Admittedly some of these similarities may arise from the traditional links between the Malinalco-Ocuilan region, situated in the valley of Toluca, and the city of Culhuacán.

A Composite Group

Certain religious parallels between Tepanecs and Matlatzincas may legitimately be drawn, but they offer no basis for far-reaching historical conclusions. The Otomí-Pame linguistic family indeed exists, but embraces tongues whose relationship is fairly remote; in particular, a wide gap divides Matlatzinca from Otomí. Soustelle states that 66 per cent of the principal words are shared by the two languages; between Otomí and Pame (north and south), the percentage is reduced to 35.[26] But in terms of glottochronology—admittedly a science still in its infancy—the linguistic separation between Matlatzincas and Otomís is estimated at fifty-five centuries, though in the case of the Mazahuas and Otomís the time interval would be much less. The difference between Matlatzinca and Otomí is almost as great as between Latin and early Russian (sixty-five centuries in terms of glottochronology). Therefore, to treat prehistoric Otomís and Matlatzincas as blood brothers may be acceptable in terms of prehistory, but not when dealing with events that span centuries, not millennia.

141

Since the two problems are connected, a few further comments on Tepanec origins will be added after reviewing their later historical development. Up to this point we have seen that the Tepanecs were traditionally associated with the Acolhuas and also at times with Culhuas and Mexicas. Equally, the worship of basically Otomí gods, and the continued presence in their cities of Matlatzinca-speaking elements is significant. Clearly some relationship existed between Tepanecs and Matlatzincas, but its closeness is hard to assess. The Matlatzincas were perhaps one of several distinct ethnic groups in Azcapotzalco and other Tepanec cities, just as Otomís lived in Tenochtitlán, Culhuacán, Texcoco, and Cuauhtitlán.

Most cities of central Mesoamerica came to acquire mixed populations, a phenomenon that was caused by voluntary migration or by forced flight after military disaster, and at times stemmed from the action of a powerful ruler, who would move people from one place to another. To cite a few examples: Tlaxcaltecas (i.e. Acolhuas) lived in Tenayuca, and Xochimilcas in the barrio of Olac in Culhuacán; in Cuauhtitlán, parts of the city were allotted to people from Tepotzotlán and other neighbors; Culhuas also took refuge in Cuauhtitlán after the disasters that befell their own home. The Mexicas were not confined to Tenochtitlán and Tlatelolco; after their defeat in Chapultepec, some went to Culhuacán, but others to Acolhuacan (Coatlichán?), Xochimilco, and Azcapotzalco; Mexicas, Tepanecs, and Huitznahuas settled in Texcoco under Techotlalatzin. Tenochtitlán itself possessed foreign quarters; apart from the Otomís mentioned above, Xochimilcas and later Huexotzincas migrated thither.[27] Such people were following a long-established tradition; archaeology demonstrates that in Teotihuacán one part of the city was inhabited by Zapotecs.

The Tepanecs, not unlike the Mexicas, may therefore be viewed as a composite group that included certain elements from the valley of Toluca. But suggestions that the Tepanecs were Toltecized are hard to reconcile with others that they came mainly from the valley of Toluca. On balance, evidence is lacking that the Toltecs conquered much of that region.

Certain similarities are apparent between the earlier Matlatzinca pottery and that of Tula-Mazapan. But Matlatzinca contacts were not confined to the Valley of Mexico, since cultural links with Cholula are also found, as well as stylistic affinities with the valley of Morelos; these links persisted in the Late Postclassic, after the fall of Tollan.[28] The written sources associate the valley of Toluca, and more specifically Teotenango, with Tollan Xicocotitlan. Chimalpain mentions wars between the two cities and writes of a subsequent migration of the Nonoalca Tlacochcalcas from Teotenango to Tollan, but he never suggests that Tollan conquered that region. Teotenango was an imposing site and enjoyed a long life span that only ended with the Conquest. It is unlikely that the city came under Tollan's sway, and its significance in the politics of the Valley of Mexico in the post-Tollan period is unknown, though both Teotenango and Calixtlahuaca—later to be absorbed into the Aztec Empire—were surely important centers. More probably only the Ocuilan-Malinalco corner of the valley of Toluca was dominated by the Toltecs; this area was a traditional Culhua patrimony, to which the Mexicas laid early claims, and the *Memorial Breve* states that the two places were subject to Culhuacán in Toltec times.

Possibly the migration from Teotenango to Tollan had something to do with Tepanec origins, but any such hypothesis belongs to the realm of pure speculation, since no proof exists. Evidence survives of Tepanec affinities with Mexicas, Culhuas, Acolhuas, and Matlatzincas. Proto-Tepanecs reportedly took part in the original Acolhua-Chichimec migration from the northwest. The fully fledged Tepanecs are more likely to have emerged after the original group had first intermingled with the Toltecized Chinampanecas of the Valley of Mexico, and had then absorbed Matlatzinca elements that penetrated the Valley of Mexico from the direction of Toluca, or possibly from the Teotlalpan. But if the Tepanecs' forebears, the proto-Tepanecs, formed part of the general Acolhua migration, their rise in status was slow, and Azcapotzalco did not play a leading role during the apogee of Coatlichán and Huexotla. No information survives concerning when the Tepanecs became Nahuatized; if they did not speak this tongue when they arrived, at all events they would have been eager to acquire such a significant status symbol; no stories exist, as in the case of the Acolhuas, of resistance to the process of Nahuatization, and they appear to have been apt pupils.

143

Xaltocan

Among the least Nahuatized of the main migrant groups were the people of Xaltocan, who never abandoned their Otomí language and traditions. Jiménez Moreno and Martínez Marín see the Xaltocans as related to the Mazahuas; however, as previously stressed, millennia, not centuries, separate the Mazahuas and the Otomís in linguistic terms, and Xaltocan is invariably described as an Otomí rather than a Mazahua stronghold. The site, like many others, had been occupied for many centuries; Aztec I pottery and even Teotihuacán IV have been found on the surface in or near the city.[29] The *Anales de Cuauhtitlán* mention those earlier, or pre-Otomí, inhabitants; during the war between Xaltocan and Cuauhtitlán in the year 8 Tecpatl, the new settlers described the original occupants as "tlilhuipilleque (the people of the black huipils), Nonoalca and Cozcateca."[30]

Don Pablo Nazareo's famous letter to the King of Spain gives a long list of provinces, townships and strongpoints (*plazas fuertes*) that served the rulers of the former señorío of Xaltocan, and the territory claimed by Don Pablo as the ancient patrimony of its rulers occupies about half the area designated as Tepanec territory in the Codex García Granados.

Many place-names mentioned by Don Pablo, such as Atotonilco, Metztitlán, Tototepec, and Tulancingo also figure in the campaigns of Tochintecuhtli and Huetzin. If, therefore, his letter is to be treated as anything more than an inflated claim designed to impress the King of Spain, it must surely refer to a period before the Tochintecuhtli-Huetzin era, not after, when the Tepanec rise to power commenced and the star of Xaltocan had already waned. Don Pablo names the Mazahua area of Xiquipilco, Xocotitlan, and Atlacomulco (also included in the Codex García Granados) as belonging to Xaltocan—a claim that presumably led Jiménez Moreno and others to suggest that the people of Xaltocan were linked to the Mazahuas.

Don Pablo also includes the present-day Otumba, near the Teotihuacán, in his list. It is not impossible that, when Chimalpain wrote of a triple alliance of Tollan, Culhuacán, and Otompan, he was not thinking of the Otumba we know, but either of Xaltocan itself, or the general region claimed by Don Pablo as belonging to that city. The notion that Xaltocan first rose to power at the same time as Coatlichán and Azcapotzalco is based on a contrived version of events and cannot be taken at its face value.

On the contrary, it will be recalled that the Codex Vaticano-Ríos situates the apogee of Xaltocan in the immediate aftermath of the collapse of Tollan, at a time when power was exercised by Culhuacán, Tenayuca, and Xaltocan; only thereafter did Azcapotzalco, Coatlichán, and "Ciaculma" become predominant.

Sahagún, dealing with the same topic, states that after the decline of Tenayuca and Xaltocan, the principal powers of the region were Azcapotzalco, Coatlichán, and Culhuacán.[31] Therefore, although the glyphs for Acolman and Culhuacán could hardly be confused, "Ciaculma," by some strange slip of the pen, appears in the Vaticano-Ríos in place of Sahagún's Culhuacán. An Acolman is listed in the Codex Boturini as having been visited by the Mexicas before reaching Cempoala. Ixtlilxóchitl moreover includes among the second dynasty *(casa)* from which many rulers descended "los de la tierra de Mextitlán, Acolman y otras partes."[32] Since he also includes in his list the dynasty of the Acolhuas of Coatlichán, the implication is clear that, whatever its etymology (meaning strictly speaking "Place of Shoulders," not "Place of Acolhuas"), he was treating Acolman in this context as a Chichimec, or more probably Otomí, rather than an Acolhua stronghold; as such, it could have been a temporary successor to Tenayuca or to Xaltocan as one of the three leading powers; it may be recalled that the *Memorial Breve* gave Otompan as the third partner in the Toltec Triple Alliance, along with Tollan and Culhuacán.

The assertion that Xaltocan played a major part in the expulsion of the Mexicas from Chapultepec (probably in 1325) may be an anachronism. According to the *Leyenda de los Soles,* the anti-Mexica coalition consisted of Culhuacán, Xaltocan, Cuauhtitlán, Acolman, Tenayuca, Azcapotzalco, Cuahuacán, Mazahuacán, Xiquipilco, Matlatzinco, Ocuilan, Cuitlahuac, and Xochimilco. This list contains an impressive proportion of people who spoke Otomí or related tongues. Incidentally, it provides further evidence that Acolman was not then a specifically Acolhua city, since the Acolhuas in general declined to join this coalition. However, the continuance of Xaltocan as a principal power until that date remains in

145

doubt; at all events the city fell an easy prey to the Mexica-Tepanecs in 1395. This Tepanec conquest was preceded by a war of attrition between Xaltocan and Cuauhtitlán, that, according to the *Anales de Cuauhtitlán,* lasted twenty-four years. After the Tepanec onslaught, the Xaltocans, including the ruler, took refuge among their kinsmen in Metztitlán, which was an Otomí stronghold (though the people were sometimes called Chichimecs); the Otomís of Xaltocan were moon worshipers, a cult shared by the people of Metztitlán (meaning "Place of the Moon").[33]

The Tepanec Dynasty

Between 1371 and 1427, the throne of Azcapotzalco was occupied by Tezozómoc, that colossus who dominated his era. His rule, which may be termed the Tepanec half-century, was highly personalized, but the deeds and even the names of the great king's forebears remain wrapped in obscurity.

Ixtlilxóchitl gives a compressed version of Tezozómoc's ancestry, stating that the first Tepanec leader, called Aculhua, was one of those three señores who arrived together at the court of Xolotl, and received the principality of Azcapotzalco. For Ixtlilxóchitl, Tezozómoc is simply Aculhua's son. But Aculhua supposedly arrived in the Valley of Mexico fifty-two years after the fall of Tollan, while Tezozómoc's reign began some two centuries later, in the 1370's. The Texcocan historian bridges the gap by crediting Acolhua with a life of two hundred years; like so many other rulers, including Ixtlilxóchitl's three kings of Tollan, he traditionally died in the year 7 Acatl.[34]

The *Anales de Tlatelolco,* a source containing fuller information on Azcapotzalco, tells a different tale.[35] The first chief of the Tepanecs was Matlacoatl, also called Acolnahuacatzin, who died in 4 Acatl. This source states that the Azcapotzalco monarchy was established 170 years before the arrival of the Mexicas in the Valley of Mexico. But this assertion is hard to reconcile with the statement that Azcapotzalco had only four rulers before Tezozómoc, i.e., before 1371. Matlacoatl went to Azcapotzalco, according to the *Anales de Tlatelolco,* and married the daughter of the Chichimec leader Tzihuactlatonac, who was ruler of Cuitlachtepec. In another passage, Tzihuactlatonac is ruler of Tenayuca.

Matlacoatl was succeeded by the following rulers:

> Chiconquiauhtzin, son of Matlacoatl, who married the daughter of Tepantzin of Xaltocan.
>
> Tezcapoctzin, son of Chiconquiauhtzin.
>
> Acolnahuacatzin, brother of Tezcapoctzin, who married the daughter of Tequanitzin, king of Tenayuca.
>
> Tezozómoc was the youngest son of this second Acolnahuacatzin, whose three elder children had been killed in Oztopolco by the señor of Coyoacan, another leading Tepanec city.

Now Tochintecuhtli is also described in the *Anales de Tlatelolco* as son of the ruler of Cuitlachtepec, and the text might therefore be taken to imply that Matlacoatl married Tochintecuhtli's sister. But in a subsequent passage, the source also states that Acolnahuacatzin of Azcapotzalco (presumably in this context Matlacoatl Acolnahuacatzin, rather that the second ruler of the same name) married the daughter, not the sister of Tequanitzin of Tenayuca, a princess called Cuetlachxóchitzin.[36] In Chapter III, Tequanitzin was identified with Tochintecuhtli; other sources such as the *Memorial Breve* also name Cuetlachxochitzin as daughter of Tochintecuhtli, and this appears to be the correct relationship.

Tezcapoctzin and the second Acolnahuacatzin, who presumably possessed an additional name, were brothers and were both grandsons of the original Matlacoatl Acolnahuacatzin. Tezozómoc, as the son of Acolnahuacatzin, was therefore separated by three generations from the founder of the Azcapotzalco dynasty, according to the *Anales de Tlatelolco,* and by four generations from Tochintecuhtli, whose active life began 120 years before that of Tezozómoc. The genealogy therefore makes sense, since a thirty-year gap between generations is reasonable, bearing in mind that Tezozómoc's father was a younger son, and Tezozómoc himself was also the youngest of four children.

The *Anales de Tlatelolco* account of early Tepanec dynastic history accordingly makes reasonable sense. Torquemada, however, gives a different list.[37]

Acolhua-Huetzintecuhtli (described as Xolotl's son-in-law)
Cuecuex
Quauhtzintecuhtli
Ilhuicamina
Matlacohuatl
Tezcapuctli
Teotlehuac (who was reigning when the Mexicas arrived in
    Chapultepec)
Tzihuactlatonac
Tezozómoc

Acolhua, or Acolnahuacatzin, as in the *Anales de Tlatelolco*
list, is seemingly another rather generalized appellation, applicable
to several successive rulers. Walter Lehmann first pointed out that
Aculhua was to be considered more as title than name. Veytia, for
instance, mentions two Aculhuas, the second of whom died in 1343
and was succeeded by Tezozómoc.[38] The *Anales Mexicanos* also
mention a son of Tezozómoc called Acolnahuacatl.[39] The *tlatoani*
Axayacatl had a son called Tezozomoctli Acolnahuacatl, while
Huitzilihuitl of Tenochtitlán also had a son called Acolnahuacatl.

The task of reconciling the *Anales de Tlatelolco* and Torquemada versions is plainly impossible. Torquemada's long list may
conceivably contain members of two dynasties that reigned simultaneously since evidence exists of the presence of two rulers in
Azcapotzalco (see below). Alternatively, two or three successive
names, such as Cuecuex (the name of a god) and Quauhtlequeztli
(a traditional title for a *teomama* on the Mexica migration) may in
fact belong to one sole monarch.

Several names occur in both lists: Tzihuatlatonac, Matlacoatl,
Tezcapoctzin, and Chiconquauhtzin (the same person as Quauhtzintecuhtli?); however, such names in Torquemada's list occur in the
reverse order to their equivalents in that of the *Anales de Tlatelolco.*
According to the *Memorial Breve,* Tzihuatlatonac (called Tzi-
huactli) and Matlacoatl were successive leaders of the Teochichimeca.
In general terms, the *Anales de Tlatelolco* version seems to be the
more consistent of the two and is probably reasonably correct.

The Institutions of Azcapotzalco

The details of Tepanec institutions in pre-Aztec times are lost to us. History belongs to the victors, and Barlow aptly stated that in the bonfire of Tepanec records after the downfall of Azcapotzalco, many secrets of their history and social organization perished. Surviving reports generally recall the institutions of Tenochtitlán-Tlatelolco; for instance, the offices of Tlacochcaltatl and Cihuacoatl existed in Azcapotzalco, and Maxtla, Tezozomoc's successor, was advised by a "council," or *tlatocan*.

As in Tenochtitlán, social stratification was apparently rigid: when Maxtla put a heavy price on the fugitive Nezahualcoyotl's head, he offered lands to anyone who apprehended his enemy, "even if he were a plebeian."[40] He thereby implied, as in Tenochtitlán, that the outright ownership of land was normally a class privilege. However, as also in Tenochtitlán, promotion from the ranks was possible; Maxtla on another occasion showed special favor to a dwarf who denounced the Mexica *tlatoani* Chimalpopoca, and made all the dwarf's relations into "knights."

In one respect, Azcapotzalco may have followed the Culhua tradition. The *Historia de los Mexicanos* states: "Tezozomoc was made lord of Azcapotzalco, one of two. There always were two rulers, and they still exist today."[41] In one passage of the *Anales de Tlatelolco* a certain Acolhua seems to rule at the same time as Tezozómoc.[42] The inference by Durán that Maxtla and Cuecuex were also joint monarchs has already been cited.

The Tepanecs Before Tezozómoc

Although Azcapotzalco, like Texcoco, can boast of Teotihuacán remains, the rise of a new or Postclassic Azcapotzalco began relatively late. Concrete evidence is lacking that the Tepanecs played a significant role in the Valley of Mexico before the thirteenth century; even their true part in the expulsion of the Mexicas in 1325 remains uncertain.

According to the *Anales de Tlatelolco* list, the historical period of Azcapotzalco began with Aculhua I (Matlacoatl), who married a sister, or more probably a daughter, of Tochintecuhtli. Aculhua I thereby becomes the approximate contemporary of Huetzin's son, Acolmiztli of Coatlichán, whose death occurred in about 1310.

The emergence of Azcapotzalco is thus linked with the Tochintecuhtli-Huetzin period, during which the city, together with its future rival Texcoco, would have played at best a minor role. Azcapotzalco was at that time merely a future contender for power, though, unlike Texcoco, it is already known to have possessed its own dynasty. Very possibly, this early Azcapotzalco was a tributary and satellite of Tenayuca; it might even have constituted a kind of lesser or alternative capital to that principality, since Tochintecuhtli and his spouse are reported to have lived there for seven years.[43] Sahagún implies the existence of such ties and tells how, in the reign of Yaotzin, son of Tochintecuhtli, the Acolchichimecas— probably in this context the Tenayucans—began to exact tribute from those of Tepanohuayan.[44]

The beginnings of known Tepanec history in the Valley of Mexico, therefore, only marginally precede those of the Mexicas. According to several accounts, when the latter arrived in Chapultepec, they occupied a territory where the borders of the Culhuas, Aculhuas, and Tepanecs converged. Although I previously felt that the Tepanecs were the prime movers in the expulsion of the Mexicas from that site, I am now more ready to question whether Azcapotzalco had yet—in 1319—acquired the status to lay valid claim to leadership of such a coalition. The Tepanecs, the Culhuas, the Xaltocans, and the Chalcas are variously mentioned as playing a principal part in the destruction of the Mexicas. But the question of who led the coalition is a tricky one, as will be seen when we come to examine early Mexica history. After reconsidering the data on the Tepanec dynasty and noting the absence of other references to Tepanecs at this time, I am more inclined to regard reports of Tepanec leadership as just another interpolation of a later situation into an earlier period. Because the Tepanecs were enjoying a brief supremacy in 1425, it later came to be assumed that they played a leading role in the events of 1325. Moreover, because the Mexicas became Tepanec dependents in Tenochtitlán, it was easy to suppose that a similar situation had prevailed in former times. Xaltocan reportedly played a prominent part in the campaign against the Mexicas, and at that time, together with Tenayuca, had not yet lost all its power and counted more than Azcapotzalco. The *Anales de Cuauhtitlán* contradict other accounts by stating that Chapultepec belonged to the ruler of Culhuacán, another doubtful assertion, since Culhuacán was already on the decline, even if it had controlled Chapultepec in Toltec times.

A surer sign of the emergence of Tepanec power dates from thirty years after the Mexicas' expulsion from Chapultepec, in the form of Quinatzin's decision to abandon his capital of Tenayuca and move his court to Texcoco. This departure, as I already showed in Chapter V, was probably involuntary and marks the passage of Tenayuca from the Acolhua to the Tepanec orbit during the reign of Quinatzin's predecessor. According to the *Anales de Tlatelolco,* certain Acolhuas (described as Texcocan) had resided in Tenayuca but departed during the reign of Acamapichtli of Tenochtitlán.[45]

Tenayuca was surely a major center in the period following the collapse of Tollan, even if some of the reports of an "empire," centered exclusively on that city, may be discounted. According to *L'Histoyre du Mechique,* Topiltzin first went thither when he fled from Tollan. Tenayuca remained important in the Huetzin-Tochintecuhtli period as a capital of the latter ruler, also called Tequanitzin.

Torquemada even says that when the Mexicas arrived in Chapultepec, Tenayuca was the leading Tepanec city.[46] Since the Tepanecs appeared relatively late upon the scene, I am tempted to think that Azcapotzalco was originally an offshoot of Tenayuca and that the satellite then absorbed its parent, just as Tenochtitlán later overthrew Azcapotzalco. Tenayuca became the first victim of the Tepanec urge to conquer, at a time when the city was still generally regarded as more important than Azcapotzalco itself. Tenayuca was reportedly conquered by the Mexicas, then under Tepanec tutelage, probably in 1370.[47] Tezozómoc of Azcapotzalco was then made ruler of the city, a year before he became the chief Tepanec monarch, just as his son Maxtla reigned in Coyoacan before he also took control of Azcapotzalco.

The possibility may exist of semi-independent Mexica initiatives at that time, in particular against Culhuacán. However, the case of Tenayuca is different, and it is most unlikely that the fledgling city of Tenochtitlán should have been allowed to indulge in a private war against a leading center lying at the very doors of Azcapotzalco.

Ixtlilxóchitl actually states that the war against Tenayuca was instigated by Aculhua of Azcapotzalco, Tezozomoc's father, who ordered
the Mexicas to attack the city.[48]

Concerning the date of this event, the Codex Xolotl places it in
the year 2 Acatl, but the Codex Mexicanus gives a figure of 8
Tochtli, while also asserting that Tezozomoc ascended the throne of
Azcapotzalco in the following year of 9 Acatl. The *Anales de Tlatelolco* state: "In the year 10 Tecpatl, the Chichimecs who lived in
Tenayuca set forth from their home." The date of 2 Acatl in the
Tenochca count would be 1351 in the Julian calendar, but if taken as
belonging to the Culhua-Texcocan count, then it becomes 1371 and
thus coincides within one year with 8 Tochtli in the Tenochca
count, (the equivalent of 1370).[49]

The Tepanecs had already begun to harbor ambitions in other
directions even before the absorption of Tenayuca. In 7 Tecpatl
(1356 in the Tenochca year-count), they established themselves in
Toltitlan in the Teotlalpan.[50] In 1370, they founded Tecpatepec,
also in the Teotlalpan.[51] Perhaps even more significant was the campaign against Culhuacán, a city that, like Tenayuca, at one time belonged to the Acolhua sphere of influence. The Codex Mendoza illustrates Culhuacán as a Mexica conquest during the leadership of
Tenoch; the *Historia de los Mexicanos* writes of a Mexica attack
against Culhuacán and of the burning of the main temple, an event
that occurred twenty-one years after the foundation of Tenochtitlán.
Since the source places the founding of the city three years earlier
than the orthodox date, I have calculated that this war against Culhuacán took place in 1363.[52] Like the attack on Tenayuca, the conquest is presented as a Mexica victory in later records, but the prime
movers were surely the Tepanecs. This was far from being the first
disaster that befell the city; almost a century before, Huetzin of
Coatlichán had usurped the throne of Culhuacán, in the face of
bitter resistance by its inhabitants. A period of limited recovery
seems to have ensued in the early years of the fourteenth century,
during which Mexica refugees helped to score a rather pyrrhic
victory against Xochimilco. At the outset of the Mexica-Tepanec
war against Chalco that began in 1375, the *Anales de Cuauhtitlan*
state, Culhuacán was under Chalca domination, and the attack

against Culhuacán in 1363 may even have been an opening shot in this long struggle.[53]

The occupation of Tenayuca and the overthrow of Culhuacán marked the outset of Tepanec ascendancy in the Valley of Mexico and the surrounding areas. The *Relación de la Genealogía* says that, after the fall of Culhuacán, the most important Chichimec ruler was the king of Azcapotzalco, who acknowledged no overlord; the next most important rulers at the time were those of Coatlichán, Amecameca, Huexotzingo, and Cuauhnahuac, who all made obeisance to the suzerainty of the king of Azcapotzalco.[54] The statement thus names the Acolhuas and the Chalcas as the leading rivals within the Valley of Mexico to Tepanec claims of supremacy, which, however, they hesitated to challenge. By this time, Texcoco would have overtaken Coatlichán as the principal Acolhua power. The mention, previously cited, of a period dominated by Azcapotzalco, Coatlichán, and Ciaculman, may be taken to refer to this period, when the Tepanecs and Acolhuas, the two surviving superpowers after the decline of Culhuacán, stood facing each other across the Lake of Texcoco.

The details of Tepanec conquests prior to the overthrow of Azcapotzalco in 1428 survive in Mexica sources, and are often shown as Mexica rather than as Tepanec victories. These Tepanec-Mexica campaigns are inseparable from the rise of the Mexicas themselves, and therefore belong to a subsequent chapter. In general terms, such conquests followed a traditional pattern, already set by Tollan Xicocotitlan, also visible in the triumphs of Tochintecuhtli and Huetzin, even if these were less ambitious. Not only are Tepanec-Mexica conquests reported in the valley of Morelos, but also in a northeasterly direction, as far as Tulancingo, and southeastwards to Cuauhtinchan, in the Puebla-Tlaxcala valley.

The Tepanec Claim

Ixtlilxóchitl asserts that the Tepanecs were descended from the Toltecs. And in effect, in a fuller sense than the Acolhuas, they became the first true pretenders to the Toltec heritage, conquering, or at least claiming, those lands that were probably subject to Tollan.

At this stage, therefore, before we come to the Mexicas, we are already better placed to review the era that separates Toltec from Aztec supremacy. In the twelfth century, after the fall of Tollan, and perhaps even before that event, groups of Otomís, accompanied by Chichimecs, penetrated into the Valley of Mexico and beyond, led by traditional heroes and exalted with divine, or semidivine, appellations such as Xolotl, Mixcoatl, and Mitl, or Amimitl. These invaders occupied much but not all of the territory previously dominated by Tollan, and thus became temporary claimants to the heritage of the fallen city, even if reports that they forged a new empire out of the wreckage have an apocryphal ring. Moreover they were not the sole heirs, since Culhuacán still survived intact and, as Tollan's partner, could lay a residuary claim as heir to the estate of the defunct city. Between say, 1200 and 1250, Culhuacán still plays a paramount role as the surviving bastion of Toltec civilization and the upholder of Toltec tradition. During this time, Xaltocan and Tenayuca became more powerful after being partly resettled by the intruders; hence the assertion in the Codex Vaticano Ríos that power was shared between Tenayuca, Xaltocan, and Culhuacán seems perfectly correct. Xolotl's easy victory over Culhuacán is as much a reflection of later disasters that befell that city as an historical occurrence of the immediate post-Tollan period.

Not until the middle of the thirteenth century did Coatlichán come into its own, when Tochintecuhtli of Tenayuca and Huetzin of Coatlichán subjugated a territory that deserved to be called an empire, and thereby became partial pretenders to the Toltec heritage, though they were far from dominating the whole Toltec patrimony and, as Acolhuas, were more often called Chichimecs than Toltecs. By a process of interpolation so frequent in Mesoamerican historical accounts, this embryo empire was pushed back to the twelfth century, and the historical Tochintecuhtli of Tenayuca and of Huexotla, his portrait blown up to beyond life size, becomes the great Xolotl, ruler of a boundless domain and forefather of all future rulers. To a certain extent Tochintecuhtli indeed played this role of father figure, since through his daughters, Cuetlachcihuatzin and Nenetzin, he became the ancestor both of the Acolhua and Tepanec dynasties.

This Acolhua-Chichimec empire lay astride the Lake of Texcoco; in the western half, bordering on Otomí territory, Tenayuca and Cahuacan dominated, while the principal cities of the eastern portion were Coatlichán and Huexotla. Huetzin of Coatlichán, the ruler of the eastern half, occupied Culhuacán for a time, and a joint campaign was conducted against the region of Metztitlán-Atotonilco-Tulancingo, whose people are described as true Chichimecs but who also had Otomí associations.

Although this mini-empire may have been short-lived, Tenayuca, Xaltocan, and Coatlichán declined fairly slowly, and only in mid-fourteenth century, about the time of the foundation of Tenochtitlán, an important change occurs with the rise of the Tepanecs, who until that moment had played a more muted role in the power politics of the region. Reports of Tepanec leadership in previous events is probably another anachronistic reflection of Azcapotzalco's subsequent bid for supremacy.

The Tepanecs first pushed the Acolhuas (whose leading city was no longer Coatlichán but Texcoco) out of Tenayuca, defeated Culhuacán, and thus established control over the land to the south and west of the Lake of Texcoco, while already threatening Xaltocan, which they were to conquer in 1395.

The key problem remains: who were the Tepanecs? Most answers to the question postulate the arrival of a homogeneous group, who came from outside the Valley of Mexico and thereafter maintained their ethnic integrity. But more probably the people who came to be known as Tepanecs did not arrive as one body, but were formed within the Valley of Mexico by the merging of different elements. The Acolhuas seem to have developed out of a blend of Otonchichimecs and Teochichimecs, with an important and varying admixture of the original Nahua or Toltec inhabitants. The Tepanecs were surely the result of a similar blend, but with a fresh ingredient added thereafter.

I view the people of Xaltocan, Tenayuca, Huexotla, and Coatlichán as the product of this kind of ethnic mixture of Otonchichimecs, Teochichimecs, and original Nahuas, though the blend was varied in each case. In particular, Xaltocan possessed a high proportion of Otomí blood, while Tenayuca probably absorbed more Teochichimecs; consequently this city came to be described in the oral tradition as Chichimec and Xaltocan as Otomí.

However, in Azcapotzalco, that had formed part of Tochinte-

155

cuhtli's domain, the true Tepanec stock developed, when to these elements were added newcomers from the valley of Toluca, probably of Matlatzinca origin; however, this does not mean that the Tepanecs all came from that region, or that they were mainly Matlatzinca.

Carrasco sees these Oto-Mangue groups as coming from the valley of Toluca in fairly recent times; he identifies them with the Otomís mentioned by the *Anales de Cuauhtitlán* as reaching Cahuacan in the reign of Tochintecuhtli, and as then settling near Tepotzotlan. But links between the valley of Toluca and the Valley of Mexico can be traced back to the time when Culhuacán, as Tollan's partner, reportedly dominated the Ocuilan and Malinalco, and peoples of Mazahua or Matlatzinca origin could have settled in the Valley of Mexico at an earlier date, and brought their gods with them.

Accordingly, the Tepanecs not only—like the Acolhuas—had Otomí affiliations, but also absorbed a second Otomangue element consisting of people of Matlatzinca derivation, who had come previously from the valley of Toluca. They perhaps also differed from the Acolhuas in having a larger proportion of Nahua or Toltec blood; no doubt Tenayuca had possessed a considerable Nahua-speaking population when the Chichimecs arrived, and Ixtlilxóchitl reminds us that the city had been important in Toltec times; many of these original inhabitants of Tenayuca may have been absorbed into the ethnic blend that came to be designated as Tepanec.

The Tepanecs who rose to power after Tenayucans and Xaltocans and the first Acolhuas belonged in a sense to a new breed of peoples whose background, like that of these other intruders, was basically Tolteca-Chichimec, but who only came to fruition when yet a further element had been added to the ethnic blend. Later it will be shown that the Mexicas and Chalcas, the two other new claimants to the imperial purple, also belong to this category.

VII. Friends and Neighbors

A Slow Recovery

Although this work deals mainly with the señoríos of the Valley of Mexico, their history is closely bound up with that of neighboring lands. Unfortunately however, little or no information survives about events in the valley of Toluca during the period in question. In the preceding chapter, documentary hints of ties between Tepanecs and the Matlatzincas were listed, along with archaeological parallels between the Valley of Mexico and the valley of Toluca. On the rulers of this region however, and on their doings, the written record is silent.

And we know almost as little of the history of Morelos, aside from Mixcoatl's brief incursion, mentioned in the Anales de Cuauhtitlán. Evidence has already been cited of links between the Valleys of Mexico and Morelos in the Tula-Mazapan period, and as well as certain signs of Toltec domination of part of the latter. In addition, affinities have come to light between ceramic styles of this region and the Valley of Mexico, and also between those of the valleys of Toluca and Morelos. For instance, Noguera and Piña Chan write of analogies in form and decoration between Matlatzinca pottery and

157

Tlalhuica laquer, corresponding to the era that runs from the fall of Tollan to the rise of Tenochtitlán.[1]

Any power dominant in the southern Valley of Mexico always felt the urge to penetrate the valley of Morelos and lay its hands on the highly prized produce of the warmer lands, such as cotton, that does not grow in higher altitudes. Whoever ruled the Valley of Mexico enjoyed no automatic right of entry into the region to the south; however, Culhuacán lay at a short distance as the crow flies from Cuauhnahuac, though separated by a formidable mountain barrier.

The Tlalhuicas reportedly settled in present-day Morelos only in the Late Postclassic period, and are named by several sources among the tribes who came singly or together from Chicomoztoc and who peopled the Valley of Mexico and the lands beyond in post-Tollan times. These Tlalhuicas, after settling in their new home, continued to enjoy close links with the Chinampa peoples. In particular, a special relationship seems to have prevailed between the Xochimilcas and Tlalhuicas, to a point where Alvarado Tezozomoc could write of "those perverse Xochimilca Tlahuicas."[2]

However, in the period with which we are now concerned, before the rise of Tenochtitlán, the Puebla-Tlaxcala valley looms larger in the history of the Valley of Mexico, and of that region's history a little more is known. Jiménez Moreno has frequently been at pains to point to the key role of the Puebla-Tlaxcala valley, and to the need for any would-be conqueror of central Mesoamerica to dominate both this and the Valley of Mexico. Ancient traditions linked the two territories. Teotihuacán, for instance, lay astride both, with easy access to each; the ruins of its Great Pyramid bear witness to the grandeur of Classic Cholula, that in later times became a center of worship and commerce for peoples living on both sides of the Sierra Nevada.

As explained in *The Toltecs,* when Teotihuacán fell, the Olmeca-Xicallancas were left in possession of the Puebla-Tlaxcala region, which they dominated during the Tula-Mazapan horizon, marked in Cholula itself by the phases Cholulteca I and II; however, the presence in that site of fair amounts of Aztec I pottery points to continued ties with the Valley of Mexico, especially with Culhuacán, where this ware abounds and may even have originated. Quetzalcoatl himself is reported by Ixtlilxóchitl and Torquemada to have visited Cholula before he ever reached Tollan; Mendieta also writes of a Quetzalcoatl who came from Yucatán to Cholula and returned eastwards without ever having visited Tollan at all.[3] Other sources tell how, on leaving Tollan Xicocotitlan, Topiltzin Quetzalcoatl visited Cholula before going to Tlillan Tlapallan. The Nonoalcas, on their way from the Gulf Coast to Tulancingo and thence to Tollan, had also skirted the Puebla-Tlaxcala valley, and visited Zacatlán.

In my previous volume, I questioned the view that Cholula had been a major rival of Tollan Xicocotitlan; at all events, the Olmeca-Xicallancas, who then occupied Cholula, fell an easy prey to the assaults of those Tolteca-Chichimec migrants, who, at the close of the Toltec era, moved thither. During its first Postclassic phase, Cholulteca I, the city was virtually abandoned; with the advent of Cholulteca II, roughly contemporary with Tula-Mazapan and Aztec I, it began to grow again, but the initial revival was modest. The evidence, cited mainly by Florencia Müller, now suggests that Cholula's true resurgence does not belong to Tula-Mazapan at all, but to the ensuing Cholulteca III phase, that marked the beginning of Cholula polychrome, and therefore comes after the apogee of Tollan.[4] On the contrary, the latest archaeological evidence reveals the local pre-eminence of the great site of Cacaxtla, that still flourished during the early Tula-Mazapan phase but declined thereafter. Cholula itself, after the collapse of the Classic, seems to have made a slow recovery that gained momentum only in the post-Tollan era.

By the time Tochintecuhtli and Huetzin in the thirteenth century began their career of conquest, described in Chapter III, Cholula was again important, and had forged new links with the peoples of the Valley of Mexico and with others, such as the Mixtecs; this connection bore visual fruit in the wonders of the Puebla-Mixtec style. Ixtlilxóchitl records that after the campaigns of Quinatzin (in this context for Quinatzin read Huetzin—see Chapter III) against the Teochichimecs of Metztitlan, Tototepec, and Tepepulco, his defeated rivals were exiled to Tlaxcala and Huexotzingo in order that the rulers of those lands could keep a close eye on them, since these princes were Quinatzin's "brothers." At that time, before Huexotzingo, let alone Tlaxcala, had become important, Cholula was again the leading city, and a special relationship had already come into being between the powers of the Puebla-Tlaxcala valley and the Acolhuas of the Valley of Mexico. Only later, when the Mexicas came to the fore, do we possess evidence of fierce rivalries between these adjacent regions.

Chichimecs and Cholulans

In *The Toltecs* aspects of the Tolteca-Chichimec migration from Tollan to Cholula were considered; in particular, doubts were expressed regarding whether a band of dissident Toltecs, who for thirty-seven years had pursued a most circuitous route to Cholula, could have then wrested that city from the Olmeca-Xicallancas, who had held it for several centuries.

The intruders admittedly did not have things all their own way, and the *Historia Tolteca-Chichimeca* gives two distinct versions of the dealings of these breakaway Toltecs with the inhabitants of Cholula, that it calls Tlachiuhualtepec, and whose rulers it names as Tlalchiach Tizacozque and Aquiach Amapane [*sic*].

According to one of these two accounts, no initial and complete conquest occurred; on the contrary, the Olmecs mocked the newcomers, made them swallow bitter food, and used them as messenger boys. Ill treated and afflicted, they only took courage at the promptings of Tezcatlipoca; adopting a strategem proposed by this deity, they asked the Olmeca-Xicallancas for old arms and shields for use in a festival of dancing and singing. With the help of this superannuated equipment they vanquished their hosts, though we are not told how much Olmec territory they actually conquered. Six years of tranquility ensued, after which the Olmecs became restive of serving as underdogs, and the Toltecs, unable to maintain their sway singlehanded, decided to go and fetch their Chichimec friends from Chicomoztoc.

In the *Historia Tolteca-Chichimeca,* the exodus of the Nonoalcas is told as if it were the first major event in the final break-up of Tollan; it therefore by implication preceded the departure of the Tolteca-Chichimecs who went to Cholula. But, as previously argued, the expedition to Cholula seems to have taken place well before the collapse of Tollan in 1175. Accordingly, the following amended order for the events of the *Historia Tolteca-Chichimeca* was proposed:[5]

    1. Initial migration of Tolteca-Chichimecs to Cholula under Icxicoatl and Quetzalehuac, in about 1130.

    2. The fetching of the Teochichimec reinforcements from Chicomoztoc.

    3. The quarrel between the remaining Tolteca-Chichimecs of Tollan and the Nonoalcas, leading to the departure of the latter.

    4. The collapse of Tollan described by other sources and mentioned indirectly in the *Historia Tolteca-Chichimeca*—probably in 1175.

The departure of the Tolteca-Chichimecs for Cholula may have coincided with an initial time of troubles, marked by the damage in the principal ceremonial center to which Acosta bears witness and that he views as happening before the final collapse. As in the former case of Teotihuacán, life seems to have gone on somewhat as before in the outlying residential districts after the ruin of certain buildings in the center.

Alternatively, if the migration to Cholula came after rather than before the fall of Tollan, then it must belong to the same period as those other movements of Chichimecs and Otonchichimecs, led, among others, by Xolotl. The story as told in the *Historia Tolteca-Chichimeca* could conceivably be another example of the recasting of events *a posteriori,* in this case designed to enhance to role of the Toltecs and to lessen that of the Chichimecs by attributing to the former the feat of having wrested Cholula from the hands of the Olmeca Xicallancas. Any migration after the collapse of Tollan would surely have included many Otonchichimecs and Teochichimecs, even if Toltecs from Tollan also accompanied them.

It still, however, seems more likely that Cholula was occupied about a generation before the fall of Tollan. The coincidences are remarkable between places and people in the *Historia Tolteca-Chichimeca* and the other sources, such as the *Leyenda de los Soles* and Muñoz Camargo, that describe Mixcoatl's migration to the Valley of Mexico prior to the birth of Topiltzin in Culhuacán, and well before his period of rule in Tollan. Therefore it was deduced that, starting from some kind of rallying point in Poyauhtlán, which these first Chichimec invaders all seemed to have visited, some of them continued their journey to Cholula, while others doubled back to Culhuacán, which they also seized.

Thus some Chichimec migration into the Valley of Mexico seems to have begun well before the end of Tollan, rather as the Roman Empire was already infiltrated by Visigoths and others centuries before it collapsed. Some of these early Teochichimec intruders were probably already led by Otomís, like those that came later. The exodus to Cholula differed only in that Toltecs, not Otomís, were in the van. Moreover if the Toltecs of Cholula acted as mentors to a group of Chichimecs, the same principle may sometimes have applied to subsequent Chichimec invaders, even if the sources seldom mention it. In the case of Chalco, Chimalpain does write of the commanding role among the migrants played by the Toltec-Teotlixcas.

As Kirchhoff also pointed out, the ethnic panorama changed radically in Cholula with the arrival of the Toltecs and Chichimecs. The city again became a metropolis, though all around lived peoples whose cultural attainments were limited and who were barely emerging from a primitive way of life.[6] For a time the seven Chichimec tribes remained united, according to the *Historia,* but once their adversaries were subdued, the newly founded principalities, such as Tepeaca and Cuauhtinchan, began to squabble among themselves.

After this more generalized account, the *Historia Tolteca-Chichimeca* in its final portion concentrates upon the affairs of Cuauhtinchán under the rule of Moquihuix, and of its rival Totomihuacan. The Cuauhtinchantlacas also had Toltec mentors, such as Coatzin, who was a *nahuatlato.* The source describes the fratricidal struggle between the two centers, and then switches suddenly from this intermediate era to the time of the Tenochca Tlatoani, Axayacatl. During this final pre-Hispanic period, Tlaxcala, Huexotzingo, and Cholula retained a certain independence, while Cuauhtinchan, conquered in 1470, Totomihuacan, and Tepeaca, bowed to the Aztec yoke.

Prior to these events, local rivalries seem to have persisted among the Chichimecs tribes, until the moment when Huexotzingo began to assume a leading role in the region. Only from 9 Tecpatl onwards, probably the equivalent of 1359, after the defeat of Cholula by Huexotzingo and its allies, does a clearer pattern emerge; from, say, 1350 to 1450, Huexotzingo dominates the scene.

Of the preceding century, when the Chichimecs were already settled in, but before Huexotzingo became powerful, history says little. The different peoples probably sought to impose their will upon their nearest neighbors, just as in the Valley of Mexico; at that time, Cholula, like its counterpart Culhuacán, was regarded more as a guardian of the ancient culture than as a dominant power. The rise of Huexotzingo—to be treated below in more detail—marked the end to any genuine claims on the part of Cholula to a position of dominance.

Archaeological evidence lends support to the account of the written sources. As already explained, a limited revival was achieved by Cholula during the Tula-Mazapan horizon. Peter Schmidt considers that Cholula polychrome started as early as A.D. 1000. He stresses (personal communication) that the beginning of polychrome —in conformity with the sources' story—coincided with an immense upsurge of population in Huexotzingo, visible in the archaeological record. His investigations suggest that the region was now coming to play a leading role in the Altiplano, and surface materials found in Huexotzingo indicate a population nearly five times larger than before. Not all Cholula polychrome was actually made in Cholula, and a mold for making this ware has been found in Huexotzingo. Archaeology demonstrates the increasing influence of the Valley of Mexico; whereas relatively minor quantities of Aztec II were found in the site, Aztec III, in association with polychrome, appears in greater profusion, together with some Texcoco black-on-red and related types.

Florencia Müller goes so far as to opine that Cholulteca III, or polychrome, that brought this cultural renaissance in its train, did not begin before Aztec III, and is therefore contemporary with the founding of Tenochtitlán, to which she gives the traditional date of 1325. It is never easy to be specific about the first appearance of a given pottery; however, Cholula polychrome and the general resurgence of the Puebla-Tlaxcala valley, marked by the empire-building enterprise of Huexotzingo, surely began earlier than 1325, and more probably shortly after the downfall of Tollan Xicocotitlan, or even before, as Schmidt proposes. In his written report, he mentions an elaborate system of terraces and water control found in Huexotzingo that bear witness to the need to increase food supplies in face of the demographic explosion. He stresses that Huexotzingo was no true "city," but a series of settlements, or *cabeceras,* exactly as in Tlaxcala, with its four divisions and four rulers, as described by the Spaniards.[7]

In Huexotzingo, four ancient *cabeceras* are perfectly identifiable, and in three of these the remains of ceremonial centers have been discovered, though of more modest proportions than, say, those of Tenochtitlán or of Cholula. The *Anales de Cuauhtitlán* actually state that at the time of the fall of Azcapotzalco in 1428, when Huexotzingo was at the height of its power, its center of government alternated among three distinct places and there were three separate rulers; at that particular moment, power was being exercised from Chiauhtzingo; on Schmidt's map, San Lorenzo Chiauhtzingo lies about four kilometers northwest of the present-day pueblo.

Refoundations

The *Historia Tolteca-Chichimeca,* while it says much of Cholula, is ostensibly a history of the people of Cuauhtinchan, and goes out of its way to stress their importance. But while the quarrels of Cuauhtinchan, Totomihuacan, and Tepeaca may be a useful study in miniature of Mesoamerican patterns of power, they lack deep significance in the history of the period.

Of greater importance was the rise of Huexotzingo and Tlaxcala, though the latter only came to the fore in Aztec times. Tlaxcalans are indeed mentioned in the *Historia Tolteca-Chichimeca* as one of the seven tribes brought by the Tolteca-Chichimecs to Cholula; they also figure collectively in other references to the seven migrant tribes in that source, but are only mentioned individually as victims of an assault by the Huexotzingans and "Acolhuas" in 9 Tecpatl.

On the other hand, Muñoz Camargo, par excellence the historian of Tlaxcala, concentrates upon the fortunes of the Chichimec group that invaded the region after the fall of Tollan, settled first in Poyauhtlán and later founded Tlaxcala. This migration, like the occupation of Cholula, forms an integral part of what I have called the Mixcoatl saga; not only are many personalities common to Muñoz Camargo and the *Historia Tolteca-Chichimeca,* but the connection is evident between these two linked accounts and those of three other sources, the *Anales de Cuauhtitlán,* the *Leyenda de los Soles,* and the *Historia de los Mexicanos por sus Pinturas.*[8] I previously concluded that the tribes in question had followed a circuitous route from the northwest, going first to Amecameca, after which they split, some bound for Cholula and others for the Valley of Mexico. The itinerary given by Muñoz Camargo for Mixcoatl, leader of the Chichimecs who later founded Tlaxcala, and the route followed by the seven Chichimec tribes of the *Historia Tolteca-Chichimeca,* both include Mazatepec, Tepanene (or Nenetepec), and Poyauhtlán. Huetlapalli, Pantzin, Cocoltzin, and Xicallan, described by Muñoz Camargo as fellow-leaders of Mixcoatl's Chichimecs, figure also in the *Historia Tolteca-Chichimeca.*

Muñoz Camargo, in addition, mentions other Chichimecs who pushed on as far as the Gulf Coast, reached also by Xolotl's forces, according to Ixtlilxóchitl. However, the historian of Tlaxcala presents these events as a mere background to his central theme, the group that stayed temporarily in Poyauhtlán, and then went on to Huexotzingo, Tepeaca, and Totomihuacan. It was some of those migrants who first made their home in Tepeaca, and later settled Tepeticpac, one of the four future *señoríos* or *cabeceras* of Tlaxcala, from which they expelled the Olmeca-Xicallancas.[9] The same source tells of the foundation of the other señoríos of Tlaxcala, Ocotelolco, Tizatlan, and Quiahuiztlan. The founders of Tlaxcala had previously settled in Tepeaca and Totomihuacan, and therefore had pursued the same route as those Chichimecs of the *Historia Tolteca-Chichimeca,* who went to Poyauhtlán, before founding Totomihuacan and other places.

García Cook worked extensively in the Tlaxcala region, and his findings are related to the written record. The most striking result of his work was the conclusion that the region reached its cultural zenith in the Tezoquiapan phase, running from about 400 B.C. to A.D. 200; out of a total of 207 sites belonging to his period, no less than 50 had ceremonial centers with fairly imposing structures of stone; agriculture was then widely practiced with the help of an irrigation network. After a longish interlude (called Tenanyecac) of relative stagnation, technical progress was resumed in the Texcalac phase (A.D. 650–1100), though the cultural achievements of the previous era were never surpassed. García Cook gained the impression that Texcalac was marked by the arrival of new immigrants.[10] Such findings would be easier to assess if they were published in more detail.

The last phase, called Tlaxcala, ran from A.D. 1100 to the Conquest, and García Cook states that the four señoríos of the immediate pre-Conquest period are perfectly identifiable. Notwithstanding the prominent political role of Tlaxcala in the final era of Mesoamerican history, the number of reported sites (totaling 136) represents a reduction on previous centuries, and García Cook thinks that the population diminished, in marked contrast to the same period in the Valley of Mexico; the proportion of sites that possess a ceremonial center admittedly increases, though the structures themselves are smaller than those of Classic times.[11] These archaeological data therefore suggest that the adverse effects of the Aztec stranglehold, described by Mesoamerican sources, and even by Cortés, might not be exaggerated. As in other parts of Postclassic Mesoamerica, the sites of the Tlaxcala phase are located on hilltops or hillsides, and suggest that warfare increased in scale.

García Cook fixed A.D. 1100 as the beginning of the Tlaxcala phase, apparently on the basis of what the sources say—in particular Muñoz Camargo—rather than on the actual evidence of his archaeological findings. He links the ending of Texcalac and the commencement of the new Tlaxcala with the arrival of additional groups that, according to Jiménez Moreno, had occurred in 1100. Following this incursion, a struggle ensued between the new migrants and the previous inhabitants, and then later between Tlaxcalans and Huexotzingans.

However the Chichimecs of Poyauhtlán seem unlikely to have "founded" Tlaxcala much before 1200. Not only was Tlaxcala's rise to prominence slow, but wars between Huexotzingo and its neighbors, including Tlaxcala, took place not in the twelfth century, but more probably in the fourteenth. Earlier data on Tlaxcala should be treated with caution; attention has already been called to the tendency for late arrivals on the Mesoamerican scene to contrive for themselves a deeper historical perspective than they could legitimately claim.

Huexotzingan Beginnings

Although Huexotzingo's development far outpaced Tlaxcala in the period with which we are directly concerned, less information is available on its early history. Torquemada states that it was also founded by Teochichimecs.[12] The *Anales de Cuauhtitlán* tell of Chichimecs who spread out after the fall of Tollan, not only over central Mexico, but as far as the Huaxteca and Yopitzingo; their numbers included tribes that settled in the Puebla-Tlaxcala valley in Tlaxcala, Tliliuhquitepec, Tepeaca, and also in Huexotzingo; the last were led by Tepolnextli, Tlanquaxoxouhqui, and Xiuhtochtli, described as the first people to reach Huexotzingo.[13]

Ixtlilxóchitl states that Tlotzin (Xolotl's grandson) gave Huexotzingo jointly to Tochintecuhtli and to two sons of Huetzin, Chicomatzin, and Tlacatlanextzin. These three princes, together with a fourth called Cuauhtlitentzin, became its first rulers. At first sight the report suggests that Ixtlilxóchitl was confusing the glyph of Huexotzingo with that of Huexotla, governed by Tochintecuhtli. However, he clarifies his statement by saying that Tochintecuhtli returned to Huexotla and left the other three to rule in Huexotzingo. The *Anales de Cuauhtitlán* mention the subsequent presence in that place of three distinct rulers.

Muñoz Camargo makes a mysterious reference to an early Huexotzingan monarch, called Xiuhtlehuitecuhtli, who asked the "Mexican" ruler, Matlalihuitzin, for help against the Chichimecs of Poyauhtlán, his mortal enemies, then governed by Culhuatecuhtli-cuanex.[14] A parallel version of the same story in Torquemada, who follows Muñoz Camargo in much of what he writes of Tlaxcala, gives a rather clearer picture. Torquemada tells how Xiuhtlehuitecuhtli of Huexotzingo was at war with Tlaxcala, i.e., with the former Chichimecs of Poyauhtlán, and requested help, not from the Mexicas, at that time hardly in a postion to help anyone, but from the Tepanec-Mexicas, that is to say, the Tepanecs of Azcapotzalco, who were ruled by Matlahuitzin.[15] Now Matlahuitzin is presumably to be identified with Matlacoatl, given by Torquemada as a later ruler of Azcapotzalco, but probably correctly named by the *Anales de Tlatelolco* as founder of the Azcapotzalcan monarchy. If it is right to suppose that Matlacoatl belonged to the next generation after Tochintecuhtli (see Chapter VI), then these early hostilities between Huexotzingo and Tlaxcala occurred in about 1300.

These settlers in Tlaxcala, Huexotzingo, and elsewhere are invariably portrayed as Teochichimecs or as Chichimecs. But like the other groups of invaders, they reveal traits that contradict this description, since they practice Mesoamerican customs and worship Mesoamerican deities. Muñoz Camargo says that Mixcoatl's Chichimecs had as their principal gods Quetzalcoatl, Camaxtli (equivalent to Mixcoatl), and Tezcatlipoca.[16] Like other Chichimecs, the Tlaxcalans and Huexotzingans probably included a leavening of Otomís, and might even, like the conquerors of Cholula, have been accompanied by Nahua-speaking Toltecs. Kirchhoff suggests that the seven tribes of the *Historia Tolteca-Chichimeca* spoke Otomí.[17] Moreover, not only did some Poyauhteca Chichimecs go to Cholula, but other Poyauhtecas (also called Panohuayas) went to Chalco, according to Chimalpain; but these Poyauhtecas were also known as Nonoalcas, a term that implies the very opposite of Chichimec.

Ample evidence exists of the presence of Otomís in Tlaxcalan-controlled territory in the immediate pre-Conquest phase, as well as in Totomihuacan, whose name, according to Jiménez Moreno, derives from Totomitl, the original form of the Nahuatl word for Otomí.[18] Indians taken from Huexotzingo and Tlaxcala by the Aztecs were always made to represent Tezcatlipoca in sacrificial ceremonies held in Texcoco.[19] However, more indicative of ethnic origins is the report that Tlaxcalan prisoners in Moctezuma II's reign were burned as well as killed by the knife;[20] some were also slain by arrows. When Moctezuma made war on Huexotzingo and took many prisoners, some were burned alive; presumably they were sacrificed to Otontecuhtli, the Otomí god who was also associated with fire, while those killed by arrows were probably offered to Mixcoatl.

More Imperialists

After describing the taking of Cholula by Toltecs and Chichimecs, the *Historia Tolteca-Chichimeca,* also called the *Anales de Cuauhtinchan,* concentrates upon events in that place, founded or refounded about the same time as Huexotzingo and Tlaxcala. However the long rivalry between Cuauhtinchan and Totomihuacan, so significant for the Puebla Tlaxcala valley, hardly affected the struggle for the Toltec succession in the Valley of Mexico. Nonetheless, the *Historia Tolteca-Chichimeca* intersperses its account of the affairs of Cuauhtinchan with references to Huexotzingo, whose nascent ambitions were focused upon its immediate neighbors, though they came to exercise a wider impact upon the central Meso-american scene.

Once the Olmeca-Xicallancas were vanquished, the town of Cuauhtinchan was established under the leadership of the original Chichimec chiefs. As long as the latter lived, the different tribes of invaders remained reasonably united and scored notable victories, sometimes over distant neighbors such as the Huaxtecs. Following this triumph, all the seven tribes, still acting in unison, went on a pilgrimage to Cholula, the home of the oracle of Quetzalcoatl, to which they made traditional offerings of quail, serpents, deer, and rabbits, together with gaudy feathers.

Following in the wake of the Chichimecs, new migrants arrived; far from being nomads, the newcomers were civilized Meso-americans. Certain Culhuas established themselves in Tepeaca, and people of Mixteca-Popoloca derivation, some of whom were from Coixtlahuaca, also came, though it is not clear exactly where they settled; one group apparently made its home in Quauhtinchan. The same thing had happened in Texcoco, where Tlaillotlacas and Chimal-panecas from the Mixteca joined the original Chichimec founders, or in Chalco, where the Teotlixcas, originally from Tollan itself, were among the last to arrive; an earlier group of migrants to Chalco was also called Tlaillotlaca, but these Tlaillotlacas reportedly came from Teotenango, near Toluca, and not from the Mixteca.

In theory these events occurred during the life of the original Tolteca-Chichimec leaders, Icxicoatl and Quetzalteueyan, and spanned a period of only eighteen years, from 2 Calli, when Cholula was first conquered by the Tolteca-Chichimecs, until the victory over the Huaxtecs in 7 Acatl. An apparently uneventful interlude ensued that, again in theory, lasted for forty-one years. Then in

9 Tecpatl a new chapter of history began, marked by Huexotzingo's dramatic entry upon the scene in that year. Berlin treats this 9 Tecpatl as the equivalent of 1228, but according to my calculations, in basic accord with Jiménez Moreno, it is more likely to have been 1352. By this reckoning, over one and one-half centuries separate the Huexotzingan bid for supremacy from the earlier doings of the Chichimec tribes—a period that forms a long but blank page in the history of the Puebla-Tlaxcala valley. During this period Cholula, as the religious and commercial center of the region and its largest city, probably continued, as previously mentioned, to play a leading political role, but more as a *primus inter pares* among surrounding Chichimec foundations than as dominant power.

In 9 Tecpatl Huexotzingo opened its campaign of conquest with an attack on Tlaxcala. A powerful coalition made up of Huexotzingo itself, together with Acolhuas (the account does not say where they came from), Toltecs (Cholulans), Totomihuacas, and Quauhtinchantlacas, defeated Tlaxcala, perhaps rather a paltry target for such an alignment of forces.

In 2 Tochtli, six years later, the next blow fell, when Huexotzingans and Acolhuas, now described as "enemies of the Toltecs" (i.e., of the Cholulans), shot arrows at the face of Quetzalcoatl; in other words, they defeated Cholula. The city faced famine, and its people were near to extinction. Jiménez Moreno places this event in 1359, though 1358 (1352 plus six) seems logically more exact.[21]

Again in 1 Tochtli, or twelve years later in 1370, the same source tells us that the Cholultecan *calpullis* were ravaged by hunger. In view of the odd similarity between the events of 1 Tochtli and 2 Tochtli, this is possibly one of those cases where two dates are given to the same events, through the use of two year-counts that vary by only one digit (as for instance the 1 Acatl and the 2 Acatl dates for the departure of Quetzalcoatl from Tollan); thus the same war is mentioned twice, once for the year 1 Tochtli, and once for 2 Tochtli.

After a victory against Chalco on the part of Cholula—perhaps acting under Huexotzingan tutelage—in 9 Tochtli, or 1378 according to the original reckoning, a further successful war was fought against Huehuequauhquechollan, though the source omits to name the victors. The Quauhquechollans were again defeated by an anonymous conqueror in 2 Acatl (1423); in 3 Acatl (1463 in the same year-count) the Totomihuacans yielded territory to the Huexot-zingans. The date should be treated with caution, and is more likely to belong to the previous calendar cycle and be the equivalent of 1411 (1463 minus fifty-two) (see below).

Other sources offer confirmation of these events. Muñoz Camargo states that in 9 Tecpatl the Huexotzingans and "Mexicas" (perhaps Acolhuas) attacked Tlaxcala and the Tlaxcalans withdrew to their hilltop fortress, where they successfully defended them-selves.[22] This report is typical of so many in which a local source— in this case Muñoz Camargo—reports a victory for his own people, whereas others write of a defeat.

The *Anales de Cuauhtitlán* give an account of this sequel of events so similar to that of the *Historia Tolteca-Chichimeca* that it seems to have a common origin, notwithstanding discrepancies over chronology and places conquered. The source lists the following occurrences:[23]

9 Tecpatl (probably 1352). The king of Huexotzingo, Miccacalcatl, besieged Tlaxcala, together with Acolmiztli, king of the Acolhuas. The outcome of the campaign is not stated. Acolmiztli in this instance can hardly be the ruler of that name who was the son of Huetzin; but the appellation was used as a title by more than one ruler of Coatlichan.

3 Acatl (1360, i.e., one year after the corresponding report of the *Historia Tolteca-Chichimeca).* Miccacalcatl of Huexotzingo defeated the Cholulans and destroyed their temple.

12 Calli (1381, or three years after the defeat of Chalco as recorded in the *Historia Tolteca-Chichimeca).* Xayacamachan, ruler of Huexot-zingo, defeated the Chalcas, with the aid of the Tlaxcalans and the Totomihuacans.

3 Acatl (1411). Huexotzingo and its allies defeated the Huehue-tecos.

3 Acatl (probably also 1411—see below). Quauhquechollan was defeated by Xayacamachan.

7 Acatl (1415). Xayacamachan defeated Totomihuacan.

13 Calli (1421). Huexotzingo again beat the Totomihuacans.

13 Tochtli (1434). Tenocelotzin of Huexotzingo defeated Ozto-ticpac. This event is confirmed by the *Anales de Tlatelolco,* that write of the defeat of the Señor of Oztoticpac, but in 2 Tochtli.

The chronology of the last five occurrences is rather confusing. According to the *Anales de Cuauhtitlán,* a whole calendar cycle passed between the first 3 Acatl, when Xayacamachan of Huexotzingo, after reigning at least four years, defeated Huehuetocan, and the second 3 Acatl, when he defeated Quauquechollan. These dates seem to credit this monarch with an unrealistically long military career. The *Historia* and the *Anales de Cuauhtitlán* versions merely differ in detail; for instance, in the former, Chalco was assaulted by Huexotzingo in 1381, while according to the latter, it was defeated by Cholula in 1378. Both sources allow for the elapse of one whole calendar cycle and part of the next before another Huexotzingan triumph in 3 Acatl (in one source over Quauhquechollan and in another over Totomihuacan), and this 3 Acatl would fall in 1463, according to the same reckoning. The 13 Tochtli, the last date in this career of conquest given by the *Anales de Cuauhtitlán,* thereby becomes 1486, or well after the Aztecs had subdued the region. Surely this is another instance when one year cycle has been mistaken for another, and the 13 Acatl in question is really 1411, not 1463. The subsequent dates, if adjusted to this calculation, also make good sense. The Huexotzingan bid for empire under three successive rulers would run from 1228 to 1463, if the sources were taken literally; but a more realistic interpretation compresses this expansion into a period from 1352 to 1434.

We are told by Alva Ixtlilxóchitl that Xayacamachan remained faithful to the Texcocan ruler, Huehue Ixtlilxóchitl, during his war against the Tepanec-Mexicas (1414–17). More probably however, Huehue Ixtlilxóchitl was helped by Xayacamachan's son, Tenocelotzin. The latter was apparently still reigning in 1428 in Huexotzingo, together with Chiyauhcoatzin and Texochimatzin—a report that offers evidence of plural rule, as in other places. In that year occurred the incident when Moctezuma Ilhuicamina, the future Moctezuma I, was captured by the Chalcas; after much deliberation, they sent him as a captive to their allies, the three monarchs of Huexotzingo, who proceeded to set him free. Another Xayacamachan of Huexotzingo was incidentally a contemporary of the Tenochca Tlatoani, Ahuitzotl.[24] In 1515 a Huexotzingan ruler, perhaps the same individual, is reported as fleeing to Tenochtitlán.[25]

The surviving evidence is perhaps too scanty to allow us to

speak of a Huexotzingan empire in the true sense of the word, but leaves us in no doubt that Huexotzingo at one time sought to dominate the Puebla-Tlaxcala valley. During this period, it launched far-flung campaigns and intervened more than once in conflicts between the powers of the Valley of Mexico. These military operations cover almost a century, and Huexotzingo was still the leading power when the Mexicas launched their bid to usurp the Tepanec Empire. In the fateful struggle, Huexotzingo was actively courted by both parties, Tenochtitlán and Azcapotzalco. Nezahualcoyotl took advantage of the traditional friendship between Acolhuas and Huexotzingans, and his entreaties carried the day; the results of this diplomatic contest were fateful and Huexotzingan forces helped to sway the balance; in doing so, they created a scourge for their own backs and set the course for the last century of Mesoamerican history.

A Complex Relationship

The supremacy of Huexotzingo spanned the latter part of the period in question, beginning with the assault on Tlaxcala in 1352. During the century that separates this event from the previous triumphs of Tochintecuhtli-Huetzin, Cholula may logically be looked upon as the leading city-state of the region. Evidence to that effect is admittedly scant, and the course of events between the arrival of the Toltec migrants in Cholula and the rise of Huexotzingo obscure. Archaeology shows that Cholula was once more expanding after the fall of Tollan, but Muñoz Camargo may be right in saying that this resuscitated Cholula led the field in commerce more than in war.[26] In the few campaigns know to history, the city suffered more defeats than victories. Postclassic Cholula was probably, even before Aztec times, more a center of trade, culture, and religion than a military power. Until the reign of Ahuitzotl, Huexotzingo should normally be read for Tlaxcala, whenever the latter is treated by the sources as the leading power of the Puebla-Tlaxcala valley. However, a certain caution is also needed in crediting Cholula with the principal role right up to 1359. Huexotzingo cannot have become important overnight, and would already have begun to make its presence felt in the earlier decades of the fourteenth century.

The crushing of Azcapotzalco by the Mexica coalition, with Huexotzingan support, and the formation of the Triple Alliance radically altered the balance of power. Notwithstanding the consistently pro-Acolhua policy pursued by Huexotzingo, the Tepanecs had confined themselves to brief incursions into the Puebla-Tlaxcala valley, such as the expedition against Cuauhtinchan; but from 1428 onwards the tables were turned, as Huexotzingo and its allies came under increasing pressure from the new and triumphant alliance of Tenochtitlán, Texcoco, and Tlacopan.

Except in broadest outline, the validity of generalizations is limited, and to treat the Puebla-Tlaxcala valley as a homogeneous unit in its relations with the Valley of Mexico may confuse the issue. In the first place, before the ascendancy of Tenochtitlán, dealings between the two valleys were marked more often by amity than by conflict, and the neglect of this good neighbor policy by Tezozomoc's successor proved disastrous.

Second, notwithstanding the tribute-gathering campaigns of Huexotzingo, the region as a whole remained somewhat balkanized, and its peoples continued to owe allegiance to a number of small and mutually hostile *señoríos*. The laconic reports of the *Historia Tolteca-Chichimeca* and the *Anales de Cuauhtitlán* refer exclusively to wars between city-states, among which no very consistent pattern of alliances emerges. All that could be said in that respect is that Tlaxcala figures more as a victim of Huexotzingo, and is only once recorded as an ally in its conquests of other pueblos.

This situation did not change in later times, and even the Aztec onslaughts—often presented in the sources as mere "wars of flowers"—failed to unite the rulers of the valley; in the decade before the Conquest, because of the internecine struggle between Huexotzingo and Tlaxcala, Moctezuma's armies were able to penetrate to within a short distance of the latter, by then the paramount power.[27] A state of affairs whereby one city-state assumed a leading role within a given region, but failed to achieve total domination, is probably more typical of Mesoamerican historical development than is the final period in the Valley of Mexico, where a single alliance became the master of all other peoples.

Aside from rivalries and alliances between the larger polities of the two regions, wars continued to take place between lesser entities, as, for instance, when Cuitlahuac attacked Tliliuhquitepec in 12 Tochtli. The *Anales de Cuauhtitlán*, however, place this event in the reign of Axayacatl, and it may therefore merely represent just another sally against Huexotzingo under Mexica auspices.[28] The special ties that bound Huexotzingans and Acolhuas had by then been loosened; however they seem to have existed during the whole pre-Aztec period, and a son of Tlotzin is said to have become the first ruler of Huexotzingo.[29]

The Huexotzingan empire-building period is roughly contemporary with that of the Tepanecs of Azcapotzalco. The Tepanec-Mexica conquests in the Atotonilco-Tulancingo area might have been regarded as an incipient outflanking movement, but were not apparently treated by Huexotzingo as a threat to its security. It is not known if assistance was offered to Cuauhtinchan when it was subjected to a Tepanec-Mexica assault, probably in 1398. Nor are we told what was the attitude of Huexotzingo during the Tepanec-Texcocan war of 1414–17.

Only after the Tepanec-Mexica victory over Texcoco did Huexotzingo begin to fear the growing Tepanec power and seek to redress the balance by favoring the fugitive Nezahualcoyotl, Huehue Ixtlilxóchitl's heir. Nezahualcoyotl first took refuge beyond the Sierra Nevada; and when Maxtla once more expelled him from Texcoco, to which he had been allowed to return, he sought sanctuary in "Atlancatepec, Tliliuhquitepec, Tlaxcala, and Huexotzingo."[30] Torquemada reports that the Huexotzingan ruler was related to Nezahualcoyotl, whom he received with a marked display of affection.[31] The Cholulans, whom the same source describes as enemies of the Tepanecs, also supported Nezahualcoyotl at this time. The culmination of this policy came when the Huexotzingans joined the war against Azcapotzalco in 1428.

Even such bonds of friendship were not proof against the hostility that later grew up between the Triple Alliance and its easterly neighbors. Tenochtitlán, not Texcoco, called the tune, and Nezahualpilli himself was constrained to lead a campaign against Huexotzingo, notwithstanding the bonds that linked him to its ruler, Huehuetzin, described by Ixtlilxóchitl as having been born on the same day and at the same hour as the Texcocan monarch.[32]

Chalco tended to be a complicating factor in the relations

175

between the Puebla-Tlaxcala valley and the Valley of Mexico, since its territory bordered on both. The Chalca confederation, hostile to the Mexicas and to a lesser extent to the Tepanecs, maintained close connections with Huexotzingo, of which the above-mentioned incident bears witness, when the Chalcans sent the captive Moctezuma Ilhuicamina to their Huexotzingan friends to dispose of him as they thought fit. And in the last stages of the endless struggle between Mexicas and Chalcas, in 1465, Chalca fugitives were welcomed in Huexotzingo and Atlixco.

While, therefore, a certain interplay of forces may be noted between the polities of the Valley of Mexico and the Puebla-Tlaxcala valley in the period between the fall of Tollan and the rise of Tenochtitlán, neither valley played a decisive part in the events of the other before the Huexotzingan intervention against Azcapotzalco in 1428. In the era known as that of the independent señoríos—i.e., of señoríos of limited power—neither region burst its bounds and sought to conquer the other.

VIII. Toltzalan Acatzalan

Migrants

After considering the early history of the Acolhuas, Tepanecs, and
their neighbors, the moment finally arrives when the Mexicas first
appear upon the stage. This work deals with the general course of
events between the fall of Tollan and the rise of Tenochtitlán; the
detailed story of one group, whose importance during most of this
period was limited, lies outside its scope.

The Mexica migration remains a source of controversy and
even the very etymology of their name is uncertain. For reasons that
are obscure, Huitzilopochtli ordered the Aztlanecas to change their
name to Mexicas. According to some, this comes from *meztli*
("moon"), symbolizing perhaps the reflection of the moon on the
waters of the lagoon in their original home, Aztlan; others, including
Sahagún, prefer a derivation from *metl* ("maguey cactus") and *citli*
("hare"). Both interpretations have Otomí connotations; the Otomís
of Xaltocan and elsewhere were moon worshipers.[1] Chimalpain gives
Mecitin as another name for Mixcoatl; but Mixcoatl is partly though
not wholly an Otomí deity.

In this chapter, such facets of early Mexica history and religion
will be considered as may help to clarify the over-all panorama or to

explain the development of other peoples in the period before the rise of the Mexicas. A vastly greater wealth of Mexica material has survived, and therefore their progress from semi-nomads to incipient imperialists may offer guidance on the history of Tepanecs, Acolhuas, and even Chalcas.

I have already written an account of the Mexicas' first steps to power, from their arrival in Chapultepec, and do not now intend to repeat the same story. In re-examining Mexica beginnings in this chapter, I seek general conclusions about how the different peoples of Late Postclassic Mesoamerica attained maturity and then played a significant if ephemeral role on the stage of history. The question that I am now asking is not just what happened to the Mexicas, but what can they teach us that is also applicable to others, for whom similar data are lacking.

According to tradition, the Mexicas were the last of many peoples that emerged from Teoculhuacán-Chicomoztoc, and then trod the familiar route to the promised land of the Valley of Mexico and beyond.

The *Tira de la Peregrinación* states that there were eight migrant tribes: Matlatzincas, Tepanecs, Tlalhuicas, Malinalcas, Acolhuas, Xochimilcas, Chalcas, and Huexotzingans.[2] Durán gives six names: Xochimilcas, Chalcas, Tepanecs, Culhuas, Tlalhuicas, and Tlaxcalans.[3] Absent from his list are the Matlatzincas and Malinalcas of the valley of Toluca, mentioned by the Tira, and the Tlaxcalans take the place of the Huexotzingans; Acolhuas, as on other occasions, seem to be confused with Culhuas.

Of the route followed, diverse accounts survive, and each tells a different tale. The simplest list of places visited, and the more easily identifiable, is given by the Codex Azcatitlan: Azcatitlan (Aztlan), Colhuacan (Teoculhuacán) Tepemaxalco, Chicomoztoc, Coatepec, Ecatepec, Apasco, Pantitlan, Chapultepec, and Culhuacan. The longer lists from other documents invariably include Coatepec, or Tollan, on their itinerary.

The details of the circuitous journey ascribed by legend to the Mexicas fall outside the scope of this work. Of more general interest is the length of time spent and the large number of places visited, not only in remoter parts, but after they were within striking distance of their ultimate goals, first Chapultepec, and then Tenochtitlán-Tlatelolco.

Radin provides a useful comparative table of the various versions of the route. In this list, Xaltocan occupies the forty-ninth position out of a total of ninety-nine place-names given by all sources, and all those listed after Xaltocan are situated in the Valley of Mexico.[4]

Tezozómoc states that after leaving the Coatepec-Tula area, the Mexicas went to Atlitlaquia, described as inhabited by Otomís, and then eventually reached Xaltocan.[5] According to the *Crónica Mexicana* and the *Crónica Mexicayotl,* they also visited a place called Acolnahuac before Chapultepec, but this seems to bear no direct relation to the latter-day Acolhuacan. Chimalpain credits the Mexicas with a fairly long stay in Xaltocan, where they constructed Chinampas, though it is not certain how far this statement can be taken literally.[6] The *Anales de Cuauhtitlán* say that the migrants spent eight years in "Amallinalpan Azcapotzalco."[7] They accordingly came into contact with leading peoples of the valley before they even reached Chapultepec.

Peculiar coincidences link the Mexica wanderings and those of other peoples. For instance, Coatlicamac and Cuextecatl Ichocayan ("where the Huextec wept") are included by several sources in the Mexica route from Teoculhuacán to Tula. But those two places were also visited centuries earlier by the Tolteca-Chichimecs before they reached Tollan.[8] Xolotl and his Chichimecs later sojourned there.[9] Even the Nonoalca-Tlacochcalcas, according to Chimalpain, went to a locality called Cuixtecatlycaca. According to the *Anales de Cuauhtitlán,* the Ixcuiname, or "she-devils," who came to Tollan from the Huaxteca, spoke to their captives in Cuextecatl Ixocayan.[10] The *Historia de los Mexicanos* states that it lay near Panuco, an assertion that led to suggestions that the Mexicas came from the east, not from the northwest.

Present among the earliest Mexica chiefs is an Iztacmixcoatl; but the *Anales de Cuauhtitlán* state that Mixcoatl, or Iztacmixcoatl, had led the Chichimecs who first penetrated the Valley of Mexico towards the end of the Toltec period—or, according to others, at its beginning. Xiuhnel and Mimich, who figure prominently in the

Mixcoatl saga, described in my previous volume, also took part in the Mexica migration.[11] The *Crónica Mexicayotl's* list of the first four Mexica *teomamaque,* or god-bearers, includes not only Iztacmixcoatl, but Chimalma and Apanecatl; the last is the name of the brother of Mixcoatl whom Topiltzin slew, while Chimalma is the mother of Topiltzin and wife of Mixcoatl.

Outstanding in the migration story is the repeated insistence on schisms within the tribe. Far from forming a single cohesive body inspired by a single deity, their numbers were depleted by constant excisions or reinforced by new elements who joined the main body.

The first event of this kind, illustrated by the *Tira de la Peregrinación* and described by Torquemada, concerned a tree that split asunder while the Mexicas slept under its branches. Following this portentous omen, Huitzilopochtli told his priests that part of the tribe must separate from the remainder; only the virtuous, who formed the God's elect, were to pursue the journey, while the wayward were left behind.

A second excision occurred in Malinalco, where Huitzilopochtli was enraged by the machinations of his sister, the sorceress Malinalxoch; she and her accomplices were abandoned in their slumbers. The final schism took place in Coatepec. In this place Huitzilopochtli was born, or reborn, and duly slew the four hundred Huitznahua conspirators, conforming to the traditional pattern set by Itzpapalotl, who slew the four hundred Mimixcoas, or by Tezcatlipoca, who killed the four hundred Huitznahuas. Coyolxauhqui, described as another "sister" of Huitzilopochtli, together with her adherents and other recalcitrant leaders, were slaughtered because of their refusal to abandon the comforts of Coatepec and face the rigors of a further march.

The story of Coatepec illustrates the rich blend of allegory in the Mexica migration story. The deeper implications of these incidents will be considered later. The Malinalco episode probably established the supremacy of the Huitznahua *calpulli* among the migrants. Coatepec may represent a schism within this *calpulli,* to which both Huitzilopochtli and Coyolxauhqui belonged (she was the sister of the four hundred Huitznahuas).

Previous to the Mexicas' arrival in Chapultepcc, their destinies were guided by priest-rulers, the four *teomamaque,* or "bearers of the god." As mentioned above, the *Crónica Mexicayotl* gives the names of the first *teomamaque:* Iztacmixcoatl, Apanecatl, Tezcacoatl, and a woman named Chimalma. The same source adds a second list: Cuauhtlequetzqui, Axolohua, Cuauhcoatl, and Ocacaltzin. Durán gives identical names: Cuauhtlequetzqui, Ococatl, Chachalaitl, and Axolohua.[12] These *teomamaque* were in theory spiritual leaders, but, like Moses, their dictates also governed politics: as Durán puts it, "They were like parent, shelter, and succor to these people."[13] The priests' interpretation of the words of the deity determined where the Mexicas went and what they did.

Notwithstanding this evidence of collective rule, a tendency already prevailed for one individual to assume the lead. According to one version, even in Aztlan the Mexicas were governed by Moctezuma, father of Mexi Chalchiuhtonac.[14] The same source also describes them as ruled by the king Mexi. Huitziton is mentioned by Chimalpain as an early leader, as well as by other sources, and the same individual is sometimes called Huitzilopochtli; Veytia says that Huitziton was also known as Chalchiuhtonac, thus identifying him with Mexi. The *Anales de Tlatelolco* treat the teomama Cuauhtlequetzqui as sole leader, and also mention Tozcuecuex as "ruler," at the moment when they reached Chapultepec. The *Crónica Mexicayotl* calls Cuauhtlequetzqui "the first of the *teomamaque,*" as if he was superior in status to the others.

The most significant of these early chiefs was Huitziton, alias Huitzilopochtli, or Mexi. While Durán and Tezozómoc describe him as a tribal god from the outset, the first Huitzilopochtli known to the Mexicas may have been a human leader of that name. The Codex Vaticano-Ríos depicts Huitzilopochtli as a warrior and as the first captain of the Mexicas.[15] Cristóbal del Castillo maintains that the Mexica chief during the early migration was really called Huitzil; because he was left-handed, they called him Huitzilopochtli.[16] The *Crónica Mexicayotl* also says that Huitzilopochtli was first a man before becoming a god.[17]

The complexities of tutelary gods and divinized heroes were discussed in a symposium in the XLII International Congress of Americanists in Paris. A consensus among the participants discerned a general rule, applicable to Mixcoatl, Quetzalcoatl, and Xolotl, whereby an embryo deity antedated the legend of a human hero. I

expressed doubts about how far this rule applied in the case of Huitzilopochtli; the god, as will be explained below, seems to have assumed
his final shape only in the Valley of Mexico, while the hero, if he is
a historical personage at all rather than an anticipatory reflection of
the future deity, belongs to pre-Chapultepec times.

The Arrival in Chapultepec

For the itinerant tribe whose wanderings form the background
to Aztec history, Chapultepec, like Coatepec, offered the illusion of
a promised land. Ancient traditions sanctified the place: Ixtlilxóchitl
names it as one of the sites where Xolotl permitted the Toltecs to
remain after their Armageddon. Huemac, the last Toltec ruler, had
hanged himself there; Toltec refugees had remained in the site after
his death, but they were few in number and had no ruler of their
own.[18]

The Mexicas are often thought of as a small group, uncomfort-
ably perched on Chapultepec, or the Hill of the Locust, an eminence
that possessed a strategic value. But probably they mostly dwelled
not on the hill but in the fertile and well-watered surroundings,
where they mingled with the earlier settlers from Toltec times. The
political situation at the time is summed up by Barlow: "The Mexicas
arrived in Chapultepec in the middle of the thirteenth century, an
era in which Azcapotzalco was disputing the hegemony of the Valley
with Acolhuacan-Coatlichan. Culhuacan still dominated the southern
portion and Xochimilco occupied a defensive position in the north of
Morelos and the south of the Valley of Mexico."[19]

I now interpret the situation rather differently and consider that
when the Mexicas arrived, whether in mid- or late thirteenth century, the Tepanecs of Azcapotzalco had not yet launched their bid
for hegemony; sources that treat them as a leading power at this
stage are once more back-dating a situation that came about a century later.

The chronology of the Mexica stay in Chapultepec can best be
approached by working backwards. I have always maintained that the
date of 1345 for the foundation of Tenochtitlán, originally proposed
by Jiménez Moreno, is correct; my reasons were set out in a table, in

which I was able to reconcile the different native dates given for the event.[20] Only by assuming the use of four different year-counts can sense be made of these figures.

The traditional date for the Mexicas' departure from Chapultepec and their arrival in Culhuacán is 2 Acatl. And since they are variously reported as having spent twenty-one or twenty-five years in Culhuacán, the 2 Acatl in question surely belongs to the Culhua-Texcocan calendar, and is the equivalent of the Julian calendar year of 1319 (in the Tenochca calendar it is 1299). This date is important, since it is the earliest in Mexica history that can be fixed with assurance, and even helps to determine the chronology of the dynasties of Culhuacán and of Tollan.

The sources disagree over the length of the Mexica stay in Chapultepec; estimates are much vaguer than for their sojourn in Culhuacán and vary from seventeen to fifty-six years. The most frequently quoted date for their arrival, 1 Tochtli, indicates a stay of fifty-three years, if it belongs to the same year-count as the 2 Acatl departure date.[21] However, the year in which they settled in Chapultepec remains uncertain, and their stay may have been fairly prolonged. As I will later explain in greater detail, I see Chapultepec as more crucial in the formative process of the Mexicas than Culhuacán. In preference to speculation on the exact date of their arrival, the entry of the Mexicas into the Valley of Mexico may be treated not as an isolated event, but as part of that general movement of Oton-chichimecs and Teochichimecs in the late twelfth or early thirteenth century; the proportion of the Mexicas' first century in the Valley of Mexico that was actually spent in Chapultepec is hard to determine.

The chronology of the Chapultepec period is confused rather than clarified by mention in the *Anales de Cuauhtitlán* of a Mazatzin, who reigned in Chapultepec as "king of the Chichimecs" and later became ruler of Culhuacán. Chimalpain states that Mallatzin (i.e., Mazatzin), had been ruler of Culhuacán for six years when the Mexicas arrived. But Mazatzin, or Mallatzin, is stated by the *Anales de Cuauhtitlán* to have died in 3 Tochtli, probably the equivalent of 1294—as explained in Appendix A; but these same dates are given for several Culhua rulers, and Mazatzin was thus only one of many appellations of a particular monarch. At all events, his death in 1294 indicates a relatively early arrival date for the Mexicas, since Mazatzin is credited with a longish reign and they supposedly came soon after his accession.

The question of which power, if any, then controlled the area is also hard to answer; certain reports suggest that at Chapultepec the boundaries of the Azcapotzalco, Culhuacán, and Coatlichán converged. But how far Culhuacán still exercised any influence in the northern Valley of Mexico, and how far Azcapotzalco had yet assumed the role of Tenayuca as the leading city of that region remains in doubt.

Leaders in Chapultepec

Tezozómoc implies that initially the four *teomamaque* were still in command in Chapultepec, but also suggests that "the priest Cuauhtliquetzqui" played the leading role.[22] The *Crónica Mexicayotl* also describes Cuauhtliquetzqui as the first of the *teomamaque.*[23] The *Historia de los Mexicanos* states that in Chapultepec the leaders were "Cucutliqueci" and "Acipa," son of "Cipayavichiluitl," who was chosen as ruler; in another passage he is simply called "Vichiluitl," i.e., Huitzilihuitl.[24]

The *Anales de Cuauhtitlán* tell of a priest named "Tzippantzin" as leader and later mention Huitzilihuitl as ruler at the time of the expulsion; the source adds that he was the son of Tlahuizpotoncaltzin, a priest of Xaltocan, or, according to other reports, a prince of Tzompanco.[25] "Cipaya" is a corruption of Tzippantzin, and the priest Tzippantzin is surely therefore the same person as Huitzilihuitl, or Cipayavichiluitl, as he is called in the *Historia de los Mexicanos.* The tendency to use several names or titles for one person sometimes results in a single individual's being treated as two distinct persons; quite possibly "Cauautliqueci" of the *Historia de los Mexicanos* is also to be identified with Huitzilihuitl. Cuauhtliquetzqui is evidently another title used to describe a series of individuals who played an important part in the priestly hierarchy during succeeding generations. Huitzilihuitl seems to have been, like the later *tlatoanis,* both priest and ruler.

Huitzilihuitl was made leader in Chapultepec, according to various other sources, including Chimalpain, Torquemada, and the

Anales de Tlatelolco. But in addition to the supreme leader, several documents give lists of "military" chiefs. Vetancurt and Torquemada mention the same twenty names; the *Anales de Tlatelolco* mention Huitzilihuitl and add fifteen other leaders, with names resembling those of Vetancurt and Torquemada. But fifteen or twenty *calpullis* reportedly then existed, as opposed to only seven in Aztlan. Therefore it is likely that these are *calpulli* leaders, and some of their names recall places rather than persons, a phenomenon that recurs in other contexts.[26]

Notions that before the emergence of this proto-*tlatoani* the Mexica destinies were guided by a "military democracy"—surely a contradiction in terms—are clearly mistaken. Any "military" leaders were really *calpulli* chiefs, and perhaps even priests of *calpulli* gods. As such, they are likely to have been subject to the general dictates of the four *teomamaque,* who had the final say in religious—and therefore in an ostensibly theocratic polity—in political affairs as well.

The question remains whether Huitzilihuitl indeed became a kind of proto-*tlatoani,* or whether this assertion is merely another of those transpositions by which later circumstances are back-dated with the object of lending greater antiquity to a monarchy that was only firmly established two generations later, in the person of Acamapichtli.

The *Anales de Cuauhtitlán* imply that Huitzilihuitl was really a priest, while other sources continue to write of Cuautlequetzqui, the god-bearer, as supreme leader; Huitzilihuitl may merely be the personal name of one of a series who bore the title Cuauhtlequetzqui, the first of the *teomamaque;* certainly Tenoch, Huitzilihuitl's successor, was both priest and ruler. It therefore becomes uncertain whether any radical political change occurred in Chapultepec, or whether the office of senior *teomama* (out of four) had not always existed, and was then occupied by Huitzilihuitl, who thus automatically took command in battle against the coalition that led to the Mexica expulsion. The sharing of power by two, three, or four rulers—of which the first was a kind of *primus inter pares*—was a common feature in pre-Tenochtitlán days; the system probably prevailed in Tollan and continued to be the norm in traditionally Toltec centers such as Culhuacán, Xochimilco, and Cuitlahuac. Even Azcapotzalco

185

reportedly had two kings (see Chapter VI), and plural rule would have been the natural form of government also for the Mexicas; the reported "election" of Huitzilihuitl is not necessarily to be regarded as a radical departure from that norm.

Huitzilihuitl, and Cuauhtlequetzqui, may have represented the dominant religious faction, based upon the Huitznahua *calpulli* (from which the *tlatoani* was always later chosen) and upon the nascent supreme deity, Huitzilopochtli, as opposed to leaders linked to the worship of Tetzahuitl and other traditional gods. At all events Huitzilihuitl was a controversial figure, and his tenacious defense of Chapultepec ran counter to the dictates of Tenoch, who had announced on behalf of the tribal deity that this was not the place where they were finally to settle.

The Expulsion

Information on events prior to the dramatic expulsion are scanty. The Mexicas were not yet in a position to make their mark in the local game of power politics; they had no allies, and were obvious candidates for the privilege of paying rather than of gathering tribute; to whom it was paid, if at all, is not clear. Their status was therefore humble, but they began to make a nuisance of themselves, and their neighbors were quick to take offense. They lacked wood and stone, and their first temple was a small oratory, made of rushes and reeds, while their dwellings were of straw.[27]

The *Crónica Mexicayotl* gives the fullest account of what followed. The source speaks of two distinct attacks on the Mexicas; the first was occasioned by the arrival of Copil, son of Malinalxochitl, Huitzilopochtli's sister, who had been left behind in Malinaltepec. This incursion is presented as an attack by Malinalco on the Mexicas, when they were supposedly still controlled by four *teomamaque,* and before any mention of Huitzilihuitl as leader. A political or religious schism was presumably involved, perhaps in the form of a conflict between the Huitzilopochtli faction and those of other gods. Copil was the nephew of Huitzilopochtli, but this does not automatically mean that he supported that deity, since related gods were often antagonistic to one another.

According to one source, Copil said, "I am the servant of Axo-

186

cuauhtli of Culhuacán."[28] The *Crónica Mexicayotl* states that "he appeared under the guise of Itzpapalotl," thereby implying Chichimec more than Culhua or Toltec associations. But Itzpapalotl was also goddess of the Cihuateteo, the women who died in childbirth and who accompanied the sun on the western half of his journey. Huitzilopochtli performed the same function for the souls of the sacrificed warriors on the earlier portion of the sun's trajectory. Therefore Huitzilopochtli and Itzpapalotl were both equals and opposites. At all events, the machinations of Copil, determined to avenge the wrong done to his mother, caused the Mexicas to be driven from their home. This was their first reverse in that place, to which they managed to return ten years later, in 11 Acatl, when Huitzilihuitl became ruler.

The baffling story of the Copil incursion aptly illustrates the conundrums and contradictions of Mesoamerican history and legend. Once more the sequence of events perplexes the European mind, untuned to the concept of duality. Cuauhtlequetzqui kills Copil, and yet a person of that name also marries Copil's daughter. Copil is thus both friend and foe; he is the bogey man, arch-enemy and conspirator, and alternatively the beloved son or hero, whose heart is buried in that hallowed spot where the Mexicas were fated to found their city.

The paradox eludes logical definition. The very name has obscure origins; according to Ixtlilxóchitl, the Acolhuas, Tepanecs, and Otomís had an image whom they called Cocopitl. Copil is partly identified with Huitzilopochtli, but acts as his enemy and his opposite—a situation paralleled by the captive enemy who becomes the tribal god to whom he is sacrificed. The key to the situation surely lay in the ties between the Malinalco-Ocuillan region and Culhuacán, dating from Toltec times. "Malinalco" may in this context be virtually synonymous with Culhuacán. Moreover, in contrast to Cuauhtlequetzqui, associated with the Huitznahuac *calpulli,* Malinalxochitl and Copil are more linked with Chalma. Van Zantwijk points out that his relationship can be deduced from their connection with the Malinalco and Chalma region and from the links between Malinalxochitl and Cihuacoatl-Quilaztli, a Chalmeca or Chinampaneca deity.[29]

The Copil episode may thus be interpreted as a clash between the Mexicas and these Chinampanecas, some of whom were also settled in the land around the Hill of Chapultepec. It will later be seen that the episode was as much a victory for Huitzilopochtli as a defeat. Huitzilopochtli, whose very name is partly derived from the Chinampaneca god Opochtli, one of the Tlaloques, can hardly have been imported in toto from marginal Mesoamerica; Opochtli, moreover, was the Calpulteotl of the Chalman *calpulli*. The death of Copil seems to constitute a sacrifice, perhaps to the nascent deity, Huitzilopochtli; in like manner, at the beginning of the Mixcoatl saga, occurs the slaying of Itzpapalotl, in whose guise Copil had come to Chapultepec. Perhaps a person dressed as Itzpapalotl was sacrificed and thus "became" the goddess herself. The killing of Copil, son of the Chinampa goddess, by Huitzilopochtli's supporters runs parallel to the later murder of the daughter of the Culhua king, described as Huitzilopochtli's bride.

The *Crónica Mexicayotl* lists all the leading powers of the time as responsible for the Mexica expulsion, except for the Acolhuas and the people of Cuauhtitlán, firm allies of the Mexicas. Other sources write of an alliance of Culhuas, Tepanecs, Xochimilcas, and Chalcas. All documents concur that the Mexicas were defeated by a coalition but differ concerning the leader. The Codex Azcatitlan says that Huitzilihuitl was captured by the Señor of Xaltocan.[30] Torquemada also speaks of the Xaltocans as the first to attack.[31] Other versions stress the prime role of the Tepanecs. Certain accounts ascribe the leadership of the coalition to the Culhuas; the Codex Xolotl depicts a war between the Mexicas and Culhuas at this time, and the *Origen de los Mexicanos* writes of Chapultepec as if it belonged to Culhuacán. Durán attributes the lead to the Chalcas; their ruler, Cacamatecuhtli, captured Huitzilihuitl, while the Mexicas fled and fortified themselves in Atlacuihuayan (Tacubaya) before going to Culhuacán.[32] Jiménez Moreno believes that Cuauhtitlán, not the Mexicas, was the real enemy against whom the coalition was directed and that this incident marked the outset of a long war of attrition against that city. The limited significance of the Mexicas at the time makes this view plausible.

After further study of Tepanec antecedents, I now consider that the latter were not yet launched on their bid for hegemony and that the role of Azcapotzalco in any coalition against the Mexicas would have been fairly minor. The *Anales de Cuauhtitlán* actually state that the Tepanecs were not yet powerful when the Mexica captivity in Culhuacán began. Xaltocan and Culhuacán were already on the decline, and Chalco therefore remains the most likely candidate for the role of leader. The Nonoalca Teotlixcas had evidently clashed with the Mexicas in Chapultepec, and are said to have arrived there a year before the expulsion, for which they were therefore quite possibly responsible, even if they also left the site shortly afterwards. The expulsion from Chapultepec might even be viewed as a curtain-raiser to the long and bitter struggle between the Mexicas and the Chalcas. The latter, as will be seen, were also ready to make a bid for empire, and were entrenching themselves in Cuitlahuac, Mizquic, and even Culhuacán.

The Captivity

The Mexicas did not proceed as one cohesive body to Culhuacán. The *Anales de Tlatelolco* give the impression that relatively few went there: some, including women, were taken to Xochimilco, and others to Cuauhnahuac, Chalco, and Xaltocan, as well as Azcapotzalco.[33] A small number of survivors took refuge in the midst of the lagoon water in Acocolco, and only later proceeded to Culhuacán.

Huitzilihuitl himself was sacrificed in Culhuacán. As to the treatment of the remainder, the *Tira de la Peregrinación* says that they were mere slaves, while Durán states that they were welcomed by the ruler of Culhuacán. At all events, they became a source of strife from the very beginning, and one wonders why the Culhuas consented to receive such migrants who were ready to act as valiant if unruly mercenaries, but whose nuisance value was considerable.

Certain elements in Culhuacán, including Achitometl and Coxcox, both described as rulers, were favorable to the Mexicas, though many of the Culhua nobility wanted to treat them harshly. According to some accounts, two señores ruled Culhuacán at that time, and conceivably as many as four (see Chapter II and Appendix A). At all events the Mexicas were kept at arms' length, since the volcanic waste of Tizapán, where they were settled, is not in the immediate vicinity of Culhuacán.

The tribe at this time was reportedly governed by several traditional leaders, or *teomamaque;* the foremost role, according to some

189

reports, belonged to Tenoch; the *Anales Mexicanos* mention another Cuauhtlequetzqui and an Axolhua as leaders in Culhuacán. Like Cuauhtlequetzqui and other names, Tenoch was a kind of title, apparently held by a succession of individuals; it is not conceivable that the same Tenoch, who already played a key part in the early years in Chapultepec, was also present when the Mexicas arrived in Culhuacán in 1319, and then presided over the foundation of Tenochitlán, living until 1363.

The successful war against Xochimilco forms the main episode of the sojourn in Tizapán. How this story alone survived, of all that occurred in those two decades, and what it signifies is unknown. Though not mentioned by the sources, Chalco was possibly again involved. The Chalcas were actively engaged in the Chinampa region; not only did they at one time settle Cuitlahuac and Mizquic, but Chimalpain even refers to Chimalhuacan Xochimilco and Tepetlixpan Xochimilco as if they were part of Chalco.

The ostensible reason for the hasty departure of the Mexicas was the flaying of King Achitometl's daughter, who was cast in the role of bride of Huitzilopochtli. The underlying symbolism of the event is obscure but significant. Flaying is connected with the rites of Xipe Totec, who often figures as the Red Tezcatlipoca. A further religious rift may be implied, perhaps involving Tezcatlipoca as well as Huitzilopochtli, but the exact meaning escapes us. The legend, moreover, again contains an element of repetition. Apart from the killing of Copil, mentioned above, the *Anales de Cuauhtitlán* tell how the Mexicas in Chapultepec had mocked Xochipapalotl, daughter of Mazatzin, ruler of Culhuacán.

The Eagle, the Serpent, and the Nopal

According to Durán, after leaving Culhuacán, the Mexicas retreated towards Ixtapalapa, proceeding as far as a place called Acatzintitlan, and thence to Mexicaltzingo. They then went to Mixiuhcan, about a mile southeast of the future Tenochtitlán, and finally reached Temazcaltitlan, as it was then called.

Here Huitzilopochtli appeared in a dream to one of his priests, Cuauhtlequetzqui, and told him that the heart of his nephew Copil, killed in Chapultepec, had been cast away in that place and had fallen upon a stone, out of which a beautiful cactus had grown. Reportedly a Cuauhtlequetzqui had been instrumental in the original slaying of Copil and the burying of his heart; here again a different individual of the same name is involved; apart from the time interval, the location where such an unusual deed was performed would be hard for its perpetrator to forget! So fine was the cactus that a magnificent eagle had made it his dwelling place, where he preyed upon the most beautiful and brightly colored birds. After this cactus the place was to be called Tenochtitlán, meaning "Place of the Cactus," or more precisely "Place of the Fruit of the Cactus."

The following morning the Mexicas saw the plant, with the great eagle perched upon it, bowing his noble head as they approached. Filled with wonder, they proceeded to found their city. Their first thought was to build a shrine to Huitzilopochtli; they cut sods from the earth, on which they made a little platform surmounted by a modest straw-covered oratory. The date of this event, as already explained, is more probably 1345 than the traditional 1325.

Torquemada writes of the site as a "place" called Temazcaltitlan, as if it was already inhabited. Furthermore, it lies so near to Azcapotzalco and Tlacopan in a northwesterly direction, and to Coyoacan and Huitzilopochco (now Churubusco) to the south, that one wonders how these ancient cities had ignored the attractions of islands so suited to the chinampa system of cultivation.

The Mexica promised land flowed neither with milk nor honey, but the prospects were much less bleak than the chroniclers tend to imply. The advantages outweighed the disadvantages; and, as Bernal writes, "The apparently absurd choice, but in reality so extraordinary, that the priests made of the place where they were to found their city."[34] Armillas has also pointed out the merits of the site: first, the abundance of fish and birds that permitted a mixed economy, based on agriculture combined with hunting and fishing of lagoon fauna; second, an environment ideal for chinampa cultivation, that is still used in Xochimilco and permits the all-year cultivation of crops watered by abundant irrigation canals; third, the possibility of communication by water, so valuable in a country that had no beasts of burden but only human backs on which to carry goods.[35]

In addition to such natural blessings, the site had the supreme advantage that it was easy to defend. Radin surprisingly describes the founding of Tenochtitlán as a rather minor event in Mexica history but makes the vital point that they never had to abandon this site.[36] After their harrowing experiences in Chapultepec and Culhuacán, they were now on their own, though surrounded by powerful foes. On their small islands they enjoyed many of those advantages that had paved the way, long before the Mexicas' time, to the greatness of Venice. Moreover, lacking space for seasonal agriculture, the population became increasingly urbanized and therefore more readily available for military service at all times of year than other peoples. This may have been a leading factor in the successes of the Mexicas against their neighbors, whose military activities were more closely linked to the agricultural cycle.

On the other hand, the Mexicas were to suffer from weaknesses that plagued them until they won for themselves an empire. Apart from the dangerous proximity of larger neighbors, they lacked raw materials, in particular wood and stone, which they had to beg from others.

The legend of the foundation does not tell us much about the early days of the new capital. The eagle and the cactus at least suggest the presence of plant growth and indicate that this rather uninviting little island was therefore habitable. Eagle and cactus, moreover, may symbolize the dual principle, masculine and feminine, characteristic of Mesoamercan thinking. The eagle that devoured other brightly colored birds was a predator, symbolic of sacrifice, and hence of the conquest and devouring of lesser peoples; the cactus fruit *(tenochtli),* both for its red hue and for its shape, represents those very human hearts which the sun, or eagle, devoured.

In Mesoamerican thinking, not only do the eagle and the cactus have special meaning, but even the very reeds surrounding the place. In Tenochtitlán the Mexicas settled down among the reeds and rushes (*motlallico* in Toltzallan, in Acatzallan). "The city among the rushes" was therefore the new Tollan, destined also to rule the world.

During the initial period in the new city, Tenoch came to play a part approaching that of the future *tlatoani,* and the Codex Mendoza (folio I) depicts him with the little blue speech glyph used to denote the later *tlatoanis,* though he wears no *xihuitzolli,* or crown.

In the Codex Mendoza he is accompanied by ten other leaders, though the *Crónica Mexicayotl* mentions only three.[37] Torquemada mentions rule by four chiefs at the time of the foundation.[38] Possibly the practice already existed of electing the supreme ruler from among only four eligible officeholders; in effect the later *tlatoanis,* elected in this way, descend in a direct line from the four or five *teomamaques,* of which one became the head.

Van Zantwijk relates the different leaders at the time to the dualistic ritual that permeated the legend of Tenochtitlán's foundation. Tenoch, as head of the Cihuatecpan *calpulli* ("the Female Palace"), personifies the nopal growing upon the stone, the symbol of the earth and of fertility. Copil, representative of the Chalman *calpulli,* magician and priest of an alien religion, is the serpent, reborn as symbol of the nether world and of the religion of the native Chinampa population, who had intermingled with the Mexicas. Cuauhtlequetzqui, "the Eagle that Unites with the Fire," embodies the eagle of the foundation legend.

A latent dualism is evident between Cuauhtlequetzqui and another leader, Axolhua, priest of Tláloc, and representative of water. Axolhua is already linked with water in the story of his immersion in the sacred fountain followed by his return from the land beyond Tlalocan, at the moment of the foundation of Tenochtitlán: Cuauhtlequetzqui, closely associated in the text with the eagle and therefore with the sun, is thus Axolhua's opposite.[39]

The symbolism underlying the foundation of Tenochtitlán thus implies a reconciliation of the migrant Mexicas and their god, Huitzilopochtli or Mexitli (related to Tlaltecuhtli), with the local population and with Tláloc, the ancient god of rain. Van Zantwijk's interpretation in this sense is both stimulating and acceptable, though I would question whether the fully fledged Huitzilopochtli was really the principal Mexica deity *before* this reconciliation between gods and peoples took place—probably in Chapultepec—and whether Huitzilopochtli himself was not more the end-product of such a reconciliation than one of two elements that were thereby fused.

Tlatelolco

Of life in the early days of Tenochtitlán, few details survive, and

193

the principal event is the foundation, or refoundation, of the sister city of Tlatelolco. Two sources state that this took place thirteen years after the establishment of Tenochtitlán; the *Anales de Tlatelolco* give a date of 1 Calli.[40]

Veytia says that the nobles were behind the move, and talks of a legend of eight families involved.[41] Torquemada, however, attributes the emigration to sheer lack of space.[42] This explanation seems plausible since the Mexicas obviously felt cramped on one tiny island, and the urge was natural to colonize a similar piece of land, that lay so close by; space was still limited on the two islets that were only later merged with others to form a great metropolis.

In this colonization a particular feature was present; a rivalry, amounting to hostility, persisted between the two cities, and they developed along rather different lines. Tenochtitlán became the leader in military affairs while Tlatelolco was dominant in commerce. The nobility of the latter was mainly oriented towards Azcapotzalco, whereas Tenochtitlán maintained closer ties with Culhuacán, Coatlichán, and later Texcoco.

According to the archaeological evidence, Tenochtitlán and Tlatelolco may have been founded much before the official dates for the event—a possibility already suggested in Chapter VI. They may therefore have had separate histories in the period before their settlement by the Mexicas; Tlatelolco in particular, in view of the near identity of the two pyramids, seems to have enjoyed very close links with Tenayuca, which I see as Azcapotzalco's precursor and which was Tezozómoc's first kingdom before he ruled in Azcapotzalco.

Previously it was thought that Aztec II pottery, already present elsewhere in late Toltec times, was only to be found in Tlatelolco. Recently, however, it has been found in fair quantities in Tenochtitlán, and both cities therefore seem to have existed in embryo well before 1345.

Beside the cathedral, at a depth of ten meters, 66 per cent of the sherds found in stratigraphic pits were Aztec II, while the remainder were Aztec III. Aztec II has now been subdivided into Aztec IIa and Aztec IIb, and only the latter variety was located in Tenochtitlán, whose Aztec II pottery is not therefore necessarily contemporary with that found in Tollan (Constanza Vega, personal communication). This ware is, of course, characteristic of Tenayuca, whose pyramid offers such exact parallels with that of Tlatelolco.

In the cathedral excavations arrowheads were also located, of which Aztec II samples date from approximately 1500 BP – 120 using the technique of obsidian dating, while a further twelve samples were put at 900 BP ±100. The presence of Aztec II pottery and the architectural similarities with Tenayuca offer tentative confirmation of the latter set of twelve dates; however the eleven earliest samples would correspond to the Teotihuacán III period, and if this were so, it would be logical to expect that sherds of that period would also be present. While, therefore, I have always accepted that Tenochtitlán-Tlatelolco was inhabited long before 1345, I would prefer to reserve judgment on the presence of any human settlement on those islets as early as Teotihuacán III until absolute proof can be offered of the provenance of the obsidian used for making the arrowheads—a prerequisite for determining dates by this method. At present it is believed that the obsidian in question came from the Sierra de las Navajas, Hidalgo.

The study of the settlement of the two island cities and the over-all symbolism of the event, offers an idea of how other cities were re-established after the fall of Tollan. No doubt, in each case, the material and the spiritual went hand in hand; the leaders of the cities, in addition to their personal appellation, surely possessed ritually ordained names or titles, related both to the elements and to the gods. Azcapotzalco, Tenayuca, Tlaxcala, and even Texcoco were relatively ancient, and the Late Postclassic mainly witnessed a process of resettlement. From the little that the sources relate, the refounding of these cities surely involved, as in Tenochtitlán, a fusion between new and old gods and peoples, thereafter reflected in the complex *calpulli* structure of each place.

The Interim

The sources are sparing in their data on events between the settlement of Tenochtitlán-Tlatelolco, and the advent of their new dynasties some two decades later. Comments on this period center upon relations with their other peoples. Durán stresses the dire poverty and wretchedness of the settlers, hemmed in by greedy neighbors; so timorous were they that they even had misgivings over the building of a small temple of dried mud to honor Huitzilopochtli.

It was first proposed to submit formally to the Tepanecs, in return for stone and wood with which to build. Finally, however, the Mexicas resolved not to depend on any single neighbor, but to obtain construction materials by trading fish and other lagoon products in the various markets.[43] Apparently they did not pay tribute to the Tepanecs at the outset, but became vassals rather later, some time between the foundation of Tlatelolco and the accession of the new dynasties.

Two events mark this initial era: the conquests of Culhuacán and of Tenayuca. These conflicts will be considered, in conjunction with the other Tepanec-Mexica campaigns, in Chapter IX, although they were seemingly initiated before the accession of Acamapichtli. The Mexicas' energies were mainly spent in the exacting task of making the chinampas and building homes and temples, albeit on a modest scale, without great changes in government or social structure.

Tenochtitlán and Tlatelolco were thus founded, as small and struggling communities closely dependent on their neighbors. The situation, obscure in detail, was dramatic in its essence; the Mexicas, still poor and despised, bereft of raw materials and initially without chinampas, had at last found a home of their own. In this modest settlement of fisher folk lay the nucleus of the imperial city at which Cortés and his men gazed in wonder a bare two centuries later as surpassing all that was known in Europe.

The Dynasties

The accession of the Mexica monarchies marks a period of complete if short-lived subordination to the Tepanecs of Azcapotzalco, under whose shadow they were to live for the following generation.

"Foundation" is a rather figurative expression in dealing with the dynasties as well as with the cities. A change of leadership was made, in conformity with the new situation, but this change harbored an element of continuity. Tenoch and Cuauhtlequetzqui are replaced by Acamapichtli and Ilancueitl—possibly not the spouse of Acamapichtli, but his male colleague. Both the old and the new leadership are counseled by other chiefs, alternatively described as four and ten in number; the daughters of the old leaders, such as Tenoch and Ocelopan, figured among Acamapichtli's many wives.

According to certain reports, Acamapichtli did not found a new dynasty at all. Vetancurt says that he was the son of Huitzilihuitl I. Mendieta writes that he was the son of another Acamapichtli, who reigned in Tenochtitlán after the death of Tenoch.[44]

Probably Tenoch was still a semi-independent leader, whereas Acamapichtli and Ilancueitl—and to an even greater extent Cuacua-pitzahuac in Tlatelolco—were Tepanec nominees. In spite of Acamapichtli's Culhua or Acolhua descent, his relations with the Tepanecs dominated his reign. Torquemada writes of the contentment of the King of Azcapotzalco at his election; Ixtlilxóchitl also states that he was appointed by that ruler, still named as Aculhua, not Tezozómoc; the same author in another passage even maintains that Acamapichtli was the son of Aculhua, and therefore himself a Tepanec.[45]

Tezozómoc stresses Acamapichtli's subordination to the Tepanecs by stating that in his reign the Mexicas first paid tribute to Azcapotzalco.[46] Torquemada also writes that Acamapichtli was not an absolute ruler, since he paid tribute to the Tepanecs; both he and Cuacuapitzahuac served Tezozómoc well, helping him to conquer his empire and backing him against rebellious subjects.[47] Sahagún confirms that the Mexicas at that time were subjects of Azcapotzalco.

The Mexicas were tributaries, and their lot was reputedly hard because of the burden they bore. Durán tells the dramatic, if apocryphal, story of the sudden doubling of the tribute by the Tepanecs and of their far-fetched demands, such as a duck and a heron on their nests, at the very moment when they were hatching out their eggs; with the aid of Huitzilopochtli, even such peculiar fiscal demands were met.

Cuacuapitzahuac's role as a Tepanec nominee is not in doubt, and acquires added significance because Tlatelolco may then have been the more important of the two cities; the *Anales de Tlatelolco*— admittedly a partial source—maintain that Tenochtitlán under Tenoch's rule even paid tribute to its sister-city.[48] The origins of the Tlatelolco monarchy present few problems; no source questions that

197

the first ruler was appointed by the Tepanec sovereign. Almost all accounts agree that the new ruler was called Cuacuapitzahuac, though Ixtlilxóchitl at times calls him by the alternative name of Mixcoatl or Coatecatl.[49] Sources also sometimes call him Epcoatl, while others insist that he was Tezozómoc's son; however, the two monarchs tend to appear as contemporaries, and Ixtlilxóchitl may be right in saying that he was the son of Tezozómoc's father, Acolhua. According to the *Anales de Tlatelolco,* the Tlatelolcas were granted a son of Tezozómoc, and then spent a year in building him a palace while he remained with his father in Azcapotzalco. He collected tribute from his people and delivered it to the Tepanecs; he married the daughter of Acolmiztli, ruler of Coatlichán, and thus, like Acamapichtli, acquired Acolhua connections.

The story of the choice of Acamapichtli is more complicated, and the different versions are contradictory. He was not ostensibly a Tepanec, even if he was their choice for the Tenochca throne. According to most accounts, he was related to the Culhuacán-Coatlichán dynasty and was therefore a representative of the old order as well as the new.

The more orthodox versions state that Acamapichtli was born of Mexica father and Culhua mother, though it may be convenient first to mention the alternative accounts of his origins. Motolinía states that he was the son of the thirteenth ruler of Culhuacán, presumably Huehue Acamapichtli, since the ruler in question is stated to have been killed by a usurper.[50] The *Relación de la Genealogía* calls the Tenochca sovereign Acamapichtli II, and affirms that he also became ruler of Culhuacán at the time of its destruction. This monarch was the adopted son of Huehue Acamapichtli, and had fled with his mother to Coatlichán, where he was named after his adopted father, though his real name was "Xilechoz."[51]

The majority of the sources, however, give the more standard version, whereby Acamapichtli was the son of Opochtli, of Mexica stock, while his mother, Atotoztli, was a Culhua princess. Atotoztli is described as the daughter of Nauhyotzin, a name that frequently crops up in Culhua king-lists; other Nauhyotzins also had a daughter called Atotoztli. Only the *Historia de los Mexicanos* puts matters in reverse, saying that Acamapichtli's mother was a Mexica and that his father was a Culhua prince.[52]

Accounts vary about whether the new monarch really came from Culhuacán or from Coatlichán; while some maintain that he was living in Culhuacán, others assert that he was fetched from Coatlichán by the Tenochcas.

The *Crónica Mexicayotl* states that the ruler of Culhuacán consented to the Mexicas' choice of Acamapichtli as *tlatoani,* and they then went and found him in Coatlichán.[53] Chimalpain also states in his seventh *Relación* that Acamapichtli was fetched from Coatlichán, where he had been reared though he was born in Culhuacán. Motolinía, however, states that, though Acamapichtli was brought up in Coatlichán, he came to Tenochtitlán at an early age; the *Relación de la Genealogía* even maintains that he had lived in Tenochtitlán for forty-six years before he became ruler.[54] Possibly, therefore, Acamapichtli was well advanced in years at the time of his accession; he is often presented as a kind of father figure, and his reign was fairly short.

According to the *Relación de la Genealogía,* Acamapichtli was never *tlatoani* and the first true holder of the title was Huitzilihuitl. Moreover, although Acamapichtli is stated to have married the daughters of the twenty *calpulli* leaders; the sons of these daughters are called his grandchildren in the *Crónica Mexicayotl.* All together five different fathers and five different mothers for this prince are mentioned by the sources; these and other discrepancies make of Acamapichtli a rather ambiguous figure. As will be seen below, the chronological data is ample, and his dates are consistent when duly interpreted; thus I believe that some change of government did take place in 1371, but am not necessarily at variance with van Zantwijk, for whom Acamapichtli bears the stamp of a semi-mythical ruler. Acamapichtli ("Handful of Arrows"), is another of those names or titles, like Acolmiztli or Coxcox, that occur quite frequently; one Acamapichtli is leader of the Mexitin in Chapultepec; another was a Toltec leader who first settled Tulancingo; and a third Acamapichtli was a ruler of Culhuacán (known as Huehue Acamapichtli), who was overthrown by the usurper Achitometl. The name might have associations with the Chichimec ceremony of occupying land by the shooting of arrows; the first *tlatoani* is called Acamapichtli Itzpapalotl in the *Crónica Mexicayotl,* and therefore bears the name of a goddess (or god) linked with this rite in other sources. Van Zantwijk suggests that Acamapichtli's real or personal name (in addition to his title) was Chilatlexochtzin; he is occasionally called Xilechoz, and Chilatlexochtzin could be his name in the Codex Azcatitlan, to judge by a glyph at his side when he is crowned in Tenochtitlán.[55]

Ilancueitl is equally enigmatic. She is usually described as older than Acamapichtli, and bore him no children; the *Crónica Mexicayotl* maintains that she was his aunt before becoming his wife.[56] She was in some way related to her husband, for she is variously reported as being the daughter of the ruler of Culhuacán, the daughter of the ruler of Coatlichán, or merely "a native of Coatlichán."[57] The *Relación de la Genealogía* states that she had previously been married to Huehue Acamapichtli of Culhuacán, but chronology makes this unlikely.[58] In another paragraph, the *Relación* calls her the wife of Achitometl II of Culhuacán, which is more plausible.

Ilancueitl, like Acamapichtli, is a fairly common name or title, applicable to a kind of mother figure. According to many sources, the wife of Iztacmixcoatl, the procreator of the different tribes in Chicomoztoc, bore this name. In Chimalpain's fifth *Relación,* a prince called Ilancueitl is ruler of Tzacualtitlan Tenanco, one of the Chalco Tecpans; like so many other migrant suitors, he married a Culhua princess; according to the seventh *Relación,* this Ilancueitl abandoned his throne after a reign of eighteen years, and went off to Coatlichán.

Caso suggested, with some logic, that Ilancueitl was not really Acamapichtli's wife but his Cihuacoatl. Without accepting in its entirety the legend of Tlacaelel, the significance of the office in Tenochtitlán is beyond question; it probably dates from earlier times, perhaps even deriving from a dualistic relationship between Huitzilopochtli and his sister, the goddess Cihuacoatl, that led to the dual offices of Tlatoani and Cihuacoatl.

Whatever changes occurred in the status of the Cihuacoatl, this office, like most Mexica institutions, springs from ancient traditions rather than from modern innovations. Like the *tlatoani* himself, Chimalpain describes the Cihuacoatl as a kind of mouthpiece of the deity, in whose name he spoke, in order to give guidance to the people. Moreover Tlacaelel was also known as Atempanecatl ("Lord of the Edge of the Water"), a title borne by legendary figures in Toltec times. Not only the office of Tlatoani, but also that of Cihuacoatl, might therefore be seen as a continuation of *teomama* traditions, under radically altered circumstances.

The *Historia de los Mexicanos* implies that Ilancueitl, not Acamapichtli, was the real ruler, and it is not inconceivable that Ilancueitl was *tlatoani,* and that Acamapichtli was originally *cihuacoatl.* Accounts, already quoted, say that he only became *tlatoani* some years after arriving in Tenochtitlán, and he is represented in the Codex Mendoza with his personal glyph, and also with that of Cihuacoatl.

Chronology

In *Los Mexicas: Primeros Pasos,* a fairly full study was made of the chronology of Acamapichtli, Cuacuapitzahuac, and Tezozómoc of Azcapotzalco. In all, twenty-eight references were listed for Acamapichtli's accession, giving a range of twelve different dates, together with twenty-seven references for his death or the accession of his successor, with sixteen dates.[59] There is no need to repeat the more complex arguments that led to the conclusion that the Tenochca and Tlatelolca monarchs came to the throne in 1371, preceded by one year by Tezozómoc, who probably nominated them.

These calculations, however, and the table on which they are based, amply demonstrate that Acamapichtli's accession and death, as given by the sources, correspond to a number of different native calendars. Only about half of the twenty-eight references for his accession are intelligible, if reckoned in the Tenochca count (1 Acatl = 1519); to maintain that the many other dates also derive from this calendar, in which they make no sense at all, is to relegate most of this chronological data to the nonsense department.

The Government

With the establishment of the two Tepanec-oriented dynasties, a new era dawns, in which the Mexicas, as auxiliaries or vassals, helped the Tepanecs to carve out their ephemeral empire; later, as partners, they acquired their own stake in the enterprise, prior to taking over the whole concern.

The social organization and government of the early Tenochtitlán falls outside the scope of this work; information is scarce, and
I have little to add to what I previously wrote on the matter.[60]

The social structure of Tenochtitlán is often presented as a
class struggle between the *pipiltin*—all ostensibly sired by the pro-
lific Acamapichtli, wedded to the twenty daughters of the *calpulli*
leaders—and the submerged nine-tenths of the population. Very
possibly a new aristocracy emerged under the Tepanec aegis, part-
Tepanec, part-Culhua, but a Mexica nobility surely existed long
before this, as implied in accounts of the migration and the stay in
Chapultepec. In Tenochtitlán the highest offices, Tlacochcalcatl and
Tlacatecatl, bore the names of two original Aztlan barrios—following a curious custom, noted by Kirchhoff, of changing names of
places or *calpullis* into titles. Other cities in the Valley of Mexico
seem also to have possessed their *tlacochcalcatl* and *tlacatecatl,* and
Huehue Tezozómoc is stated to have summoned these two digni-
taries from many different places when he was about to attack
Xaltocan.

It is widely assumed that Acamapichtli produced a vast progeny;
by a process of geometrical progression, Tenochtitlán was therefore
plagued with supernumerary *pipiltin* by the time of the Conquest.
But evidence to back this notion is scarce, except for the report that
the first *tlatoani* married twenty wives (or twenty-one, if we include
the barren Ilancueitl, possibly his aunt, possibly a man). Even if the
view of Acamapichtli as a semilegendary figure is rejected, the story
of the twenty wives from the twenty *calpulli* leaders patently bears
the stamp of a fable. While no data survive regarding *pipiltin* population in Tenochtitlán at the time of the Conquest, figures from other
centers, such as Huexotzingo, suggest that the proportion was fairly
modest.[61] It is easy to forget the constant waste of *pipiltin* on the
battlefield or on the sacrificial altar. As every source insists, not
only was the *pipil* trained as a warrior but was judged by his performance in combat and by the captives he took; the gods were fastidious
about their victims, and the Mexica *pipiltin* could become captives as
well as captors, forming a natural target for enemies in search of
choice offerings for their own favorite gods.

Probably the new ruling class, irrespective of its size, was linked
in some way to the old *calpulli* system, though its increasing land-

holdings were quite separate. The *calpullis*—perhaps of totemic origin—had functioned more as religious and ethnic entities, but in imperial days were restricted to the role of controlling the common lands and acting as recruiting agencies for *macehual* cannon fodder required for wars of conquest. With the consolidation of the state under the aegis of the tutelary gods, Huitzilopochtli and Tezcatlipoca, the claims of such units on the citizens' loyalty was reduced; the political significance of the *calpulli* shrank as the traditional leaders lost their importance. In Tlatelolco, additional *calpullis* were formed of merchants and artisans, though as trade and commerce increased, the merchants were increasingly subjected to the dictates of the Tlatoani and the high command, and the *pochtecas* were used as a spearhead in the Aztec career of conquest.

Who Were the Mexicas?

In asking who were the Mexicas, the question first arises: Who were their gods? In trying to reconstruct the history of one people, and hence of all Mesoamerica, we rely on information relating mainly to the final period before the Spanish Conquest; and in this instance, the official story is somewhat contrived and expurgated, as Sahagún makes quite clear. Moreover, we possess a picture derived from the Spaniards that is far from a complete version of what was really known to people before the Conquest; Durán complains that many of the books were burned and that, even in his day, few old people could be found to act as informants.

The successive excisions during the Mexica migration, that should tell something of their ethnic background, remain a puzzle. They ostensibly concern Huitzilopochtli; however, if, as I suggest, this deity only came fully into his own after his people had entered the Valley of Mexico, then these schisms, represented as having occurred in remoter places, really symbolize later events within the Valley, including the Chapultepec period, where the Mexicas may have stayed longer than history relates. Moreover, these excisions, that *a posteriori* accounts ascribe to more specific causes, may have partly derived from a natural tendency for tribes to divide if numbers swelled unduly. Nowadays, in southern Venezuela, on the upper reaches of the Orinoco, primitive native groups will often split into two halves when the total reaches about 150 people; a similar tendency might have prevailed among the Mexicas.

Close ties linked the Malinalco-Ocuilan region with Culhuacán; the *Anales de Cuauhtitlán* tell how Cuauhtexpetlatzin, ruler of Culhuacán, sent his vassals to Ocuilan and Malinalco, where they settled; equally Malinalxochitl is associated both with Malinalco and with the Chinampanecas. Therefore, in effect, the excision in Malinalco and the conflict in Chapultepec involving Copil seem to form a single series of events. Copil is both friend and enemy of the Mexicas, just as the chief protagonist in a prior schism in Coatepec, Coyolxauhqui, the war goddess and sister of Huitzilopochtli, is both his companion and his foe. This concept of the enemy who is part associate is present in the *xochiyaotl,* or war of flowers, and the notion of the deified foe is basic to human sacrifice.

Tetzahuitl figures as the original Mexica deity during the migration. Van Zantwijk sees him as both lunar and earth deity, and he is often presented as a kind of proto-Huitzilopochtli. Chimalpain writes of "Tetzauhteotlytoca Huitziltin," as if Tetzahuitl was hero as well as god and as if the original leader Huitzilihuitl was as much precursor or prototype for Tetzahuitl as for Huitzilopochtli. Tetzahuitl the sorcerer, however, is more akin to Tezcatlipoca than to Huitzilopochtli, and the final Huitzilopochtli logically came into being after, not before, the Mexicas came into contact with the Chinampa peoples. Possibly during the migration neither a Tetzahuitl nor any proto-Huitzilopochtli reigned supreme; Durán says that the Mexicas brought seven other gods with them, probably corresponding to the seven original *calpullis.*

The formative process of the god Huitzilopochtli—as often occurs in Mesoamerica—is partly the repetition or reflection of a former event, in this instance the birth of the human Topiltzin Quetzalcoatl in the Chinampa region, from an Otonchichimec father and a local Toltec mother, called Coatlicue, like Huitzilopochtli's own mother. Copil is also linked with Quetzalcoatl; his heart was buried, and Tenochtitlán founded, in the Place of the Red and the Black, formerly visited by Topiltzin Quetzalcoatl on his way to Tlillan Tlapallan. Like Topiltzin, Copil is just another offspring of Mother Goddess and local ruler, in this case described as king of Malinalco, a dependency of Culhuacán.

The same event, the marriage of the non-Toltec with the Toltec-Culhua princess or deity, is then re-enacted, not only in these two instances, concerning a god, but also by Nopaltzin, the Chichimec invader, who marries the daughter of a Culhua ruler and (in a more historical context) by Huetzin, the Acolhua conqueror, who weds Atototzin, daughter of Nauhyotzin of Culhuacán; Acamapichtli stems from another of these prototype marriages; his father is Opochtli, a tribal dignitary, and his mother is a Culhua princess, also called Atotzin, daughter of another Nauhyotl. Huactzin, ruler of Cuauhtitlán, reputedly a Chichimec settlement, also married a daughter of Coxcox, señor of Culhuacán.[62]

In Chapultepec the lagoon way of life, that reached its culmination in Tenochtitlán, was probably already introduced. And Huitzilopochtli, the Humming Bird of the South, came into being as a fusion of the colibri tradition—represented by Huitzilton, leader during the migration—with Opochtli, a typical lagoon fisherman's god, stated by Sahagún to have been one of the Tláloques; Opochtli was also called Atlexeliuhqui ("The Left One who Divides the Water").

Kirchhoff puts it slightly differently. He also sees the Mexicas as a blend of lagoon dwellers with migrants from farther afield; however, he regards the people of the lagoon as "Chichimecs" (Atlacachichimeca), being primarily gatherers of lacustrine products, while it is the wandering Mexicas who are the "Toltecs." Kirchhoff, however, was the first to point out that the difference between Toltecs and Chichimecs was apt to become blurred, and the distinction is therefore a fine one.[63]

The religion and mythology of the Mexicas reflect their complex ethnic background. Van Zantwijk views them as primarily composed of Nahua Toltecs (Chinampanecas), to whom were then added Tolteca Chichimecs and finally Chichimecs; the tribe from which the legend of the migration stems formed the Chichimec element in the racial blend, while for Kirchhoff the migrants are the Toltecs, and the lagoon dwellers the Chichimecs.

I accept van Zantwijk's definition, with certain reservations. Reversing his order, I see the Mexicas as consisting of a blend of:

1. The Otonchichimec tribe (with a sprinkling of Teochichimecs) of the migration legend.

2. Nahua Toltecs (=Chinampanecas).

3. Further elements that were added later, such as Tlacochcalcas in Chapultepec and Culhuas in Tizapan.

The historical relevance of certain details of the captivity in Culhuacán are easy to overstate, and accounts of the eating of snakes, the ear-cutting war against the Xochimilcas, and the sacrifice of King Achitometl's daughter are puzzling. However, the story of constant intermarriage with the Culhua population must contain a kernel of truth. The Mexica insistence on their Culhua-Toltec ancestry may be rather contrived, though most of the evidence points to a connection in the female line between the new rulers of Tenochtitlán —installed only a generation later—and the Culhua-Coatlichán royal house; this dynasty did not originate in Tollan, but sprang from a marriage between the Acolhua Huetzin and a bride drawn from that never failing supply of Culhua princesses. Notwithstanding Motolinía's statement that the Culhuas and the Mexicas were the same people, the *Relación de la Genealogía* may be nearer the mark in stating that the latter were not true Toltecs, but "a low kind of people" *(gente baja),* i.e., basically Otonchichimecs.

With certain differences in emphasis, I agree with van Zantwijk that the whole migration story must be treated with caution and concur about the manner in which Huitzilopochtli rose to be the tribal deity. Van Zantwijk regards the immigrant group called Mexicas or Mexitin as basically Teochichimec; I however think that they were Otonchichimecs with an admixture of Teochichimecs, as were also the Acolhuas, Xaltocamecas, and Texcocans; I suspect, moreover, that they arrived in the Valley of Mexico at about the same time as these other peoples. The *Anales de Cuauhtitlán* actually state that the people who came to that city had stayed together with the Mexicas in Tollan, Tequizquiac, Apazco, Citlaltepec, and Tzompango; in other words, the two peoples had been fellow migrants, and the Mexicas had also sojourned in Cuauhtitlán itself. The Mexicas by all accounts were well on the way to becoming Mesoamericanized when they came to Chapultepec, and were no more pure Teochichimecs than were those Chichimecs of Xolotl and other peoples so described by Ixtlilxóchitl. Moreover the group that arrived in the Valley of Mexico, far from being homogeneous, was the product of a series of excisions from and additions to the original body. Kirchhoff thought that the migrant Mexicas were a blend of two elements; in a sense I agree, since both Otonchichimecs and Teochichimecs were involved, though I now think that not two opposing groups but a whole series were involved.

The respective leaders are not easy to relate to the different elements later present in Tenochtitlán. Tenoch, according to the Codex Ramírez, was an Otomí; Cuauhtlequetzqui is associated with Axolhua, priest of Tláloc, but is also an Otomí chief.[64] These leaders, therefore, mentioned as prominent in Chapultepec, might be connected with Otonchichimec migrant elements. Even Huitzilihuitl is described by the *Anales de Cuauhtitlán* as descended in the male line from the nobility of the Otomí stronghold of Xaltocan. The Chinampanecas in general, and the Culhuas in particular, are hard to distinguish from each other, though Malinalxochitl and her son Copil are basically linked to the Chalman Calpulli (i.e. to the Chinampanecas), while Acamapichtli, Ilancueitl, and other later leaders reportedly derive from Culhuacán proper.

The situation remains confused; Cuauhtlequetzqui, the human leader, married a daughter of Copil, essentially a Chinampaneca; but Cuauhtlequetzqui belonged to the Huitznahuac *calpulli,* whose members descended from the Mexica migrants, and which became one of the leading *calpullis,* with which par excellence Huitzilopochtli was associated. In like manner the tribal deity, as patron of the migrant Huitznahuas and as son of Coatlicue, Mother Goddess of Culhuacán, represents a fusion of the two main elements, the migrant and the settled.

Van Zantwijk seems at times to regard the migrant *calpullis* as less significant than those native to the Valley of Mexico. But the Tlacochcalcas, who took part in the migration, and the Huitznahuas, were supreme in war and were therefore very important.

A Further Riddle

In the complex problem of Mexica origins, a further riddle remains unsolved, since no simple explanation exists for the near identity between the pyramids Tlatelolco II and Tenayuca II.[65] The only possible solution surely lies in an early affinity between Mexicas and Tepanecs, both somehow linked at that point with Tenayuca.

Although the Tepanecs were the first of the two to become powerful, the earliest settlements both in Postclassic Azcapotzalco and Tenochtitlán-Tlatelolco might conceivably be viewed as political offshoots of Tenayuca. Possibly not all the Mexicas went to Chapultepec, any more than they all went to Culhuacán. In the late thirteenth and early fourteenth century some Mexicas could have settled in Chapultepec, while others had already gone to Tlatelolco and become dependents of Tenayuca, when that city was the local power, before the rise of Azcapotzalco; as adherents of Tenayuca, they then went so far as to build an identical temple. Eventually, after the expulsion from Chapultepec and Culhuacán, other Mexicas arrived and fused with their kinsmen, already settled in the islands of Tenochtitlán-Tlatelolco.

Alternatively, some other migrant *calpullis*—not Mexicas at all, but also a mixture of Otonchichimecs and Chinampanecas—perhaps came to the future Tenochtitlán-Tlatelolco long before 1345, the year when they were first joined by *calpullis* of Mexicas coming from Culhuacán; the two groups, of which the earlier, or non-Mexica element had built the Tlatelolco pyramid, then linked up to form the Mexica or Aztec polity. Both groups would have been users of Aztec II pottery, current at that time in Culhuacán and characteristic of Tenayuca, on whom the pre-Mexica Tlatelolco had thus depended. As a third alternative, the Tlatelolco pyramid could originally have been built in pre-Mexica days, not by any migrant tribe but by native Chinampa peoples who had lived there for some time.

I tend to favor the first hypothesis, since I question whether all the Mexicas went to Chapultepec and thence to Culhuacán and whether some of their kin were not established at an earlier date in Tlatelolco and perhaps in Tenochtitlán. A special relationship existed between Tepanecs and Mexicas, as described in Chapter VI. As Tenayuca dependents, the two peoples would have thus been closely linked from the outset, long before they each in turn assumed the supreme role in the Valley of Mexico, first as subordinates and then as successors of Tenayuca.

Tenayuca, an important city in Toltec times, capital of the legendary Xolotl and of the historical Tochintecuhtli, was a member of the ruling confederation in partnership with Culhuacán and Xaltocan, and thus an early claimant to the Toltec heritage, being in this respect the predecessor of Azcapotzalco and of Tenochtitlán. The usage has developed of calling Tenayuca's inhabitants Chichimecs; probably, like their Mexica and Tepanec neighbors, they were a blend of local Nahuas and of invading Otonchichimecs and Teochichimecs.

The conquest of Culhuacán by the Mexicas. Codex Telleriano-Remensis.
Courtesy Bibliothèque Nationale, Paris

210

Tezozómoc of Azcapotzalco tells his three sons—Maxtla, Tlatoca Tlix-patzin, and Tayatzin—about dreaming of Nezahualcoyotl's revenge. Codex Xolotl, plate VIII. *Courtesy Bibliothèque Nationale, Paris*

Tepanec warrior takes Chimalpoposa of Tenochtitlán prisoner. Codex
Xolotl, plate VIII. *Courtesy Bibliothèque Nationale, Paris*

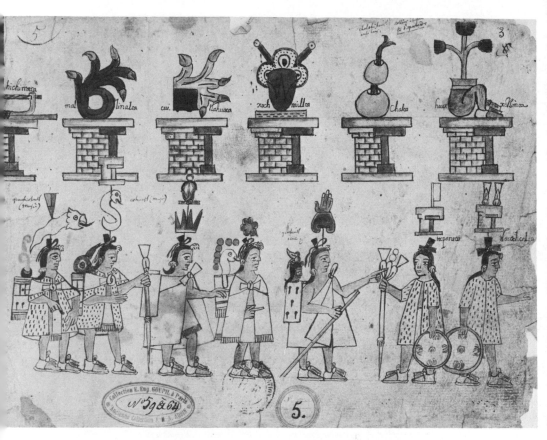

The leaders of the seven tribes leave Chicomoztoc. Codex Azcatitlan.
Courtesy Bibliothèque Nationale, Paris

213

Huitzilopochtli born in Coatepec. Codex Azcatitlan. *Courtesy Bibliothèque Nationale, Paris*

214

The defeat of the Mexicas at Chapultepec. Codex Azcatitlan. *Courtesy Bibliothèque Nationale, Paris*

The Mexicas fight the Xochimilcas during the captivity in Culhuacán.
Codex Azcatitlan. *Courtesy Bibliothèque Nationale, Paris*

Chichimec hunter kills rabbit. Codex Telleriano-Remensis. *Courtesy Bibliothèque Nationale, Paris*

IX. The Will to Conquer

The Initial Campaigns

Chapter II told the story of Culhuacán until the time of Tezozómoc, and studied the complexities of the Culhua king-lists; reports that the Mexicas took control of Culhuacán before their escape from captivity in 1343 were seen as exaggerated. Whatever their ambitions, they still lacked the muscle to tackle such a major center. Moreover, supposing that the Mexicas had indeed overthrown Culhuacán at this time, they would logically have stayed there; no motive would have existed to abandon the scene of such triumphs, in order to found their own fledgling capital elsewhere; as masters of Culhuacán, they would not later have deigned to become Tepanec vassals. It was also suggested in Chapter II that reports of a break in the Culhua king-list and of an empty Culhua throne more probably resulted from a changeover from one calendar count to another, that revealed an *apparent* gap of some twenty years between the death of Huehue Acamapichtli, successor of Coxcox, and the accession of Achitometl II, who usurped the throne in about 1336. The dynastic upheaval occurred before the flight of the Mexicas, who, as a parting gesture, flayed the daughter of Achitometl, thereby gruesomely re-

218

enacting the ritual "marriage" of an outsider to a Culhua princess—
the bridegroom on this occasion being their own tutelary god.

It was calculated in Chapter II that Achitometl probably reigned
until 1371—the accession date of Acamapichtli of Tenochtitlán.
Following an apparently short interregnum, another Nauhyotzin,
sometimes called Nauhyotzin II, was installed on the Culhua throne
as a Mexica nominee after the Mexicas' onslaught upon that city,
which literally seems to have fallen apart after the death of Achitometl. I previously concluded that, notwithstanding civil strife,
symptomatic of a declining polity, the final fall of Culhuacán was due
more to the Tepanec-Mexica offensive, to which the city fell an
early victim.

This was not the first Mexica attack, since Culhuacán, together
with Tenayuca, are the two "conquests" attributed by the Codex
Mendoza to the proto-*tlatoani,* Tenoch, acting presumably under the
aegis of the Tezozómoc's predecessor, Aculhua of Azcapotzalco.
Such feats before the Tezozómoc-Acamapichtli era are open to
question, though, as explained below, I incline to the belief that some
Tepanec-Mexica aggression against Culhuacán did occur in the
1360's, between the foundation of Tenochtitlán and the accession
of Acamapichtli, even if the *coup de grâce* was delayed until 1377.

Once more chronology rears its ugly head. It becomes hard to
decide whether we are genuinely faced with two separate but related
events—a first attack on Culhuacán in the 1360's and a second in the
1370's—or whether Culhuacán was really the victim of a single
assault, that the chroniclers reduplicate. Where two or more dates
are given for such wars, the obvious assumption that we are concerned with two separate conflicts is not necessarily valid; Appendix
A demonstrates that in many cases a single event is involved, though
its dates are presented in different ways and thereby appear to refer to
two or more separate occurrences.

The accession of Tezozómoc to the throne of Azcapotzalco in
1370 and of his Tenochcan and Tlatelolcan nominees in 1371
heralded the great era of Tepanec expansion and of the Tepanec-
Mexica bid for supremacy in central Mesoamerica.

I advisedly use the phrase "Tepanec-Mexica"—in that order—
as the best means of describing what occurred. As already explained,

every shred of evidence suggests that the Mexicas remained for a time Tepanec vassals and tributaries. Doubts arise over the duration of this condition; in Chapter XI I shall insist that the portrayal of the Mexicas as Tepanec menials until 1428, when the worm suddenly turned, is part myth; signs exist that from about 1400 onwards the Mexica tail was visibly beginning to wag the Tepanec dog.

This chapter concerns the early period of Tepanec-Mexica conquest, when the Tepanecs were in undoubted control. Why, therefore, should we write of Tepanec-Mexica conquests at this stage? Could not the Mexicas be omitted altogether from the equation and the process be described as a purely Tepanec operation? Yet the Mexicas must be included because they seemingly played a major part as leading auxiliaries; moreover, when the Mexicas overthrew Azcapotzalco in 1428, many Tepanec records were burned, and surviving accounts of the previous period concentrate upon Mexica rather than on Tepanec triumphs. On the system of government in Azcapotzalco or in Tenochtitlán at this time, information is scanty. Nonetheless, where the phrase "Tepanec-Mexica" conquest is used, it should never be forgotten that the master-mind behind the strategy was that of Tezozómoc, not of Acamapichtli or his successor Huitzilihuitl, and that the high command operated from Azcapotzalco, not Tenochtitlán.

The Mexicas were far from being mere Teochichimecs, however loudly they proclaimed their nomad descent while vaunting almost in the same breath their Culhua or Toltec ancestry. However, at this moment, when Tenochtitlán and Tlatelolco (despite its Tenayuca-like pyramid) were still fairly modest chinampa-type settlements, the two cities hardly vied with Azcapotzalco as bastions of the surviving Toltec culture. The Mexicas in 1371 were first and foremost warriors, notwithstanding their intellectual efflorescence in later times, when they were to build the lagoon city whose glories bedazzled the conquistadors and still captivate the modern mind. At the outset they seem to have possessed a unique talent for war, and were thus an invaluable instrument in the hands of Tezozómoc, that he could employ in crucial sectors of his campaign for supremacy. The use of auxiliary levies was not uncommon in Mesoamerica; the Aztecs in their far-flung campaigns later recruited the peoples of the Valley of Mexico and beyond, including Culhuas, Xochimilcas, Tlalhuicas, and Matlatzincas. While Tezozómoc could draw on a number of Tepanec cities for levies, it is not clear how far he was able to call on the services of other tributary peoples in his wars, since our information comes primarily from Mexica sources that mainly feature their own campaigns.

Apart from the evidence of the Codex Mendoza, already cited, the *Historia de los Mexicanos* also insists upon a Tepanec-Mexica attack on Culhuacán before Tezozómoc's reign.[1] It states that twenty-one years after the foundation of Tenochtitlán, the Mexicas attacked Culhuacán and burned its temple; but this source gives not the traditional 1325 for the foundation of the city, but 1322, or three years earlier. On the supposition that the traditional date should be interpreted as 1345, not 1325, then the calculations of the *Historia de los Mexicanos* (that dates its events by the number of years elapsed since the foundation of Tenochtitlán) should be based on a starting point not of 1345 but of 1342; twenty-one years thereafter then becomes 1363. Now, according to the *Anales de Tlatelolco*, Tenoch died in 4 Tochtli, or 1366, Tenochca count.[2] Chimalpain and the *Crónica Mexicayotl* report that he died in 1 Acatl, or 1363.[3] It therefore seems likely that some attack on Culhuacán was indeed made in the early 1360's; the Mexica military machine, that later became so formidable, was then beginning to flex its muscles. Culhuacán was by that time debilitated, and Achitometl II's reign was neither legitimate, popular, nor peaceful. The *Origen de los Mexicanos* insists that the process of disintegration had already begun during the controversial reign of Achitometl, a ruler alien to the traditional dynasty and murderer of its last scion, Huehue Acamapichtli.

The Codex Mendoza describes Tenayuca as a Mexica conquest under Tenoch. Ixtlilxóchitl and the Codex Xolotl also mention a war between the Mexicas and Tenayuca in the year 2 Acatl (for which the chronicler gives the Christian equivalent of 1195). Unlike certain sources, Ixtlilxóchitl insists that the Mexicas acted under Tepanec auspices and actually states that they (the Mexicas) received their orders from Aculhua of Azcapotzalco, Tezozómoc's predecessor. The Tenayucans were then led by Tenancacaltzin, uncle of Quinatzin, supposedly left in charge when his nephew transferred his capital to Texcoco. The Mexica levies defeated Tenancacaltzin, who fled to

Xaltocan, whose sovereign was also his nephew, though he turned a deaf ear to his uncle's pleas. The Mexicas first sacked Tenayuca and then went to Azcapotzalco to give an account of their success to their overlord, Aculhua. As a result of this victory, Aculhua was able to claim the title of Chichimecatecuhtli, that traditionally pertained to the rulers of Tenayuca since the time of Xolotl.[4]

Sahagún reports that Cuacuapitzahuac of Tlatelolco, not Tenoch, conquered Tenayuca.[5] The Codex Mexicanus mentions a Mexica attack on Tenayuca in 8 Tochtli (1370, Tenochca count); according to the same source, Tezozómoc became ruler of Azcapotzalco in the following year, 9 Acatl. The *Anales de Tlatelolco* confirm this report by stating that in 10 Tecpatl (1372) the Chichimecs of Tenayuca set forth from their city; in the previous year, the Tlaxcalans who lived in Tenayuca had also left.[6]

Ixtlilxóchitl reports that Tezozómoc ruled in Tenayuca before he ascended the throne of Azcapotzalco, and any Mexica incursion against Tenayuca in 1370 or 1371 therefore appears in the light of a support operation for their overlord Tezozómoc, with the aim of quelling rebellious subjects in a city not primarily inhabited by Tepanecs.[7] Tenayuca was, like Culhuacán, a natural candidate for incipient Tepanec military ambitions, since it was a leading center of long standing and lay close to Azcapotzalco.

The two apparently conflicting dates of 2 and 9 Acatl for attacks on the city are easy to reconcile; Jiménez Moreno has already suggested that Ixtlilxóchitl's date of 2 Acatl derives from the Culhua-Texcocan count, in which it is the equivalent of 1371, and thus coincides exactly with 9 Acatl Tenochca, the year given by certain accounts for the accession of Tezozómoc, Acamapichtli, and Cuacuapitzahuac.

The Grand Monarch

The Mexicas participated from the start in the Tepanec bid for aggrandizement, developed by the forceful Tezozómoc. Not surprisingly, Culhuacán and Tenayuca figured at the top of his shopping list; not only were they by then debilitated, but both retained an aura of prestige, as the former "Toltec" and "Chichimec" capitals of the region.

Despite the relatively remote era in which he lived, a wealth of information on Tezozómoc survives, concerning his personal attributes, his military victories, and his political machinations. The sources quote his words and describe his nightmares when faced with the specter of a Texcocan *revanche,* inspired by the intrepid Nezahualcoyotl. Ixtlilxóchitl even offers details of how the grand monarch was cosseted in his old age and placed in the sun for warmth, swathed in garments made of feathers; the pomp and ceremony attending his funeral is minutely described, though the account patently draws on material taken from the burial rites of the Aztec emperors.

Yet, notwithstanding these pen portraits of the tyrant, the temptation lingers to question how far Tezozómoc is a truly historical figure, looming larger than life on the Mesoamerican scene, and to ask whether he is not just another part legendary personage—a kind of latter-day Xolotl. Peruvian ethnohistorians have even expressed doubts over the historicity of Huayna Capac, father of Huascar and Atahualpa, though he died a bare five years before Pizarro arrived and was therefore personally known to many of those whom the conquistadors met. How far can we rely upon records of a Mesoamerican ruler born some two hundred years before the Conquest? Certain of their more colorful details would present no challenge to the imagination of a chronicler versed in Tenochca court ceremonial; however, the more concrete facts and dates of Tezozómoc's reign do tally to a degree that supports the general validity of such Mesoamerican records, whatever their failings when sympathies were overcommitted to a particular cause. In the case of Tezozómoc, this particular factor is less in evidence, since neither the Texcocan nor the Mexica chroniclers laid special claim to the Tepanec dynasty as its ancestor; the Texcocans preferred to descend from the Chichimec Xolotl, and the Mexicas from the Toltec Culhuas.

In this instance, certain historical processes were not so much initiated as accelerated by the action of one man who enjoyed a long reign. The urge to reconstruct the Toltec power persisted, and the Tepanecs were the obvious candidates for a new attempt; but Tezozómoc's own single-minded urge to make himself master of all he surveyed, by fair means or foul, gave added impulse to the dictates of destiny.

The Chinampa Front

As a first step to fulfillment of the will to conquer, Culhuacán, already under attack some years previously, was a prime target for Tezozómoc. The *Anales de Cuauhtitlán* endow the attack with the status of a mercy mission and tell how Ilancueitl—Acamapichtli's alter ego, as spouse or sponsor—was so overcome with pity in the face of the disintegration of Culhuacán that in 2 Calli (1377), he, or she, resolved to confer on the ailing city the blessings of rule by a Mexica nominee, known as Nauhyotzin II (several other Nauhyotzins had reportedly occupied the throne of Culhuacán from the fall of Tollan onwards; however in Appendix A, they are shown to be one and the same ruler. But the Nauhyotzin who became king in 2 Calli must be a different person, even if his dates oddly resemble those of his namesakes). Ixtlilxóchitl, in writing of this Mexica attack on Culhuacán in 2 Calli, adds that Acamapichtli himself seized the Culhua throne—a statement that may arise from a tendency on the part of chroniclers to confuse Acamapichtli of Tenochtitlán with the former Culhua ruler, Huehue Acamapichtli, or Acamapichtli I.[8] Ixtlilxóchitl's statement that many Culhuas fled from the city after the attack may be linked with his previous report of these Culhuas (some of whom were described as Tepanecs and Mexicas), who arrived in Texcoco in the reign of Techotlalatzin. The Codex Mexicanus gives a date of 6 Tochtli for a Mexica conquest of Culhuacán.[9] This date can be related to the more frequently cited 2 Calli, if 6 Tochtli is taken to belong to the year-count that I previously designated as *Anales de Cuauhtitlán* V; 6 Tochtli follows three years (in the same count) after the 3 Acatl given in the *Anales de Cuauhtitlán* for the beginning of the Chalca war, an event that can be dated from other sources, such as Chimalpain, to 1375—that in the Tenochca count would be not 3 Acatl, but 13 Calli.[10]

The conclusion may therefore be drawn that in 1377, or thereabouts, the subjection of Culhuacán was completed by Tezozómoc, who used for the purpose his Mexica auxiliaries; a Tepanec-Mexica nominee mounted the throne of what remained of the city and its inhabitants.

All accounts coincide in placing this final conquest of Culhuacán, together with that of Xochimilco, Cuitlahuac, and Mizquic, in the years following the outbreak of the Chalca war against the Tepanec-Mexicas. In dealing with these and other Tepanec-Mexica conquests, I prefer to postpone mention of the Chalca war itself, and to deal separately with this complex struggle in the following chapter, when the Chalca involvement in the Chinampa region will be more fully considered. At this point it need only be said that the war started, probably in 1375, in Techichco, then described as a dependency of Chalco and situated between Culhuacán and Ixtlapalapa. Mizquic and Cuitlahuac had at some point been occupied by Chalca elements. Therefore the campaign against Culhuacan, followed by the conquest of its Chinampa neighbors, may be viewed in the light of the Chalca war, of which I tend to regard such operations as an initial phase. The Chinampa dependencies, or ex-dependencies, of Chalco were the immediate object of a Tepanec-Mexica offensive once Culhuacán had been subjected.

The following sources attributed to Acamapichtli the conquests of Cuitlahuac, Mizquic, and Xochimilco, together with Cuauhnahuac: Codex Mendoza, *Anales de Cuauhtitlán,* the Letter of Don Pablo Nazareo, and the *Historia de los Mexicanos.* The Codex Azcatitlan attributes the conquests of Mizquic, Cuitlahuac, and Xochimilco to this ruler, but significantly omits Cuauhnahuac. The *Anales de Tlatelolco* list all four cities as conquests, but attributable to Cuacuapitzahuac. Chimalpain mentions a conquest of Xochimilco in 3 Tochtli, while Ixtlilxóchitl writes of the subjection of Mizquic and Cuitlahuac in 1 Tochtli, mainly by the Tlatelolcas.

A certain caution is needed when studying these conquest lists, whose derivation from a single source is at times evident; in particular, the lists of the Codex Mendoza, the Codex Azcatitlan, Don Pablo Nazareo, and the *Anales de Cuauhtitlán* display similarity, and at times identity, while close parallels can be found between Chimalpain and the *Historia de los Mexicanos.*

Supporting evidence for such conquests comes, however, from other sources; moreover, the chronology of the different accounts coincides so well as to increase the probability that facts and dates are correct. For instance, the 3 Tochtli dates of Chimalpain and the *Anales de Tlatelolco* for the conquest of Xochimilco fall implicitly in the same year (1378) as the date of fifty-six years after the foundation of Tenochtitlán, given by the *Historia de los Mexicanos*. The adjusted dates for the subjection of Cuitlahuac coincide even more closely, as I previously demonstrated in a more detailed study of these conquests. The subjugation of Xico can also be fitted into the same pattern.

In all these early but so-called independent Mexica conquests, the Tepanecs themselves inevitably take a hand at some stage in the proceedings. For instance, the *Anales de Cuauhtitlán* state that Tezozómoc himself, not the Mexicas, swooped down on Cuitlahuac in 4 Tecpatl and killed the ruler of Cuitlahuac Ticic, while another señor of Cuitlahuac was slain by his own people.[11] In the following year, Tezozómoc himself installed Tepolotzmaitl as sole ruler of Cuitlahuac, perhaps as a justifiable measure of retrenchment, leaving the city to manage with one monarch rather than with two or four as reported by other sources. In spite of Tepanec incursions, most accounts agree that the Mexicas bore the brunt of the fighting in the Chinampa region; Ixtlilxóchitl even states that the war against Cuitlahuac was the first waged by the Mexicas on behalf of the Tepanecs.

Further Gains

The identity of the Cuauhnahuac that is coupled in so many conquest lists with the Chinampa cities, must remain in doubt. Ixtlilxóchitl does, however, describe a campaign waged by Quinatzin on behalf of Acamapichtli in the valley of Morelos; possibly, therefore, some foray in this direction was made in the reign of Acamapichtli, though on a more limited scale than the subsequent penetration of the area by Huitzilihuitl. The romantic story of the wooing of the daughter of the ruler of Cuauhnahuac by Huitzilihuitl is told in detail in the *Crónica Mexicayotl*—a courtship that ended in hostilities and in a struggle that, according to the same source, lasted for forty years.[12] The conquest of Yecapixtla is reported in the *Anales de Cuauhtitlán* for 6 Acatl; this, if taken to belong to the Tenochca count, is the equivalent of 1407, given by the *Historia de los Mexicanos* for the taking of "Capisela," clearly the same place.[13]

The drive towards the warm lands is a salient feature of the reign of Huitzilihuitl; this is confirmed by Torquemada, who says that in this monarch's reign the Mexicas first began to wear cotton clothes in preference to more rustic garments made of fabrics native to the Valley of Mexico. The *Anales de Tlatelolco* also mention a conquest of the Cohuixcas at this time, in the north of present-day Guerrero, but the attack was launched by the rulers of Culhuacán and not by the Mexicas themselves, who, however, partook of the spoils, and may have been concerned with this expedition, undertaken by people whom they had already conquered.[14] Evidence therefore abounds of Huitzilihuitl's intervention in the valley of Morelos, though the reported conquest by Acamapichtli of Cuauhnahuac may be another case of "backdating," whereby one ruler is credited with the conquests of his successor.

For the reign of Huitzilihuitl, the Codex Mendoza lists the following conquests: Toltitlan, Cuauhtitlán, Chalco, Tulancingo, Xaltocan, Otumpa, Acolma, and Texcoco. Other sources give comparable data. The *Anales de Cuauhtitlán* give: Tollan, Cuauhtitlán, Azcapotzalco, Chalco, Otompan, Acolhuacan (Texcoco?), and Tollantzingo; the letter of Don Pablo Nazareo: Tollan, Chalco, Otumpa, Tollantzinco, Aculman, and Cuauhtitlán; the *Anales de Tlatelolco* (conquests attributed to Tlacateotzin of Tlatelolco): Toltitlan, Cuauhtitlán, Chalco, Acolhuan, Otenpan, Acolhuacan, and Tollantzinco. The *Historia de los Mexicanos* gives rather different information: Cuaximalpan, Capiscla (Yecapixtla?) Cuauximalco, Tezquiaque, Puchitlan, Xaltocan, Tazcuco, and Tepepan. Ixtlilxóchitl mentions the following as conquered by the Tepanecs at this time: Xaltocan, Cuauhtitlán, Tepotzotlán, and Xilotepec. The *Anales de Tlatelolco* give an additional list (of people, not places) for Huitzilihuitl: Mizquicatl, Xochimilcatl, Cuauhnauacatl, Cuitlauacatl, and Tepanouaya.

The first four lists are closely related; the Toltitlan-Cuauhtitlán-Xaltocan region in the north of the Valley of Mexico will be discussed separately below, and the conquest of Texcoco and its neighbors, Acolman and Otumba, belongs to Chapter XI; in this chapter the possibility will also be examined that the Mexicas did participate in some campaign against Azcapotzalco—while in theory still its vassals—as implied by mention in conquest lists of Azcapotzalco, or of Tepanohuayan. But as in the case of Chalco, also included in certain texts, even if a temporary victory was won, no true conquest ensued. The inclusion of Tulancingo is noteworthy; all would-be conquerors of central Mesoamerica, whether Toltecs, Acolhuas, or Tepanecs, seem to have been drawn towards the Tulancingo-Atotonilco area, perhaps as the gateway to the Huaxteca and to the highly prized produce of the coastal regions.

Concerning the version of the *Historia de los Mexicanos:* Cuauh-ximalpan is probably Cuauhximalco, about twenty kilometers to the south of the City of Mexico on the road to Toluca: Capisela may be Yecapixtla: Tezquiaque is Tequizquiac in the north of the Valley of Mexico (see Map 2); Tepepan is Tepechpan, near Acolman: Puchitlan is Huepochtla, that formed part of the territory of Cuauhtitlán. The identity of the Tollan and Xilotepec mentioned in two lists will be discussed below; they were probably both situated, not in the Teotlal-pan, but in the vicinity of Huepochtla in the northern Valley of Mexico.

One place not mentioned in these lists presents a problem: Cuauhtinchan, lying to the southeast of Cholula. The *Historia Tolteca-Chichimeca* says that in 10 Tochtli the Tlatelolcas defeated Cuauhtinchan; the wife of the ruler of that city was then taken to Tlatelolco and married to its ruler, Cuauhtlatoa.[15] The *Anales de Cuauhtitlán* give a parallel version of the defeat of Cuauhtinchan by Cuauhtlatoa, but state that Acamapichtli was then ruler of Te-nochtitlán; in the following year, 11 Acatl, Cuauhtinchan prisoners were sacrificed in Cuauhtitlán by the ruler, Xaltemoctzin; a third source, the *Anales de Tula,* confirms the date of this event.[16] The *Anales de Tlatelolco* give a different year, 3 Tochtli, in which Cuauh-tinchan was conquered and prisoners were sacrificed by Cuacuapit-zahuac; the account mentions that Xochimilco was conquered in that year. The same source gives also 10 Tochtli for the event, the same date as the *Historia Tolteca-Chichimeca,* in another passage.[17]

The mention of Cuauhtlatoa as conqueror and of the date of 3 Tochtli, or 1430 in the Tenochca count, has inspired doubts that a place so remote as Cuauhtinchan, in the Puebla-Tlaxcala valley, was conquered as early as 1398, or 10 Tochtli Tenochca, the usual date given for the occurrence. But 3 Tochtli, if taken to belong to the Culhua Texcocan count, *is* precisely 10 Tochtli in the Tenochca count or 1398. Thus, far from disagreeing, the sources coincide in indicating that 1398 is the correct date; moreover, mention of Xalte-moctzin, ruler of Cuauhtitlán, is significant, since he was later killed

by Tezozómoc, who died in 1426. Regarding the report that Cuauhtlatoa was the conqueror: the *tlatoani* of that name, who succeeded
Tlacateotl in about 1427, was not the first Tlatelolcan prince to be
called Cuauhtlatoa; it is even possible that Cuacuapitzahuac bore
this additional name.[18] According to the *Anales de Tlatelolco,* the
fifth and seventh children of Cuacuapitzahuac, both daughters,
married into the ruling family of Totomihuacan, Cuauhtinchan's
neighbor, surely a good indication of Tlatelolco's interest in that
region as early as the reign of its first *tlatoani.*

That the Mexicas, or even the Tepanecs, should have ranged so
far afield at this stage is, of course, open to question; however Cuauhtinchan is not much farther from Azcapotzalco than Cuauhnahuac and
Tulancingo, also mentioned as conquests. Tlatelolcan merchants,
who later were to cover such vast distances, may have been used by
the Tepanecs as a kind of advance guard in an early attempt to break
out of the Valley of Mexico, not only into the warmer lands of the
valley of Morelos, but also towards the Gulf Coast—bypassing the
Puebla-Tlaxcala valley via Cuauhtinchan to the south and Tulancingo to the north.

But even if Cuauhtinchan itself was temporarily occupied, any
Tepanec designs on the region would have faced opposition from the
rulers of Huexotzingo, who were making their own conquests at the
time, and even penetrating the Valley of Mexico.

In general terms, during the reigns of Acamapichtli and Huitzilihuitl, the Tepanecs, with Mexica support, expanded in all directions: east to Tulancingo and possibly Cuauhtinchan: south beyond
the Chinampa cities into present-day Morelos: north to Tequizquiac,
Huepochtla, and Xaltocan: west as far as Cuajimalpa. However, the
extent of such Tepanec-Mexica conquests is apt to be exaggerated;
long-range ambitions seem to have been focused on the warmer
lands to the south and east that held out prospects of tribute in the
form of gaudy feathers and precious stones for the use of the new
nobility; conquests to the north and east were of modest proportions.
The Aztecs were to learn to their cost that forays in the valley of
Toluca met with stiff resistance, while prospects of gain were not
alluring.

For the short reign of Chimalpopoca, coinciding with Tezozómoc's last years, the *Anales de Cuauhtitlán* name only Tequiz-

quiac, already attributed to Huitzilihuitl, and Chalco, undoubtedly assaulted, but scarcely conquered at this stage. Mention of a conquest of Ahuilizapan (Orizaba, on the road to Veracruz) in 10 Tecpatl is more likely to relate to a later reign, though 10 Tecpatl in the Tenochca count is the equivalent of 1424 and falls in the reign of Chimalpopoca.[19] The same source also mentions Tulancingo as a conquest by Tlacateotl—another example of the reconquest of one center by two or more succeeding *tlatoanis*.

Xaltocan and Cuauhtitlán

The hard-fought war between Azcapotzalco and Texcoco will also be considered separately in Chapter XI. This major conflict was preceded by an important victory by the Tepanec-Mexicas over Xaltocan. That city, together with Tenayuca, had been the principal successor state to Tollan in the northern Valley of Mexico, while Culhuacán still predominated in the south. Probably as Coatlichán came to the fore, the importance of Xaltocan waned, as well as that of Culhuacán, which became a fief of Coatlichán. The first Acolhua Empire, based on Coatlichán and Tenayuca, did not apparently fight or conquer Xaltocan; Tochintecuhtli reportedly married the daughter of its ruler. The royal house of Xaltocan continued to play an important part in local dynastic alliances, and even Huitzilihuitl, ruler of the Mexicas in Chapultepec, is said to have been of Xaltocan descent.

The power of Xaltocan, already on the decline before 1300, was further circumscribed by involvement in an interminable and fruitless struggle with its neighbor, Cuauhtitlán, from 1319 onwards, already mentioned in the previous chapter. This Cuauhtitlán-Xaltocan war forms a backcloth to the whole period stretching from the Mexica expulsion from Chapultepec in 1319 until the fall of Azcapotzalco in 1428. Jiménez Moreno even suggests that the attack on the Mexicas in 1319 may be viewed in the light of this struggle, of which it constitutes a mere incident. The anti-Mexica coalition sought the adherence of Cuauhtitlán but the ruler, Huehue Quinatzin, refused his support; the Mexicas and the people of Cuauhtitlán had always been friends and had journeyed together during those migratory years, spent in Tollan, Atlitlalaquia, Tequizquiac, Apazco,

Citlaltepec, and Tzompango. Cuauhtitlán even comforted the Mexica remnants after their disaster, sent them modest gifts, and freed some prisoners that Xaltocan had taken. Quinatzin married the daughter of the Mexica ruler Huitzilihuitl, called Chimallaxochitl.[20]

The story of Cuauhtitlán's hundred years' war with Xaltocan derives, somewhat naturally, from the *Anales de Cuauhtitlán*: scholars more often direct their gaze towards the light shed by that source on the wider panorama, and pay less attention to those penetrating beams directed towards Cuauhtitlán itself; nonetheless that microcosm, portrayed in its own annals, forms a prototype for situations that might have existed in a broader context, as well as in other individual *señoríos*, of which so much less is known. For the rival city of Xaltocan no such records survive, if we exclude the ambitious territorial claims of Don Pablo Nazareo, framed in his famous letter to Philip II of Spain.

The Xaltocan-Cuauhtitlán war is presented in the *Anales de Cuauhtitlán* as a sequel to the Mexica expulsion from Chapultepec; the reverse is more likely, and the expulsion may be viewed as an early episode in that struggle. Presumably the anti-Mexica coalition was short-lived, since it is hard to see how Cuauhtitlán, any more than the Mexicas, could have long resisted such an all-embracing alliance, if it ever existed.

In 2 Acatl, while the war was still in its early stages, Huehue Quinatzin (not to be confused with Quinatzin of Texcoco) died and was succeeded by his son Tezcatecuhtli; like the dynasties of Culhuacán, studied in Chapter II and in Appendix A, the king-list of Cuauhtitlán is full of puzzles, though from the time of Quinatzin onwards its rulers have every appearance of being historic personages.

The doubts surrounding earlier rulers recall those that arise in the case of Culhuacán. Legend relates that the first ruler of Cuauhtitlán, Huactli, was appointed by the goddess Itzpapalotl to the accompaniment of typical Chichimec rites, with the shooting of arrows towards the four cardinal points; the date was 1 Tecpatl, that classic favorite as the inaugural year for Mesoamerican dynasties.[21]

But as in other king-lists, an element of repetition is present: another Huactzin succeeded the Tezcatecuhtli mentioned above, and both these Huactzins reigned for sixty-two years. By coupling several rulers' reigns, as in Culhuacán, "ritual" reigns can be identified,

231

running from approximately 7 Acatl to 7 Acatl, (the legendary figure repeated many times over by Ixtlilxóchitl for different rulers of Tollan). For instance, the third king of Cuauhtitlán, Ayauhcoyotzin, ascends the throne in 8 Tecpatl (7 Acatl plus 1), and the fifth, Mecellotzin, dies in 9 Calli (7 Acatl plus 2); thus in effect three notional reigns complete the magic 7 Acatl to 7 Acatl cycle. Mecellotzin and his two successors reign until 11 Acatl (7 Acatl plus 4) thus almost completing another cycle. Tezcatecuhtli and his successor, the second Huactzin, together rule from 1 Tochtli to 13 Calli, and their reigns therefore form a further fifty-two year cycle, though not based on 7 Acatl.

Therefore, as in the case of Culhuacán, ritual dates for early rulers tend to be confused with real ones for their descendants. In addition, rather odd coincidences emerge between the dates of the señores of Cuauhtitlán and of Culhuacán, as also given by the *Anales de Cuauhtitlán,* and by other sources. Out of eighteen rulers of Cuauhtitlán listed before Xaltemoctzin (who was roughly contemporary with Tezozómoc), eight rulers' reigns almost exactly coincide with those given for Culhua rulers:

Cuauhtitlán	*Culhuacán*
Huactli I — 1 Tecpatl to 10 Calli	Acamapichtli I — 1 Tecpatl to 13 Tecpatl (10 Calli plus 3)
Nequamexochtzin — 11 Acatl to 12 Calli	Nauhyotzin — 10 Tochtli (11 Acatl minus 1) to 12 Calli
Mecellotzin — 13 Tochtli to 9 Calli	Matlacxochitl — 1 Acatl (13 Tochtli plus 1) to 10 Tochtli (9 Calli plus 1)
Iztacxillotzin — 13 Tecpatl to 11 Acatl	Achitometl II — 13 Tecpatl to 11 Acatl
Eztlaquencatzin — 11 Acatl to 2 Acatl	Xiuhquentzin — 11 Acatl to 2 Acatl
Huactzin II — 3 Acatl to 13 Calli	Chalchiuhtlatonac — 3 Acatl to 13 Calli
Ehuatlycuetzin — 6 Tecpatl to 10 Tecpatl	Yohualtlatonac — 3 Calli (6 Tecpatl minus 3) to 10 Tecpatl
Tlacateotzin — 4 Acatl to 1 Calli	Achitometl — 4 Acatl to 5 Calli (1 Calli plus 4)

Five of these eighteen Cuauhtitlán rulers thus have dates identical with Culhua or Toltec monarchs (a single year's difference is without significance and often arises simply from the way of counting the length of a reign, inclusive or exclusive; in addition, in some sources each monarch's reign begins in the year that his predecessor dies, while in others he ascends in the following year). Moreover, three further rulers have dates that are very close to those of Culhuacán. This constitutes a very strange coincidence, to say the least. Of equal interest is the apparent changeover from the Culhua-Texcocan to the Tenochca count—to be explained below— also identifiable in Toltitlan.

Assuming, as in the case of Culhuacán, that the earlier dates belong to the Culhua Texcocan count, the reigns of the Cuauhtitlán rulers from Huehue Quinatzin onwards may be given as follows:

Huehue Quinatzin	8 Acatl to 2 Acatl
Tezcatecuhtli	2 Acatl to 2 Tochtli
Huactzin	3 Acatl to 13 Calli
Iztactotol	13 Calli to 5 Acatl
Ehuatlycuetzin	6 Tecpatl to 10 Tecpatl
Temetzacocuitzin	11 Calli to 3 Tochtli
Tlacateotzin	4 Acatl to 1 Calli
Xaltemoctzin	2 Tochtli to 7 Tecpatl

This is a plausible king-list, and traces the Cuauhtitlán dynasty back to within a century of the fall of Tollan; the previous ten rulers, starting with the first Huactli, seem in some form or other to be little more than an alternate version of the second eight.

A Pyrrhic Victory

As in the early stages of the Mexica-Chalca conflict, the war between Cuauhtitlán and Xaltocan was initially fought on a limited scale during the reigns of Quinatzin and Tezcatecuhtli. The tempo of hostilities rose under Huactzin. However, after a spectacular Cuauhtitlán victory—according to our Cuauhtitlán inspired account—the conflict ground to a halt at Acpaxapocan, a place that belonged to Xaltocan. After this intensified struggle, followed by stalemate, no further fighting is mentioned until 7 Acatl (probably 1395), after Xaltemoctzin, portrayed as a ruler of some consequence, had ascended the throne of Cuauhtitlán. He was at first unable to win the war with Xaltocan, basically perhaps the more powerful city of the two. Only in 1395 were the tables turned, when Xaltocan collapsed;

233

after long withstanding the unaided assaults of Cuauhtitlán, it succumbed to a Tepanec-Mexica offensive, mounted on behalf of Xaltemoctzin, who had previously helped the Mexicas by attacking Chalco and taking prisoners. The Xaltocans were routed in Teconman, the modern Santa Cruz Tecama in the municipality of Tecama de Felipe Villanueva. Many Xaltocans took refuge with their kinsmen in Metztitlan, while others went to Tlaxcala, also partly populated by fellow Otomís. The Tepanec intervention may have followed some Cuauhtitlán defeat, since the *Anales de Cuauhtitlán* state that the Xaltocans took away captives from Cuauhtitlán to Metztitlan and Tlaxcala.

Ixtlilxóchitl also writes of the defeat of Xaltocan, and states that the war had begun in 5 Tecpatl, when Tezozómoc and his Mexica allies attacked Xaltocan; the chronicler rather confuses the issue by asserting that the Tepanecs simultaneously fought against Cuauhtitlán and Tepotzotlán—whose dynasty, according to the *Anales de Cuauhtitlán,* was closely related to that of Cuauhtitlán.[22] Techotlalatzin of Texcoco gave land in Otumba to some of the Xaltocan refugees. According to Veytia, the Tlatelolcans and Tenochcas received part of the territory of the defeated enemy, and Clavijero says that the war contributed greatly to the enhancement of the Mexicas' status.[23] We are not told if Cuauhtitlán itself received any spoils, though its bounds seem to have been provisionally extended; in 7 Acatl, Xaltemoctzin set his frontier posts in Tzompanco, Citlaltepec, Huehuetocan, and Otlazpan, places forming an arc some ten miles northeast of Cuauhtitlán itself.

At all events, any triumph shared by Cuauhtitlán was shortlived; Azcapotzalco was a dangerous ally, and in due course the city fell victim to Tepanec ambitions. In 7 Tecpatl, at the invitation of the Tepanec ruler, Xaltemoctzin visited Azcapotzalco, accompanied by a numerous retinue; expecting to be regaled with banquets, he was unceremoniously hanged by the neck. Thereafter, reportedly no king reigned for nine years, until Tecocomatzin of Tlatelolco usurped the throne in 4 Tochtli.

For Cuauhtitlán, the elimination of Xaltocan was a Pyrrhic victory since it merely led to the replacement of one foe by another, Toltitlan, a Tepanec foundation that now became Cuauhtitlán's arch-enemy; its ruler at that time was Epcoatl, son of Tezozómoc.

The *Anales Tepanecas* and the *Crónica Mexicayotl* report that this Epcoatl, son of Tezozómoc, was ruler of Atlacuihuayan (Tacubaya) while Ixtlilxóchitl names him as the first ruler of the Tlatelolcas; but another Epcoatl, according to the *Anales de Tlatelolco,* was son of Cuacuapitzahuac of Tlatelolco or, alternatively, son of Cuacua-pitzahuac's successor, Tlacoteotl. Following the demise of Xalte-moctzin, Tezozómoc was resolved to install his son on the throne of Cuauhtitlán, but its resistance to the would-be usurper was implacable. Epcoatl continued to reign in Toltitlan, and his death coincided with the downfall of Azcapotzalco; after this, an interregnum also reportedly occurred in Toltitlan, where no sovereign ruled for twenty years, after which Ocellotlapan became king, followed by Acolmiztli, who reigned only forty days, and was then succeeded by Citlalcoatl, who was still reigning at the time of the Spanish Conquest. These names alone survive of an obviously truncated list of the later rulers of Toltitlan.

A Chronological Milestone

Chronology of the final chapter in the story of the native dynasty of Cuauhtitlán, before its destruction by the Tepanecs, is uncertain but significant. Again, as in the case of Culhuacán, the chroniclers report a gap, or interregnum, in the king-list; again, the gap occurs in 7 Tecpatl, just as in Culhuacán, where the interregnum begins in 10 Acatl (three years after 7 Tecpatl), or alternatively in 7 Tecpatl itself. By an equally odd coincidence, in precisely the same year, 7 Tecpatl, an apparent interregnum of twenty years emerges in yet a third king-list, that of Toltitlan (see Appendix A).

The 7 Acatl date of the defeat of Xaltocan has been taken to belong to the Tenochca count and to be the equivalent of 1395; in the Culhua-Texcocan count 7 Acatl would be 1415. But 1395—or two decades before the Tepanec war against Texcoco—is a more likely date for Tezozómoc's assault on Xaltocan; moreover, the event, in which the Mexicas participated, would more probably be given in the Tenochca count. However, I have little doubt that while the Xaltocan war is dated according to the Tenochca count, the Cuauhtitlán king-list, as well as the lists of Culhuacán and Chalco, continued to correspond to the Culhua-Texcoco count, at least until

235

the overthrow of Azcapotzalco; therefore, the killing of Xaltemoctzin is more likely to have occurred, not in 1408 (7 Tecpatl Tenochca), but in 1428 (7 Tecpatl Culhua-Texcoco).

Admittedly the *Anales de Cuauhtitlán* say that he was killed by Tezozómoc, not Maxtla; however, when sources of this nature list events year by year, they evidently amplify the bare facts with some background information, such as the name of the señor who was presumed to be reigning at a given moment; for instance, Chimalpain credits Tezozómoc with the Mexicas' expulsion from Chapultepec, though he gives a date of 1199 for the event, or nearly two centuries before Tezozómoc's accession. In the case of the killing of Xaltemoctzin, the chronicler, thinking only in terms of the Tenochca count, was in no doubt that this occurred in 1408, and merely by way of comment attributed the deed to Tezozómoc, who then ruled in Azcapotzalco. But the elimination of Xaltemoctzin in 1408 is recounted as an isolated occurrence, and if it really happened in that year, lacks any apparent motive; Cuauhtitlán had proved to be a staunch ally of the Tepanec-Mexicas, and few reasons appear to have existed for killing him then. The *Anales de Cuauhtitlán* portray Xaltemoctzin as an important ruler who enlarged the temple of his city, extended its territory, and enjoyed a fairly long reign before his untimely end.

The same source describes in greater detail the subsequent quarrel of Cuauhtitlán and Azcapotzalco in 3 Tochtli (the Tenochca equivalent of 1430). In point of fact, the correct date for this occurrence is probably two years earlier, in 1 Tecpatl, just prior to the Mexica-Tepanec war; as amply demonstrated in Appendix A, such lesser discrepancies are universal in Mesoamerican chronology. On this occasion, Maxtla is named as Tepanec ruler, and Epcoatl is mentioned as his contemporary. The war against Cuauhtitlán probably came a few months before the final struggle between Azcapotzalco and the Mexica coalition; it was hard fought and may have sapped the strength of Azcapotzalco. The Tepanecs enlisted the aid of Cuauhtitlán's neighbors, not only Tepanec Toltitlan, but Tepotzotlán, Cuauhuacán, Cilaltepec, and Tzompango. A Tezozomoctli of Tlatelolco is mentioned as ruler of Cuauhtitlán, but he is a rather shadowy figure, and possibly reigned, if at all, for less than a year. This Tezozomoctli committed suicide when Cuauhtitlán was crushed, after taking refuge in Huehuetoca, which had remained loyal to his cause. The Tepanecs burned the temple of Cuauhtitlán, and took many prisoners. Maguey cactus was planted in the ceremonial center, and the important slave market was transferred to Azcapotzalco.

It is much more likely that Azcapotzalco defeated Cuauhtitlán once, not twice, and that this victory occurred not in 1408, but in 1428 or thereabouts, when war with Cuauhtitlán's allies, the Mexicas, was imminent. The deaths of Xaltemoctzin and of Tezozomoctli seem to have become confused with each other, and the Tepanec assault may have been a preventative war, designed to crush in advance such a firm friend of the Mexicas. The *Anales de Cuauhtitlán* state that the city paid tribute on only two occasions to Azcapotzalco; but if the Tepanec ruler had really killed Xaltemoctzin as early as 1408, he would certainly have imposed tribute on its citizens thereafter, and they would then have paid this for twenty, not two, years. Furthermore, the source describes the Tepanec-Cuauhtitlán war as a direct result of the fury of its people at the killing of their king, Xaltemoctzin; their reaction was clearly immediate, and they could scarcely have nursed a silent grudge from 1408 to 1428.

Thus the death of Xaltemoctzin, attributed to 7 Tecpatl, surely belongs to the Culhua-Texcoco count, in which it is the equivalent of 1428, not 1408; following the uncertain and short reign by the Tlatelolcan Tezozomoctli, the next ruler, Tecocohuatzin, was installed in 3 Tochtli, which is 1430 in the *Tenochca* count; the dates of his reign, and those of his successors, certainly belong to that calendar. Thus, once more, as in the case of Culhuacán and of Toltitlan, instead of a most improbable interregnum of nearly twenty years, again beginning in 7 Tecpatl with the death of Xaltemoctzin, we are surely faced with an identifiable changeover from the Culhua-Texcoco calendar to the Tenochca—perhaps a minor milestone in Mesoamerican calendrics; the death of Xaltemoctzin is given as 7 Tecpatl, in the Culhua count, and is therefore 1428, while the accession of Tecocohuatzin in 3 Tochtli belongs to the Tenochca count, and is the equivalent of 1430.

More Ex-Chichimecs

The *Anales de Cuauhtitlán,* describing events, provide some interesting information on the people of Cuauhtitlán. Once again, the historian is confronted with an impeccably Chichimec background. Not only was the first ruler, Huactzin, a typical Chichimec hero, but so intense was the pride taken by the inhabitants of that city in their Chichimec blood that they taunted their Xaltocan enemies as being Nonoalcas and Cozcatecas (i.e. Olmeca-Xicallancas), and therefore typical non-Chichimecs, as if that were the worst insult that they could offer.

The source is vague about the deities originally worshiped in the city, and tells of a water god called Acpixapo, a peculiar figure with a body like a great serpent but with a woman's face, coiffure, and fragrance. This strange creature would seem to embody the notion of Cihuacoatl, or woman snake, a form of the mother goddess and later a kind of grand vizier to the *tlatoani* of Tenochtitlán; Acpixapo, like Huitzilopochtli, is more easily identifiable with the Chinampa region of Culhuacán than with the arid Chichimec homeland.

The people of Cuauhtitlán, like the Mexicas themselves and the Chalcas, became rather unaccountably involved in the Chinampa region of Culhuacán. The *Anales de Cuauhtitlán* speak repeatedly of a Cuauhtitlán presence in Techichco, and state that Eztloquencatzin, who occupied the throne some time before Huehue Quinatzin, possessed his house of straw in Techichco, and even began to construct a palace there. Huehue Quinatzin is actually stated to have been enthroned in that place in 8 Acatl, where he also had his palace.

The source's information is rather ambiguous; on the one hand it associates Techichco in an earlier passage with Tehuiloyocan, apparently situated in the vicinity of Cuauhtitlán itself. But, when referring to the Mexica-Chalca war, Techichco is stated to belong to Chalco, at a time when the Chalcas also claimed Culhuacán, and is additionally named as Techichco Culhuacán.

Techichco is identified by Trautmann as situated near to Ixtapalapa.[24] Probably it lay on the border between Chalca and Culhua territory, and it seems unlikely that the *Anales de Cuauhtitlán* were referring to two distinct Techichcos in separate contexts.

The whole story, therefore, points to an involvement of Cuauhtitlán in the Culhuacán region and, more significantly, to a participation in the Mexica-Chalca war, said to have begun in Techichco.
If the Mexicas were able to campaign in the Chinampa region, no
reason exists for denying the same privilege to their Cuauhtitlán
friends, and yet another example arises of some kind of interrelation
between people who called themselves Chichimecs and others who
called themselves Toltecs, each of whom had something to contribute to the other; both terms are relative, since the people of Cuauhtitlán were well on their way to becoming Toltecized, just as the
Culhuas were already part-Chichimecized!

The existence of some indefinable link between Culhuacán and
Cuauhtitlán is confirmed by the decision of some Culhuas to take
refuge in Cuauhtitlán when their city was devastated by the Tepanec-
Mexicas. They probably arrived at the beginning of the reigns of
Tezozómoc and Acamapichtli in 1370. They built their own temple
in Cuauhtitlán and installed their various gods and goddesses, including Toci and Xochiquetzal; according to their *Anales,* the poor
Chichimecs of Cuauhtitlán previously had no proper temples and
confined themselves to primitive ceremonies, formerly taught to
them by the Chichimec patron goddess, Itzpapalotl. The Culhuas
instructed the people of Cuauhtitlán in the gentle art of human
sacrifice and other Mesoamerican religious practices, and they came
to love and respect these Culhua mentors, giving them lands to
cultivate and the hands of their daughters in marriage. For the first
time in Cuauhtitlán men were sacrificed who had been captured in
the Xaltocan war. On the other hand, the Culhuas reportedly also
taught the building of houses and the making of pottery.

It becomes unnecessary to insist on the allegorical nature of this
account. Long previous to this event, a ruler of Cuauhtitlán had
already wedded a daughter of Coxcox of Culhuacán, and this marriage
would have sufficed to transform the city into a Mesoamerican community, if it was not already so. Moreover, the rulers Huactzin and
Iztactototl are described as priests of Mixcoatl, to whom they erected
a straw temple or oratory; Mixcoatl, like Itzpapalotl, is in part a
Chichimec god but at the same time remains a typical Mesoamerican
deity, as well as the father of the human Topiltzin Quetzalcoatl. The
continuance of a primitive Chichimec way of life until the advent of

the Culhuas is as inconceivable in Cuauhtitlán as formerly in Tena-yuca. By this time the people of Cuauhtitlán, like many others, were more ex-Chichimec than Chichimec.

The story, however, illustrates two points: first, it portrays the intense loyalty of such ex-Chichimecs to Chichimec traditions; thus the fiction endured that people of a given polity had in theory con-tinued to live like Chichimecs long after they had in practice become Mesoamericanized; second, it offers a good example of the mechanics of the civilizing process in Postclassic Mesoamerica. While Cuauh-titlán was already part Mesoamericanized, the Culhua immigrants, as in Texcoco, provided a new cultural impetus, and their presence served to complete the education of their hosts. Unfortunately, in this instance the intellectual leavening was of little avail, since Cuauhtitlán was soon to suffer a fate scarcely better than Culhuacán itself when its ceremonial center was razed to the ground by the Tepanecs and replanted with maguey. Before the arrival of the Culhuas, Cuauhtitlán was probably a fairly typical Valley of Mexico community of the period, with an ethnic blend of Otonchichimecs and Teochichimec migrants, combined with local survivors from Toltec times, probably dedicated to chinampa-type agriculture and possessing a chinampa deity. Acpixapo was seemingly a water god— perhaps inherited from the local people—and the Cuauhtitlán ruler, Xaltemoctzin, also used the traditional title of Atecpanecatl ("Lord of the water Palace"), since Cuauhtitlán was situated on the edge of the lagoon.

The Tepanec Empire

I have said more about Cuauhtitlán than about Xaltocan in con-nection with the Tepanec overthrow of the two cities, though probably the conquest of Xaltocan was the more important since for the Mexicas it constituted a milestone on the road to power. Less is known of the situation in Xaltocan at this time, though it was cer-tainly a major principality and one of the leading cities of the Valley of Mexico before the rise of Azcapotzalco.

Estimates of the extent of Xaltocan's territory absorbed by the Tepanec Empire have been inflated by the famous letter of Don Pablo Nazareo, claiming land as far distant as Ojitipan. Chimalpain, who may have known the existence of Don Pablo's letter, lends force to this notion by describing Xaltocan as possessing a dry and extensive land.[25]

The true boundaries of the Tepanec domain are hard to assess, and basically two schools of thought exist; on the one hand those who, like Carrasco, favor a relatively large empire, and on the other hand Trautmann, who opts for a smaller one. Carrasco provides his own map of the Tepanec Empire.[26] He includes extensive territories to the north, based on Don Pablo's letter, in which were listed the ancient lands of Xaltocan, to which he himself laid claim. To the west of Azcapotzalco, Carrasco's map embraces the province of Xilotepec, including Tollan Xicocotitlan, and also the valley of Toluca. Putative Tepanec occupation of this valley is based on the *Memorial de los Pueblos sujetos a Tlacopan,* that lists the tributaries of Tlacopan in the final pre-Hispanic period. To the northeast, this Tepanec Empire includes Atotonilco and the Mezquital valley; in the south it extends as far as Tlaxco Guerrero (the modern Taxco), of which Torquemada said that Maxtla was ruler, and Cohuixco, mentioned by Barlow as conquered by Cuauhnahuac, allied to the Mexicas.[27] Jiménez Moreno, who also writes of a fairly extensive Tepanec domain, tends in this respect to support Carrasco.[28]

Trautmann, however, rejects such extensive frontiers for Tepanec rule. He sets out his reasons succinctly, indicating that the *Memorial de los Pueblos* is fundamental to Carrasco's reasoning, and insisting that this document delineates the western frontier of Aztec, not Tepanec, territory. Equally basic to Carrasco's interpretation is Don Pablo's letter, in which he names the dependencies of the Otomí kingdom of Xaltocan.

Trautmann explains how Xilotepec, claimed for the Tepanecs, is probably a misreading for Xilotzingo, situated in the northern Valley of Mexico; he adds that mentions of Matlatzinca conquests by the Tepanec-Mexicas offer little concrete information. Equally, any inclusion of Cuaochpa (Michoacán) and of Huexotzingo should not be taken at its face value; on the contrary, Huexotzingo is named by several other documents as an independent *señorío.* Trautmann equally doubts that Tlachco and Cohuixco in Guerrero belonged to the Tepanecs.[29] He summarizes his views by stating that only in the northeast and south did the territory of Azcapotzalco stretch beyond the Valley of Mexico. Provinces that Trautmann assigns with more assurance to the Tepanecs are, in the north, Xaltocan, Cuauhtitlán, and Tulancingo: in the south, Cuauhnahuac: in the west, Quahuacán: in the east the provinces of Otumba, Chalco, and Texcoco.

With Trautmann's main conclusions I am in basic accord, though I regard Chalco as a somewhat unrealistic claim, comparable only to the inclusion of Azcapotzalco itself in the conquest list of Huitzilihuitl. The *Memorial de los Pueblos* is a colonial document, and Trautmann is right in stressing that territory assigned, perhaps for mere administrative convenience, to Tlacopan, junior partner of the Triple Alliance, cannot be automatically included in the former Tepanec Empire. Admittedly Ixtlilxóchitl might be cited in support of such an assertion when he states that Itzcoatl and Nezahualcoyotl endowed the señor of Tlacopan with the kingdom of the Tepanecs; but Ixtlilxóchitl makes it quite clear that he had in mind Cuauhtitlán and Tepotzotlán, as well as the Chinampa cities, rather than Tepanec territories in a more general sense.[30]

The same principle applies to Don Pablo Nazareo's imposing claims; these pretensions bear some relation to certain Aztec tributary provinces in the Codex Mendoza, with whose basic content he was perhaps familiar. Also included in Don Pablo's list is Mazahuacan, and pueblos of Ixtlahuacan and Atlacomulco. This inclusion may have inspired the suggestion that the Mazahuas and Xaltocans were related, since this Mazahua region is not contiguous with the rest of the territory claimed for Xaltocan by Don Pablo.

Yet another document relating to later times deserves mention: Kirchhoff suspected that the cities listed by the Codex García Granados in connection with Tlatelolco might have some bearing on the extent of the former Tepanec Empire. Many centers illustrated in this codex and situated to the north of Azcapotzalco correspond with those given by Don Pablo; in addition, the Codex García Granados lists a number of pueblos in the southern Valley of Mexico and in the valley of Toluca that were not claimed by Don Pablo.

I find it hard to accept any such latter-day claims, related to the Aztec Empire, as a reliable guide to the bounds of the Tepanec domain, and some of the more inflated ones do not stand up to closer examination. For instance, in the west, Tula, or Tollan, is probably not Tula de Allende in Hidalgo but the Tula that is listed as an *estancia* of Temascalpa.[31] Xilotepec surely is not the equivalent of Jilotepec de Abasolo near Tula de Allende, but of Jilocingo in the municipio of Hueypoxtla; such identifications are in conformity with Ixtlilxóchitl's grouping in a single context of the four places, Temascalapan, Tula, Xilotepec, and Citlaltepec.[32] In another passage he mentions Xilotepec in close conjunction with Citlaltepec, Tepotzotlan and Cuauhtitlán as places occupied by the Tepanecs. Such statements could hardly refer to Xilotepec de Abasolo and to Tula de Allende, geographically too far removed to fit into the same picture as the other places. On the other hand, Temascalapa and Huepoxtla are situated near to Tequizquiac, repeatedly named as a Tepanec-Mexica conquest.

I therefore concur with Trautmann in conceding more restricted boundaries for Xaltocan lands taken by the Tepanecs; while more credit is usually given to Don Pablo's more flamboyant claims, the Xaltocan frontier posts listed by the *Anales de Cuauhtitlán* are often overlooked; this list includes the following places, identified by Trautmann (see Map 2): Tepemaxalco, Ecatepec, Tecama, Tonanitla, Zumpango, and Xaltenco.[33] As may be seen, they offer a more modest but perhaps realistic frontier for that sector of the Xaltocan (and Tepanec) border. In addition, to the north of Azcapotzalco, Toltitlan was a Tepanec city and in the *Anales de Cuauhtitlán* Quahuacan is associated with Cuauhtitlán, conquered by the Tepanecs; the same source mentions Otlazpan, Huepoxtla, and Citlaltepec as occupied by Cuauhtitlán in its war against Xaltocan.

Concerning the southern limits of Tepanec expansion, I concur that the Tepanec-Mexicas penetrated into Morelos, occupying Cuauhnahuac and Yecapixtla, and that they also made conquests as far west as Ocuilan, that traditional dependency of Culhuacán. However, Tepanec occupation of the northwest part of the state of Guerrero seems much less likely. The mention by the *Relación de Iguala* of certain areas of Cohuixco where Matlatzinca was spoken has been cited as evidence of Tepanec penetration, on the unproved assumption that the Tepanecs were Matlatzincas or that they had occupied other Matlatzinca territory.[34] The Tlachco assigned by Torquemada to Maxtla's realm, and to which he reportedly fled, has been identified as the modern Taxco, Guerrero. But the *Anales de Cuauhtitlán* mention a Tlachco where Chichimec refugees from Cuauhtitlán were settled which apparently lay much nearer to Cuauhtitlán itself.

Chimalpain gives a much simpler explanation of Maxtla's flight to Tlachco in 4 Acatl (1431); according to his third *Relación,* Maxtla was greatly upset as a result of what had occurred in "Tlachco"— in this instance not a distant pueblo but simply, in its literal sense, the site of an important ball court. Maxtla went to this Tlachco, i.e., the ball court, in the middle of the night, accompanied by his sorcerers; there he was the loser in a ceremonial ball game, and thereupon died there: "Auh yn Maxtlaton, yuh quitohua yn huehuetque, ompa miquito yn Tlachco, ynic aoccan nez y ma nel ypilhuan yxhuihuan ypampa ca yehuatl concahuilli yn altepetl yn tepanecayotl" ("As for Maxtlaton, according to the old people, he died there in Tlachco, and neither he nor his children and grandchildren were anywhere to be seen, because he left the city and the Tepanec nation").

That this bare statement should have given rise to a report that Maxtla was king of the modern Taxco, and that he fled to this Guerrero domain when defeated in Azcapotzalco, illustrates with what ease the facts of Mesoamerican history can be leavened with misleading embellishments. Suggestion of Tepanec control over parts of Michoacán are no less acceptable. Alva Ixtlilxóchitl reports that Tezozómoc received help from the people of Michoacán in his war against Huehue Ixtlilxóchitl of Texcoco.[35] Carrasco in addition points out that the *Anales Tepanecas* mention Cuaochpan as a tributary of Azcapotzalco and that Cuaochpame is another name for Tarascans or Michoaques. But this claim is surely inspired by a certain patriotic fervor on the part of the Tepanec sources, and is more to be compared with assertions that Huexotzingo, itself an empire builder at the time, belonged to the Tepanecs.

On the other hand, it may be easier to accept that the Tlatelolcans, under Tepanec auspices, launched some kind of expedition against Cuauhtinchan, to the southeast of Huexotzingo. Tulancingo was also probably occupied, at least temporarily, since it is included in various conquest lists; Ixtlilxóchitl mentions Atotonilco, another pueblo of that region.

Accordingly, in my view, the Tepanec Empire embraced the approximate area covered by Map 2, with the exception of the Tollan-Xilotepec region in the northwest corner; it thus roughly coincides with the Mexica conquest lists for that period. In addition, the Empire included Tulancingo, lying to the northeast of the area shown on the map, and possibly Cuauhtinchan, at some distance to the southeast of the Great Volcanoes. In effect, therefore, a record of Tepanec conquests survives, but they are credited to the Mexicas, who were mere participants.

Even this more restricted domain represents a maximum rather than a minimum extension of Tepanec territory. The inclusion of Tulancingo is questionable, since Alva Ixtlilxóchitl states that this city helped Huehue Ixtlilxóchitl against Tezozómoc, though it might have been absorbed by the Tepanecs after the Texcocan defeat. Tezozómoc fought his war against Texcoco with forces including only Tepanecs and Mexicas, reinforced by levies from the Chinampa cities; the same account, however, makes it clear that the Citlaltepec-Zumpango region was Tepanec territory. It is difficult to say for certain that the Tepanecs conquered more than the territory of Xaltocan to the north, Culhuacán and the Chinampa cities to the south, and Acolhuacan to the east, together with the possible addition of a slice of Morelos.

In the process of Mesoamerican empire building, an intermediate category of places may exist that are neither subject nor free at any given moment; they may have been the object of initial attacks by their would-be assailant without having been fully subjugated; the same names thus recur with unfailing regularity in the conquest lists of successive Aztec Tlatoanis. For the Tepanecs, Cuauhtinchan may have been a case in point; a penetration may have occurred in that direction, but without any outright conquest or the imposition of annual tribute. In certain instances, the possibility even exists that some form of tribute was paid from time to time to a potential conqueror in Mesoamerica, as a kind of Danegeld—that is to say, not as a formal acknowledgment of political suzerainty, but, on the contrary, as the price of remaining autonomous and as a bribe to the intended overlord to persuade him to stay away.

At all events, Tepanec ambitions, whether or not they were fully realized, follow the pattern of the conquests of Tollan and of the first Acolhua Empire of Tochintecuhtli-Huetzin, of which Tezozómoc is in a sense the heir. He was himself directly descended from Tochintecuhtli, whose daughter had married Aculhua, founder of

MAP 2

TEPANEC—MEXICA CONQUESTS

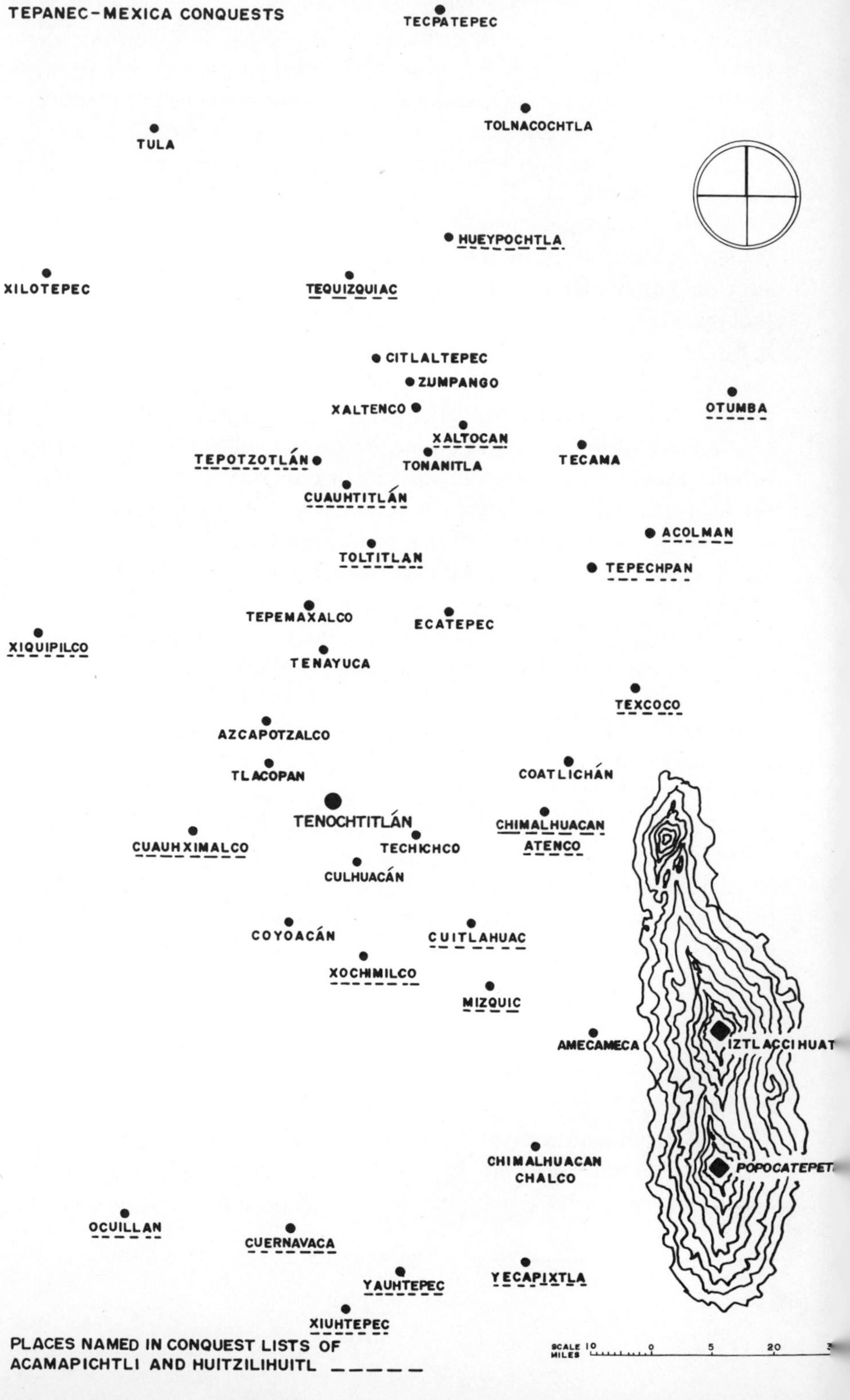

TECPATEPEC

TOLNACOCHTLA

TULA

HUEYPOCHTLA

XILOTEPEC

TEQUIZQUIAC

CITLALTEPEC

ZUMPANGO

XALTENCO

OTUMBA

XALTOCAN

TEPOTZOTLÁN

TONANITLA

TECAMA

CUAUHTITLÁN

ACOLMAN

TOLTITLAN

TEPECHPAN

TEPEMAXALCO

ECATEPEC

XIQUIPILCO

TENAYUCA

TEXCOCO

AZCAPOTZALCO

TLACOPAN

COATLICHÁN

TENOCHTITLÁN

CHIMALHUACAN

CUAUHXIMALCO

TECHICHCO

ATENCO

CULHUACÁN

COYOACÁN

CUITLAHUAC

XOCHIMILCO

MIZQUIC

AMECAMECA

IZTLACCIHUAT

CHIMALHUACAN

CHALCO

POPOCATEPET

OCUILLAN

CUERNAVACA

YAUHTEPEC

YECAPIXTLA

XIUHTEPEC

PLACES NAMED IN CONQUEST LISTS OF
ACAMAPICHTLI AND HUITZILIHUITL _ _ _ _ _

SCALE 10   0   5   20   3
MILES

the Azcapotzalco dynasty; like Tochintecuhtli, he killed a number of lesser señores; like Nopaltzin, he slew a ruler of Culhuacán called Nauhyotl; moreover, he first reigned in Tochintecuhtli's ancient capital of Tenayuca.

Because Tezozómoc's deeds are better documented, he looms larger than Tochintecuhtli and Huetzin as successor to the rulers of Tollan and as predecessor to those of Tenochtitlán. He serves as a prototype for Moctezuma I and Ahuitzotl; evidence suggests that, like the Aztec Tlatoanis, he was motivated more by the will to conquer and the quest for tribute than by thoughts of religious proselytization. Aztec conquests are sometimes presented in the peculiar guise of a crusade to implant the worship of Huitzilopochtli, but the same can hardly be said of the Tepanecs, whose deity seems to have been Tezcatlipoca, who was equally revered by the main adversaries of the Tepanec-Mexicas, the Chalcans, and by their principal victims, the Texcocans.

By a study of the relevant year-counts, Tezozómoc can be logically stripped of an absurd longevity, and thereby portrayed as a figure of history rather than of legend. The true impact of this titanic figure upon the Lilliputian city-state world of his time remains uncertain. The historian may infer that by the fourteenth century centrifugal forces were already on the wane; perhaps some new attempt to reunify the broken fragments of Tollan's empire was now due in any case. Tezozómoc's predatory genius gave added impetus to the process.

X. The Third Claimant

The Early Chalco

In writing of some of the more sweeping triumphs of the Tepanec-Mexicas, I have said little of the war against Chalco, which was no easy victory but a bitter struggle, lasting for a century. Chalco was no ordinary rival; not unlike other centers in the Valley of Mexico in the post-Tollan era, the Chalco region came to absorb a whole series of migrant elements, that were molded into a confederacy of thirteen *tecpans* or principalities. This formidable grouping successfully defied the Tepanec-Mexica bid for supremacy; the Chalca problem thus became a key factor in relations between the Tepanecs and the Mexicas and has a bearing on the rise of the latter. Moreover, while Chalco was an ancient foundation, its revitalization by migrant groups started relatively late and therefore more or less coincided with the rise of the Tepanecs of Azcapotzalco, aided and abetted by the Mexicas.

Like most other places that came to the fore in post-Toltec times, Chalco had existed for many centuries before the fall of Tollan. At nearby Xico, a localized Teotihuacán site has been found, as well as much Coyotlatelco material; Chalco itself has yielded an abundance of Aztec I pottery that is roughly contemporary with the Tula-

Mazapan horizon. Although Culhuacán has been often regarded as the dispersal center for Aztec I, its presence in such quantities in Chalco led O'Neill to suggest that this site was another focus for Aztec I in early Postclassic times. Moreover Chalco polychrome, though exclusive to Chalco, is closely related to Aztec I, with which it shares many decorative motifs. By way of contrast, Aztec II, characteristic of the northern Valley of Mexico, is scarce in Chalco, where it is found only in association with Aztec III, a pottery that marks the era of Mexica expansion.[1] Chalco polychrome is described by O'Neill as being also very Cholulan in character; this resemblance, coupled with the abundant presence of Aztec I in both Chalco and Cholula, suggests that fairly close bonds linked the two cities in pre-Aztec times.

Such connections between Chalco and the Puebla-Tlaxcala valley find confirmation in the written sources; Muñoz Camargo writes of the arrival at Chalco of Olmeca-Xicallancas, who occupied the Cholula region in Toltec times.[2] His story is at times confusing, since he makes out that these Olmecs came from a northwesterly direction; this is surely a misunderstanding on the part of the chronicler, since the Olmeca-Xicallancas were par excellence non-Chichimecs, confined to lands lying east of the Sierra Nevada, and had nothing to do with the stream of Chichimec and Tolteca-Chichimec migrants who came from northwestern Mesoamerica. The *Memorial Breve* also says that the Olmeca-Xicallancas of Chalco came from the north *(mictlampa)*, but this report probably emanates from the same original source as Muñoz Camargo's statement.[3]

The Chalco of the Tula-Mazapan horizon might thus be seen as a westerly outpost of Olmeca-Xicallanca territory, that may have stretched as far as the Gulf Coast in the opposite direction. Chalco's situation offered easy communications with peoples who lived both east and west of the Great Volcanoes; it is not therefore unreasonable to suppose that in Toltec times its population derived partly from the Valley of Mexico and partly from the Olmeca-Xicallanca strongholds to the east. These links were never severed and at times led to hostilities; the Chalcas not only came into armed conflict with the Tepanecs and Mexicas, but fought wars against Xayacamachan, ruler of Huexotzingo in the late fourteenth century; subsequently the Chalcas and Huexotzingans became friends, and when the Mexicas finally overthrew Chalco in 1465, several of its rulers fled to Huexotzingo.

The former presence of Olmeca-Xicallancas in Chalco is further confirmed by Chimalpain's assertion that the Totolimpanecas, the leading Teochichimec element among the latter-day immigrants, fought in Amecameca against the Olmecas who were then in occupation. As in other instances, the Olmeca-Xicallancas were cast in the role of victims, and many were sacrificed by the new occupants.[4] Thus written and archaeological evidence suggest that Chalco in both Toltec times and thereafter was connected both with the Valley of Mexico, of which it formed part, and with the Puebla-Tlaxcala valley, on which it bordered.

Equally significant for Late Postclassic Chalco—with which we are now concerned—is the provenance of the various groups who arrived at intervals and constituted its thirteen *tecpans,* some time after the fall of Tollan and the earliest Teochichimec and Otonchichimec invasions of the Valley of Mexico. A fair proportion of these settlers in Chalco-Amecameca reportedly came from Teotenango in the valley of Toluca; however, Aztec III and IV are much in evidence in Late Postclassic Chalco rather than Matlatzinca pottery.

Chalco, according to Chimalpain, is not an ancient name, but was bestowed on the site by these latter-day settlers. His *Memorial Breve* credits the site with the hallowed appellation of Tamoanchan, whose uncertain etymology I discussed in *The Toltecs* without reaching any very sure conclusions. The original Olmeca-Xicallanca settlers supposedly arrived there chanting, "We seek Tamoanchan." In this context, Tamoanchan is described as an earthly paradise; the name is clearly applicable to more than one locality, and is generally treated as pertaining to the home of gods rather than of mortals; its use in this context bears witness to Chalco's antiquity and to the reverence and affection of its latter-day citizens for their homeland.

Chalco means literally "Place of Green Stone"; Chimalpain tells us that the first of the new arrivals, the Acxotecas, called the people Chalcas and the land Chalco, because in a remote past the Toltecs had built a Chalchiuhcalli ("House of Green Stone") in Atentlipan, on the edge of the lagoon. The Acxotecas found the temple columns still standing when they arrived. The third *Relación* says that the name Amaquemecan was also given by these new arrivals because of the earlier inhabitants' custom of wearing paper ornaments for important ceremonies; the place was previously called Chalchiuhmomozco (the "Place of the Altar of Green Stone").

The *Memorial Breve* also refers to the original Chalco as Chalchiuhtepec and even as Chalchiuhmomozco, though this name seems to apply more particularly to the place later known as Amecameca. In the late Postclassic, as today, an important shrine stood on the adjacent peak.

Among the first tribes to migrate to Chalco were the Teotenanca Tlaillotlaca Cuixcoca Temimililolcas; of the new settlers, these were the most closely connected with Teotenango, and had reportedly lived there for three hundred years.[5] Chimalpain portrays the splendors of the sanctuary of the god Nauhyotecuhtli in Teotenango; his account recalls allegorical reports in other documents of Tollan itself, and the city possessed a house of green stone, a house of turquoise, a house of quetzal feathers, and a house of red spoonbill feathers. Like the descriptions of such exotic structures in Tollan, Chimalpain's account probably either refers simply to buildings painted in different colors, or alternatively to miniature shrines and oratories made of precious materials. Chimalpain even reports that these Tlaillotlacas came into conflict with Topiltzin of Tollan, who was envious of such splendor. But even if it is not to be taken too literally, the story serves to emphasize that, while Chalco's previous inhabitants, the Olmeca-Xicallancas, already enjoyed a high standard of culture, many of the newcomers were also deeply versed in Mesoamerican traditions long before they reached the new Tamoanchan, the terrestrial paradise of Chalco Amaquemecan. In addition to the Tlaillotlacas, the Teotlixcas, another group who settled in Chalco, acted as a link with the Toltec past; these two peoples had sojourned in Tollan itself. Moreover, Ixtlilxóchitl, who describes it as a former Toltec center, tells how Tlotzin, Xolotl's grandson, lived mainly in Chalco "among the Toltecs and Chalcas."[6]

Some of Chalco's new settlers seem to have been linked not only with Tollan but with the Toltecized Chinampa peoples of the southern Valley of Mexico; Torquemada writes of "Chalco de los Culhuas," while Durán tells how Chalcas and Xochimilcas were connected and lived peacefully side by side. As will be seen later, Chalco came to be particularly associated with two of the Chinampa cities, Cuitlahuac and Mizquic. A special relationship seems to have existed between Chalcas and these Chinampa peoples, who were their immediate neighbors; both regions had at one time been extensive users of Aztec I pottery.

Chalco, Our Father and Mother

The surviving evidence suggests that Chalco Amecameca developed into a formidable power in the period following the arrival of its new settlers, from about 1300 onwards. The *Anales de Cuauhtitlán* state that Culhuacán itself was at one time under the sway of Chalco, but without saying when this occurred.[7] The Chalca zone of influence had certainly extended well beyond the subsequent limits of its territory and included the Mizquic-Cuitlahuac area, already mentioned above.

According to Chimalpain's third *Relación,* the Tlaillotlacas had originally arrived at "Tizatepec Cuitlahuac" before going on to Chalco, though in another context he treats Tizatepec and Cuitlahuac as two distinct places. The Chalcas seem to have remained in possession of Cuitlahuac for some time, since in 2 Calli, after they finally left Tizatepec to settle in the Chalco region in Tlalmanalco, their ruler, Cuauhuitzatzin, was once more residing in Cuitlahuac, having returned thither from Tlalmanalco; in that year he was visited in Cuitlahuac by Itzcauhtzin, ruler of the Tzacualtitlan *tecpan* of Chalco-Amecameca. In his seventh *Relación,* Chimalpain even refers to the "Cuitlahuacas Chalcas" in connection with the subsequent conquest of Cuitlahuac by the Mexicas.[8] When the latter occupied the Chinampa cities in 2 Acatl, probably 1403, the Chalcas left the region, where some of them had apparently remained until then. The *Anales de Cuauhtitlán* mention this occurrence, stating that the Chalcas of Tlahuacan (Cuitlahuac) left Xico in 13 Calli, or two years before the 2 Acatl in question. The *Anales de Cuauhtitlán* also say that Cuitlahuac Tizic was ruled by the Chalcas.[9]

The *Memorial Breve* goes so far as to suggest that the Tlaillotlacas were the founders of Mizquic, so named because they encountered there a very old mezquite tree. They obtained a small enclosure *(conmacehuato chinantzintli),* and the place came to be called Mizquic; according to the same source, it later stood on the boundary of Chalca territory.

Ixtlilxóchitl equally states that Mizquic, together with Acatlan, belonged, in the time of Quinatzin, to Amintzin, señor of Chalco Atenco, when Cuitlahuac was already a Mexica tributary.[10] The account implies, probably erroneously, that the Chalcas and Mexicas were campaigning together against the Chinampa cities of Cuitlahuac and Mizquic, whereas this region was in reality not a joint conquest but a bone of contention between two rivals.

Chalcas also seem to have been involved in another city of Toltec derivation, Xico, that stood on an island in the lagoon lying to the west of Chalco Atenco and to the north of Mizquic. Trautmann includes Xico in Chalca territory, but without stating his reasons.[11] The *Memorial Breve* implies that, in addition to settling in Mizquic and Cuitlahuac, the Tlaillotlacas sojourned there before proceeding to Chalco. It also states that Huitznahuatl, son of the first ruler of the Acxotecas, stayed in Xico for some time before they went to Chalco; Huitznahuatl's son, Toteoci, was born there, and later became ruler of the Acxotecas in their new home in Acxotlan Calnahuac. Huitznahuatl died in Xico, having lived there for many decades, and Toteoci first ruled in that city before the Acxotecas went to Chalchiuhtepec and came to call themselves Chalcas. The *Anales de Cuauhtitlán* also state that Tozquihua, ruler of Chalco, died in Xico in 3 Acatl and was succeeded by "Acatl."[12] The transposition of names, as already stressed, is frequent in Mesoamerican records, and there can be little doubt that Chimalpain and the *Anales de Cuauhtitlán* are referring to the same two monarchs under different names. The various names cited in this source for rulers of "Chalco" bear absolutely no relation to Chimalpain's more copious lists of señores of the various *tecpans*. The *Anales de Cuauhtitlán* confusingly mention another "Aca," ruler of Chalco, who died in Xico in 3 Tecpatl and who was Tozquihua's predecessor.

Chalco seems also to have enjoyed some special relationship with Xochimilco; Chimalhuacan Xochimilco is named in the third *Relación* as one of the four divisions of Chalco. In the seventh *Relación,* Chimalpain writes of Tepetlixpan Xochimilco, where Caltzin Tlatquic was ruler, as if it were part of the Chalca federation.

This application of the name Xochimilco to pueblos or *tecpans* of Chalco probably reflects some previous link with the other Xochimilco, rather as certain *tecpans,* such as Tzaculaltitlan Atlauhtlan, also bore the additional name of Tenanco. Chimalpain further states that when the Mexicas had to leave Culhuacán, they went to Mexicaltzingo before reaching the future Tenochtitlán, and that Mexicaltzingo was then a dependency of Chalco-Amecameca.

Not content with partial occupation of the Chinampa region by the Tlaillotlacas and Acxotecas, in the period just prior to their final settling in Chalco-Amecameca at the beginning of the fourteenth century, members of the Chalco confederation later fought wars and made conquests much farther afield. The seventh *Relación* states that the Poyauhtecas of Amecameca had at some time defeated Tulancingo. In the opposite direction, the third *Relación* reports that the Tlacochcalca Teotlixcas conquered Tenancingo and Ayotla in 2 Acatl (1351?). It is not, however, clear whether this is the Tenancingo of the valley of Toluca, since an Ayotla lies quite near to Chalco itself. In another passage, however, the same *Relación* states that in 11 Tochtli the Chalcas defeated the Matlatzincas; 11 Tochtli, if taken as belonging to the same year-count, falls seventeen years before 2 Acatl.

The *Anales de Cuauhtitlán* mention a war between Chalco and Tepotzotlan; it is not stated who was victorious, though the ruler of Tepotzotlán was killed.[13] The same source writes of a Chalca defeat at the hands of the Huaxtecs, and of a war between Cuauhtitlán and Chalco; in a period when Chalco no longer controlled Cuitlahuac, a conflict took place between the two cities. Various wars in mid-fourteenth century between Chalco and Xayacamachan of Huexotzingo were already mentioned in Chapter VII. Such reports usually imply that Chalco was defeated, but they probably derive from sources partial to Huexotzingo.

Mainly, however, Chalco seems to have pushed into the present-day state of Morelos on its southern border. Like the Mexicas, the Chalcas sought the luxury products of the warmer lands. The priest-ruler of the Teotlixcas, Quetzalcanauhtli, had his nose ceremonially pierced in Yecapixtla in 9 Tecpatl; a Quetzalcanauhtli is also mentioned as priest-ruler of the Teotlixcas during their stay in Chapultepec—i.e., before 1319—but this is probably another individual of the same name. As will be explained below in connection with problems of chronology, this 9 Tecpatl, like many of Chimalpain's dates, more probably belongs to the Culhua-Texcocan than to the Tenochca count, and would therefore be the equivalent of 1352, not of 1332; the same text mentions that the Chalcas arrived in Yecapixtla just before the Mexicas colonized Tlatelolco. By way of explanation, the seventh *Relación* states that in 9 Tecpatl some of the Teotlixcas had gone off to Yecapixtla because of the offensive way in which other inhabitants of Chalco had treated their deity, Tlatlauhqui Tezcatlipoca.

Ixtlilxóchitl, writing of the reign of Quinatzin, and therefore of about the same period, states that Huaxtepec belonged to Acacitzin, one of the señores of Chalco.[14] Chimalpain however mentions no Acacitzin except as a Mexica leader who was a contemporary of Tenoch.

The connection between the Chalco region and neighboring Morelos also appears to have been of long standing. The *Anales de Tlatelolco* report that Timal, the Nonoalca leader who conquered Cuauhnahuac after the fall of Tollan, had also occupied Chalco.[15] The same source tells how the señor of Cuauhnahuac cast envious glances upon Tzacualtitlan, one of the *tecpans* of Chalco. This Chalca expansion, whether in Morelos or elsewhere, seems to belong to the period preceding the onset of hostilities with the Tepanec-Mexicas, probably in 1375. It may be added that Trautmann makes interesting comments on the boundaries of Chalco territory, not only in the immediate pre-Conquest period, but also in mid-fourteenth century. In accordance with the Relación de Coatepec Chalco, he places the latter-day boundary just beyond Chimalhuacan and Coatepec.[16] However, on his map of frontiers in about 1350, he, somewhat inexplicably, places Coatepec within Acolhua territory and states that the Acolhuas had reconquered the city.[17] On Chalco's western border with Cuitlahuac stood the pueblos of Tlapitzahuayan, Ayotzingo, and Cuitlatelco, where the Acxotecas first arrived from Cuitlahuac and Tizic; Atlauhtlan, one of the *cabeceras* of Amecameca, marked the common frontier that Chalco shared with Xochimilco, to the south of Cuitlahuac.

Yet more striking than references of this kind to its expansion is a general impression of the greatness of Chalco, not only conveyed by Chimalpain—a rather partial witness—but attested by other sources.

Sympathy for Chalco by other peoples of central Mexico is demonstrated by their joint reaction when in 6 Acatl (probably 1407) the Mexicas are stated to have occupied it and driven out most of its rulers; a powerful coalition was formed, including, oddly enough, the Mexicas' Tepanec partners, together with many other peoples. They exclaimed with one accord: "Is the Chalca not our father and our mother? . . . Was it not they on whom in bygone days so many peoples depended, and was it not the Chalcas whom twenty-five rulers of cities took as an example and a guide, receiving from them the ceremonial investiture?"[18]

Chimalpain further relates how the single *tecpan* of Tzacual-titlan Tenanco was an important polity ruled by two señores. The leading señor was to be compared with a duke [*sic*], with various other princes placed under his tutelage.[19]

Clearly Chalco was not only formed by tribes who joined forces to build a community both variegated and civilized; in addition, . before the Tepanec-Mexica assaults began to take their toll, its radius of action was wide and its power respected.

In fact, the Chalcas' whole center of gravity may have shifted from an original base in the southern Valley of Mexico; previously the Acxotecas and Tlaillotlacas had established themselves in the Cuitlahuac-Mizquic area (and possibly even in Culhuacán itself). Thence they extended their control in a northeasterly direction, occupying lands that were to be their final home in the Chalco-Amecameca region. The move from Cuitlahuac-Mizquic was hardly voluntary and took place under Tepanec-Mexica pressure, supported by Quinatzin's Acolhuas.

More Chronology

In writing of the expansion of Chalco, I have anticipated events, in order to stress its over-all significance and its formidable challenge to the Tepanec-Mexicas.

It still remains to examine how the Chalcan confederation originally sprang from the diverse groups that settled in that region; but before studying the process of merger, the order of their coming to Chalco must first be put into its right chronological perspective.

At first sight, no problem exists. For Chimalpain, unlike other chroniclers, obliges the reader by giving both the native dates and their Julian calendar equivalents; for instance, in one of the earliest years listed in the third *Relación,* 9 Tecpatl, or 1072, Nauhyotzin, king of Culhuacán died, and was succeeded by Cuauhtexpetlatzin; in another 9 Tecpatl, given as 1176, (i.e. two year-cycles later), the Acxotecas, the future settlers of Chalco, left Tizic and moved to Cuitlatelco. On the face of it, matters are therefore simple, and we can happily dispense with those involved calculations that beset our studies of other sources.

Moreover, it may be argued, if doubts persist concerning Chimalpain's reckoning of the Julian year equivalent, they can best be resolved by cross-checking with other events that he names, unrelated to the history of Chalco. In particular, references to Chalco and its dynasties are made to coincide with the accession or death of Culhua rulers, such as Coxcox and Nauhyotzin.

However, mere mention of the death of a Culhua ruler, alongside other data included under the same Christian and native date heading, has unfortunately little significance. For this approach takes no account of the method generally used by the chroniclers, who clearly took their facts and the respective native dates from several different documents; this information they would then collect and recapitulate as pertaining to the years in the native calendar, listed in succession. Unfortunately they often had to rely on pure guesswork in judging to what native year-cycle (and hence to what Christian year equivalent) a given event or series of events should be ascribed. Accordingly, under a single Julian calendar year, and even under a single native year, entries may be listed whose true dates are decades if not centuries apart. The chroniclers' errors in this respect are compounded by the assumption that the Tenochca count can be used for calculating all Julian calendar equivalents.

The phenomenon can be illustrated by the *Anales de Cuauhtitlán.* According to this source, in 13 Acatl, towards the end of the reign of the *tlatoani* Axayacatl (1469–81), occurred the death of Ixtotomahuatzin, señor of Cuitlahuac, who was succeeded by "don

Mateo Ixtliltzin." But quite aside from the anomaly of a señor bearing the title of "don" reigning in Cuitlahuac half a century before the first Spaniard set foot in Mexico, the source's next reference to Ixtliltzin of Cuitlahuac states that he was still alive in 12 Tecpatl, one year after the death of Ahuitzotl, the second *tlatoani* after Axayacatl. He is again mentioned under 10 Acatl, the year that is also given for the death of Nezahualpilli (who died in 1515) and he was still reigning when the Spaniards arrived. Thus events can be arbitrarily grouped under the heading of a particular year 13 Acatl that clearly belong to different calendar cycles, or—as in this particular case—probably to different year-counts.[20]

And even if only one year-count is being used in any particular instance, the problem does not disappear; as mentioned above, an event belonging to 3 Tochtli may be listed by the chronicler as following immediately after another happening in 2 Calli, whereas in reality the 3 Tochtli in question is not one year but fifty-three (52 plus 1) years after 2 Calli, not to mention even greater differences relating to happenings separated by several calendar cycles.

This problem is not absent in Chimalpain's case, just because he gives us his own Christian year equivalent; moreover, even such a notable twentieth-century commentator as Walter Lehmann fell into the same trap and merely confused the issue with an oversimplified series of Christian year equivalents in his otherwise admirable translation of the *Anales de Cuauhtitlán.*

One of the simplest examples of Chimalpain's assignment of an event to the wrong calendar cycle is his statement that a solar eclipse took place in 12 Tochtli, 1478; astronomers now calculate that this eclipse really occurred in 1426, or fifty-two years before (i.e., the date actually given for this event in the Codex Telleriano Remensis).

Countless other instances may be cited where Chimalpain's Julian calendar equivalents of native dates either contradict each other in different *Relaciones,* or are not in accord with accepted facts. As a simple illustration, the following example may serve: Chimalpain in his third *Relación* lists both 7 Calli and 1 Tecpatl for the accession of Acamapichtli of Tenochtitlán, and in the seventh *Relación* 5 Acatl is given for the same event (in all, I have found twelve different years proposed for this ruler's accession, provided by twenty-three sources). Now Chimalpain translates all native dates into their Julian equivalent by assuming that they belong to the standard Tenochca count (1 Acatl = 1519). Thus his three dates for Acamapichtli's accession become in his own reckoning 1369, 1376, and 1367—for the same event. Moreover, in the third *Relación,* Acamapichtli is made ruler *(motlahtocatlalli)* in 7 Calli (1376), and then, a mere fifty-four words later in the Nahuatl text, the reader is told that he died in 1 Calli, interpreted as 1389 by Chimalpain, who nonetheless asserts that Acamapichtli reigned for twenty-one years. By the same token, in addition to 1 Calli, the seventh *Relación* give 12 Acatl as the year of Acamapichtli's death.

Now, leaving aside for the present the possible use of different year-counts, the conclusion is already plain; if a chronicler gives several different native dates for a single event of a once-and-for-all nature, such as the death of a sovereign, then his Christian year equivalents cannot all be right, and some at least must be mistaken. Equally, in connection with the same reign, the chronicler in his sixth *Relación* gives both 12 Acatl (1387) and 1 Tecpatl (1376) for the beginning of the Chalca-Mexica war, and in the seventh *Relación* he repeats the 1 Tecpatl date. The near identity of the words he uses to describe the event in each case eliminates any possibility that he is referring to two quite different happenings.

Even more patent examples of Chimalpain's confusion in correlating native and Julian dates—even within a single *Relación*— may be taken from the earlier part of his story: according to the third *Relación,* in 6 Acatl, given as 1199, Tezozómoc, señor of Azcapotzalco, formed a coalition of powers who drove the Mexicas out of Chapultepec; this report is clearly not concerned with any preliminary skirmish, but with the final expulsion of the Mexicas from that place, since we are told in the same paragraph that Huitzilihuitl, the Mexica ruler, was led captive to Culhuacán, an event given in a variety of sources as marking the end of the Mexica stay in Chapultepec. But in the same *Relación,* under the year-heading 1 Tochtli (1298), we are told that the Mexicas had at that time been in Chapultepec for nineteen years. Now, if 1199 is the correct date for the expulsion, how were they still in occupation in 1298? After their captivity in Culhuacán, they founded Tenochtitlán, and no no source suggests that they went back to Chapultepec.

Chimalpain in his seventh *Relación* confirms this sequence of events and tells (listed under events for 13 Acatl, 1323), how the Mexicas spent twenty-five years in Culhuacán and then left for Mexicatzingo, en route for the future Tenochtitlán. In the seventh *Relación* he reiterates his statement made in the third *Relación* to the effect that in 1 Tochtli (1298) the Mexicas had been for nineteen years in Chapultepec—i.e., they had arrived in 1279, or 9 Tecpatl; he adds that they were led by Huitzilihuitl, whom, in his third *Relación,* he had killed off one hundred years before in a year 6 Acatl that he equates, not to 1303, as in the seventh *Relación,* but to 1199—or two whole cycles earlier. Both statements cannot be correct.

Yet Zimmermann persisted in the belief that Chimalpain's Julian calendar equivalents were to be taken literally, in spite of such evidence to the contrary, plain for all to see. In his edition of Chimalpain's Nahuatl text, he did not adopt the obvious procedure of publishing each *Relación* as a whole as written by the chronicler; instead, he pulled the *Relaciones* apart, and put them together again after his own fashion by taking the Christian year equivalents one by one in consecutive order, and giving the events listed by Chimalpain for that particular Christian and native year in *all* his *Relaciones,* starting with A.D. 1064, and ending in 1521. Notwithstanding Zimmermann's invaluable contribution to the study of this chronicler, in this respect he merely confused the situation since his method is based on Christian year equivalents, many of which are manifestly mistaken.

The task of the modern investigator is surely to find out what really occurred by comparing the chronology of one source with that of others, rather than to blindly accept, as do Zimmermann and even Lehmann, inconsistencies that make no sense, thereby repeating and even compounding the errors of those earlier writers who were chroniclers in the literal sense of the word; by copying different documents, they concocted a chronicle, not an analysis as befits the modern historian.

The problem outlined above applies to the case in point—the chronology of the arrival of the different groups of migrants in the Chalco-Amecameca region. The same anomalies immediately arise, and it again becomes clear that even if Chimalpain's dates are sometimes right, they cannot always be so because they are not consistent.

Of this, one example may suffice: the arrival of the Temimililolca Cuixcocas. According to the third *Relación,* they reached Tizatepec Cuitlahuac in 8 Tochtli, 1162, and in 9 Tecpatl, 1176, went on to Cuitlatelco (southwest of Mizquic). They were led by Totoltecatl Tzompachtli Tlaillotlac Tecuhtli, to give him his full title.

But in the second *Relación,* the Teotenanca Temimilolca Cuixcocas, led by Totoltecatl Tzompachtli, arrived in Tizatepec in 3 Calli, 1209. To remove any doubts that the two accounts concern the same events, the actual text may be quoted: "Nican ypan in y huel mellahuac ynic oncan Tiçatepec yn inahuac Tulyahualco Xuchimilcatlalli ypan yn acico, ynic oncan motlallico yn huehuetque yn quintocayotiaya y Eztlapictin Teotenanca Teochichimeca Cuixcoca Temimilolca Yhuipaneca Çacanca. Auh yn quinhualyacan yn tlahtohuani hualmochiuhtia ytoca Totoltecatl Tzompachtli tlayllotlac teuhctli, ychuatl Quihualmamatia yn inteouh diablo yn quitocayotiaya Nauhyo teuhctli yn Xipil, ypial hualmochiuhtia. Auh yn icihuauh quihualhuicac omotoneuh tlahtohuani Totoltecatl Tzonpachtli ytoca Cuauhxuchtzin yn cihuapilli tehuan hualla." ("Here is the truth that there in Ticatepec, next to the Xochimilca land of Tulyahualco they arrived, and there the elders settled who were called the Eztlapictin Teotenanca Teochichimeca Cuixcoca Temimilolca Yhuipaneca Çacanca. And heading them was he who became ruler called Totoltecatl Tzompachtli Tlayllotlac. They made him the bearer of their god called Nauhyoteuhctli the Precious Prince, and he became his keeper. And the ruler Totoltecatl Tzompachtli brought his wife, called Cuauhxuchtzin, and she was a princess.")

The latter part of this text is repeated word for word in the third *Relación,* this time said to have occurred in 8 Tochtli, 1162. The sole difference is that in the third *Relación* the glyph for Totoltecatl's wife has been interpreted by the chronicler as Xiuhtoztzin, whereas in the second *Relación* the same person is named as Cuauhxochtzin.

The date 3 Calli would fall a mere five years before 8 Tochtli in the same calendar; as already stressed, differences of a few years are common if not universal in dealing with such remote dates, probably because of an accumulation of errors of one digit, arising from causes explained in Appendix A.

But whereas the native dates for the coming of the Temimilol-cas hardly differ in the two *Relaciones,* a major discrepancy emerges in the two Julian calendar equivalents because the event is ascribed in one instance, and probably in both, to the wrong calendar cycle. If 8 Tochtli is not taken as 1162, as in the third *Relación,* but as 1162 plus 52, i.e., 1215, then it approximately accords with the 3 Calli, 1209, given in the second *Relación.* Later we shall see that the 3 Calli in question should probably be placed yet two further calendar cycles later, and really coincides neither with 1157 nor with 1209 but with 1313.

In addition, as part of the same account, we are told in the *Memorial Breve* that Totoltecatl died in 6 Tochtli, 1238, after a reign of twenty years in Tizatepec (by inclusive reckoning, explained above, 1238 *is* twenty years after 1209, named as the year in which he and his people arrived). In all, he had reigned thirty years over the Tlaillotlacas; he was suceeded by his son Quahuitzatzin.

However, according to the third *Relación,* Totoltecatl died in 1187; this *Relación* nonetheless states that Quahuitzatzin died in 2 Tochtli, 1338, after a reign of seventy years. Now, adding a 52-year cycle to 1187, the third *Relación* date for the death of Totolte-catl, we reach 1239, or a single year after 1238, the year given by the *Memorial Breve* for that event. The patent absurdity of a reign of one hundred years for Quahuitzatzin, stated to have died in 1338, heightens the probability that the different Julian calendar equiva-lents of both the second and the third *Relaciones* are wrongly cal-culated, as will be explained in more detail below. For the moment it may suffice to insist that Chimalpain's *Memorial Breve* and his third *Relación* patently attribute the same events to two or more year cycles, and thus to quite different dates in the Christian calendar.

Accordingly, before studying the absolute chronology of the migrant groups and of the order in which they came, it has been established beyond reasonable doubt that Chimalpain's Christian year equivalents, for these and other events, cannot be taken literally and require close analysis and interpretation. The further question remains as to whether these native dates can be taken as belonging to the Tenochca count (1 Acatl = 1519), and whether, therefore, the Christian equivalent can always be determined by adding or subtracting fifty-two years, or multiples of fifty-two years, to Chimalpain's figures, based upon that year-count. Evidence will be cited to show that this is often not the case.

The Order of Their Coming

The *Memorial Breve* relates that the Acxotecas were the first of the new migrants to reach Chalco, followed by the Teotenanca Tlaillotlacas; in the seventh *Relación* Chimalpain repeats the statement that the Acxotecas arrived before the Tlaillotlacas.

Paradoxically, the Acxotecas had originally come to Tizatlan after the Tlaillotlacas, who left when they arrived. Nonetheless, the Acxotecas were the first to get to Chalco, accompanied by the Tlaltecahuaques, Contecas, and Mihuaques, portrayed as their vassals. "Mihuaques" are presumably Michuaques; in another context, Chimalpain also writes of "Mihuacan", meaning Michuacan.[21]

In the *Memorial Breve* the chronicler further states that the Tlaillotlacas (though coming after the Acxotecas), reached Chalco before the Totolimpanecas and the Tzacualtitlan Tenancas Tecuanipas. The third *Relación* affirms that the Nonoalca Poyauhtecas, one of the last to appear upon the scene, came ten years after the Tecuanipas; the same *Relación* describes these Tecuanipas as the third group to arrive; by implication they had left Chicomoztoc and reached Chalco after the Totolimpanecas. In the seventh *Relación* it is stated that, of all the tribes, the Nonoalca Teotlixca Tlacochcalcas were the last to arrive. A conflicting report that they came first may be discounted, since the text on several occasions makes it plain that this was not really so. The *Anales de Cuauhtitlán* incidentally state that these Teotlixcas arrived in Chalco in 1 Tecpatl.

Accordingly, a fairly clear picture emerges of a series of migrations, occurring in the following order:

> Acxotecas (and their three auxiliary groups)
> Teotenanca Tlaillotlacas
> Totolimpanecas
> Tecuanipas
> Nonoalca Poyauhtecas
> Nonocalca Teotlixca Tlacochcalcas

263

The question still remains: When did they each arrive? How are we to square Chimalpain's reasonably consistent native dates with his rather erratic Julian calendar equivalents, and correctly relate the Chalca migrations to other events whose chronology is easier to determine?

The tacit assumption that the dates for the migrations all belong to a single native calendar—but not necessarily the Tenochca—in itself gives rise to no anomalies. For instance, if we are told that in 8 Tochtli the Tlaillotlacas reached Tizatepec, led by Totoltecatl, and then read that Totoltecatl died in 7 Acatl after ruling for twenty-six years, no problem arises, since (by inclusive counting) 7 Tecpatl *is* twenty-six years after 8 Tochtli. In terms of native chronology it accordingly becomes possible to follow year by year a fairly long sequence of events involving many comings and goings of tribes. The dates for the accession and death of their respective rulers raise certain other problems, that do not require detailed treatment in this context except when they help to clarify the arrival dates of the different peoples. This is often not the case: for instance, the third *Relación* states that Totoltecatl, ruler of the Tlaillotlacas, died in 7 Acatl, 1187; his son, Cualtzin, then reigned from 7 Acatl until 6 Tochtli, 1238, when he in turn was succeeded by his son, Cuahuitzatzin, who reigned until 2 Tochtli, 1338. But in the *Memorial Breve* it is Totoltecatl, not Cualtzin, who dies in 6 Tochtli, 1238, and Cuahuitzatzin is no longer his grandson and second successor, but his son and immediate heir. Apart from such anomalies, the dates for Totoltecatl appear to be more ritual rather than historical; as previously mentioned, Ixtlilxóchitl and Torquemada give 7 Acatl or 6 Tochtli for the accession and death of several Toltec rulers; and several early Cuauhtitlán monarchs also ruled for a 7 Acatl to 7 Acatl cycle.

A marked inconsistency has already been noted between the Julian calendar correlations given in the third and seventh *Relaciones*. In the case of the earliest migrants, the equivalents provided in the third *Relación* precede those of the seventh *Relación* by as much as two calendar cycles, or 104 years. The third *Relación*'s first reference to any migration to the Chalco region concerns the coming of the Tlaillotlacas to Tizatepec Cuitlahuac in 8 Tochtli, given as 1162; shortly thereafter, the same account reports the arrival of the

Mexicas in Chapultepec in 11 Acatl, 1191. But in the *Memorial Breve,* the Tlaillotlacas reach Tizatepec *one* year-cycle later, while the seventh *Relación,* concerned with the same sequel, only begins its account of events with the year 2 Calli, 1272, and places the arrival of the Mexicas in 1 Tochtli, 1298, *two* year-cycles (plus 3 years) later than the third *Relación* figure.

Now the dates of the Mexica stay in Chapultepec and Culhuacán provide a better basis for the fixing of Chalca chronology, since Mexica doings can be correlated with such key events as the foundation of Tenochtitlán.

Bearing in mind this important factor, and—with reservations— accepting the later of Chimalpain's different calendar dates for the Mexica stay in Chapultepec, I assume initially that his later alternatives are also more nearly correct for the moves of the Chalca settlers whenever he gives two or more Julian calendar equivalents for identical happenings.

In the seventh *Relación,* he states that the Poyauhtecas arrived at the relatively late date of 7 Tecpatl, 1304—only three years removed from his third *Relación* figure of 10 Acatl, 1307. According to both the third and seventh *Relación,* the Tecuanipas arrived in 11 Acatl, 1295; however, the third *Relación* also asserts that the Tecuanipas came ten years before the Poyauhtecas—a statement in perfect accord with the seventh *Relación* report that the Poyauhtecas arrived in 1304. In the fifth *Relación* Chimalpain tells us that the Poyauhtecas reached Chalco thirty-five years after the Totolimpanecas; the latter according to the third *Relación* came in 9 Calli, but in this instance 9 Calli is given as 1241 (or sixty-three rather than thirty-five years before the Poyauhtecas). According to the *Memorial Breve,* the Tlaillotlacas came in 10 Calli, 1229, and in 6 Tochtli had already lived for 10 years in Cuitlatelco Atentlipan. On the basis of these figures, a reconstruction of the native dating becomes possible, if only on a somewhat eclectic basis. But before seeking any absolute chronology for these tribal migrations, we must pay attention to a crucial factor so far ignored. According to my calculations, these earlier native dates given by Chimalpain really belong to the Culhua-Texcoco calendar, not to the Tenochca; therefore, in order to reach the right equivalent, we must first assign them to the correct native year-cycle and then add to Chimalpain's Julian calendar dates an extra twenty years, the necessary process of adjustment from the Tenochca to the Culhua count. For instance, the seventh *Relación* 7 Tecpatl date for the arrival of the Poyauhtecas no longer falls in 1304, but in 1324, and so forth.

Jiménez Moreno has consistently affirmed that before the foundation of Tenochtitlán the use of the Tenochca calendar is very limited, and that the year-count commonly though not universally employed is what he named the Texcocan, but that I prefer to call the Culhua-Texcocan, since it was mainly used before Texcoco itself rose to prominence. In particular, the use of that count leads to Jiménez Moreno's conclusion that Tenochtitlán was founded in 1345, not 1325, an assertion that has seldom been contested, and whose accuracy I have supported in tabular form. Chimalpain, among others, gives 2 Calli for the event, or 1345, Culhua count.

Without repeating these calculations, it is important to note the evidence that Chimalpain in certain instances did use the Culhua-Texcocan count, or some year-count other than the Tenochca. Indeed, certain of his dates make little sense unless explained by the use of a different calendar. For instance, the third *Relación* gives 8 Calli (also cited by Ixtlilxóchitl) for the death of Quinatzin of Texcoco and for the succession of Techotlalatzin; in the Tenochca count, 8 Calli is either 1345 or 1397. Neither of these dates can be taken as correct; Quinatzin cannot have died in 1345, since by all accounts he was an ally and co-belligerent of Acamapichtli of Tenochtitlán, who came to the throne in 1371 or thereabouts. Equally, Quinatzin can hardly have died as late as 1397, since Techotlalatzin was reportedly already ruler in 1395, during the Xaltocan war; this monarch, who is generally credited with a longish reign, died in 1409, when he was succeeded by Huehue Ixtlilxóchitl. On the other hand, the Culhua equivalent of 8 Calli, 1377, makes perfect sense for Quinatzin's death, since only the end of his reign coincided with that of Acamapichtli.

The use by Chimalpain of yet other year-counts can be demonstrated in other ways. He gives one date of 12 Acatl for the beginning of the Chalca war against the Tepanec-Mexicas; but in another context, he states, in almost the same words, that the war began in 1 Tecpatl. These dates can only be reconciled by assuming that the

266

12 Acatl in question belongs neither to the Culhua nor to the Tenochca, but to what I have called the Cuitlahua count, in which
12 Acatl is the equivalent of the Tenochca 13 Acatl (i.e., one year
before 1 Tecpatl). These one-digit differences, as in the case of the
1 Acatl and the 2 Acatl dates for Topiltzin's flight from Tollan, or
the 12 and 13 Tecpatl given for Xolotl's death, crop up so frequently
that they can only be explained by the use of such alternative year-
counts (as opposed to variations of, say, 1 Calli and 2 Tochtli for one
event, that occur for a different reason).

Whether or not it is agreed that Chimalpain's 2 Calli for the
founding of Tenochtitlán really refers to 1345 rather than to 1325,
such doubts become harder to sustain in the case of his 10 Tecpatl
for the birth of Tezozómoc of Azcapotzalco, which surely belongs
to the Culhua count. In the Tenochca count 10 Tecpatl falls in 1320,
and in the Culhua-Texcoco count in 1340. Now Tezozómoc's death
is universally described as having occurred in 1426 (12 Tochtli in
Chimalpain's third *Relación),* or in 1327, or just before the outbreak of the Mexica-Tepanec war. Reports agree that he was a very
old man; his birth in 1340 therefore makes perfect sense, and accords him a lifespan of eighty-six years; but to suggest that he was
born in 1320 and was still in active control of events when he was
106 years old amounts to sheer fantasy and almost rivals Xolotl's
example of legendary longevity. Therefore, historians who doubt
their own capacity for solving the conundrums of Mesoamerican
chronology, when already 106 years old, should concede that Chimalpain's date for Tezozómoc's birth (but not his death) belongs
to the Culhua-Texcoco, rather than to the Tenochca calendar.

This Culhua-Texcocan count seems to have been in common
use in the early fourteenth century and applies in particular to Mexica and Culhua dates of this period (though in Appendix A I have
shown that a likely change-over to the Tenochca count occurred in
the 1330's affecting dates for the death of Huehue Acamapichtli
and the accession of Achitometl II of Culhuacán). I therefore logically assume that Chimalpain's dates for the Chalcan tribal migrations of a few decades previous really belong to the Culhua count, and
that the right correlation can best be deduced by taking the later of
the chronicler's two or more Julian calendar equivalents and adding

twenty years to such figures, to convert them from Chimalpain's Tenochca count calculations into the correct Culhua-Texcocan correlation.

The dates for the arrivals of the respective groups in the Chalco-Amecameca region may then accordingly be read as follows:

> Acxotecas: no precise dates given, but they arrived shortly before the Tlaillotlacas.
> Tlaillotlacas: 9 Tecpatl, 1300
> Totolimpanecas: 9 Calli, 1313
> Tecuanipas: 11 Acatl, 1315
> Poyauhtecas: 7 Tecpatl, 1324
> Teotlixcas: 1 Tecpatl, 1324

In the case of the Teotlixcas, the 1 Tecpatl date comes not from Chimalpain but from the *Anales de Cuauhtitlán.* I strongly suspect that this is the only date for the arrival of a tribe that belongs to the Tenochca count, since 7 Tecpatl in the Culhua count would fall in 1344, which seems to be too late; moreover, as can be seen in Appendix A, other instances arise where 7 Tecpatl in one source is the equivalent of 1 Tecpatl in another, a phenomenon that can only be explained by a change from one year-count to another.

Reports of the deaths of certain rulers of Chalco accord with these dates for tribal migrations: Quautlehuatzin, señor of the Tlaillotlacas, died in 2 Tochtli, and his predecessor in 6 Tochtli, as previously mentioned. This 2 Tochtli may now be calculated as 1358, and he was probably the second, not the first, ruler after Totoltecatl, who died before his people reached Chalco. Tliltecatzin, first ruler of the Totolimpanecas in Chalco, died in 7 Tecpatl, or 1324, and the reign of Atonaltzin, leader of the Tecuanipas, ended in 10 Acatl, or 1327 Culhua count (the same year as Coxcox of Culhuacán). In the *Memorial Breve,* Atonaltzin, Tliltecatzin, and Quahuitzatzin figure as contemporaries, and an important ceremony is described in which they jointly participated.

These peoples and their leaders were to establish the thirteen *tecpans* that made up the Chalco-Amecameca confederation in Aztec times. However, in spite of the common use of certain names, such as Tecuanipan Huixtoco, it is hard to relate the original groups with a single *tecpan,* except perhaps in the case of Panohuayan Amaquemecan, founded by the Poyauhtecas or Panohuayas. At times a given people would move from one part of the extensive Chalcan territory to another; for instance, the Teotenanca Tlaillotlacas in 9 Calli migrated from Chalco Atenco to Tenanco Texocpolco and one year later went to Amecameca. The name Amecameca is associated in one way or another with no less than four out of the six original groups, the Totolimpanecas, Tecuanipas, Poyauhtecas, and Teotlixcas. In all, out of thirteen *tecpans,* three are called Amaquemecan: Tecuanipan Pochtlan Amaquemecan, Tehoacan Amaquemecan, and Panohuayan Amaquemecan. The situation is further confused because the Teotenanca Tlaillotlacas, not the Tecuanipa Tzacualtitlanecas, ended up in control of Tzacualtitlan Tenanco. Moreover, not only do cases arise where one group, e.g., the Teotenanca Tlaillotlacas, is associated with several *tecpans,* but conversely several peoples, the Acxotecas, Tlaltecahuaques, and Mihuaques are apparently confined to one *tecpan,* since they are reported as forming the four barrios of Tlalmanalco. A further complication arises from the subdivision of certain peoples into *calpullis;* in the case of the Teotenanca Tlaillotlacas, but not in most others, we are given the names of these *calpullis* that had their own "kings" (intlatocauh). The people of one of these *calpullis* were called the Tlacatecpantlaca; Tlacatecpan was also a principal *calpulli* of Tenochtitlán. One of the first Chalca immigrant tribes, the Tlacochcalca, also bore the same name as an original Mexica *calpulli.* Moreover, in addition to the Tlaillotlacas of Chalco, other people of that appellation settled in Texcoco in the reign of Techotlalatzin (see Chapter V). The heads of the Tlaillotlaca *calpullis* also bore the title of *tlatoani:* an Ilancueitl is so named and referred to as the leader of the Atlauhtecas, or Atlauhtecatecuhtli; these were people of another *calpulli* belonging to the Tlaillotlaca group.[22] Thus, not content with the possession of thirteen *tecpans,* each governed by one or more rulers, the *tecpans* in turn tend to be subdivided into *calpullis,* each with its own *tlatoani.* The Chalca confederation therefore was well supplied with "kings," who are easily confused one with another in the record.

Sylvia Rendón gives a list of the various *tecpans* and their dynasties, though she does not include Tepetlixpan Chimalhuacan, and gives a total of twelve, rather than thirteen, as mentioned by

Kirchhoff and by Jaqueline de Durand. In associating these *tecpans* with one of the six original migrant groups, Rendón assigns four to the Tlaillotlacas. The exact affiliation of each *tecpan* is not easy to determine and lies outside the scope of this book, though I understand that this problem will be studied in de Durand's comprehensive work on Chimalpain, in course of preparation. The problem is multiplied by the presence in one place of more than one señor; for instance, the seventh *Relación* mentions two señores of Amaquemecan, but without saying whether they ruled over the same *tecpan.*

A Varied Blend

In his account of the rise of Chalco, Chimalpain provides a unique narrative that helps to illustrate the way in which other people who inhabited central Mexico in the Late Postclassic may also have developed. Chalco, with its thirteen *tecpans,* may constitute an even richer ethnic blend than most of the others, and may have absorbed an even wider range of diverse elements. However, the principles remain the same, and in general terms what occurred in Chalco could also be applicable in the case of other peoples.

Tenochtitlán-Tlatelolco is a case in point, though not an exact analogy, since the Mexicas were originally confined within the lagoon to such a limited space that a greater homogeneity might be envisaged and a lesser admixture of successive immigrants. The Tepanecs are perhaps more comparable to the Chalcas; they occupied a larger area, and although Azcapotzalco became the capital, the sources list at least three additional centers, Tlacopan, Huitzilopochco, and Coyoacan, quite apart from other places such as Toltitlan, where Tepanecs also settled. Tlaxcala, with its four separate *cabeceras,* might also be compared to Chalco, as well as Acolhuacan, with its relatively more extensive home territory containing the various Acolhua cities, even if in pre-Aztec times they occasionally lacked cohesion.

But the relationship between peoples of different cultural levels, the Chichimecs and non-Chichimecs, who came together to form a new polity is better documented in Chalco's case than in others; the process described in Chalco therefore merits further observation concerning the leaders, religion, and ethnic affiliations of each group, in the order in which they arrived:

Acxotecas (together with the Tlaltecahuaques, Contecas, and Mihuaques). The *Memorial Breve* states that the Acxotecas had come from Tollan, where their first king, Xallitecuhtli, had died; they brought with them their god called Acollacatl ("Shoulder Person"). Acollacatl was also called Nahuatecuhtli. They first went to Chalchiuhtepec, where they set up a market, such as they had possessed in Tollan. They built a temple to their god, then constructed a wall round the existing palace, and even made a prison. When they arrived in Chalchiuhtepec, their leader was Toteocitecuhtli, who had become ruler during the time when they had settled in Cuitlahuac before coming to Chalco. The seventh *Relación,* in telling of the Acxotecas' social structure, uses the term *toltecayotl* (government by nobles); on the other hand, the Mihuaques and the two other tribes that accompanied them had no nobles but only military chiefs.

Tlaillotlaca Tenanca Cuixcocas. They arrived in 8 Tochtli in Cuitlatetelco, then part of Chalco, led by Totoltecatl, whose wife, Xiuhtototzin, was a noblewoman *(cihuapilli).* They were worshipers of Nauhyotecuhtli. Totoltecatl fulfilled the classic role of *teomama,* and bore the image of the god on his back *(quihualmamatia).* They had spent twenty years in Tollan, though the seventh *Relación* states that they originally came from Mollanco (possibly the Molango near to Metztitlan). Their real place of origin, however, was Teotenango, in the Toluca valley. The *Memorial Breve* states that they spent three hundred years in that city; they had known Topiltzin and had fought wars against him. The source describes the fabulous buildings they had erected in Teotenango in honor of their deity. Before reaching Chalco, they had also lived in Tizatepec and Cuitlahuac, where they first came into contact with the Acxotecas.

Totolimpanecas and Tzacualtitlan Tenancas. The *Memorial Breve* states that they left Aztlan before the Mexicas, and describes them as the true founders of Amecameca, where they arrived in 9 Calli. Here they defeated the Olmeca Xicallancas, some of whom stayed behind. At this time they were led by two brothers, Toltecatzin and Atonaltzin (usually referred to as Chichimecatecuhtli). The latter seems to have subsequently become leader of the Acxotecas.

The Totolimpanecas differ fundamentally from the other groups, since Chimalpain describes them as true or Teochichimecs. In the third *Relación,* he makes it quite clear that they were firmly wedded to Chichimec customs and religion: they performed arrow-shooting ceremonies like those of the Teochichimecs described in the early part of the *Anales de Cuauhtitlán,* their god was a white eagle, who descended upon the back of the red jaguar (also mentioned in the *Anales de Cuauhtitlán).* They called the place where they performed the rites to the white eagle Cuauhtli Itlaquayan ("Place Where the Eagle Devours").

Tecuanipas. They arrived in 11 Acatl, two years after the Totolimpanecas, and Chimalpain suggests that they came from Aztlan. In Huixtoco Tecuanipan they had been first led by Ocelotzin, who was succeeded by Tziuhtlacahui; they then settled in Tecuanipan Amaquemecan Chalco. Tziuhtlacahui is described as a great warrior and as *"teuctli teomama";* in this role he bore the image of the god Citecatl, mentioned in the fifth *Relación;* in another passage Citecatl is described as the equivalent of Mixcoatl.

Nonoalca Poyauhtecas. They reached Amecameca ten years after the Tecuanipas. In the seventh *Relación* they are also described as people of Panohuayan (Rendón gratuitously but erroneously adds that Panohuayan is the invariable equivalent of Panuco—an identification that Sahagún makes in a single and quite different context). Their leader was called Nochuetzin Tlamaocatl Teuhtli; the *hualteomama,* or bearer of the god, was named Tlotliteuhctli. They settled in Panohuayan Amaquemecan, where they seem to have remained. It will be recalled that other Poyauhtecas, described not as Nonoalcas but as Chichimecs, went to found Tlaxcala, according to the account of Muñoz Camargo.

Nonoalca Tlacochcalca Teotlixcas. In spite of a single statement to the contrary, Chimalpain in general makes it clear that they were the last to arrive. They also had been twenty years in Tollan (probably they had remained much longer; in the *Historia Tolteca-Chichimeca,* the Nonoalcas are also stated to have been in Tollan for twenty years, but they were one of the two principal ethnic groups in that city, where they probably remained for centuries). The Teotlixcas had originally come from Huetlapallan in the east and had crossed the great sea. They were people of the highest cultural attainments, spoke the Nonoalca language, and possessed painted codices.

The early part of the seventh *Relación* gives a fairly ample account of their attainments and achievements. They first went to Chapultepec, arriving one year before the Mexicas were expelled; I tend to regard them as the prime movers in this affair, notwithstanding Chimalpain's statement in the *Memorial Breve* that it was the Tlaillotlacas who were instrumental in driving out the Mexicas. The Teotlixcas had also been in Teotenango, and were therefore easy to confuse with the Tlaillotlacas, with whom they had thus had previous contacts.

The Teotlixcas were worshipers of Tlatlauhqui Tezcatlipoca—the equivalent of Xipe Totec: they practiced the *xochiyaotl,* or war of flowers, that would have provided captives for Xipe's sacrificial rites.

Before making further comments on the status and cultural level of the various peoples, it is worth noting that Chimalpain offers certain clues to their mutual relationships. The seventh *Relación* states that on the one hand the Tlaltecahuaques, Contecas, and Mihuaques, who were without nobles, were in effect vassals of the more civilized Acxotecas; on the other hand, faced by a period of famine, the Acxotecas and their attendant tribes put themselves under the guidance of the Teotlixcas.

Thus the Acxotecas, who were not Toltecs but who had sojourned in Tollan, occupied an intermediate rung on the ladder between true Toltecs, such as the Teotlixcas, and pure Chichimecs, the category to which the Mihuaques and the Totolimpanecas belonged. We are told that they were at times influenced by the Acxotecas, who brought them to the temple of their god Acollacatl; they led them into the shrine and introduced them to the worship of a true Mesoamerican deity. However, when it came to hostilities against a common foe, it was the more martial Totolimpanecas who played the leading role and drove out the Olmeca Xicallancas; at that time they even gave orders to the Acxotecas and told them to leave Atenco Chalchiuhtepec, to which they returned three years later.

A kind of love-hate relationship seems to have developed between the more backward and the more advanced peoples. The former, who were the most warlike, would at times give vent to their resentment of the latter's cultural pretensions and go to the extent of driving them away; but at other times, anxious to benefit from the possession of superior knowledge and skills, the Teochichimecs would seek both technical aid and religious solace from their more sophisticated neighbors. From Chimalpain's description, it becomes clear that in the long run brain tended to prevail over brawn; the Teotlixcas, portrayed as originally poor, were intellectually the most advanced and came out on top in the final analysis. But they had to fight for their privileges; Chimalpain says that in 1 Tecpatl, before the Tepanec-Mexica war on Chalco, the Teotlixcas fought a *xochiyaotl,* or war of flowers, against the Chalcas.

Reports on Teotlixca origins are particularly conflicting. As de Durand points out, their very name embodies a contradiction. Zimmermann translates "Teotlixca" as "People of the East," a meaning that implicitly links them with the people who came to Tollan from Huetlapallan; Chimalpain mentions that they did come from there and calls them Nonoalcas. But while de Durand agrees that they form part of an ancient tradition, dating back even to Teotihuacán times, she also points out that the Tlacochcalcas were not only one of the seven Mexica Calpullis in Aztlan, but that the name Tlacochcalco ("House of Spears") is inseparably linked with the north and with the land of the dead, and was also the land of Mixcoatl (ostensibly the northern hunting god), as well as of Tezcatlipoca Tlacochcalcayotl ("Warrior of the House of Spears").[23]

De Durand makes the logical suggestion that the Tlacochcalcas had come from the north and had then joined forces with the Nonoalca Teotlixcas to form a composite group. The paradox thus arises that not only was Chalco a melting pot for a whole series of migrant bodies named by Chimalpain, but, in addition, each Chalca group was a kind of ethnic cocktail. As their composite names imply, these groups were themselves the likely product of a complex blending process before they ever reached Chalco. In certain cases, such as that of the Acxotecas and Mihuaques, two or more peoples traveled together, but without fully merging.

However, as de Durand also implies, the antecedents of the Mexica Tlacochcalca *calpulli* cannot be taken for granted, and the name might have been given *a posteriori* by the Aztecs as a sign of Chichimec antecedents and thereby as a token of prestige. In this respect, the joint presence of the Tlacochcalca Teotlixcas and the Mexicas in Chapultepec is significant; conceivably the Mexicas could have "borrowed" the name from such prestigious neighbors—and as Durand implies—conferred it *a posteriori* on one of their own tribes.

Chimalpain's account stresses that, whatever their origins, the Tlacochcalcas were "palace people" *(tecpantlaca);* mention of their Gulf Coast affiliations, their skill in writing, their worship of Tezcatlipoca squarely places them among the non-Chichimecs, or Toltecs.

Their salient quality is not so much their superior culture, as their capacity for civilizing their neighbors. The seventh *Relación* tells how in 6 Acatl, after the Teotlixcas had withdrawn for five years to Xallipitzahuacan (near Ixtapalapa, and therefore outside the traditional Chalco territory), they still exercised a controlling influence over Chalco-Amecameca as a whole, that they proceeded to divide into two halves, centered on Itzcahuacan and Opochuacan; tribute was to be split into two parts and stored in special enclosures. In 6 Acatl, other Chalcas came to pay their respects to the Teotlixcas, including the ruler of Xochimilco Chimalhuacan, Pocatzin, on whom the Teotlixcas conferred the title of Teohuatecuhtli.

While the Teotlixcas thus came to acquire a unique prestige, most of the other Chalca groups with whom they came into contact were already fully fledged Mesoamericans, even before they arrived, rather than Teochichimecs. Some were more advanced than others, and each occupied its own segment of the cultural spectrum. Probably the Poyauhtecas came next in the pecking order after the Teotlixcas, since they are also called Nonoalcas, i.e., par excellence non-Chichimecs.

But not far down the list were the Tlaillotlacas; not only had they come from Teotenango, a center that in its day vied with Tollan, but the accounts of their former temples and palaces dazzle the imagination. They had also spent twenty years in Tollan itself, to complete their education as Toltecs. The cultural attainments of the Tecuanipas and Acxotecas were more modest and probably comparable one with the other. Both peoples, unlike the Chichimec Totolimpanecas, already possessed rulers and nobles, and worshiped Mesoamerican deities, complete with *teomamaque,* who bore their gods' images, when they were on the move. The Acxotecas came accompanied by three subordinate and humble tribes, who had no nobility, but only military leaders.

The Totolimpanecas are unequivocally portrayed as Chichimecs. They were sky worshipers and performed arrow-shooting ceremonies. But they were the most bellicose of all and had borne the brunt of the fighting against the Olmeca-Xicallancas, from whom they wrested the control of Amecameca. Paradoxically, symptomatic of their love-hate relationship with the other groups was their capacity to give orders to the Acxotecas under the stress of war, accompanied by a humble urge to learn the rites of the Acxoteca god.

Above all, from Chimalpain's unique documentation, we learn once more that to divide the peoples of Mesoamerica into Chichimecs and non-Chichimecs oversimplifies the issue. The martial skills of the Totolimpanecas help us to understand why certain Chichimec qualities were so cherished and why many were apt to call themselves Chichimecs who had little claim to that title. Three kinds of peoples can be identified in Chimalpain's account and are the equivalent of Toltecs, Tolteca Chichimecs, and Teochichimecs. To the first category belong the Teotlixcas and probably the Nonoalca Poyauhtecas; the Acxotecas, Tlaillotlacas, and the Tecuanipas conform to the general pattern of Tolteca Chichimecs; and the Totolimpanecas, together with the Tlaltehuaques, Contecas, and Mihuaques, are evident Teochichimecs.

In such a configuration, if the Chichimecs assumed the lead at the outset, the main need was for fighting, to overcome the previous inhabitants. However, culture and learning came into their own as soon as a more settled polity developed and the possessors of these gifts gained the upper hand.

Whatever the origin of the name Tlacochcalca, the Teotlixca Tlacochcalcas had come from Tollan and were in effect Toltec. Their presence in Chalco raises the interesting question of whether other migrants into the Valley of Mexico—Tepanecs, Mexicas, or Acolhuas—had not also come accompanied by elements that were by definition Toltec, or had immediately joined forces with similar elements in their new surroundings. Such Toltecs would tend to assume an ascendancy over the remainder of any migrant group that was thereby reintroduced to Toltec culture, notwithstanding the traditional pretensions to virile Chichimec origins. Certainly the Mexicas not only boasted of Culhua ancestry, but were ruled by part-Culhua princes, supported by Culhuanized or Toltecized *pipiltin.* In like manner the Teotlixcas, though not native to Chalco, set the tone in that center.

The Outbreak of War

During the reigns of Acamapichtli, Huitzilihuitl, and Chimalpopoca, the sources' reference to hostilities between Tepanec-Mexicas and Chalcas recur with unfailing regularity; usually the Mexicas get the upper hand, but no decisive result is achieved. Several texts name Chalco as a conquest of the Mexica *tlatoanis* but while victories may have been won, they were not conclusive, since the war continued and the Chalcas only finally succumbed in the reign of Moctezuma I in 1465, a generation after the defeat of Azcapotzalco.

Indirectly at least, Mexicas and Chalcas were related, since both had connections with the Chinampa peoples of Culhuacán, Xochimilco, and Mizquic. The Mexicas had, moreover, as mentioned above, been in contact with the Teotlixcas of Chalco in Chapultepec; and after their defeat in that place, some Mexicas went to Chalco rather than to Culhuacán. According to the *Anales de Cuauhtitlán,* when a ruler of Chalco, Xipemeztli, died in 3 Acatl (probably just before the first outbreak of hostilities with the Tepanec-Mexicas), his successor Yacatecuhtli went to Tenochtitlán, where his son was educated.[24]

As described in Chapter IX, the Mexicas intervened in Culhuacán, some time after their expulsion in 1343, at a moment when by all accounts the Chalcas also laid claim to that city and still occupied Xico, Mizquic, and Cuitlahuac. Therefore, when Acamapichtli mounted his throne, the rivalry between the two peoples was not new but had already started with the expulsion of the Mexicas from Chapultepec, followed later by some form of confrontation in the Culhuacán region.

Tezozómoc of Azcapotzalco took advantage of these antagonisms to further his ends, and at the outset the Chalca war was primarily a Tepanec rather than a Mexica affair. According to the

Anales de Cuauhtitlán, the war was undertaken by the Tepanecs and started in 1 Tecpatl (1376) in Techichco, described as a Chalca dependency at the time. Trautmann identifies Techichco as lying between Ixtapalapa and Azteopan, now Santa María Aztahuacan.[25] Cuauhtitlán played a part in these early hostilities, and Huactzin, ruler of that city, had reportedly established himself in Techichco, and was therefore at this stage implicated in the incipient struggle.[26]

The *Anales de Cuauhtitlán* contradict their assertion that the Mexicas were not initially involved by reporting in another passage that they engaged in a war of flowers with the Chalcas, that took place in Techichco (where the war had started) and lasted for nine years. The source states that after the initial nine years, i.e., in 10 Calli (1385), hostilities took a new turn; the intensified struggle was no longer a war of flowers and lasted seventy-two years (or until the reign of Moctezuma I).[27]

Chimalpain's information coincides reasonably with the *Anales de Cuauhtitlán;* clearly the two accounts derive partly but not wholly from a common source. Chimalpain follows a similar chronology for the war, even if his information on the dynasties of Chalco differs radically from briefer references to these rulers in the *Anales de Cuauhtitlán.* The third *Relación* confirms that the Mexica-Chalca *xochiyaotl* began in 1 Tecpatl (1376) and lasted for eight years; it was a mild affair, and both sides even released their prisoners; in subsequent hostilities this never occurred. Chimalpain also mentions a previous *xochiyaotl* fought between the Teotlixcas and other Chalca peoples; possibly it was in this war of flowers among Chalcas that the prisoners were really returned rather than in the first skirmishes with the Mexicas; little of what we know about Chalca-Mexica relations—or about Mesoamerican war in general—suggests the observance of such a gentlemanly rule.

The Teotlixcas were worshipers of Xipe, and Kirchhoff thought that the concept of *xochiyaotl* might even have originated in Chalco. The whole idea of a *xochiyaotl* between Mexicas and Chalcas, as opposed to a tourney of this kind between different Chalca groups, should be treated with caution; from the very outset conquest and victory over their Chalcan rival were more plausible Tepanec-Mexica objectives, rather than the mere urge to gain sacrificial victims. The concept of the *xochiyaotl* has a certain romantic appeal for chroniclers and even for modern writers, but the Chalco-Mexica war was a savage struggle, even if the ritual Mesoamerican proprieties were observed.

The *Anales de Cuauhtitlán* give both 1 Tecaptl and 3 Acatl for the commencement of the Chalca war; Chimalpain's seventh *Relación* also names 1 Tecpatl, and the sixth *Relación* offers 12 Acatl as an alternative; though the dates differ, the event in the two *Relaciones* is identically described as a *xochiyaotl* in which prisoners were spared the sacrificial knife and sent safely home. The 1 Tecpatl given by both sources most probably belongs to the Tenochca count and relates to 1376; Chimalpain's 12 Acatl date for the same occurrence must surely belong to the Cuitlahua count, in which it is the equivalent of 1375; otherwise, it makes no sense.[28] The 3 Acatl mentioned by the *Anales de Cuauhtitlán* for the start of the war may belong to yet another year-count, to which the *Anales de Cuauhtitlán* date of 13 Tecpatl for the accession of Tezozómoc also belongs. The Chalca war is generally reported to have started a few years after the accession of Tezozómoc, followed by that of Acamapichtli and of Cuacuapitzahuac, probably occurring in 1370 or 1371. Chimalpain incidentally also writes of a bitter battle that took place in the vicinity of Ixtapalapa in 5 Acatl (1367?), in which the Ixtapalapans fought on the side of the Tepanec-Mexicas. But since the sources insist that the war started after the accession of Tezozómoc and his Mexica colleagues, the date of 1367 is unlikely to be correct. More probably the date corresponds to the Culhua-Texcocan count, and should be read as 1387, not 1367; this would be just two years after the moment when hostilities took a new turn in 1385. The statement by Chimalpain that Cacamatzin Tecuhtli of Tlaillotlacan Amaquemecan died in this episode hardly affects the issue, since there were at least two rulers of Amecameca of that name, and reports of their dates are conflicting. The *Crónica Mexicayotl* mentions that there was no ruler called Cacamatzin, but only a distinguished warrior who never became a ruler.[29] The *Anales de Cuauhtitlán* confirm the death of Cacamatzin in 3 Calli, the same year as that of Huitzilihuitl, probably 1417.[30]

The War Continues

Acamapichtli was succeeded by Huitzilihuitl in 1391, and the war went on unabated in this *tlatoani*'s reign. Accounts of hostilities for its opening decade are lacking; however, the *Historia de los Mexicanos* reports a Chalca setback for 1406 in a struggle that continued for two years and ended in a Chalca defeat.[31] The *Anales de Tlatelolco* confirm this occurrence and describe a truce in 7 Tecpatl, or 1408 in the Tenochca calendar. The same source implies that this truce followed a Chalca success: "In 7 Tecpatl we surrendered the edge of the lagoon to the Chalcas. . . . they remained our friends for 120 days and then rebelled again."[32] The source also mentions another Chalca "rebellion" that had occurred nine years earlier.

For Chimalpain the year previous to 7 Tecpatl, 6 Acatl, marked a turning point in the war, when the Chalcas suffered a shattering defeat that was due in part to internal dissension. Apparently in that year three dissident Chalca leaders named as *cuezconpiaia* (keeper of the silos), or *cuexconpixque,* went to Huitzilihuitl in Tenochtitlán and to Itzcoatl, who at that time occupied the office of *tlacateccatl.* These *cuezconpixque* had apparently been appointed by the Mexicas to obtain the dry maize that the Chalcas were obliged to deliver. To the Mexica leaders they "spoke falsities" of various Chalca rulers *(quintentlapiquico),* and in particular against Toteoci Teuhctli, ruler of the Acxotecas. Several rulers of the Chalcan *tecpans* then took flight, and went to Amomolloco Huitzillac, near to Yecapixtla. The Mexicas sent an expedition to Chalco to kill these señores, but found that they had already fled; the cuezconpixque were then put in control of Chalco; Chimalpain describes them as mere *macehuales,* not true rulers: "auh macihui yn tlahtocatque yn cuezconpixque, yece ca çan macehualtin. ca çan quichtecque yn tlahtocayotl."[33]

This spectacular success on the part of the Mexicas alarmed other peoples, who rushed to Chalco's defense; as already cited, they recalled the former greatness of that center, from which so many other señores had depended for their titles in former times, referring to Chalco as "our father and our mother." This coalition included not only peoples of the Puebla-Tlaxcala valley, usually well disposed towards Chalco, but also of the Chinampa cities, nominally then under Mexica control, as well as important elements from places in the Toluca valley described as Mazahuacan, Matlatzinco, and Xiquipilco; even Cuauhtitlán, staunch ally of the Mexicas, took part.

Strangest of all, the anti-Mexica grouping included the Azcapot-zalcans, supposedly their overlords.

Huitzilihuitl, the Mexica *tlatoani*, faced with such an awesome array, gave way and promised to restore to their thrones the Chalcan señores who had fled; the *cuezconpixque*, whose machinations had set the crisis in motion, were to be killed. Toteocitecuhtli of Acxot-lan and Ixmacpaltzin of Itzcahuacan were duly reinstated in their *señorios;* the latter died three years later, after a reign of thirty years, during four of which he had lived in exile under the Mexica occupation.

The incident raises many questions: first, a close examination of Tepanec-Mexica relations in the next chapter will stress the in-congruity of the ranging of Tepanecs and Mexicas on opposite sides in several conflicts at a time when the latter were still vassals of the former. As I will later demonstrate in more detail, by this stage the Mexicas seem to have been more partners than subjects of Azcapot-zalco, and this might explain any temporary falling out, since two allies may differ on a single issue, whereas a mere vassal cannot so easily defy his master with impunity. Apparently, therefore, in about 1410 the Mexicas under Huitzilihuitl, profiting by Chalca dissen-sions, did score a spectacular success in their war of attrition, but were then restrained from virtually controlling Chalco by the Tepan-ecs and others, already alarmed by their overweening ambitions.

I suspect that the story has been rather oversimplified, if not exaggerated. In the first place, among the complex and petty rival-ries of central Mesoamerica at this time, a virtual consensus among the different peoples, including not only the leading powers of the Valley of Mexico, but also of the Puebla-Tlaxcala and Toluca val-leys, is surely unprecedented. Normally, if some cities took one side in a quarrel, the rest would rally to the opposing group. Agreement on a concerted action is uncharacteristic of the politics of the period, and even the alliance against Azcapotzalco twenty years later was not so all-embracing. It is more probable that the Tepanecs of Azcapot-zalco, feeling that they had overstimulated the Mexicas' zeal to crush Chalco, took fright at the success of their proteges, and sought to restrain them—a course of action which certain neighbors gladly supported.

But even conceding a growth of Mexica power and influence,

their ability to overthrow Chalco at such an early stage in their career of conquest remains in doubt. Chimalpain's story probably combines two quite separate episodes in the long-drawn-out Mexica-Chalca conflict; whereas the Mexicas indeed scored some victory in 1410 or thereabouts, and were then restrained by the Tepanecs, such a sweeping success against Chalco is more likely to have occurred after, not before, the fall of Azcapotzalco in 1428. By 1430 (or 7 Tecpatl in the Culhua Texcocan count), the Tepanecs were no longer in a position to intervene, but very possibly the peoples of the Puebla-Tlaxcala and Toluca valleys, as yet unconquered by the Aztecs, then appealed to them to act with moderation in dealing with a city so revered for its former glories.

Following the incident of 1410, the Chalcas actually supported Azcapotzalco in the Tepanec war against Huehue Ixtlilxóchitl of Texcoco, from 1414 to 1417; however, in 1428 (1 Tecpatl, Tenochca count) the Chalcas, according to Chimalpain's seventh *Relación,* captured the future Moctezuma I, who was on a diplomatic mission to Huexotzingo, and were about to sacrifice him, if he had not managed to escape.

But in the years following the fall of Azcapotzalco, notwithstanding this flagrant insult to a great Mexica warlord and future *tlatoani,* we know nothing officially of any punitive expedition against the Chalcas. Surely Moctezuma and Itzcoatl would have been swift to avenge this humiliating incident, and Chalco would in any case have been a natural target for Mexica aggression after their other triumphs. While nothing can be proved, I question whether two incidents have not been rolled into one, and whether, while part of the story of the *cuezconpixque* relates to 1410, or 7 Tecpatl, Tenochca count, this has not also been confused with a more sweeping triumph in about 1430, or 7 Tecpatl, Culhua Texcoco count— the equivalent of 1 Tecpatl in the Tenochca calendar.

Certain support for such a view may be cited from other sources. Chimalpain generally employs the Tenochca calendar when dating incidents affecting the Mexicas and emanating from Mexica documents, but his Chalca king-lists apparently belong to the Culhua count, and his own Julian correlations for their reigns are therefore twenty years too early. Confusion could thereby arise; the incident concerning the *cuezconpixque,* described as beginning in 9 Tochtli and taken from a Mexica source, would indeed have taken place in 1410, since the 9 Tochtli belongs to the Tenochca count. However, dates for the flight of any Chalca ruler, that resulted in the termination or suspension of his reign, would derive from the Chalca king-list, copied by Chimalpain from another source using the Culhua Texcocan count; these escapes would thus have occurred in the *Culhua* 9 Tochtli, that is the equivalent of 1430, not of 1410. The Chalca ruler who absconded to Huexotzingo would accordingly have been motivated by a second and more resounding triumph over Chalco, shortly after the fall of Azcapotzalco, when the Mexicas were in a position to assert themselves to the full.

Such a proposition might seem at first sight to complicate matters unduly, but it helps to explain two otherwise unaccountable phenomena: first, the all-too-sweeping success of the Mexicas as early as 1410, that is hardly commensurate with their strength at that stage; second, if Chimalpain had used the Culhua count for his Chalca king-lists, at what point did he switch to the Tenochca count that he was obviously using for the dates of rulers in the immediate pre-Conquest period?

It seems that by 1465 Chimalpain's native dates can be correctly related to the Tenochca count; 12 Calli, the Tenochca equivalent of 1465, is a well-attested date, and in that year the Mexicas finally overthrew Chalco and made a clean sweep of Chalca rulers, who again fled to Huexotzingo; such reigns according end abruptly in or about 1465. But this story has one very odd feature. According to Chimalpain's Julian calendar correlations, of these fugitive señores, several had by that date already reigned for inordinately long periods: Cuauhtlehuac of Tzacualtitlan Tenanco Chiconcoac since 1418: Cohuanecatzin of Teohuacan Amaquemecan since 1411: Ayocuantzin of Itztlacozauhuacan Amaquemecan since 1411: and Cuateotzin of Itzcahuacan Chalco since 1417. Apart from these four, the only other *señorío* for which Chimalpain provides a consecutive king-list covering this period is Tlalmanalco Opochuacan, whose señor in 1465 had only reigned for fourteen years. Therefore, in the case of the five Chalca dynasties for which a succession of rulers is given between 1400 and 1465, two monarchs had in 1465 been reigning for fifty-four years, one for forty-eight years, and one for forty-seven. The reigns of the kings of England need only be recalled once more to realize that such figures are far-fetched. Of the forty sovereigns between William the Conqueror and Elizabeth II, only three reigned for fifty years or more. Of the nine Tenochca *tlatoanis,* the longest reign, that of Moctezuma I, lasted a mere twenty-eight years. And yet we are asked to believe that four out of five Chalca señores had passed or were nearing their golden jubilee in 1465 and were still alive.

A more feasible explanation does exist, namely, that the accession date of these rulers corresponded to the Culhua or some other count, while their deposition in 1365 belonged to the Tenochca calendar. In such a case, the true accession date of each monarch has to be put forward at least twenty years, and the length of their respective reigns becomes just acceptable. The only alternative is to discard the dating of these rulers as semi-legendary, and to treat their reigns as ritual rather than historic, since they approximate loosely to the length of a fifty-two year cycle.

The question of change-overs from one calendar to another is one of the major problems of Mesoamerican chronology, since by the time of the Conquest, most dates are clearly given in the Tenochca count. In the case of Culhuacán, it has already been shown in Chapter II that this adjustment to the Culhua count had probably taken place over a century earlier, at a time when the Mexica-Tepanecs were becoming involved in Culhuacán. The changeover was made between the reigns of Coxcox and Huehue Acamapichtli, the first Culhua sovereign whose dates seem to correspond to the Tenochca count.

Chalcan Finale

Chimalpopoca succeeded Huitzilihuitl in 1415, 1416, or 1417. During his reign hostilities against Chalco continued; certain episodes are mentioned, though details are lacking. According to the *Anales de Tlatelolco,* a war against Chalco occurred two years after Chimalpopoca's accession, and Chalco was reportedly occupied by the Mexicas.[34] The Codex Mexicanus mentions a Mexica-Chalca war in 7 Calli, or 1421.[35] Chimalpain in his third *Relación* writes of another confrontation in 11 Calli or 1425; the *Anales de Cuauhtitlán* give Chalco as a conquest both for Huitzilihuitl and for Chi-

284

malpopoca, but like certain other "conquests," this may be an ephemeral victory rather than a true occupation. During the following years Chalco fared better, since it was being actively wooed by both parties to the coming conflict between Azcapotzalco and its enemies. In the end Chalco remained neutral; by missing this golden opportunity of revenge, the fate of the city was sealed.

It was not until 1465, however, that Moctezuma I finally subjugated Chalco, after nearly one hundred years of warfare. Even then, Chalca enmity towards the Mexicas failed to subside. The *Anales de Cuauhtitlán* state that the many leaders who then fled to Huexotzingo continued to incite the Huexotzingans against the Mexicas.[36]

According to the surviving accounts, Chalco, during its long war with the Tepanec-Mexicas, was usually on the defensive. However, both its pristine glory and its staunch defense make of Chalco a power in its own right and a potential, if thwarted, contender for the Toltec heritage.

XI. The Disputed Heritage

The General Situation

In the last decades of the period usually called the "Age of the Independent *Señorios*," few such *señorios* survived and the remainder were clasped in the greedy embrace of the king of Azcapotzalco.

I have previously stressed the need for caution in appraising Tezozómoc and his achievement. Certain episodes, such as the epic of Coyohua, told by the *Anales de Cuauhtitlán,* have an apocryphal ring; Tezozómoc's funery rites seem partly to be taken from those of Axayacatl; the story of how the ailing Tezozómoc had no warmth in his body and was wrapped in thick robes exactly recalls the description of the old age of King David in the Book of Kings. Nonetheless, in the main his feats are well documented, and many colorful episodes, such as the dispatch of raw cotton to Huehue Ixtlilxochitl, to be woven in token of submission, could have been well illustrated in pre-Conquest codices. The Coyohua saga seems more apt to have been passed by word of mouth from one Calmecac generation to the next. In assessing the historicity of Mesoamerican traditions, it is surely a useful but baffling task to separate the wheat of codical recording from the chaff of oral tradition that so easily becomes garbled with the passage of time.

286

Xaltocan had been overthrown in 1395, following the Tepanec-Mexica intervention in Cuauhtitlán's ceaseless struggle against that city. Cuauhtinchan, in the Puebla-Tlaxcala valley, was probably the victim of assault rather than conquest in 1398. By 1400 the Tepanecs, reinforced by the Mexicas, had rivaled the feat of arms of Tochintecuhtli and Huetzin over a century before. The Tepanec Empire clearly embraced many a conquest of the first Acolhua Empire: the northern Valley of Mexico, Culhuacán and the Chinampa cities in the southern valley, the Ocuilan-Malinalco enclave of the valley of Toluca, and in a northeasterly direction, both empire builders had advanced towards Tulancingo. The Tepanecs, however, had not so far subdued the heartland of Acolhuacan, a twin pillar of the Huetzin-Tochintecuhtli domain. On the other hand, they had pressed forward into Morelos, where the previous contenders seemingly did not penetrate though they held Culhuacán, the gateway to the region; Chalco had remained unconquered in both instances. Accordingly, the two realms had managed to absorb most of what I regard as the confines of Toltec power.

The bounds of the first Acolhua Empire and the nature of its politico-military system are ill defined. In the case of the Tepanecs, the situation is also far from clear. For instance, both in the reign of Maxtla and in late pre-Conquest times indications exist that there were two rulers in Azcapotzalco; however, we know of no second tyrant who presumed to share a throne with the imperious Tezozómoc.

A Cuckoo in the Nest

Details of Tepanec imperial policy are obscure, and in particular their relationship with the Mexicas is enigmatic. It is far from clear whether control lay solely in the Tepanecs' hands; alternatively, from a vassal status, had the Mexicas already risen to the rank of partners in a kind of dual alliance? Many people take for granted that the Mexicas continued to serve as the menials of Azcapotzalco until the very moment of reckoning in 1428, when these humble servants in a few eventful weeks turned the tables on their masters. Barlow in particular supported this view, on the strength of a partial backing in certain sources.

I have previously argued at greater length that the Tepanec hold on the Mexicas was loosening well before 1428, and that they by then were more partners than tributaries.[1] Without doubt, after the foundation, or refoundation, of Tenochtitlán and Tlatelolco, the Mexica sovereigns became vassals of Azcapotzalco, if not their nominees. This situation prevailed during Acamapichtli's reign, but certain doubts persist concerning his achievements; in particular, some of his conquests follow all too closely those of his successor.

Huitzilihuitl married Tezozómoc's daughter; as a son-in-law he became as much equal as underling of Tezozómoc. Huitzilihuitl also wooed the daughter of the ruler of Cuauhnahuac; no evidence survives about how far this move formed part of any Tepanec master plan and whether the Mexica advance into the valley of Morelos was made under strictly Tepanec auspices. It seems to have stemmed from an increasing Mexica hold on the Chinampa region that served as a springboard for such a venture.

Significantly, the Mexicas do not seem to have remained mere tributaries; that is to say, people forced to disgorge their annual surplus as tribute in kind or in service to the Tepanec imperial power. On the contrary, the Tepanec, or Tepanec-Mexica Empire, far from impoverishing the Mexicas, became a source of gain. We learn how, following Huitzilihuitl's conquests in the valley of Morelos, Mexica nobles for the first time shed their rustic garments of maguey cactus fiber and donned clothes of cotton. By this time Mexica tribute to the Tepanecs was reduced to minimal proportions; following Huitzilihuitl's marriage to Tezozómoc's daughter, only a nominal tribute of ducks and other lagoon produce was paid.[2]

In several instances, the Mexicas, former payers of tribute, advanced to the receiving end of the line. After the Xaltocan war, they gained a share of Xaltocan territory. Clavijero in particular tells how the war against Xaltocan enhanced their status.[3] A prince from the ruling house of Tlatelolco was later imposed upon the throne of Xaltocan.[4] Ixtlilxóchitl relates that after the Acolhua defeat in 1418, Texcoco was placed under Tenochca rule, while Tlatelolco assumed control of Huexotla. According to the same writer, although Texcoco payed tribute to the Mexicas, it recognized Tezozómoc as supreme lord.[5] Torquemada also insists that sovereignty rested in Tezozómoc's hands.[6]

Nonetheless, even if Torquemada is right in maintaining that the ultimate control belonged to Tezozómoc as a kind of king of kings, the sources concur that the Mexicas had by then joined the ranks of tribute-gatherers and stood to gain by the triumphs of the Tepanecs. Far from being mere mercenaries, they were beginning to vie with their overlords and to become a cuckoo in the Tepanec nest.

The supposition that the Mexicas were cast in the role of humble suppliants of Azcapotzalco until 1428 rests more than anything on the harsh treatment of Chimalpopoca, Huitzilihuitl's successor, leading to his assassination. But, as will later be explained in detail, reports on the liquidation of that ruler are contradictory, and Chimalpopoca more probably fell victim to a palace revolution in Tenochtitlán, prompted not by the Tepanecs of Azcapotzalco, but by their dissident kinsmen of Tlacopan.

Quite possibly Tezozómoc's grandson, Chimalpopoca, tended to submit to the dictates of the Tepanecs during his short reign. But the Tenochca challenge to Azcapotzalco probably gathered strength more gradually than Barlow and others have suggested, just as the rise to power of Texcoco in Acolhuacan at the expense of Coatlichán was not brought about in a day, as a result of a single battle.[7]

The case of Chalco illustrates the ambiguities of Tepanec-Mexica relations. As related in Chapter X, in 1411 the Mexicas intervened massively in the affairs of Chalco-Amecameca, and its various *tecpans* were overthrown and their rulers expelled. Even though as already suggested, some of Chalco's misfortunes really occurred twenty years later, the Mexicas in about 1411 certainly dealt a heavy blow to this adversary, even if we ignore its exact nature. But the Tepanecs, far from sponsoring the venture, opposed it and joined a coalition that rushed to the defense of Chalco and forced the Mexicas to give way; this alliance, it may be recalled, included Matlatzincas and Mazahuas from the valley of Toluca, as well as Cholulans and Huexotzingans.[8] While the Mexicas were thus the sworn enemies of the Chalcas, the Tepanecs blew hot and cold and were as often ranged on the side of the latter as of the former. The Chalcas declined to join the anti-Tepanec coalition in 1428, and Maxtla reportedly fled to Chalco after his defeat. After the initial war of 1376, the Tepanecs seem to have been ready to leave Chalco to its own devices, and were at times more intent upon restraining the Mexicas in their zeal for final victory.

Much further evidence points to divergences between Mexicas and Tepanecs *before* the final struggle in 1428: In the *Anales de Cuauhtitlán,* the following passage concerns a confrontation between the two in 1 Acatl: "1 Acatl [A.D. 1415]. Ye ypan inyn xihuitl yancuican yaotique yn mexitin yn ompan tepanohuayan. Ypan inyn çan oc tepiton quimoquauhtlaltica çan oc ynneyxcahuil." ("1 Reed [A.D. 1415]. In this year the Mexicas made war in Tepanohuayan for the first time. In this year for the first time they had established for themselves a small piece of war-land, as their own exclusive possession.")[9]

For events occurring two years later, the report runs: "Yn ipan ey tochtli yc oppa quimixnamicti yn tepanecatl yn mexicatl achtopa matlacxihuitl omome. Ynic otlayecoltique tepaneca yn opa tenoch-titlan ypan çe acatl quinpehua yquac çan oc ochiton yn iquauhtlal contlalica mexitin." ("In 3 Rabbit [1430], for the second time the Mexicas fought with the Tepanecs. First for twelve years the Te-panecs served strangers there in Tenochtitlán. In 1 Reed [1415] they had been defeated. And besides, the Mexicas had established their war-land.")

Some of the pitfalls of Nahuatl translations are illustrated by the Velásquez translation, which treats the last passage as the record of a Tepanec victory in 1415 over the Mexicas, who had merely "piled up a little wood" ("cuando ellos solos habían amontonado un poco de leña").[10] Walter Lehmann appears to be correct in conveying the opposite meaning, in which the Mexicas figure as victors and the Tepanecs as vanquished; he clearly derives the word *"quauhtlaltica"* from the noun *quauhtlalli,* for which Siménon's dictionary gives the meaning "land containing detritus of wood, fertile land, excellent for cultivating maize. Derivation: *quauitl, tlalli."* However, for Leh-mann, *quauhtlatica* and *iquauhtlal* are formed from the prefix *quauh* (plus *tlalli*) deriving from *quauhtli* (eagle) and thus having a warlike connotation, rather than from *quauhuitl,* meaning "wood."

If the two dates belong to the same year-count, then 1 Acatl falls thirteen years before 1 Tecpatl, the date given by most sources for the final war, and fifteen years before 3 Tochtli, quoted in other documents. 1 Tecpatl is the Tenochca calendar equivalent of 1428, and 1 Acatl is 1415, as noted by Lehmann. Now Jiménez Moreno regards this 1 Acatl as belonging what he calls the Culhua II count, in which it would fall in 1427. I have also identified the use in certain cases of this particular native calendar, as for instance by Ixtlilxóchitl for the death of Acamapichtli, for the beginning of the war against Xaltocan and of the war against Texcoco.[11]

I consider, however, that the 1 Acatl in question does belong to the Tenochca count and that 1415 is the correct Julian calendar equivalent. In the first place, while the *Anales de Cuauhtitlán* employ various native calendars, I have not so far identified their use in other cases of "Culhua II." Moreover, this source reports that in the same 1 Acatl Tepolitzmaitl, ruler of Cuitlahuac-Tiçic, died after a reign of twenty-three years; it states in a previous passage that this monarch ascended his throne in 5 Calli, which would fall twenty-two years before 5 Calli in the same calendar (or twenty-three years by the exclusive method of counting). It is surely unlikely that the *Anales de Cuauhtitlán* would have thus twice repeated the use of this Culhua II count, so hard to find anywhere else in the document. Moreover, 1 Acatl, 1415, falls very near to 1416, when other indications occur of a falling out between Mexicas and Tepanecs.

Dibble also reads signs in the Codex en Cruz, associated with the year 1 Acatl, as indicating that a war was fought by the Tepanecs in that year, but the source does not relate against whom.[12] The glyph in question, that Dibble interprets as signifying Tepanecs, consists of a stone *(tetl)* and a flag *(pantli)* surmounted by a shield and a kind of club or sword. Eight years later, in 9 Acatl (1423 Tenochca count), the same people, presumably the Tepanecs, were involved in a second war against an unnamed enemy. But, most significantly, this date differs by only one year from 8 Tochtli, given by Chimalpain for an encounter between Tepanecs and Mexicas; therefore, the unnamed enemy may have been Tenochtitlán. It is surely difficult to consign Chimalpain's 8 Tochtli to any year-count that would place it as late as 1428, or thereabouts.

The *Anales de Tlatelolco* mention another conflict that apparently involved Tepanecs and Mexicas on opposite sides: "In the ninth year of his reign [Tlacateotl] made war upon the *tecpantlacalque"* (for the use of Tecpanecatl for Tepanecatl, see Chapter VI).[13] According to the same source, Tlacateotl ascended the throne of Tlatelolco in 12 Acatl, probably Texcoco-Culhua count and therefore 1407. His ninth year would thus be 1416, which coincides with the great offensive of Huehue Ixtlilxóchitl of Texcoco against Azcapotzalco, that will be described below. The *Anales de Tlatelolco* again mention this offensive in another passage, that tells how Tepanohuayan was defeated when four sovereigns advanced on the city; this happened in the reign of Huitzilihuitl, though no date is given. While it does not name the four sovereigns in question, the source tells of the ruler of Tlatelolco as a one-time Tepanec adversary and thereby hints that at some stage in the Tepanec-Texcocan war the Mexicas changed sides and thereby shared in an ephemeral triumph. The inclusion of Azcapotzalco in the *Anales de Cuauhtitlán* list of "conquests" by Huitzilihuitl is not without significance, while Tepanohuayan figures in the *Anales de Tlatelolco* conquest list for the same ruler.

Four sources accordingly contain quite different suggestions that a falling out occurred in 1415, 1416, or 1417 between the Mexicas and the Tepanecs. To these should be added other reports of friction over royal betrothals. When Maxtla was ruler of Coyoacan, some time before his accession in Azcapotzalco, he was angry with Huitzilihuitl and opposed the Tenochca ruler's marriage to his sister, Ayauhcihuatl.[14] Huehue Ixtlilxóchitl is said to have refused the hand of the daughter of Tezozómoc and then to have married Huitzilihuitl's sister. But a Mexica ruler so utterly subservient to the Tepanecs would scarcely have dared to offend them by wedding his daughter to a sovereign who had spurned the great Tezozómoc's own child.

Dynastic rivalries involved the Mexicas and Tepanecs in other quarrels. Epcoatl, son of Tezozómoc, became king of Toltitlan, but was enraged by the Mexicas who had the audacity to encourage the people of Cuauhtitlán to reject one of his sons as ruler.[15]

A substantial body of evidence therefore suggests that disputes between Mexicas and Tepanecs arose before 1428, and that the Tepanecs could not always control their former vassals. On a number of occasions, the Mexicas figure as partners, allies, or even rivals more than as underlings.

The Last Bastion

Culhuacán, Tenayuca, and Xaltocan, the centers that dominated the scene after the fall of Tollan, had now been vanquished. Chalco was beleaguered though intact, but a greater thorn in the flesh of Tezozómoc was Texcoco, still a bastion of independence within the Valley of Mexico.

Even before the reign of Huehue Ixtlilxóchitl, beginning in 1409, Texcoco had become the principal city of Acolhuacan, if not the undisputed leader. The loyalty of certain Acolhua princes to Quinatzin and to his son Techotlalatzin remained doubtful. Huehue Ixtlilxóchitl at least exercised a firm hold on Huexotla and Coatlichán, and his mother, Tozquentzin, was the daughter of Achitometl of Coatlichán.

The process whereby power passed from Coatlichán to Texcoco remains obscure. If hostilities occurred between the two cities, no record survives. Coatlichán retained a certain prestige, and several sources trace Acamapichtli's lineage to that city, whose dynastic links with the royal house of Culhuacán had not yet been severed.

Attention has already been drawn to the confusions created by Alva Ixtlilxóchitl's insistence that Quinatzin was contemporary both of Huetzin and of Acamapichtli, who reigned one hundred years later. Probably the early Quinatzin was the same person as Huetzin, ruler of Coatlichán. The later, or second, Quinatzin enjoyed a long reign, and consolidated Texcoco's leadership among the Acolhua centers. This second Quinatzin lived until 1377 and aided Acamapichtli in wars against the Chinampa cities and possibly also in the valley of Morelos. Techotlalatzin, his son, maintained a rather low profile; particularly during Tezozómoc's war against Xaltocan, he refused to help Xaltocan, but nonetheless gave lands to fugitives from that city after the conflict was over (see Chapter V). Both reigns witnessed an influx of sophisticated migrants, and by 1400 Texcoco was both powerful and civilized. Its original inhabitants may by then have been left in a minority and the names of the six principal barrios of the city recalled the various migrants: Mexica-pan, Colhuacán, Huitznahuac, Tepan, Tlaillotlacan, and Chimalpan.

The latter-day Texcocans were hardly therefore pure Acolhuas, and such ethnic diversity was surely an addéd source of strength, even if the royal house remained basically Acolhua while retaining links with Culhuacán. The city also had certain ties with Chalco; the Tlaillotlacas and Chinampanecas had spent some time there before some of them settled in Texcoco. Of equal significance were the special ties that bound Texcoco to the peoples of the Puebla-Tlaxcala valley—to a point where Quinatzin could speak of the rulers of Tlaxcala and Huexotzingo as "brothers."[16]

Techotlalatzin seems to have reached a kind of *modus vivendi* with Tezozómoc, but with the accession of his son, Huehue Ixtlil-xóchitl, everything changed. He was a man of a different stamp, who claimed full leadership over the Acolhuas, proclaiming himself heir to the ancestral title of Chichimecatecuhtli. He stood up to Tezozó-moc, and even spurned marriage with the Grand Monarch's daughter when Tezozómoc refused to recognize him as Chichimecatecuhtli. Instead he had married Matlacihuatzin, daughter of Huitzilihuitl. This match profoundly influenced events since, as a result, Neza-hualcoyotl was born half-Mexica.

Following Huehue Ixtlilxóchitl's accession and his renewal of ancient claims, Tezozómoc was not slow to act. He had a dual motive: first, the assertion of his supremacy over the Acolhuas; and second, the instigation of preventative action against an insidious rival. He first sent for the Mexicas, told them that he would not recognize Ixtlilxóchitl as Chichimecatecuhtli, and inveighed upon his haughtiness and presumption. Tezozómoc would himself be "emperor" and his grandchildren, Chimalpopoca of Tenochtitlán and Tlacateotl of Tlatelolco, would be the twin pillars of his throne; together, the three would rule the earth.[17] Tezozómoc reminded his listeners that some Acolhua rulers were his relatives and would support him against the upstart Texcocan.

Tezozómoc's tirade is pregnant with meaning; it underscores the enhanced status of the Mexicas as allies more than servants and even hints at the formation of a new triple alliance; equally, it stresses the discord that prevailed among the Acolhuas. Veytia incidentally says that Tezozómoc also summoned other señores to his presence but that they were less important than the Mexica rulers.[18]

As a preliminary to his designs against Texcoco, Tezozómoc now sent cotton to Huehue Ixtlilxóchitl, and demanded that it should be woven and returned to him as a token of submission. The first consignment was sent in 1410, and each year the quantity was increased. Even at this stage, Ixtlilxóchitl was plagued with disloyalty, and some of his allies refused to help him; for lack of resources, he did not dare to punish them.

The Lining Up of Forces

By the year 11 Calli, or 1413, the line-up of forces for the coming conflict was almost complete, according to Alva Ixtlilxóchitl. He mentions some kind of battle in the Huexotla region; however, in view of repeated assertions that the war only lasted four years, this can have been no more than an initial skirmish.

Tezozómoc now sent even more cotton to Huehue Ixtlilxóchitl than before. But this time the Texcocan flung down the gauntlet and refused to weave it, saying that he would rather use it to make protective arms. Tezozómoc once more promised to partition Acolhua domains with the Mexicas and to give one-third each to Tlatelolco and Tenochtitlán.[19]

The Texcocan ruler on his side mustered his allies, in particular Huexotla and Coatlichán, who had remained faithful. Ixtapalapa and Chalco are mentioned, though they later changed sides. Representatives from Acolman and Tepechpan also attended, but from the outset their rulers were really on the side of Tezozómoc. Torquemada tells how the kings of many places themselves favored Ixtlilxóchitl but could not command the loyalty of their subjects to his cause.[20] In the following year, 1414, the Texcocan ruler had himself crowned as "universal monarch" in Huexotla; only his two most stalwart allies, the señores of Coatlichán and Huexotla, were present. Then, as a precautionary move, he placed guards on the frontiers of Chalco and Ixtapalapa, which he rightly mistrusted.[21] Lack of unity among the Acolhuas and their allies is thus a salient feature of this war, though certain evidence, previously cited, suggests that Tezozómoc was not always master in his own house, any more than his Texcocan rival.

The War

In 1415, Tezozómoc ordered a major offensive. He summoned a powerful force, including not only Mexicas but also contingents from Coyoacan, Tlacopan, Huitzilopochco, Mizquic, Cuitlahuac, and Culhuacán. This army made a surprise attack on the Acolhua city of Iztapaloca, but the assault was repulsed, and Tezozómoc was irate that his vassals had failed to crush the enemy resistance.

Nonetheless, the Tepanec monarch contained his anger and halted his attack, although the Mexicas were eager to resume the campaign. Instead, he launched a diplomatic offensive that was much more rewarding, since he managed to win over to his side the rulers of Otompan and Chalco. This move was decisive; previously Tezozómoc had disposed of levies drawn only from the Tepanecs and Mexicas, reinforced by the Chinampa cities, and they had proved unequal to the Acolhua forces as long as other neighbors remained neutral. Moreover, in spite of previous defections, Alva Ixtlilxóchitl gives an impressive list of places that supported the Texcocans, including contingents from Zempoala and Tulancingo.[22]

These desertions from his cause spurred Huehue Ixtlilxóchitl to make a desperate counter-move at the beginning of the year 3 Calli, or 1417. Leaving Chalco on one side, as too powerful to conquer, he marched in a northeasterly direction to subdue Otompan, and then veered northwest through Axapochco and Temascalpan. Beyond this place he fought a major battle, pressed on to Xilotepec, then turned down to Citlaltepec, and fought a second battle at Tepotzotlán; he caught up with the Tepanecs at Tecpatepec, and, after again defeating them, reached Temacpapalco, near Azcapotzalco, which he besieged for four years, according to Alva Ixtlilxóchitl.[23] Veytia, however, says that the siege lasted four months, which is much more feasible. Huehue Ixtlilxóchitl's route, cited above, includes a place named Tula, as well as a Xilotepec. However, as explained in Chapter IX, I now adhere to the view that the places in question are a Tula that is an *estancia* of Temascalpa, and Jilocingo, in the *muni-*

cipio of Huepochtla. These localities form part of a logical line of march for Huehue Ixtlilxóchitl, as can be seen on Map 3. Tula de Allende and Jilotepec de Abasolo would have constituted a vast and pointless diversion from this route. By the same token, this identification for Tula and Jilotepec is more in keeping with realistic estimates of Tepanec territory, and Ixtlilxóchitl had no reason to use up his strength in an advance to Tula de Allende.

The role of the Mexicas during this phase of the struggle has already been discussed; the intriguing possibility remains that they momentarily changed sides. There is little evidence that they rushed to the rescue of Azcapotzalco at this crucial point; any temporary change of alliance might have been motivated by the Chalcas, who had been won over to the Tepanec side, thereby perhaps pushing the Mexicas into the opposing camp.

Huehue Ixtlilxóchitl's daring but abortive assault on Azcapotzalco apparently petered out and was followed by a new Tepanec offensive. According to Alva Ixtlilxóchitl, the Acolhua attack at one point caused Tezozómoc to lose his nerve, and he virtually sued for peace, persuading the Texcocan ruler that if he would raise the siege and go home, he would be recognized as Chichimecatecuhtli.[24] But this is a surprising tale, even from the pen of a Texcocan apologist reluctant to admit defeat. There was surely scant cause to abandon a successful campaign in return for such nebulous promises, and other reasons have to be sought.

A study of the chronology reveals that Tezozómoc's big offensive, described by Ixtlilxóchitl and the Codex Xolotl as occurring much earlier in the war, really took place at this stage, just after the attack on Azcapotzalco. Accordingly it is more likely that Tezozómoc, seeing that Huehue Ixtlilxóchitl had left his homeland undefended, decided that attack was his best form of defense.

In developing this strategy, Tezozómoc cunningly pretended that his attack was to be concentrated on Chiconauhtla, north of Texcoco, whereas in fact his main army moved on Huexotla, to the south of that city. A kind of pincer movement followed, in which, as illustrated in the Codex Xolotl, one prong was directed against the Acolhuas of Huexotla, Coatlichán, and Coatepec, while the other reached out towards Chiconauhtla and Otumba.

The codex, interpreted by Ixtlilxóchitl, maintains that the attack

MAP 3

THE TEPANEC — TEXCOCAN WAR

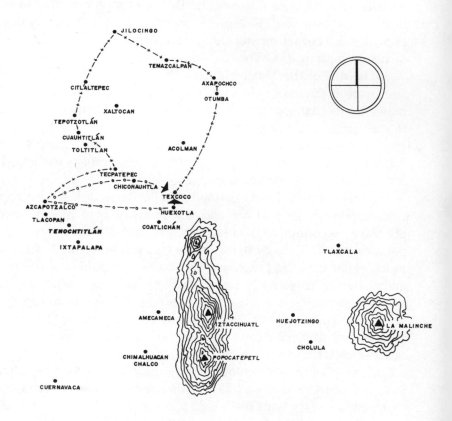

JILOCINGO

TEMAZCALPAN

AXAPOCHCO

CITLALTEPEC

OTUMBA

XALTOCAN

TEPOTZOTLÁN

CUAUHTITLÁN

TOLTITLAN

ACOLMAN

TECPATEPEC

CHICONAUHTLA

TEXCOCO

AZCAPOTZALCO

HUEXOTLA

TLACOPAN

COATLICHÁN

TENOCHTITLÁN

IXTAPALAPA

TLAXCALA

TOLUCA

AMECAMECA

IZTACCIHUATL

HUEJOTZINGO

LA MALINCHE

CHOLULA

CHIMALHUACAN

POPOCATEPETL

CHALCO

CUERNAVACA

—+—+—+—+ IXTLILXÓCHITL'S OFFENSIVE

—o—o—o—o TEZOZÓMOC'S FINAL ASSAULT

SCALE 10 5 0   10   20   30
MILES

was repulsed; but assuming that it took place in the last year of the war, when Huehue Ixtlilxóchitl was defeated and slain following serious damage inflicted on Texcoco, we can conclude that the offensive succeeded since the Texcocan king would not have yielded if still unbeaten. Alva Ixtlilxóchitl explains his downfall as the result of treachery; the chronicler goes so far as to say that Huehue Ixtlilxóchitl could not defend his capital, because most of the Acolhua rulers had been won over by Tezozómoc.[25]

At this juncture, when in desperate straits, Huehue Ixtlilxóchitl appealed to Otumba and Chalco for help. Not unnaturally, these fair-weather friends refused. Nonetheless, the cause of his final defeat and abandonment of Texcoco remains unexplained, though it presumably followed Tezozómoc's 4 Tochtli offensive. At all events, Ixtlilxóchitl was killed by the people of Otumba and Chalco, and his "empire" fell apart. On the point of death, the fallen ruler exhorted his sons, and especially Nezahualcoyotl, to remember that they were Chichimecs (i.e., Acolhuas) and to strive to recover the empire. Nezahualcoyotl retired to the Sierra and thence sought refuge in Tlaxcala and Huexotzingo.

Another Problem of Chronology

The chronology of the Tepanec-Acolhua war is at first sight rather bewildering. But in this case a solution to the riddle can be found, and affords an excellent example of how sense can be made out of apparent chronological nonsense once it is realized that several year-counts are involved, even within the text of a single source. Table B therefore provides an exposé in miniature of the use of different calendars, of which several were demonstrably employed in this instance.

In Appendix A to *Los Mexicas: Primeros Pasos,* a more detailed commentary was given on the contents of Table B.[26] Without repeating in full these explanations, the table speaks for itself. Most of the dates provided by the principal sources, Ixtlilxóchitl, the Codex Xolotl, and Veytia, plainly belong to the Tenochca count, and pose no problem of interpretation. Certain others, however, become nonsensical if converted into the Julian calendar using as a key the Tenochca count (based on 1 Acatl as A.D. 1519). Alva Ixtlilxóchitl's 12 Tochtli for the swearing-in of Huehue Ixtlilxóchitl, just

TABLE B

Chronological Table of the War Against Texcoco

Christian year	Tenochca year-count	Cuitlahua year-count	Ixtlilxochitl VII year-count
1409	8 Calli Death of Techotlalatzin Accession of Ixtlilxóchitl. (Ixtl. II: 80–81)	7 Calli	9 Calli
1410 Tezozómoc sends cotton to Ixtlilxóchitl. (Veytia I: 384)	9 Tochtli	8 Tochtli	10 Tochtli
1411 Tezozómoc sends cotton to Ixtlilxóchitl. (Veytia I: 384)	10 Acatl	9 Acatl	11 Acatl
1412 Tezozómoc sends cotton to Ixtlilxóchitl. (Veytia I: 384)	11 Tecpatl	10 Tecpatl	12 Tecpatl
1413	12 Calli	11 Calli Initial skirmishes (Ixtl. I: 153)	13 Calli
1414	13 Tochtli	12 Tochtli Swearing of Ixtlilxóchitl as chichimecatecuhtli (C. Xolotl: 92)	1 Tochtli Ixtlilxóchitl swears as chichimecatecuhtli (Ixtl. I: 153)

1415	1 Acatl Tezozómoc's offensive against Itztapalapan (C. Xolotl: 90; Veytia I: 394; Ixtl. I: 150)	13 Acatl Ixtlilxóchitl summons his allies. (Ixtl. II: 86)	2 Acatl
1416	2 Tecpatl Ixtlilxóchitl prepares counteroffensive (Veytia II: 9)	1 Tecpatl	3 Tecpatl
1417	3 Calli Ixtlilxóchitl makes counteroffensive (Veytia II: 11) Tezozómoc's diplomatic offensive (Ixtl. I: 161)	2 Calli	4 Calli
1418	4 Tochtli Final offensive of Tezozómoc and death of Ixtlilxóchitl (C. Xolotl: 91; Ixtl.: 161; Ixtl.: 95)	3 Tochtli Death of Huitzilihuitl (Veytia I: 389)	5 Tochtli
1419 Division of Texcocan lands (Veytia II: 33)	5 Acatl	4 Acatl	6 Acatl
1420	6 Tecpatl Tezozómoc hands out Acolhua lands (Ixtl. I: 184; Ixtl. II: 103; C. Xolotl: 101)	5 Tecpatl	7 Tecpatl

before the war started, is the Tenochca equivalent of 1374, long before Huehue Ixtlilxóchitl became ruler; or it could be taken as 1426 (1374 plus 52 years), which falls eight years after his death. Equally, Alva Ixtlilxóchitl's second figure of 1 Tochtli for the same event would be 1402 in the Tenochca count, or seven years before the Texcocan ruler ascended the throne. At all events, both of Ixtlilxóchitl's dates for the same occurrence cannot be correct if ascribed to the same Julian calendar correlation; either one or both are careless mistakes, or else they belong to distinct native year-counts. The simple explanation as shown in Table B is that the 12 Tochtli date belongs to the Cuitlahua count, in which it is the equivalent of 1414; 1 Tochtli, on the other hand, derives from what I have termed the Ixtlilxóchitl VII count, used by that author on several other occasions; 1 Tochtli *in that count* corresponds to 1414.

Further proof of the occasional use by Alva Ixtlilxóchitl of other year-counts is offered by his date of 11 Calli for the birth of Nezahualcoyotl. The more usual native date for this occurrence is 1 Tochtli, given by the *Anales de Cuauhtitlán,* the Codex Mexicanus, the *Anales de Tula,* and by Ixtlilxóchitl himself in another context. In the Tenochca count 1 Tochtli is 1402, and accords perfectly with all reports that Nezahualcoyotl was a very young man when his father was killed in 1418. But 11 Calli in the Tenochca count is 1373, which would make Nezahualcoyotl forty-five years old at the death of his father, and ninety-nine years old when he himself died in 1472. This 11 Calli date of Ixtlilxóchitl apparently belongs to yet another count, that I previously called Anales de Cuauhtitlán VI, and that is not included in Table B, as not relevant to the Tepanec-Texcocan war. In this count, 11 Calli falls in 1401. Among other dates, the *Anales de Cuauhtitlán* figure of 8 Tochtli for the foundation of Tenochtitlán also belongs to this calendar.

The Aftermath

Like wars in modern times, the conflict sowed the seeds of others that followed; Tezozómoc first proclaimed himself supreme monarch and then proceeded to exact harsh retribution from his fallen foes.

Many accounts suggest that the spoils of victory were divided equally between Azcapotzalco, Tenochtitlán, and Tlatelolco. However, Alva Ixtlilxóchitl says that Tezozómoc took Coatlichán for himself, together with two-thirds of the tribute of that province, leaving the remaining third for the local ruler, who retained his throne. Tlacateotl of Tlatelolco was given Huexotla, while Chimalpopoca of Tenochtitlán took Texcoco. Tezozómoc made Coatlichán into a collecting center, where all the Acolhua tribute would be gathered.[27] Vetancurt confirms that the Texcocans had to pay tribute to the Mexicas; while recognizing Tezozómoc as supreme sovereign, some of the Acolhuas had to give obedience to either Tlacateotl or Chimalpopoca.[28]

Torquemada also states that the other rulers had to pass on part of their own share of the booty to Tezozómoc.[29] This author mentions an interesting detail: the joint protest of the Acolhuas to the Tepanec ruler. A deputation was headed by a "Toltec" and a "Chichimec," who both spoke up, saying that the war had left them too poor to be able to pay all the tribute asked of them. The story illustrates the composite nature of the Texcocan population.

The Texcocan Comeback

Tezozómoc had defeated Texcoco but had failed to quell the spirit of its people. Rather as Bismark after 1870 never freed himself from the fear of a French revanche, so Tezozómoc was haunted in his dreams by visions of a resurgent Texcoco and a triumphant Nezahualcoyotl.

The politico-military systems of Mesoamerica offered no ready solution to Tezozómoc's Texcocan problems; once he had removed their legitimate sovereign (though he allowed the Coatlichán ruler to keep his throne), he had no proper means of controlling the implacable Texcocans. Even the Aztecs had no proper garrisons on the Roman model and relied on punitive expeditions to keep their vassals in order.[30] The Tepanecs surely suffered from the same deficiency, and Tezozómoc's expedient of parceling out the Texcocan domains to his minions did not solve the dilemma.

The Tepanecs seem to have nursed few aspirations to anticipate the Aztecs' drive northeastward to the Gulf Coast or southeast to Oaxaca. Azcapotzalco was perhaps for the moment a sated power, intent on digesting what it had seized. But Tezozómoc still had to reckon with Nezahualcoyotl, from whom he could steal his kingdom but not the affection of its citizens.

As a young man, Nezahualcoyotl combined personal charisma with a prestige only bestowed by legitimacy, and commanded the unswerving loyalty of his rightful subjects. He could rely on the support of most of the Acolhua cities, even if a few had favored the victor.

The *Anales de Cuauhtitlán* give the fullest and the most dramatic account of Nezahualcoyotl's life between the death of his father and that of Huehue Tezozómoc. The story is told in epic form, and Walter Lehmann has described it as unique among the writings of Mesoamerica.

After Huehue Ixtlilxóchitl was killed before their very eyes, his two sons, Nezahualcoyotl and Tzontecochtzin, were brought to Cuauhoztoc, where they were joined by their faithful follower, Coyohua, who figures prominently in the narrative. They followed a tortuous route, as they fled from Tepanec pursuit towards their friends beyond the Sierra Nevada.[31]

Emissaries reached them from Itzcoatl, their uncle, who was not yet *tlatoani;* he acted as an adoptive father and arranged to have them brought up in Tenochtitlán. This close association with his uncle in his formative period was to have important consequences to Nezahualcoyotl. In spite of past experience, he emerged from this period in Tenochtitlán as much Mexica in outlook as Texcocan.

The *Anales de Cuauhtitlán* tell how Nezahualcoyotl made his first prisoner in Zacatlán, and then captured others, under the guidance of Coyohua; these he took to Azcapotzalco and presented to the aged Tezozómoc; however ardent his desire for revenge, he knew that he must first placate the tyrant, whom he even addressed as "Xolotl," thus accepting him as successor of the original Chichimecatecuhtli and as his own overlord. The Texcocan prince then joined in a war against Chalco in which he also took prisoners, and again delivered them to Tezozómoc; this may have been the Mexica war against Chalco, reported by Chimalpain in the year 11 Calli, or one year before Tezozómoc's death.

Nezahualcoyotl thereafter managed to return to Texcoco and

established himself there at the bidding of Itzcoatl, though other sources state that Tezozómoc himself allowed him to go back. The old king, however, had second thoughts on the matter, and sent for Coyohua, telling him that he had had a hideous nightmare in which he was attacked in turn by an eagle, a tiger, a wolf, and a viper; these assailants he identified with Nezahualcoyotl, who was out to destroy him.

Tezozómoc accordingly tried to persuade Coyohua to kill his charge, but he refused to obey and returned to Texcoco to warn him of his danger. The saga ends abruptly, at the moment when Nezahualcoyotl visited Azcapotzalco, in spite of the risks involved, from which Coyohua managed to save him.

The other account of Nezahualcoyotl's actions is given by Alva Ixtlilxóchitl, and follows events up to the war against Azcapotzalco. After the death of his father in 1418, Nezahualcoyotl retired to Tlaxcala, and then returned to Chalco. However, the Chalcans, still friends of Tezozómoc, rejected his claims and imprisoned him, though he was later allowed to escape The incident further illustrates the ambivalent attitude of the Chalcas, whose leaders Nezahualcoyotl finally managed to befriend.[32]

Ixtlilxóchitl's story in general follows the *Anales de Cuauhtitlán* and tells how Nezahualcoyotl was first allowed to go to Tenochtitlán; his aunts, not Itzcoatl, are given the credit. The greedy old Tezozómoc could not resist the glittering assortment of jewels offered by these ladies as a ransom for their nephew; he merely stipulated that Nezahualcoyotl was not to leave the bounds of Tenochtitlán and Tlatelolco. After he had lived in these cities for a short period, his aunts again went to Tezozómoc and by their blandishments arranged for his return to Texcoco.

The account then relates Tezozómoc's dream; beset in his sleep with eagles and jaguars that tore at his entrails, he told his sons to kill Nezahualcoyotl. He died shortly after this, in 1426, and his heir, Maxtla, was not slow to give effect to his father's deathbed injunctions. He appointed a bastard brother of Nezahualcoyotl as ruler of Texcoco; this usurper tried to kill him, but he escaped and made his way once more to the principalities of the Puebla-Tlaxcala valley, hotly pursued by the Tepanecs.

The Death of Tezozomoc

As long as Tezozómoc still lived and a pliant grandson reigned in Tenochtitlán, no dramatic change in the balance of power was to be expected. Nezahualcoyotl remained a virtual exile from his Texcocan kingdom, even if its inhabitants resented the Tepanec yoke. Certain Acolhua cities, such as Acolman and Coatlichán, were more subservient, and Tezozómoc had adopted the expedient of bestowing on them the headship of the Acolhua nation.[33] For the moment, towards the close of his life, Tezozómoc reigned supreme, as universal monarch.

Nonetheless, at the very end of his reign, the king may have been losing his grip, since the year of his death, 12 Tochtli or 1426, witnessed stresses within the Tepanec polity. An anti-Mexica faction was gathering strength, and various notables objected to supplying the Mexicas with materials to build an aqueduct from Chapultepec to Tenochtitlán; the matter caused quite a stir, and those who opposed this concession sought to rouse the rabble of Azcapotzalco.[34]

Tezozómoc's successor, Maxtla, was prominent among the anti-Mexica lobby; it was even mooted that Chimalpopoca should be carried off to Azcapotzalco, but this proposal merely increased the prevailing discord. Alvarado Tezozómoc even suggests that his subjects killed Huehue Tezozómoc.

Durán and Alvarado Tezozómoc leave the reader in no doubt that the Tepanecs were already at odds among themselves as their king's life ebbed, and tensions mounted further at his death. The *Anales de Cuauhtitlán* confirm the outbreak of strife at this moment. The succession itself was contested, before Maxtla became ruler, ceding his own principality of Coyoacan to Tayauh, whom his father had designated as heir.

Dissension among the Tepanecs accordingly ran deep and involved other cities such as Tlacopan and Coyoacan. Barlow even contends that the Tepanec Empire was already breaking up before it actually fell.[35] Like many great rulers, Tezozómoc had failed to provide for his succession. The Mexicas were inevitably involved and had by this time become so self-sufficient that, Ixtlilxóchitl states, they no longer paid tribute to Azcapotzalco.[36] Torquemada goes so far as to assert that Tezozómoc had asked the rulers of Tenochtitlán and Tlatelolco to protect his chosen successor, Tayauh.[37]

The King Must Die

The untimely deaths of Chimalpopoca and his Tlatelolcan colleague, Tlacateotl, are a major turning point. Accounts vary about what happened. Alvarado Tezozómoc states that, after the accession of Maxtla, the Tepanecs went to Tenochtitlán and killed Chimalpopoca and his son, Teuctlehuac, and the Durán account of events is similar. Torquemada, Ixtlilxóchitl, and Veytia give versions of the story that are in basic accord with Durán and Tezozómoc. They tell how, after Maxtla seized the throne, Chimalpopoca advised Tayauh to kill the usurper, but was overheard by Maxtla's dwarf servant, who told his master. Maxtla thereupon murdered Tayauh.

According to Ixtlilxóchitl, Maxtla next proceeded to confine Chimalpopoca in a cage; Nezahualcoyotl came to visit the captive ruler and was told to join forces with his uncle, Itzcoatl, in order to overthrow Maxtla; the latter then had Chimalpopoca killed.

Torquemada also tells of Chimalpopoca's support for Tayauh, and of the latter's subsequent death; his story differs only in stating that Chimalpopoca committed a kind of ritual suicide, when he knew that Maxtla meant to kill him. Dressed in the robes of Huitzilopochtli, he performed a ceremonial dance and then offered himself up for sacrifice. But at this crucial moment Maxtla's contingent of Tepanecs arrived upon the scene, put Chimalpopoca into his cage, and carried him off, still dressed in the full regalia of the god— surely an unsuitable attire for such cramped conditions. The *Relación de la Genealogía* agrees that the ruler of Azcapotzalco had Chimalpopoca put to death; it adds that he entrusted the deed to henchmen drawn not only from Azcapotzalco, but also from Tlacopan, Tenayuca, Coyoacan, and even Texcoco.

The *Anales Mexicanos,* or *Anales Mexico-Azcapotzalco,* tell a rather different tale from the other sources, which agree in naming Maxtla as the murderer of Chimalpopoca and Tlacateotl. According to the *Anales Mexicanos,* Tlacateotl was not killed at the same time as Chimalpopoca, but was hanged some time afterwards by the Tepanecs in Atzompan. This source adds that this ruler had always been friendly with the Tepanecs. Indeed, at some stage, the Tenochcas and Tlatelolcas may have disagreed about the right policy to adopt; of the two, it may be remembered that the Tlatelolcans had always been the more closely linked with Azcapotzalco.

According to the *Anales Mexicanos,* when Chimalpopoca was humbled by Maxtla, Teuhtlehuac (described as his *tlacochcalcatl,* not his son as in Tezozómoc) overcome by shame, told the ruler that his life was no longer worth living, and then killed himself, but not Chimalpopoca.[38] After this, at Itzcoatl's bidding, Tlacaelel went and told Acolnahuacatl, ruler of Tlacopan, with whom he was on good terms, that "perhaps" Chimalpopoca was destined to die in the night, an obvious hint that he should be killed. The ruler of Tlacopan thereupon sent people to strangle Chimalpopoca. This alternative account is of the utmost significance, and finds confirmation in the *Crónica Mexicayotl,* that also names the Tepanecs from Tlacopan as the slayers of the Tenochca ruler.[39]

The orthodox version of Chimalpopoca's death, that he was publicly killed by Maxtla, is unconvincing. Either Maxtla had him assassinated privately or, more probably, he was dispatched by his own people and their associates. Ixtlilxóchitl indicates that he by then lacked popular support in Tenochtitlán.[40] The Mexicas may have been caught at a disadvantage by Maxtla, but surely not to the point of allowing a band of Tepanecs to saunter through the city and publicly kidnap the ruler, unless they *wanted* to see him killed.

Dissension may also have arisen in the Mexica camp regarding how to deal with the Tepanec menace. In particular, Itzcoatl, Moctezuma, and Tlacaelel were by now in open opposition to Chimalpopoca, but hesitated to act as regicides. They would therefore have welcomed friendly Tepanecs ready to do the deed for them. Thereafter the triumvirate would be free to take over the government and pursue a harder line towards Azcapotzalco, while driving a wedge through Tepanec solidarity by making friends with Tlacopan.

Apart from the colorful tale of the eavesdropping dwarf, no real evidence exists that Chimalpopoca ever opposed Maxtla; even if he did so, Itzcoatl and his partners perhaps resented his lack of ardor. Moreover, the *Anales Mexicanos* refer to Tlacateotl as Maxtla's ally, and few motives existed for murdering that ruler, whatever his attitude towards Chimalpopoca.

It is hard to see why Maxtla, if he were in a position to kill Chimalpopoca, could not then install a reliable puppet on the Tenochca throne instead of allowing Itzcoatl to succeed. According to the official version, the Mexicas were at that moment little more than helpless spectators in the unfolding drama, powerless to oppose any ruler nominated by Maxtla.

The story of Chimalpopoca's murder by Maxtla is not necessarily true just because it is told many times over. It bears the stamp of a single account, copied by a number of sources; it may amount to a solitary piece of evidence presented in variegated form—a phenomenon that besets any student of that short span of Mesoamerican history for which meaningful records exist. Itzcoatl is known to have destroyed tell-tale documents that might have revealed a different story, and the alternative account given by the *Anales Mexicanos,* and that somehow survived, is more likely to be true. Chimalpopoca was weak and submissive to Tepanec dictates, and his death benefited Maxtla's enemies more than it helped Maxtla himself. This version better explains the stiffer attitude of the new regime towards Azcapotzalco, as well as the process by which the Tlacopans deserted their kith and kin and joined the winning side.

A New Administration

According to the *Anales Mexicanos,* the accession of Itzcoatl was more a conspiracy than a legitimate succession. Durán tells us that Itzcoatl was "elected" by common accord, without saying who took part in the election. Tezozómoc is equally vague about the method of choice, and simply says that the Mexicas met together to select a new ruler.[41]

Tlacaelel now came to be known mainly by his title of Cihuacoatl, and certain accounts, particularly those of Durán and Tezozómoc, insist that he, not Itzcoatl, held the reins of power, assisted by his brother, Moctezuma Ilhuicamina. Tlacaelel was however very young at the time, and there is little reason to doubt that Itzcoatl, who was the more experienced member of the triumvirate and who as *tlatoani* spoke in the name of the deity, was ruler in fact as well as name. It has at times been suggested that the *"Crónica X"* (from which Durán and Tezozómoc notionally derive) was written by a descendant of Tlacaelel anxious to magnify the part he played; moreover, his ascendancy over Itzcoatl is flatly denied by Torquemada, who stresses that the Tlatoani was a mature man of forty-six when he ascended the throne, having already held high office for a long time.[42]

At all events, the Tepanecs realized that the new ruler was a man of a different stamp and put guards on all roads leading to Tenochtitlan. According to Tezozómoc, they saw that hostilities were inevitable, and put their city on a war footing.

The official version, told by the *Crónica X,* states that the common people of Tenochtitlán now took fright and even pressed Itzcoatl to humiliate himself by delivering the image of Huitzilopochtli to the Tepanec ruler.

At this point, according to the *Crónica X,* Tlacaelel stood forth as the opponent of abject submission and volunteered to go as ambassador to Azcapotzalco. In a vein of feigned humility, he there begged Maxtla to have pity on the old people and the children of Tenochtitlán. Maxtla replied that he must first take counsel before giving his answer. Itzcoatl thereupon told Tlacaelel to go again to Azcapotzalco and find out if the Tepanecs really were bent on war; if so, he was to anoint the ruler with oil, as prescribed by ritual. Tlacaelel then went back, and was told by the Tepanec ruler that he did not want war but that his subjects were unrelenting in their hostility to the Mexicas.

At this stage the people of Tenochtitlán became even more alarmed and wanted to abandon the city. Itzcoatl consoled them, and in order to gain their co-operation in war, a most unusual bargain was struck. The Señores told the people: "if we are unsuccessful in our undertaking, you may take your vengeance and devour us in dirty and broken pots." The people in their turn replied to the nobles: "And we thus pledge ourselves, if you should succeed in your undertaking, to serve you and pay tribute, and be your laborers and build your houses, and to serve you as our true lords."[43]

Any notion that the people should thus conditionally give up their rights to the ruling class is rather suspect. This "revolution" is described only by the official Tenochca sources. The story that the *macehuales* put themselves into the hands of the señores of their own free will, as the price of deliverance from the Tepanecs, is more likely to have been written into the record in order to gloss over the inequitable sharing of the spoils after the war. Vast stretches of Tepanec territory were taken over by the military hierarchy, while the *macehuales* and the *calpullis* went almost empty handed.

Any change is more likely to have been an act of deliberate

policy by Itzcoatl, to complete the revolutionary process and to transform Tenochtitlán into a unitary state, dedicated to war. The step marks the final consolidation of power in the hands of the military nobility, involving an even greater degree of submission on the part of the *macehuales,* and of the ancient *calpulli* organization. It may, however, be doubted whether, before 1428, much real authority still resided in the *calpulli* organization, and whether by that time the *macehuales* still had any power to lose. Even after these changes, the socio-political system of the Mexicas probably differed only marginally from that of their neighbors.

The *calpullis* seem to have played a more significant role in earlier Mexica history, even if the ill-conceived description of the tribe as a "military democracy" was never accurate. As in the case of any people cast in the role of conqueror, power of necessity became concentrated in the hands of the military hierarchy; this process was surely begun long before the time of Itzcoatl, and he merely completed it. In this respect, Tenochtitlán can hardly have been unique; previous claimants to the Toltec heritage, such as the Tepanecs and Acolhuas, were presumably ruled by a warrior king and a military caste. A broader power base, implying stronger local or *calpulli* influence, would represent an earlier stage in the development of the Mesoamerican city-state.

The War of Succession

The stage was now set for the final act in the drama that was to determine who was to be guardian of the Toltec heritage during the century before the Spaniards appeared and themselves became the residuary heirs.

The key factor was the reversal of alliances, leading to a full accord between the Mexicas and the Texcocans; this reversal set the seal upon a *de facto* reconciliation, that had already taken place when Nezahualcoyotl lived in Tenochtitlán after the killing of his father.

Both the Mexicas and Texcocans had been victimized by the Tepanecs, but the prime cause of war was more the weakness than strength of Azcapotzalco. It seems to have been triggered off by Tepanec dissensions, originating before the death of Tezozómoc; these were accentuated by the usurpation of Maxtla, a man of violent

311

disposition with a gift for making enemies, even among the traditional friends of his people.

Maxtla acted in the opposite manner to his father, who was adept at playing off the Mexicas against the Acolhuas, for the new ruler went out of his way to antagonize both. Whether or not he killed Chimalpopoca, he provoked the Mexicas in other ways and made renewed demands for tribute. Furthermore, he offended Itzcoatl's wife.[44] The usurper apparently resented the enhanced standing of the Mexicas and longed to reduce them to the more lowly status they had occupied in the days of Acamapichtli; he complained bitterly that they had been relieved of tribute payment.[45]

Maxtla never enjoyed even a brief spell of peace after his accession, and was perhaps already losing control of the situation before the alliance against him was cemented.

The Mexicas, seeing that war was inevitable, were automatically drawn towards Nezahualcoyotl, and an embryo Triple Alliance came into being—or rather a Dual Alliance, since the part played by the dissident Tepanecs, the Tlacopans, is at this stage less well defined. Nezahualcoyotl, in spite of bitter memories, was in sympathy with the new regime in Tenochtitlán, over which his uncle, Itzcoatl, presided. The *Anales Mexicanos* relate that, when the Mexicas first appealed for help, he gave the unequivocal answer that he himself was a Tenochca. Nezahualcoyotl's own position at this time was not strong, since many of his Acolhua subjects supported the Tepanecs.

It thus became inevitable that the Mexicas and Nezahualcoyotl should join forces; the question of whether the Triple Alliance came into existence in 1428, or a few years later, is not of major significance. The wartime league, whether dual or triple, was already a reality and arose out of a common hostility towards the Tepanecs. The formal Triple Alliance, including Tlacopan as Azcapotzalco's successor, was merely a projection into peacetime (if that term can ever be applied to the Aztec Empire) of an alliance made in war, with the important addition of a defeated rival—rather as the Holy Alliance was formed after the Napoleonic wars, with the significant accession of France to the councils of the victorious powers.

The Tepanec subjugation of Cuauhtitlán prior to the war

against the Mexicas has already been discussed in Chapter IX. Cuauh-titlán had previously held its ground against the Tepanecs; this time, however, it was crushed, and its market place was sown with maguey plants. The Mexicas apparently stood aside from this war, though the ruler of Cuauhtitlán at the time was reportedly a Tlate-lolcan prince; his successor, Tecocohuatzin, joined with the Mexicas in appealing for help to Huexotzingo.[46]

A crucial point at issue was the allegiance of the powers of the Puebla-Tlaxcala valley and in particular of Huexotzingo, much more powerful at the time than Tlaxcala. Since Tezozómoc had eliminated his main rivals in the Valley of Mexico, few states of importance survived in that region, and the attitude of the Huexotzingans would be vital to the outcome, if not decisive.

At this juncture, roughly corresponding to the preliminaries of war in Tenochtitlán, Nezahualcoyotl had again sought refuge in the Puebla-Tlaxcala valley, which he succeeded in reaching after a haz-ardous journey. The story of the subsequent courting of Huexot-zingo and its neighbors is revealing, since the efforts to woo them were not confined to Nezahualcoyotl. Maxtla himself sent an em-bassy, that bore costly gifts to Huexotzingo and left other presents with the rulers of Chalco. The Tenochcas sent delegates, who were followed by the envoys of the exiled ruler of Cuauhtitlán, bringing meager presents, which were all that he could afford. A delegation also arrived from Tlatelolco and made cogent pleas for help.

Finally the Mexica and Cuauhtitlán delegates convinced the Huexotzingans of the iniquities of Maxtla, whose envoys were killed publicly in front of the god Camaxtli—an example of the occupa-tional hazards of serving as ambassador in Mesoamerica, where diplomatic immunity was not always respected.

The Mexicas reportedly sent a deputation to Chalco, led by Moctezuma in person; somewhat naturally it was ill received, and Moctezuma was lucky to escape with his life. This courting of the Chalcas is surprising; for the latter, it was one thing to help Neza-hualcoyotl recover his kingdom, but quite another matter to assist the hated Mexicas. According to Veytia, the Chalcas were willing to support Nezahualcoyotl against Maxtla. Their offer of assistance was refused on the grounds that it was not needed.[47] One wonders if it was ever made. At all events, the Chalcas at least did not join the opposite side, an omission that surely affected the outcome, and was perhaps due to Nezahualcoyotl's deft diplomacy.

The War

A detailed description of the conflict hardly forms a part of this work, concerned more with political issues than with military campaigns; in my previous work on the subject, I set out in detail what each source has to say.[48]

Accounts of the ensuing hostilities are given by Ixtlilxóchitl, Veytia, Torquemada, the *Anales de Cuauhtitlán,* Durán, and Tezozómoc. According to Ixtlilxóchitl, Nezahualcoyotl, after recovering Texcoco, agreed to go to the help of the embattled Mexicas. After first dealing with a revolt led by his own captain-general, he set forth and disembarked in Tlatelolco; shortly after, the Huexotzingan and Tlaxcalan force arrived, and battle commenced. The allied army consisted of three contingents: the first, led jointly by Nezahualcoyotl and Xayacamachan of Huexotzingo, contained part of the Huexotzingan levies; the second, led by Itzcoatl, included the rest of the Huexotzingans; the third was under the command of Moctezuma and Cuauhtlatoa of Tlatelolco. The war lasted 115 days, and the Tepanecs, who fought valiantly, were finally defeated; Maxtla hid in a bath, and was killed by Nezahualcoyotl.

Veytia follows Ixtlilxóchitl's Texcocan version of events in general outline, but provides a fuller and rather different story, describing in greater detail the siege of Azcapotzalco. Since such embellishments can hardly have been invented by the historian, they must have been taken from some document still available in the eighteenth century but now vanished. Veytia describes the Azcapotzalcan lines of defense and the assault on them in considerable detail. After 114 days of siege, Maxtla in desperation appealed to Cuauhtitlán (of all places!), Xochimilco, Coyoacan, and other centers, asking them to rally in Tenayuca. However, the Mexicas and their allies overcame this rescue force, and Maxtla was killed in a fierce battle to the northwest of Azcapotzalco after he had attempted a sortie. Veytia's account is interesting, but perhaps rather more reminiscent of European siege warfare than of Mesoamerican military techniques.

The official Mexica account of the victory, told by Tezozómoc and Durán, maintains that the Mexicas defeated the Tepanecs without any assistance, after a short battle, and drove them into the mountains. This version of events is less plausible. The *Anales de Cuauhtitlán,* in a briefer report, tend to bear out the Texcocan story, and confirm the participation of Huexotzingo. Moreover, the Texcocan account seems in this instance the less biased, since it does not claim all the laurels for Nezahualcoyotl and acknowledges the role of the Mexicas and Huexotzingans in the battle.

However, the Mexicas surely made the main military contribution, and Nezahualcoyotl's strength remained limited, even after the victory over Azcapotzalco. Ixtlilxóchitl admits that he had to deal with a mutiny in his own camp at the moment when he set out from Texcoco. Moreover, after the triumph, he only gradually quelled the resistance of Acolhuas who had opposed his rule, and was so dependent on Mexica help to achieve this end, that he actually spent four years in Tenochtitlán before returning to Texcoco.

The Outcome

At this stage in the development of Mesoamerica, it can be seen that we possess accounts that are truly historical, even if caution is needed in their interpretation. After all due allowance is made for error and distortion, the causes of the war can be analyzed, the search for allies examined, and the course of hostilities unfolded. Descriptions even survive of such details as the gifts sent by Cuauhtitlán to Huexotzingo, or of the fate of Maxtla's ambassadors to that place; in most cases the facts are presented in a way that gives the modern historian no cause to suspect that they are invented.

By contrast, our knowledge of how Huetzin of Coatlichán made himself master of Culhuacán, then still a leading power, is confined to a single paragraph in Chimalpain's *Memorial Breve.* Concerning the fall of Tollan, Topiltzin's state of mind is described in mystico-religious terms, but his military maneuvers are unrecorded.

According to the different accounts, the outcome of the war against Azcapotzalco, like that of many Mesoamerican conflicts, depended less on the forces that a single ruler could master than on the allies that he secured. The city-states were usually too small to win a major war unaided, and success or failure depended on the shifting pattern of alliances. In this field Nezahualcoyotl showed his talents and made his contribution to victory.

To combine with the Mexicas was a bitter pill to swallow, and a lesser man might have refused. But Nezahualcoyotl's real triumph was to secure the adherence of Huexotzingo and its neighbors to his cause; Chalco temporized, but at least was dissuaded from supporting Maxtla.

In this vital contest for support, Maxtla's efforts were woefully inadequate. He not only failed to enlist the help of such inveterate enemies of the Mexicas as Chalco, but was unable to count on the whole-hearted support of his own people. Among the Tepanec shortcomings, the greatest was the lack of unity between their two leading centers, Azcapotzalco and Coyoacan, who allowed themselves to be defeated singly; the latter was conquered by the Mexicas in a separate campaign after the fall of Azcapotzalco. According to some accounts, other Tepanec centers, such as Toltitlan, offered help only belatedly, while Tlacopan joined the enemy.

The resulting triumph was therefore due first to the support of the peoples of the Puebla-Tlaxcala valley, who tipped the balance: second, to the diplomatic genius of Nezahualcoyotl, who forged the alliance; and last but not least to the military prowess of the Mexicas. Success was facilitated by the ineptitude of Maxtla and by the disunity of the Tepanecs. In short, victory was secured, as might be expected, by superiority in both generalship and diplomacy. Through the fullest exploitation of such assets, the way now lay open to the Aztec achievement of the coming century.

XII. Civilization and Savagery

Guidelines

This study has covered the latter part of a cycle in Mesoamerican history, spanning the two centuries from the collapse of Tollan to the rise of Tenochtitlán. When that city rose to power as the new Tollan, the cyclical process began anew, but with marked differences.

History never repeats itself exactly, even though in Mesoamerica, as elsewhere, a repeating pattern emerges: an empire is formed, expands to maturity, falls asunder, and after a while a new one takes its place. Some of Toynbee's other dicta may be open to question, such as his treatment of the Maya land and the Altiplano as two separate civilizations; however, his general hypothesis seems to apply to Mesoamerica.

The situation in modern Europe is not quite the same, since no nation ever attained a supremacy equal to, say, Rome in its heyday or even Tenochtitlán. First Spain, France, England, and finally Germany fought for pre-eminence, but none swept all before them, if we exclude the fleeting triumphs of Napoleon and Hitler.

However, the course of Mesoamerican history adhered more closely to the pattern set by the ancient kingdoms of the Old World: in Egypt, the Old, Middle, and New kingdoms, and in Mesopotamia,

Sumer, Babylon, and Assyria. In both regions, the crumbling of each empire was followed by a period of confusion and chaos, marked by the irruption of more backward tribes.

In the only part of South America that can be compared to Mesoamerica, the same forces were at work: following the demise of Chavin, two cultures, Nazca and Moche, came to the fore, at a time when Teotihuacán was predominant in Mesoamerica. After their decline, Tihuanaco-Huari rose to be a power at the time of the Toltec Empire, and finally the Incas, contemporary with the Aztecs, conquered far and wide. We ignore the process of decline of Nazca and Moche in Peru; indications exist, however, that the Yauro, people of lower cultural attainments, played a part in the overthrow of Huari, just as Chichimecs' incursions sapped the strength of Tollan.

In the New World, periods of stability and chaos often followed one another more swiftly than in the Old. Different causes may be cited; in particular, New World empires, with their rather static technology, easily became top heavy. As the urban populations grew, the means of production and the methods of transportation could not match up to the challenge. Tenochtitlán was perhaps on the way to overcoming such limitations. Its lagoon site provided excellent short-range communications, since canoes convey goods more efficiently than human carriers. At the same time, long-range imports were ensured by the regular levy of tribute from regions with diverse ecologies. The elaborate storage system of the Incas went far to mitigate the same problems of supply.

Empires in the New World may present special features. Nonetheless, better-documented situations in the Old help to clarify the over-all sequence of events in the New World, even if America and Eurasia lived separate lives. Writing in another context of possible links between the civilizations of the two hemispheres, I was forced to conclude that such contacts had not taken place for purely logistic reasons, if for no other. Therefore, faced with undeniable similarities in style and custom, we have to fall back on other explanations, that may appear obvious though seldom discussed. Unless one concedes that Alexander's fleet brought enlightenment to the New World or that Chinese mandarins built Teotihuacán, those uncanny likenesses, of which I listed many, can only suggest that humankind all the world over, under given circumstances, may act in like manner and produce like objects.

Lévi-Strauss compares the successive stages in man's ascent to a continuous card game, in which each culture is like a player who takes his place at the table and picks up cards that he has not invented. Every deal in the game is the result of a contingent distribution of the cards, unknown to the player at the time; he must accept the hand he is given and employ it as best he can. Different players may vary their approach to a similar hand, even if the rules set limits on the game that can be played with a given set of cards.[1]

The human mind all the world over shares a common heritage, derived from an unfathomable past, and that underlies its art forms, myths, and rituals. This heritage has its parallels in the animal kingdom. Innate in the nervous system of many creatures are instincts that make them react spontaneously and without teaching to the perils that beset them. Chicks with eggshells still adhering to their tails will dart for cover when a hawk flies overhead, but not when the bird is a gull, heron, or pigeon; if a wooden model of a hawk is drawn over their coop on a wire, they react as though it were alive unless it be drawn backwards, when there is no response.

As between the chick and the hawk, so in human history a kind a lock-key relationship seems to exist; a given society, like the card player, has a range of possibilities limited by the cards in hand and may react in a specific way, as to a releasing mechanism. The simile can be applied to parallels in art forms and rituals, the living expression of the myths of each people. The myths that produced the art forms in turn may derive from the shamanistic dreams of those Ice-Age hunters, some of whom ended up in America, while others stayed in Asia.

The more serious studies of Old World similarities with the New concentrate upon China and Southeast Asia. China, moreover, is the most likely point of departure for those hunters who crossed Beringia and begat the American Indian. In America and China the birth of higher civilization more or less coincided after the stage had been set by the discovery of plant cultivation. The two peoples had then been separated for some 350 generations, since the Bering land bridge was finally submerged. But this interval amounts to only about one-300th of man's estimated existence, and peoples who later

319

lived on opposite sides of the boundless Pacific had for thousands of generations shared those same dreams that inspired the earliest myths and rituals of prehistoric man. The contemporary civilizations of archaic China and Mesoamerica might be likened to two card players who sat down to the table about the same time. They could not play identical games, since each had different, if comparable, hands. But there was something in common between their cards and the way they handled them; as a result, uncanny resemblances were visible in the outcome.[2]

Such observations might be regarded as the product of a rigid determinism. But while general principles, applicable to most if not all human civilizations can and should be sought, it is better to think in terms of guidelines rather than of immutable laws. And in this respect, much can be learned by viewing Mesoamerican and Andean history in the light of Old World models and vice versa.

In my previous volume on the Toltecs, I concluded that Julian Steward's classification of the stages of human history was also valid for the empires of the New World. Steward establishes general patterns rather than set rules, and in seeking to apply these to Meso-america, I differ from pure evolutionists who view the progress of American man as subject to any iron laws. In the first place, not all peoples even *want* to follow the same path of evolution. Developing countries nowadays are apt to wax indignant if lectured by richer nations and told that they must seek the millennium by following exactly the same path. Yet the very people who nowadays insist that their own country should pursue an untrammeled course, free of the dictates of overweening neighbors, will proclaim almost in the same breath that ancient cultures "must" have developed in a particular way, in obedience to these iron laws of human development.

Secondly, due allowance has to be made for god as well as mammon in man's motivation, and for the role of religion as a de-cisive factor that varies from one culture to another. The mystico-religious approach to life of Mesoamericans and other ancient peoples bewilders the modern mind. Yet the spiritual factor cannot be dis-missed as a mere opium for the people, produced by the same red poppy in many a cornfield. Nor, for instance, can religion be re-garded as merely "a subsystem within a given socio-political system," a phrase used by Johanna Broda in her otherwise very informative study on social distinctions in Mesoamerican ritual.³ Alternatively, it cannot just be treated as a handy means of lavishing the surplus value of a community upon the foibles of the idle rich, nor is religious change to be viewed simply as a by-product of alternations in the modes of production—that in Mesoamerica were anyway slow to change. Far from being a product of economic necessity, complex ritual rules may act as a brake on material progress, as in modern India. Moreover, human sacrifice was not, as Dr. Harner would have us believe, merely a means of solving a protein deficiency in Mesoamerica; human flesh was consumed in the main by those who were not short of other proteins.⁴

Morgan formerly tended to think that the path of progress followed by man was pre-ordained; but its disjunctive nature is now better understood and Mesoamerica offers many examples. Accordingly, nowadays, few anthropologists would deny, regardless of their doctrinal stance, that evolution is not continuous, but proceeds in fits and starts, both in Mesoamerica and elsewhere.

Students of the stages of Mesoamerican history should therefore beware of being overdogmatic. Mesoamericans were not at all times logical in their behavior, and it is useless to pretend that their history "must" have conformed to a logical pattern, ordained by a set of rules invented in modern universities, not in ancient kingdoms. We should use the word "may," not "must," and be prepared to judge each case on its merits, and look for the exception as well as for the rule.

The distinction between "may" and "must" can be applied to the parallel history of Mesoamerica and the north Andes region. Given common formative period backgrounds, North and South America were likely to progress on the same lines in some ways but not in others. It was not altogether improbable that the stages in their development should roughly coincide in time: the first plant cultivation and pottery, the proto-historic Chavin and Olmec, the theocratic Teotihuacán and Moche, and the militaristic Toltecs and Huaris. So far so good; but to push this comparison too far, and to say that some law of history decreed that precisely in the early fifteenth century of our era great ecumenical empires "must" arise in each region—apparently for the first time—is manifestly absurd. On the basis of Steward's classification, the two Americas, having given birth to civilizations with an apparent theocratic basis, might have been expected to proceed to the stage of "regional conquests" (Toltec and Huari) and then to engender their military empires (Inca and Aztec). But the two regions were not in immediate contact, and direct diffusion is thereby excluded; this final stage might then easily have come about in the one several centuries before it happened in the other. The almost exact coincidence in time between the spread of the Inca and Aztec empires is surely the result of chance, even if their formation was the logical outcome of past events, and conforms to a given, if general, set of rules.

Finally, many phenomena do not permit a sole explanation; their underlying causes can be complex and involve several factors. I have previously tried to account for the Aztec urge for ever wider conquests that often seem to lack clear economic motives. Tribute lists suggest that the cities of the Triple Alliance already exacted more of certain items, such as cotton mantles, than they could possibly consume; to cover on foot yet vaster distances in order to conquer a remote and rebellious Soconusco and thereby to acquire an even greater profusion of blue, red, and green feathers—the main tribute of that province—was hardly an economic proposition. Even the addition of forty ocelot skins, also included in Ahuitzotl's shopping list, did not make the trip worth while.

Lacking a single compelling cause, one may better envisage an interplay of religious and material factors, combined with an urge for lavish display that cannot be viewed solely in terms of economic gain.[5] It could even be argued that, far from being guided by purely material motives, the Aztecs abstained at times from profitable conquest; thereby a few neighbors remained independent, and could be invited as "foreign" guests to the sardanapalian displays, in which surplus tribute was dissipated. The sources at times give the impression that this urge to display wealth was the major motive in acquiring it.

Bad Neighbors

The interaction between settled peoples and their Chichimec neighbors is the key factor in Mesoamerican history, for the Toltecs were not the only people to have been exposed to incursions from marginal Mesoamerica. The Aztec Empire was to some extent screened from a direct Chichimec menace by Otomí buffer states. But the Tarascan kingdom of Michoacán had to undertake punitive expeditions against nomad Chichimecs, with whom it shared a common frontier. At times the Tarascans penetrated well beyond the Río Lerma and established defensive frontier posts or strong points at Puruándaro, Yuriripundaro, Acambaro, and Maravatio.[6] Armillas quotes Stresser Péan as saying that the Huextecs had similar problems.[7] An over-all view of relations between nomad and non-nomad in other regions therefore serves as a necessary background in order to understand what went on in Mesoamerica itself. For such comparisons, the most obvious place to look is Mesopotamia; like Mesoamerica, it was seldom dominated by a single power, and equally, when empires were formed, their life span was often short.

Egypt was more monolithic, and points of comparison are therefore fewer. But though Egyptian history represents a long continuum, interruptions were not lacking. The first, occuring after the VI Dynasty, was the outcome of internal discord, a factor seldom absent in Mesoamerica. The second, at the end of the Middle Kingdom, produced the invasion of the Hyksos from Asia; but this irruption followed a period of internal collapse and was not therefore the direct cause of the breakdown. Like later conquerors of the kingdoms of Asia, the Hyksos were mounted and (unlike the Egyptians) possessed war chariots; though they were expert archers, they could hardly thus be described as "Chichimecs."

Mesopotamia was more fragmented than Egypt, and power tended to be shared by a number of city-states, as in Mesoamerica. Conquerors emerged from time to time, but their triumphs were often short-lived. Sargon's Akkadian Empire (c. 2400 B.C.) was even more ephemeral than Tollan; as in Postclassic Mesoamerica, the general aim was to acquire tribute. Sargon himself faced a major revolt of subject cities during the latter part of his reign; his two successors, his sons Rimush and Manishtusu, both apparently murdered in palace conspiracies, could only resume their campaigns along distant frontiers after a long struggle to reconquer nearby cities. Following the reign of Naram Sin, Saragon's grandson, a precipitate retreat began from claimed frontiers that virtually encompassed the known world.[8]

These Akkadian empire builders were never in full control of their conquests, and their empire declined in face of the incursions of Gutian mountaineers. And, as Georges Roux points out, the rise and fall of the Akkadian Empire offers a perfect preview of the course of later Mesopotamian empires: rapid expansion followed by ceaseless rebellions, palace revolutions, constant wars on the frontiers, and in the end the *coup de grâce* given by the highlanders: Guti now, Elamites, Kassites, Medes, or Persians tomorrow.[9] If "Chichimecs" are substituted for "highlanders," the same could perhaps be said of Mesoamerica, to judge by the relatively little that we know of events before the fall of Tula. As Roux stresses, for a civilization based on agriculture, as in Iraq, to be viable, two things were needed: a perfect co-operation between its socio-political units, and a neutral attitude on the part of neighbors. Neither in Mesopotamia nor in Mesoamerica were these factors often both present for long.

The Sumerian Empire that followed in the twenty-first century B.C. fell a prey to the nomadic Amorites who roamed the Syrian desert; since early dynastic times these wandering Amorites were well known to the Sumerians, because some—not unlike Sahagún's Chichimecs—had left their tribe to come to live and work in the cities, where their uncouth way of life was regarded with contempt.

The Babylonian dynasty of Hammurabi endured for a bare three hundred years (1894–1595 B.C.), and collapsed under the assault of the Kassites. These people might be compared to those who invaded central Mesoamerica after the fall of Tollan; their culture was more rudimentary than that of the Babylonians, but they at least restored order in the region and reinstated the gods of the former empire; not unlike the various Tolteca-Chichimecs, they were essentially half-civilized.

The Romans had comparable problems, though they were less concerned with pure nomads along the greater part of their long frontier; this is because the peoples who, over a period of several centuries, seeped into the border provinces, settled there, and eventually overthrew Rome itself, were essentially farmers, and at least half-civilized; even the Picts who lived beyond Hadrian's Wall in Scotland left behind them a series of indecipherable inscriptions.

The Chinese were particularly conscious of the nomad menace and sought their own solution. Shih Huang Ti, the Chi'in Dynasty

Emperor (246–209 B.C.) went to the vast expense of erecting the Great Wall for a length of 1,500 miles in order to keep out the barbarians. These people were not pure nomad food-takers, like the true Chichimecs of Mesoamerica, but semi-barbarians who possessed flocks and herds. They inhabited what are now Outer and Inner Mongolia, and were known as Hsiung-Nu; they had even previously formed an empire of their own that broke up in the first century A.D. They were possibly the ancestors of the Huns, who under Attila attacked the East Roman Empire from about A.D. 370 to 450, and also of the White Huns, who became a menace to the Persian Empire from about 420 to 550.

In the Old World some empires were toppled by peoples who were indeed nomads, but these, like the Hyksos and Hsiung-Nu, were mainly horsemen or herdsmen, and bore little comparison with the brutish and grub-eating Chichimecs whom the Spaniards found beyond the confines of Mesoamerica. Of these Old World nomads, the most fearsome of all were the Tartars, possible descendants of the Hsiung-Nu, and Genghis Khan made himself master of half the known world only at the expense of massive slaughter. His conquests ranged from China to Persia, while after his death Subotai Bahadur even advanced into Hungary.

The Tartars before their career of conquest had lived in the Gobi Desert, where Genghis Khan's original home had been his tent. Their mobility distinguished them from those frontier tribes who lived within the shadow of the Great Wall of China and who were more or less settled there; the latter may be more easily compared with the Mesoamerican Pames, who practiced a limited form of agriculture.

In a few respects, the Tartars recall the Chichimecs. They were expert archers and were even known as "the Bow and Arrow People"—viz. Sahagún's Tamime. Like the Chichimecs who shot arrows towards the four cardinal points, the Tartars made libations to the four winds. Both peoples were strictly monogamous, in contrast to their sophisticated neighbors. Recalling Nopaltzin's marriage with a Toltec princess, Genghis Khan took a wife from the Chinese reigning family.

But the Tartars had reached a level of civilization unknown to such typical Teochichimecs as the Guamares. They developed a fairly complex economy, based on their flocks and herds, from which they drew many necessities of life, including hair to make felt and ropes for binding the *yurts,* their special kind of tent, as well as leather for saddles and harness. They filled their *yurts* with looted treasures, including carpets from Bokhara or Kabul, and hung their walls with objects of inlaid silver, ivory, and bamboo. They even became expert road builders and could not have controlled their vast empire without an administrative machine unknown to any Chichimec adventurer. The Tartar way of life had little in common with that of the cave-dwelling Chichimecs of Xolotl, as shown in the traditional accounts. Nonetheless, the recorded feats of Genghis Khan may have inspired Ixtlilxóchitl's concept of the barbarian invasion that sweeps all before it.

The Khazars who came after the Huns and Avars and preceded the great Mongol Empire were originally also nomads, and spent most of their lives in tents; but they later built large urban settlements and surrounded their kingdom in South Russia with a line of fortresses.

In South America the situation was rather different where empires and nomad neighbors were concerned. Although evidence exists that the Huari Empire was overrun by uncivilized Yauros, more often than not mountain or jungle barriers separated the civilized from the non-civilized. Many of the latter remained tucked away in the jungle, where some are still to be found today and afford an example of peoples who became more or less settled, but whose culture nonetheless recalls that of the true Chichimecs of Mesoamerica. For instance, the Yanomamis, who today live on the upper Orinoco in Venezuela, do move from time to time, and such moves are generally occasioned by defeat in war. In a new settlement, they first erect temporary villages before they build dwellings of a more permanent nature; but in other respects they are Teochichimecs; they do not make pottery or wear clothes. They have cultivated gardens, and therefore, like the Pames, are semi-agriculturists, but part of their diet comes from grubs, caterpillars, and even spiders.

While less exposed than the empires of Mesoamerica, the Incas were not wholly immune from attack. The Gran Chaco is covered by a thin crust of salt, and is therefore not well suited to cultivation. When the Spaniards arrived, it was inhabited by wild and warlike

Indians, certain groups of which would move westward and loot the border tribes of the Inca Empire. A Portuguese sailor, Alejo García, shipwrecked mariner of the Solís Armada, joined one of these expeditions some five years before the arrival of the conquistadors in Peru.[10]

Accordingly, a nomad problem of some kind faced most peoples in both the Old World and the New. Toynbee's external enemy was always at the gates.

The Chichimecs

The nomads of Mesoamerica, however, were rather different from these Old World historical counterparts. Many native codices and written chronicles refer to people whom they call Chichimecs or Teochichimecs, but they seldom describe them, though passing references are made to Chichimec rituals, such as the shooting of arrows in the direction of the four cardinal points. Chichimec customs and modes of life are depicted in rather more detail by European or Europeanized writers, such as Ixtlilxóchitl and Muñoz Camargo, as well as by the codices of the Texcocan school, in particular the Codex Xolotl; such accounts are colored by the need to present Chichimecs in a particular light, as ancestors of the Texcocan dynasty. Moreover, the scant data that the sources in general provide on Chichimec religion may well be oversimplified; Chichimec rites are portrayed as very primitive, but studies of the Australian aborigines, as well as of primaeval tribes on the upper Orinoco and the Amazon, demonstrate that simplest peoples often possess the most complex religious and social structures.

In Chapter IV, various sources were quoted that tell something about these Chichimecs. But not only is more known about comparable tribes in Mesopotamia and other parts of the Old World. In addition, a problem of nomenclature arises in Mesoamerica that confuses the study of its history: that of deciding who are Chichimecs and who are not, since the name is apt to be applied to people of different cultural attainments. Were they more to be compared with the destructive Amorites or with the semi-civilized Cassites?

The anomaly arises partly through what I have termed the "rags to riches" complex among the more advanced peoples, including the Mexicas, who vaunted their Chichimec descent but with equal pride called themselves "Toltecs" or "Culhuas." Kirchhoff insists that the use of one name or another was an essentially arbitrary choice on the part of those concerned: "In order to designate any one of these peoples who had something of the Chichimec and something of the Toltec, as of one class or other, one of a great number of possible criteria had to be selected to the exclusion of all others. That selection inevitably was ethnocentric, that is, it depended on whether the speakers considered themselves Toltecs or Chichimecs. They could base their characterization of a given people on its present or on its past condition. If they selected the present, and the people concerned were composed of two or more separate elements, of different language or culture or political history, they could choose any one of these elements among that people as the basis for its characterization, and for any number of reasons. . . .

"If on the other hand, they selected as their basis of classification the past of those to be characterized, they might think of their earliest history as they knew it, when they either were still mere Chichimecs in the north or, on the contrary, Toltecs in Mesoamerica; or they might think of a somewhat later, intermediate stage, when the former had already ceased to be food takers, or when the latter had migrated to the north, "the land of the Chichimecs.' . . . The way to an understanding of the complexities of the history of Toltec-Chichimec relations, in which civilized Indians proudly called themselves Chichimecs, will be open only if and when we have understood the principles involved in these classifications and the reasons, both generic and specific, for the apparent confusions and contradictions."[11]

The problem is compounded because many intermediate steps exist between Chichimecs and non-Chichimecs and because the term Chichimec was used not only for these savage food-takers, but also for simpler farming peoples because they also lived in the north. The Mesoamericans complicated matters for their future historians by adopting confusing and even false labels. Probably the distinction between Chichimecs and non-Chichimecs, or Toltecs, is best defined by Sahagún, who insists that the latter not only had rulers, and nobles, but lived in cities; it was this last trait that distinguished the ancient Greeks from the barbarians.

Kirchhoff finally remarks that, notwithstanding the stress laid by Mesoamerican sources on relations between civilized farmers and wild, roaming food-takers, little of this data has ever been used in world-wide studies of the process of acculturation. He further notes that, with the exception of the copious Chinese chronicles, other ancient records have little to say about relations with pure nomads—or food-takers. This remark is rather surprising, since data are quite plentiful on other relationships between savage and civilized peoples, not to speak of reports on nomad communities, such as the Australian aborigines, who are still with us today.

The Moving Desert

Certain Nomads are perfectly capable of destroying empires and even of founding their own. But the true Chichimecs of northern Mexico hardly enter this category if Spanish descriptions of their primitive ways are correct. However, as previously stressed, the people who moved into the Valley of Mexico after the fall of Tollan were surely not these backward nomads, but semi-civilized peoples, best defined by the hybrid term of Tolteca-Chichimec—that is to say, tribes whose cultural level might better be compared to the Tartars and Khazars, though they differed radically in lacking horses and therefore mobility.

Swift-moving nomad horsemen were probably less eager to be encumbered with other groups whom they encountered, even if they recruited a number of camp followers. But in Mesoamerica, if the reports are to be taken literally, migrants moved at a more leisurely pace, and were apt to gather moss in the form of other itinerant bodies, as they meandered from place to place before reaching their final destination; the resultant ethnic blend was probably therefore more varied.

Since those migrant Mesoamericans were so different from the mobile nomads of the Old World, one is entitled to ask, why did they move at all? The most probable answer is the changing ecology of the region. In contrast to many parts of the Old World, a marked but unstable frontier between cultivable and non-cultivable land divided Chichimec from non-Chichimec in Mesoamerica. The semi-settled and part-time farmers, who came to be known as the Chichimecs of

329

Xolotl, hailed from certain marginal areas between savannah and land suitable for agriculture. Only in China did a comparable division between nomad and agricultural land exist, and neither the Chi'in nor the Han dynasties maintained a permanent hold on the Ordos Desert, just beyond the limits of land that could be cultivated.

Because of this climatic divide, Mesoamerica provides an excellent field for study of the confrontation of nomad and non-nomad, or of civilized and savage; not only did an ecological frontier more or less coincide with the bounds of civilization, but changes in its location can be mapped. Armillas explains how, towards the sixth century A.D., a rise in temperature occurred, producing an intensified rainfall and the northward extension of a meadow climate into regions that had formerly been steppe; as a result, the limits of cultivated land also moved northwards. The improved climate paved the way to the Teotihuacán-period colonizing movement, particularly in the region of Zacatecas and Durango.

In the twelfth century, this process was reversed, and a decline in average temperature set in, culminating in the Little Ice Age between the fifteenth and nineteenth centuries. This deterioration seems to have been the principal factor in the collapse of the Viking colonies in Greenland, and the gradual freezing of the soil has been dramatically demonstrated in the excavations of Norlund in the vicinity of Cape Farewell. To quote Armillas: "As a consequence of this temperature drop, the climatic zones in the northern hemisphere moved southwards towards the Equator. In the Mexican Altiplano, the zone of steppe climate must have once more expanded southward and westward towards the foothills of the Sierra Madre Occidental, obliging the sedentary peoples of the frontier to withdraw to a better climate. The peoples of the western marches, obliged to emigrate by the drought, constituted the invading hordes who transformed the history of the center of Mexico in the 13th century."[12]

Modern Instances

The effects of climatic change on both true nomads beyond the bounds of Mesoamerica, and on marginal cultivators on its periphery must have been traumatic. The true impact can be gauged by parallel cases in modern times. In the great drought that struck certain latitudes of Africa between 1974 and 1977, the annual rainfall fell from 200 mm. to less than 50 mm., and only the terrible drought of 1911 had been more severe. The hardest hit were the nomadic peoples, the Tuareg and Fulani in the west, and the Somalis in the east. Even in good years their way of life is precarious, but at the height of the drought it suffered a catastrophe from which many observers claimed that it would never recover. In West Africa the herds were stricken, between 100,000 and 250,000 people died, and thousands more trekked despairingly southwards in a mass exodus, to end as squatters on the outskirts of cities. Such are the uncertainties of nomad life even today, and such is its exposure to climatic upset.

The same kind of thing has been happening more gradually in a dry-land farming area in India. The Luni Block covers nearly two thousand square kilometers on the eastern rim of the Rajasthan Desert; its rainfall lies within the arid and semi-arid range, and averages 310–90 mm. per annum. Here, because of overcultivation and overgrazing, valuable trees and perennial grasses have given way to annual plants and inedible species. To these pressures on crops and vegetation must be added the villagers' continuous search for firewood and the burning of cow dung for cooking. The result has been the steady encroachment of sand. By 1950, 25 per cent of the Block was affected, and by the mid 1970's a further 12 per cent of the land was in decline.

Thus even today—with all the benefits of modern research, backed by massive international funds—a delicate balance exists between the arid and the fertile, whether in Africa, Asia, or America. The frontier between nomad and non-nomad, or between agriculturists and hunter-gatherers, remains mobile. Any demarcation line applies at best to a given century and often to a given decade.

Because of the whims of nature and the havoc wrought by man, the nomad is always beset with uncertainty, and opinions vary regarding the blessings and curses of his way of life. Even if we do not fully accept Marshall Sahlin's view of the typical hunter-gatherer as enjoying the "good life," conditions nevertheless vary greatly between one set of nomads and another.

Robert McNetting also insists that nomads are not always worse off than their more civilized neighbors. For instance, the

Hadza of Tanzania are better protected from famine than the agricultural peoples in their vicinity because the bush plants on which they rely give a more regular yield and are less vulnerable to drought, insects, and birds than the cultivated crops. He also suggests that only Eskimos and other specialized hunters, subject to extreme weather conditions, run the risk of starvation.[13]

The Hadza have the advantage of limiting themselves to fairly small groups, and many hunting-gathering peoples seem to have managed to keep their population at a low density, partly because they tend to die young. For instance, the King Bushmen in Africa in 1963–65 utilized about one thousand square miles, or the equivalent of forty-one persons per one hundred square miles. But in many cases, population increase may have caused nomads to migrate to cultivated regions.

One may suspect that the Chichimecs of northern Mexico, if Spanish accounts are anything to go by, were among the poorer rather than the richer nomads. Moreover, their numbers may have been swelled by the advance of the limit of the arid zone, that struck a mortal blow at the way of life of the marginal cultivators on the periphery of Mesoamerica and made them into nomads.

Problems of Infiltration

Armillas suggests that the post-Tollan invaders of Central Mexico were in effect these marginal cultivators, who became neo-nomads, having been driven to adopt a more primitive way of life by the dessication of their homelands, where they previously farmed. The phenomenon of reversion to nomadism also arises in Mesopotamia, where traditional irrigation agriculture was maintained in an unstable ecosystem. Great variations in rainfall and river flow, increased salinity with rising ground-water level, periodic infestations by blights and pests are repeatedly attested in the historical record, and are still in evidence today. Such fluctuations led there also to a delicately shifting balance between nomad and settled people.[14]

In the early Dynastic and Akkadian periods of Mesopotamia some of the open country beyond the immediate vicinity of the cities was inhabited by peoples who had been forced into a semi-nomad way of life by the deterioration of the soil or the breakdown of irrigation.

As Leo Oppenheim puts it: "The number of these [i.e., people driven to a semi-nomad existence] was increased by infiltrating groups from the mountains and deserts round Mesopotamia. Thus the ranks of this fluctuating element of the population could swell at times of crisis to a dangerous degree, even engulfing the cities, and—if led by an energetic and efficient political or military leader—it could transfer the rule over the city, and even that over the whole country, into the hands of outsiders or newcomers."[15]

Adams, in comparing Mesoamerica with Mesopotamia, cites Barth, who, in his work on the nomadic Basseri of southwestern Iran, says much that is applicable to ancient herdsmen in neighboring Mesopotamia. Barth stresses that nomadic life cannot be understood as an isolate; on the contrary, there is a constant dependence upon nearby agricultural zones; this causes a continuing feedback into settled areas by groups who have no choice but to trickle into the cultivated regions as a disorganized, landless, and depressed labor force.[16]

The Chinese faced a comparable problem of "Chichimec" infiltration into settled areas—for climatic or other causes—and tried to devise their own solution; the Great Wall was built with the precise intention of keeping out these nomads and of avoiding the continuing feedback described by Barth. Joseph Needham emphasizes that the wall was built not simply to keep the nomads at bay, but to check the drift of Chinese groups towards coalescence with nomad life and the formation of mixed economies: "It was realized that any fusion would be likely to react back later in the form of 'tribal' inward military pressure. How justified this premise was, can be seen from the many subsequent centuries during which large parts of North China were held as independent states by barbarians or semi-barbarian nomad houses able to call upon Chinese technicians and peasants as well as the resources of their own pastoral background. There was in fact a fairly clear line of cleavage between the territories and peoples who could advantageously be included within the centralized agrarian empire, and those which could not. Hence the course taken by the Wall depended on the possibility of agricultural productivity. Dividing the steppe from the sown, it was designed to keep the peasant population in, no less than to keep the nomad horsemen out."[17]

In Mesoamerica, there was no wall to keep out the barbarians,

333

even though the Tarascans built some defenses. Settled empires were poorly protected from the Chichimecs living beyond their confines; moreover, in the last pre-Hispanic period and probably before, there was a Chichimec feedback into the settled communities that could act as a disruptive force and encourage other Chichimec tribes to cross the dividing line between civilization and barbarism. Sahagún, as previously mentioned, writes of these true Chichimecs present in Tenochtitlán, whom he contrasts with Otomís and other semi-civilized elements. They may have formed a kind of urban proletariat, rather like the barbarians whom the Romans admitted both to their frontier regions and to their cities. Students of Mesoamerican social organization do not always reckon with these resident Chichimecs when they inquire who performed the more menial tasks within the cities.

Modern examples may also serve to shed some light on the social frictions caused when peoples of nomadic instincts cohabit with more advanced peoples. Even England has its gypsies, who still move from place to place and cause problems for the government by their need for camping sites, that local authorities are loth to provide; they engage in simple trades and buy consumer goods, and thereby demonstrate that not all nomads dress in skins or live in caves, but at times even participate in a system of monetary exchange.

In Australia the problems of adapting the nomads to modern life can be seen at their most acute. The surviving aborigines live mostly on farms rather than in the cities and do manual work for most of the year. Certain of them, however, remain partly true to a tribal and nomad way of life, living by hunting, going naked, and having no settled abode. But from time to time the domesticated aborigines from the farms may be overcome by an instinct to return to their former mode of life and to "go walkabout"; they then vanish from their place of employment and rejoin the wandering tribe. Quite recent travelers in the Australian bush have encountered people with a good command of English and a knowledge of farming skills, in the process of enjoying their walkabout, having gone back for a while to a nomad existence, their naked bodies freshly painted in the tribal tradition.

However, the second generation of aborigines that settle among white farmers lose all knowledge of the hunting life: their own culture and mythology is then lost, though twentieth-century civilization fails to provide a substitute to their ancient lore. People who occupied the status of "ex-Chichimecs" found it less hard to adopt Mesoamerican gods and rituals, but to face modern life in Australia is another matter, and Aborigines who live on the farming stations and whose bodies were formerly lean and almost skeletal, now merely develop pot bellies, supported and served by thin, bony limbs; having lost thier ancient skills, they are slow to learn new ones. In some ways, the few Australian aborigines who retain their primitive state vividly recall the Chichimecs, as described by Las Casas and others. The Aranda tribe still exists, though it is now almost extinct. The men continue to hunt with boomerangs and spears; the women scour the land for seeds and bulb roots, edible fungi, birds eggs, snakes and the pupae of moths, butterflies, and flies.[18]

A more harmonious modern example of how the process of Chichimec acculturation might have worked in Mesoamerica is provided by the nomad pygmies of Central Africa, whose relationship to settled village life may be compared in some ways to the original status in Chalco of the Chichimec Totolimpanecas, faced with the more advanced Tlaillotlacas and Teotlixcas, as described in Chapter X.

The pygmies live in the upper reaches of the River Congo, in the Ituri Forest, a vast expanse of dense, damp, and inhospitable darkness. They have no fixed home, go nearly naked, live by hunting, and have no nobles, chiefs, or formal councils. Their way of life, therefore, exactly recalls that of the Teochichimecs, though not of the more advanced "Chichimecs" of Xolotl.

While their own religious notions are rudimentary, they feel a need for spiritual and ceremonial guidance; when a pygmy dies, they call upon neighboring non-pygmy village Negroes to conduct a suitable ceremony, designed to lead the spirit of the departed safely away; the ritual employed often appears comic to the pygmies and makes them laugh. The Negroes prescribe a formal mourning period and even supply the appropriate food for a feast to mark the end of this interval. The Negroes also try to exert control over the pygmies by arranging that they should be married according to elaborate Negro rites; another method is to insist that pygmy boys undergo the intricate initiation ceremonies of the settled peoples; the villagers believe that in this way they gain ultimate mastery over their troublesome menials, who otherwise cannot be relied upon to behave as the Negroes require.

To quote Colin Turnbull: "the relationship between the two people [pygmies and village Negroes] is a strange one, full of ambivalence and uncertainty. By and large, the village was their only common meeting place, for the negroes disliked going into the forest, except when absolutely necessary. And the village was the world of the negro, so he assumed a natural position of authority and domination in that world. But it was a position without any foundations, for the pygmy had only to take a few steps to be in his own world. The negro was unable to exercise any physical force to maintain his control over the pygmies, so he created and maintained the myth that there was a hereditary relationship between individual pygmies and families, and individual negroes and families.

"It was not a question of slavery but rather of mutual convenience. The cost to the negro was often high, but it was worth while. The pygmy was able to do all the necessary chores for him that necessitated going into the forest, and could bring him game that supplemented an otherwise largely vegetarian diet. And in latter days, with compulsory maintenance of larger plantations, the negro found the pygmy a useful source of additional labor. But for all this he had to pay, and he was always uncertain as to how long any one pygmy or group of pygmies would stay with him. They were frequently miles away in the heart of the forest, and if hunting was good, no amount of coaxing would bring them back."[19]

Parallels cannot be pushed too far; moreover, only a few of those who entered central Mesoamerica after the fall of Tollan stood at the "pygmy" level of culture, and most had advanced well beyond it. However, whether on the frontiers between sedentary and nomad peoples or within the confines of lands inhabited by farmers, the process of Mesoamericanization had to begin somewhere, and this modern example of relations between nomad pygmies and settled Negroes may help to define both the problems and their solution. In both instances, religion seems to have been a key factor, and the respect of the primitive for the more advanced peoples rested on the awe which they felt for the gods and rituals of the latter and on belief in their power to control nature. A parallel surely exists between the Negroes who conduct ceremonies for the pygmies and the Acxotecas who led the Chichimec Totolimpanecas into the temples of their Mesoamerican gods. Another parallel may be sought; we are not told who hunted the game, such as deer and hares, that supplemented the diet of Tenochtitlán and other cities, nor whether the settled agriculturalists of the *calpullis* were themselves trained in such tasks or relied on migrant nomad hunters.

The process of acculturation in Mesoamerica perhaps took two forms. On the one hand, the well-documented case of the sky-worshiping Totolimpanecas and of the Acxotecas has been cited. Equally, migrants to Chalco represented all shades of the cultural spectrum, from pure Chichimecs, such as these Totolimpanecas, to the fully Toltecized Teotlixcas; most tribes, such as the Tlaillotlacas and Tecuanipas, stood at intermediate levels; they were in effect therefore Tolteca-Chichimecs. Though more advanced than the Teochichimeca Totolimpanecas, these people still had much to learn from the more fully Toltecized Teotenancas, who eventually came out on top and ultimately set the tone. The Mexicas were basically also a blend of Chichimec and Tolteca-Chichimec, in which the latter predominated. In addition, they mixed with the original Chinampa inhabitants of the Valley of Mexico. But the truly Toltec element is to be sought in this case, not among the migrants themselves, as in the case of Chalco, but among the Culhuas, whom the Mexicas did not bring with them but encountered in the Valley of Mexico.

The Role of Culhuacán

So far many points in common have been noted between the ascent of man in the Old World and in the New, not only in the realm of art forms, but in the life-cycle of empires and their reactions to the ruder peoples living beyond the bounds of civilization. This question is crucial for the troubled period after Tollan's fall. The reader may ask whether much is really to be learned from comparisons with Eurasia. However, while closer studies are clearly needed, even the generalized remarks made in this chapter show that parallels do exist between the two hemispheres. Better-documented Old World examples demonstrate that empires followed a comparable course and faced comparable problems as in America, in facing up to their nomad neighbors. Thus at least it can be seen that the Mesoamerican sources are telling a story that conforms to human reality all the world over.

In Egypt as in Mesoamerica, internal strife played a major role in causing kingdoms to crumble; at the same time it can be seen how external forces almost always hastened the process of collapse. In Mesopotamia, these invaders were usually semi-civilized rather than purely barbarian, and the same criteria may be applied to the case of the Chichimecs or ex-Chichimecs who came into the Valley of Mexico after the fall of Tula. It also becomes clear that in Mesoamerica, as in ancient China, climatic changes had a part to play and that the divide between settled and nomad often coincided with the shifting limits of cultivation. The same forces are still at work in the world today. In other regions also, the nomad menace was a permanent factor, not only in times of trouble; for instance, in Mesopotamia there was a feedback of more primitive peoples into the cities, and Sahagún implies that this also took place in Mesoamerica. Only in China did the Great Wall represent a rather vain attempt to stop the process.

Common also to both hemispheres was a deep veneration for set traditions. As a result, the new or peripheral peoples were always most eager to learn the ways of those who stood for the former culture, even if they sometimes treated their preceptors harshly. And nowhere was this hankering after legitimacy felt more keenly than in Mesoamerica, where, after the fall of Tollan, it was centered upon Culhuacán.

The desire to marry a Culhua princess or to conquer Culhuacán itself was ever present. Many examples have been cited of how this urge found expression: Nopaltzin, Xolotl's son, married Azcaxochitl, daughter of the ruler of Culhuacán; Huetzin married Atotoztli, daughter of another ruler; the father of Acamapichtli of Tenochtitlán reportedly wedded a second Atotoztli, also a Culhua princess; not to be outdone, Chalca and Cuauhtitlán monarchs allied themselves with offspring of the Culhua dynasty. The search for a Culhua bride was a pursuit both human and divine; Huitzilopochtli demanded the daughter of Achitometl as his wife: Cuauhtlequetzqui, the Mexica *teomama,* married the daughter of Copil, son of Malinalxochitl,

338

a form of the Culhua mother goddess; previously the semi-divine hero, Mixcoatl, father of Topiltzin, had married Cihuacoatl or Coatlicue, this same mother goddess under other names.

Ironically, perhaps, the Mexicas, the very people who proclaimed themselves the chosen heirs of Culhuacán, gave the *coup de grâce* to the power of a city that had survived so many disasters. Culhuacán was something more than a typical petty state of the Valley of Mexico; it was a major center of religion and culture, as had been Tollan in the previous era. Possibly the Tenochca urge to destroy Culhuacán derived from a feeling that the Mexicas could only become the undisputed successor of Tollan and of Teotihuacán when they had ruined and devoured Culhuacán, the immediate heir to those traditions.

The story of Culhuacán conveys another lesson, since it has been possible to show that at a given moment the city (together with Cuauhtitlan and Toltitlan) almost certainly changed from the use of the Culhua-Texcoco to the Tenochca native calendar. This in itself is revealing in that it offers one of the surest proofs of the existence of different year-counts. Such studies of these year-counts are much more than an empty exercise in arithmetic, for there can be no true history without chronology. The hopeless confusion over dates between the different sources suggests that much of the surviving information was transmitted orally; nonetheless, a closer study of the chronological data from the fourteenth century onwards does show that the rulers concerned were indeed historical figures, not the product of mere legend. By correlating such dates, as given in several native year-counts, and by showing that they can be reduced to a single Julian calendar equivalent, one can demonstrate that they were not invented; if that had been the case, the attempt at correlation would not have worked.

Crumbling Columns

In the first volume on the Toltecs, events leading to the collapse of Tollan Xicocotitlan were analyzed in detail. My conclusions, along with those of Armillas and others, mainly view the new settlers as members of marginal cultures, themselves forced to move by the pressure of true nomads from still farther to the northwest. I increasingly believe that these invaders lacked the Tartar capacity to destroy a kingdom still in its prime, but were at least able to speed the fall of a declining realm.

The empires of Mesoamerica and Peru were rather fragile structures, and their might crumbled before a handful of Spaniards. The latter triumphed not merely because of their guns and horses; at the very nadir of their fortunes after their flight from Tenochtitlán, the Spaniards crushed the Aztecs at Otumba, at a time when they had lost all their artillery and had only twenty-three debilitated horses. Notwithstanding displays of heroism, of which the siege of Tenochtitlán is an example, a lack of Indian staying power is in evidence. Backward technology may offer a partial explanation, but political weaknesses also played a part in their defeat.

This is particularly true of Tollan Xicocotitlan. The Tula River surely produced a regular supply of water, and even in the worst of years its flow could be expected to irrigate enough land to feed, say, sixty thousand people. But the Toltecs may never have boasted of a stable system of government, any more than the Tepanecs, whose empire was forged by one ruler and fell apart under his successor.

Toltecs and Tepanecs were not alone in this state of affairs. Not only were the Texcocans at times disloyal to their earlier rulers, and in certain instances to Nezahualcoyotl; after the death of Nezahualpilli, their cohesion again broke down, and Texcoco was a divided and disillusioned city when the Spaniards arrived.[20] Chalco in 1410 was given over to the Mexicas by the Tlaillotlacas, one of its own leading tribes; the final Mexica victory in 1465 was won after the Chalcas had again been betrayed by some of their own citizens.

The monolithic façade erected by the official Tenochca historians may not tell the whole story. Certain sources suggest that Tizoc's performance against Metztitlan was dismal and that he was murdered as a consequence—by witches, according to Torquemada.[21] Ahuitzotl's death is ascribed to a blow on the head when he was "escaping" from the floods caused by his ill-devised public works program. A faction may have existed in Tenochtitlán who found this blow rather timely. Axayacatl's reign lasted a mere twelve years, and he probably died in his early thirties; his demise occurred not very long after his utter humiliation at the hands of the Tarascans. Chimalpopoca, whom only two reigns separated from Axayacatl, was definitely murdered.

Inca history is a continuous tale of unconcealed conflict between rival claimants to the throne; the civil war that raged between Huayna Capac's two sons when Pizarro arrived had been preceded by countless "rebellions." The suspicion lingers that equally in Tenochtitlán the transfer of rule from one *tlatoani* to another was not always so smooth as we are led to believe, and that fierce intrigue, if nothing worse, often accompanied the choice of a new monarch. The absence of a fixed succession and the tendency for the throne to pass from brother to brother strengthen such suspicions; it was not for nothing that Turkish sultans would kill off their younger brothers to guard against rivals to the throne. Any system that lacked a firm order of primogeniture on European lines, whether Peru, Rome, or Mesoamerica, at times lay at the mercy of palace revolutions and personal vendettas.

The New and the Old

Compared with the more gradual rise and fall of many Old World empires, the wheel of fortune sometimes turned more swiftly in Mesoamerica; Tollan in particular enjoyed only a brief spell of grandeur. If civilizations, with few exceptions, tended to wax and wane in the course of a few centuries, it may be due to many causes. In particular, those of the Altiplano were forever exposed to pressures from the northwest, whence all newcomers arrived in Mesoamerica. The tendency for Mesoamerica to be led from the periphery rather than from the center magnified the menace; Tollan was a case in point, and Tenochtitlán was another; to reach Soconusco, Ahuitzotl's armies had to march some eight hundred miles, whereas in the opposite direction, beyond Tollan, the imperial frontier was less than eighty miles from the Aztec capital.

The technical and geographical shortcomings of Mesoamerican empires are obvious, but if their staying power was thus limited, additional reasons are not to be sought so much in religious schism, sometimes advanced as the main cause of collapse, nor in fissures in the internal social structure. Factional rivalry among rulers of different centers seems a much more significant factor than tensions

341

between antagonistic classes within a given polity. The nobles may have had their own differences among themselves in the choice of ruler, but any suggestion that they were engaged in an endless conflict with the rest of the population is quite another matter.

Nowadays it is sometimes argued that Mesoamerican society was split down the middle into two opposing factions, the oppressors and the oppressed. An admirable publication, edited by Pedro Carrasco and Johanna Broda, entitled *Social Stratification in pre-Hispanic Mesoamerica* even contains one paper on Cuauhtinchan-Tepeaca whose suggestive title includes the words "tributary despotism," a state that the article traces back to before the Aztec conquest. In another paper the Tarascans are boldly divided at the outset into two categories, the "dominant" and the "dominated" class.[22]

But other chapters in the same work stress the existence of countless steps in the social ladder between the richest *pipiltin* at the top and the poorest *mayeques* at the bottom. For instance, Dyckerhoff and Prem are at pains to show that, aside from the great property owners, among the nobility of Huexotzingo there was a large group of landholders who were by definition *pipiltin,* but who held far smaller and more compact plots. The two authors stress that their lack of political pull divided these poorer *pipiltin* from the top class of nobles, and at the same time reduced the difference between them and the *macehuales.* Dyckerhoff and Prem state that many such *pipiltin* enjoyed a standard of life little different from the *macehuales.*[23]

Carrasco writes that within a given *tecalli* (an entity controlled by a single *tecuhtli)* the lower stratum of the nobility, i.e., the *teixhuihua* of Tlaxcala and their equivalent elsewhere, performed duties that ranked as intermediate in the social scale, such as palace service and the finer forms of craftsmanship.[24] Carrasco, writing of conditions in Morelos, states that the *macehuales* could also possess servants, both for household duties and for cultivation.[25] He thereby stresses the socioeconomic differences present among the *macehuales* themselves and the great disparity between *macehual* landholdings, some of which were twenty times greater than others. He concludes by stating that in Mesoamerica we are in the presence of a society in the process of transition to a real nation state.

Those who uphold the existence of a supposedly two-class society in Mesoamerica say little of the merchants, let alone of the artisans, who constituted 20 per cent of the economically active population of Huexotzingo. Apart from such vital questions, it is hard to see how people can be arbitrarily divided into two opposing classes in a society in which in certain instances the lowliest nobles and the richest commoners lived in much the same way and in which such marked differences in wealth—amounting to a ratio of twenty to one—divided the richest from the poorest *macehuales.* If some of the nobility belong to the exploited and if some of the *macehuales* to the exploiters, lording it over their plebeian employees, who was then exploiting whom? What remains of any theoretical cleavage between oppressors and oppressed if some of the *pipiltin* were themselves little better off than the victims of their oppression, and if some of the *macehuales* indulged in oppression by acquiring twenty times as much land as less favored members of their class, some of whom they employed as their own menials? In Mexico today, anyone who acquired a piece of land twenty times the size of a typical peasant holding would presumably rank, in terms of hectares, as possessing a "small property" *(pequeña propiedad).* But nowadays owners of these "small properties" are apt to be branded in the modern idiom of class warfare as belonging to the exploiting class rather than to the exploited proletariat.

We again return to Kirchhoff's contention that in Mesoamerica black often turns out to be white, and white, black; just as Toltecs are apt to pose as Chichimecs, and Chichimecs learn to be Toltecs, so precise labels ill befit a situation where some of the *macehuales* are well-to-do, and some of the *pipiltin* are hard up.

Political stability in Mesoamerica was surely more often undermined by social cleavages between communities than between classes. During the post-Tollan period, before Tenochtitlán's rise, each petty *señorío* waged an endless struggle to impose tribute on its neighbors; when successful, it exacted a heavy toll. People in Mesoamerica thus did tend to be divided into categories—citizens of tribute-gathering and of tribute-paying states. The Aztecs repeated this pattern on a vaster scale, and the history of their empire is one long record of rebellions arising from attempts to avoid their tribute levy and of reconquest, leading to the imposition of an even larger levy. The Spaniards' first encounters in coastal Mexico confirm that the burden of tribute weighed heavily on the outposts of empire: Cortés proved a ready listener to the lamentations of the Fat Chief, whose jewels Moctezuma had purloined. He later met the five Aztec tax gatherers, who were held in such dread that they could travel freely in Totonac territory armed with no weapon more lethal than a fan.

There is no reason to suppose that Toltecs or Tepanecs were any less greedy in taxing their subjects. Ixtlilxóchitl gives some details of Tepanec methods, and the Acolhuas were treated more harshly by Tezozómoc than were the victims of most Aztec conquests. Excessive demands, with no corresponding benefits, probably speeded the breakup of the Tepanec Empire, whose military organization was unequal to such situations. The Azcapotzalcans seem to have received little support, except from a few Tepanec centers, when their own partners and former vassals organized a coalition against them.

Agricultural producers, unlike nomad hunters, can under most circumstances be forced to provide a surplus over and above their own basic needs. But in Mesoamerica much of this surplus went to swell the coffers of an outside conqueror, to augment his store of jewels, to embellish his palaces, and even to supply his zoos with specimens. Correspondingly less wealth accrued to the *tlatoani* of the local pueblo and to the well-being of his nobles and subjects.

A predatory system therefore operated that produced have and have-not principalities. This process was probably gaining momentum, just as today the gap between the poor and rich nations, far from narrowing, widens as the rewards for size, military strength, and economic efficiency increase.

If a state of imbalance prevailed in Mesoamerica, it was due to differences between communities as much as between individuals. Thus, both in Aztec times and before, conquest led to no true stability because many subject peoples resented their status. And to overcome any lack of cohesion, unlike the Incas, the Aztecs, as I have often stressed before, had few regional garrisons and no real standing army for the control of conquered peoples, relying instead upon punitive expeditions to suppress frequent rebellions.[26]

A Time of Troubles

Of the time of troubles that followed the ending of the Teoti-huacán hegemony or "empire"—as some people call it—we know very little. Information on the period of political fragmentation that followed the end of Tollan Xicocotitlan leaves many gaps, but, as this work has tried to show, a coherent story can nonetheless be told. Nurtured on the legend of the glory of Tollan, the urge to reconstitute order out of chaos lived on. Culhuacán upheld the Toltec tradition during the late twelfth and early thirteenth centuries, when the Valley of Mexico was overrun by "Chichimecs." Then before Tenochtitlán finally assumed the Toltec heritage, two previous claimants arose, the first Acolhua Empire in the thirteenth century, and the Tepanec in the fourteenth. Their rise and fall have been described in the previous chapters.

Adams, in his comparison with Mesopotamia, writes of the decline that followed in the wake of eras of integration under the aegis of centers like Teotihuacán, Tollan, and Tenochtitlán. He suggests that such periods of decline were more marked in Meso-america than in Mesopotamia, but concedes that similar forces were at work in both regions: "What seems overwhelmingly most impor-tant about these differences is how small they bulk, even in aggregate, when considered against the mass of similarities in form and process. In short, the parallels in the Mesopotamian and Mexican careers to statehood, in the forms that institutions ultimately assumed as well as in the processes leading to them, suggest that both instances are most significantly characterized by a common core of regularly occurring features. We discover anew that social behavior conforms not merely to laws but to a limited number of such laws."[27]

The thirteenth and fourteenth centuries in the Valley of Mexico form an identifiable interlude in the process of such "careers to statehood." In Toynbean terms, the age was unquestionably a time of troubles, though it may be hard to judge just how troubled it was and how deep the trough it represents in any graph of the course of Mesoamerican civilization.

The period scarcely ranks as a true dark age; Culhuacán, in spite of all reverses, continued to act as a diffusion center for the old culture. Many of the former peoples survived and helped to

educate the new. These newcomers were already half Mesoamericanized and were apt pupils in the arts of civilization.

The setback in the rise of Mesoamerican man to a new level of
socio-political complexity was therefore limited. For the succeeding
phase, the Aztec Empire was no mere repetition of past history; in
conformity with Steward's definition, a true "conquest state" was
then formed, as opposed to mere "militaristic polities" that had
gone before. The Aztecs were the first conquerors known to have
broken loose from a more restricted pattern and to have amassed
an ecumenical empire, rather than a localized *Reich;* given time, they
might have evolved new political forms and economic systems
hitherto untried in Mesoamerica. The thirteenth and fourteenth
centuries, still often called the Era of the Independent *Señorios,*
may therefore be viewed not as a bridge leading from one like structure to another, but as the springboard for the launching of a new
Tollan that was a bold departure from previous norms.

Appendix A.

The General Problem

In Appendix B of *The Toltecs,* in order to establish some kind of chronology for the last rulers of Tollan, an attempt was made to determine the dates of the principal dynasty of Culhuacán until the time of Coxcox, who reigned when the Mexicas arrived in Chapultepec in 1319—a date that was pinpointed with reasonable assurance. Working backwards from Coxcox, a tentative figure was then reached for Topiltzin and Huemac, the last rulers of Tollan.

Such calculations derive mainly from two sources, the *Anales de Cuauhtitlán,* and Chimalpain's second *Relación,* or *Memorial Breve.* Chimalpain, in certain *Relaciones,* gives additional dates, some of which are the same as his *Memorial Breve* figures, and others of which are different.

Torquemada, Ixtlilxóchitl, the *Relación de la Genealogía* and the *Origen de los Mexicanos* give king-lists for Tollan and Culhuacán. However, while they are of some use for cross-checking rulers' names, they offer little help for chronology. Ixtlilxóchitl gives dates for the reign of each monarch, but these are ritual, not historical, and most sovereigns in his list rule for one year-cycle of fifty-two years, usually from 7 Acatl to 7 Acatl or 6 Tochtli.

In seeking to rationalize the ostensibly meaningless jumble of names and dates, I found one salient feature. To begin with, the list of rulers of Tollan from Nauhyotzin onwards, given in the *Anales de Cuauhtitlán,* were designated as list A, and the first five rulers of Culhuacán named by the same source (also beginning with Nauhyotzin), were classed as list B. The first five rulers of Culhuacán in the *Memorial Breve* (starting with Tepiltzin Nauhyotzin) were labeled list C, while the next six rulers of Culhuacán in that source (beginning with another Nauhyotzin) became list D.

Setting these lists A, B, C, and D not in consecutive order, but side by side, the fact emerged that we are really dealing not with four lists but with one. In other words, with lesser variations, the same list is repeated twice over in the *Anales de Cuauhtitlán;* the source, however, refers to the kings in list A as rulers of Tollan and to those in list B as the first rulers of Culhuacán.

If the list of the first twelve rulers of Culhuacán in the *Memorial Breve* is then cut in half (Chimalpain names only eleven, but one name is clearly missing), and if these two sets of names (i.e., the first six and the last six) are placed side by side and called lists C and D, then they are seen to coincide to a remarkable degree with lists A and B of the *Anales de Cuauhtitlán.*

The dates of the first six names of the *Memorial Breve* Culhua kings are somewhat scrambled and include a few maverick figures; it is the second *Memorial Breve* list (or list D, the Table B of Appendix B of *The Toltecs)* that corresponds so closely to the *Anales de Cuauhtitlán* lists A and B. The names in the four parallel lists may vary, but the dates follow identical patterns. To give one example: not only do *all* the lists begin with a Nauhyotzin; in *each* of the four, the third ruler (allowing for one missing king in list C) ascends his throne in either 1 Calli, 2 Tochtli, or 3 Acatl; of these four rulers, whose accession dates are so close, three died in 9 Tochtli. Faced with such parallels, one sees that a close relationship between the four lists is irrefutable.

Such were the results of previous efforts. On this occasion, however, being more directly concerned with the Culhuacán than with the Tollan dynasty, I made a closer study of the later Culhua rulers, who came after these first twelve, or, in reality, the first six rulers repeated twice over. Incidentally, the practice of presenting a short list, twice repeated, as a longer single series is not confined to Culhuacán; in Chapter IX above it was explained that the *Anales de Cuauhtitlán* probably repeat the same list twice over, starting each time with a Huactli, who reportedly ruled in Cuauhtitlán in each case for sixty-two years.

Far from clarifying the situation, the so-called later rulers of Culhuacán add to the confusion. Repetition is again clearly involved, and it can be seen at a glance that the *Memorial Breve* list is not a consecutive series. However, the same exact logic did not apply for these last rulers as for the first. A tendency to repeat names and dates is visible, but no longer in an orderly manner. A kind of replay of the rulers or dates of lists A, B, C, and D emerges, but in jumbled fashion, more like an echo of the previous pattern than a strict repetition.

Names such as Quauhtlix, Chalchiuhtlatonac, and Xihuil-temoc appear over and over again but always in a different order; the dates attached to their names are not identical but somehow related, though a particular pair of dates will be ascribed to one ruler in one list, and to his successor or predecessor in another. For instance, in Torquemada's list, Achitometl comes near the top and precedes Coxcox by seven reigns; in Chimalpain's third and seventh *Relaciones,* Achitometl comes after Coxcox; in the *Memorial Breve,* Achitometl is sixth from last in the list, while Coxcox is the last. In fact, omitting from the *Memorial Breve*'s long list of Culhua rulers the first six names (that basically parallel the second six) Torquemada's list and that of the Memorial Breve coincide exactly in names (Torquemada omits dates), and obviously derive from a single source. The *Relación de la Genealogía* and the *Origen de los Mexicanos* give almost the same names, in the same order, but omit the last two.

The Different Year-Counts

In *The Toltecs,* Appendix B, the chronology of those rulers of Culhuacán whose dates seemed to coincide with the arrival of the captive Mexicas in 1319 was expressed in tabular form, based on the assumption that several different year-counts were being used. With the help of this table, it was proposed that, as several sources affirm,

Achitometl and Coxcox were approximate contemporaries, and both reigned during the first decades of the fourteenth century.

It was further questioned whether Chalchiuhtlatonac was not the same person as Coxcox, and whether the dates of 3 Acatl for the accession of Chalchiuhtlatonac and of 4 Acatl for Coxcox were not both the equivalent of the year 1307, according to two different native calendars. Often, as previously explained, two year-counts will give for one event dates that differ in this way by only one digit. Equally, the deaths of Coxcox in 10 Acatl and of 13 Calli for Chalchiuhtlatonac were treated as perhaps relating to a single event, on the same assumption regarding the use of two different calendars.

However, after further study applied to Culhua rather than Toltec rulers, I now consider that the peculiar coincidences between the dates of the last rulers, even if the same dates seldom apply to the same name in two instances, imply that in fact one year-count was generally used, and that anomalies have to be explained within the framework of that year-count, except in a few cases where the Culhua-Texcocan and Tenochca counts are both in use, as will be explained below. This modification in no way affects the certainty regarding the general tendency to use multiple year-counts. This has been amply demonstrated in a more comprehensive table in my book on the early Mexicas, for whom so much more data are available.

If we possess only a few jumbled dates for distant events, the temptation automatically arises to explain their discrepancies as caused by the use of several calendars. When a whole series of dates are available (as for the early Mexica monarchs), such assumptions can be cross-checked and shown to be valid. But in the case of, say, Achitometl and Coxcox, no such plethora of dates exists, and, while several year-counts may be involved, they are hard to pinpoint and conclusions must be tentative.

For the Culhua dynasty or dynasties, unlike others, I tend to the view that only occasionally were two or more native calendars used, and that most dates belong, somewhat naturally, to the Culhua-Texcoco count; the approximate Julian calendar equivalent is reached by taking the Tenochca official count (1 Acatl = 1519) and adding twenty years; this is the same count that Chimalpain employed for most of his earlier dates—see Chapter X. In that respect therefore, in this appendix, the methods may vary, but the change hardly affects the conclusions, since previous calculations were in any case basically derived from dates reckoned in the Culhua count, and the possible use of other counts was mooted only to confirm this evidence.

Whereas I still believe that Culhuacán had more than one dynasty, there was nonetheless always a principal ruler, and it seems that we are basically dealing with the dates of this leading dynasty, though certain rulers given in the king-lists may be contemporaries; alternatively, they may turn out to be the same person with two distinct appellations.

Grouped Dates

Re-examination of the Culhua king-lists has revealed a certain consistency between the different sources, including the dateless lists of Torquemada and the *Relación de la Genealogía,* in the order of succession of rulers, though at times two rulers are named as contemporary, and at others as successors one of the other. For instance, in the *Anales de Cuauhtitlán* and the *Memorial Breve* Mallatzin, or Mazatzin, is successor of Cuauhitonal, whereas Torquemada makes them out to be contemporary kings. In the *Anales de Cuauhtitlán* Nonoalcatl follows after Huetzin, but the *Memorial Breve* treats them as reigning together.

Even limited variations of this kind hopelessly confuse the dates of their respective rulers. This is easy to illustrate: let us suppose that King William and King Henry are given by source A as contemporary corulers, who died and were followed by King Peter. On the other hand, source B, writing of the same dynasty, states that King Henry was not King William's coruler but his successor, and that Peter in turn succeeded Henry. Then perforce King Henry comes to occupy the same dates in list B as does King Peter in list A; King Peter of list B does not have the dates of the King Peter in list A, but those of Peter's successor in list A, and so on, down the line. The error is compounded when multiple discrepancies among different lists accumulate. A real identity is evident between *reign* dates, but no two sources then agree about the ruler to whom such dates are to be applied. Matters are then further confused when the various lists give different names for the same king.

351

In this context, the word "identity" requires definition. Assuming that a number of dates of reigns belong to the same year-count and that those dates differ one from the other by a few years only, it soon becomes clear that such slight divergences in fact express the same date, or dates, rather than a different set. This point is basic to any understanding of most Mesoamerican king-lists.

For instance, in Chart B, of which an explanation follows, it can be seen that column T (that will later be designated as marking the end of Culhua reign IV) embraces dates of 6 Acatl, 7 Tecpatl, and 9 Tochtli. These dates if taken as belonging to the Tenochca count (1 Acatl = 1519) and to the last years before the Conquest, become the equivalent of 1511, 1512, and 1514. At first sight, these are genuinely different dates, belonging to different events. But in studying pre-Columbian chronology, it must first be grasped as an almost invariable rule that where several sources give dates for the accession or death of given ruler, or for other once-and-for-all events, these dates are seldom identical, but tend to fall in a cluster, usually closely grouped, but sometimes varying by five or more years. For instance, the death of Huehue Ixtlilxóchitl of Texcoco is recorded in one source as 2 Tecpatl (probably 1516), in two others as 4 Tochtli, and by a further two as 5 Acatl. His death almost coincided with that of the Tlatoani Huitzilihuitl, for which one source gives 13 Tochtli, two give 1 Acatl, two give 2 Tecpatl, five give 3 Calli and one gives 4 Tochtli. This spread is not unusual, and covers five consecutive years. The anomaly prevailed right up to the Conquest, and even for Moctezuma II three accession dates, 9 Calli, 10 Tochtli, and 11 Acatl exist.

Such discrepancies embrace three consecutive years for a major event within living memory in 1519, and stretch to five years for the death of Huitzilihuitl, a remoter figure but nonetheless important a century before the Conquest. Small wonder therefore that such differences and even greater ones crop up in the case of the earlier and more garbled king-lists of Culhuacán; in fact, such lists lack meaning unless it is understood that dates in series, such as 1 Calli, 2 Tochtli, and 3 Acatl, almost invariably refer to one king and not to several. Thus in the case of the year groups, designated with letters from P to U in Chart B, I am confident that one is dealing with the same event, i.e., the death of the same monarch, regardless of whether the year is described in one source as 6 Acatl, in a second as 7 Tecpatl, and in a third as 9 Tochtli.

The question remains: why does this spread occur? First, in Mesoamerican records both the inclusive and exclusive counting methods are used: thus a reign running from 1 Tecpatl to 9 Calli may be described either as lasting eight years (exclusive counting) or nine years (inclusive counting). Dates for a certain ruler that, to our way of thinking (exclusive counting), amount to, say, fifteen years, are often followed by a comment on the part of the chronicler that the monarch in question reigned for sixteen years.

Particularly if a given sovereign came to the throne at a date easy to remember in oral tradition, such as 1 Tecpatl (that so often marks the beginning of dynasty), and it is related that he reigned nine years, then the date of his death becomes either 9 Calli or 10 Tochtli; if a similar discrepancy occurs in the case of his successor, who reigned, say, for twelve years, the range would accordingly be widened, and his death could be memorized as falling in 8 Calli, 9 Tochtli, or 10 Acatl, based on an accession in either 9 Calli or 10 Tochtli, and a reign of twelve years counted either inclusively or exclusively. Over a whole king-list, such differences could be compounded, and an even wider disparity then emerges between several versions.

The same kind of disparity can arise in another way, because in certain king-lists—for instance that of the *Anales de Cuauhtitlán* for their own rulers—if one king dies in, say, 4 Acatl, his successor's reign is said to begin one year later, in 5 Tecpatl, in contrast to the more usual practice of dating the successor's reign from the year of death of the previous king.

Such anomalies presuppose oral as well as written transmission of dates; for it is hard to conceive that a *tlacuilo* would make repeated mistakes in copying two dates, e.g., 13 Calli and 1 Tecpatl, since both signs and numerals would be hard to confuse. Groups of dates for one event, as for Huitzilihuitl's death, suggest that certain formal numbers, such as 1 Tecpatl for the accession of Acamapichtli of Tenochtitlán, were memorized, and that the dates of following rulers were then repeated orally, as lasting for a given number of years. This could only be the case if most extant king-lists were post-Conquest reconstructions, based on oral tradition and written down in chronicles and codices *after* a correct written records had vanished. Such reconstructions would obviously vary in detail; thus though the *Anales de Cuauhtitlán* and the *Memorial Breve* repeat the same traditional data on Toltec and Culhua monarchs, they seem to be copying from two different reconstructions of the original lists. Possibly these lists no longer existed when the Spaniards came. Thelma Sullivan, among others, insists that there was a tendency to destroy codices after a given period. But surely to burn a codex and to keep a facsimile would run counter to the whole spirit of ritual iconoclasm, whether the object in question was a painted codex or a Maya stela (known to have been ritually smashed in many cases). Thus the likelihood arises that only inaccurate versions survived, based on memorized data. A priest who consigned a document to the flames and then pulled out of his briefcase an exact copy to insert into the record would have made a hollow farce out of a sacred rite.

The other problem now comes to the fore: not only did the dates in these lists vary by three or four years or perhaps more; in addition, these dates—or date groups—were then attributed to different rulers' names in different lists, as related above in connection with Culhuacán. Such confusions are not hard to explain in the case of monarchs who reigned two centuries or more before the Conquest; continuous oral repetition could easily lead to the dropping or forgetting of one ruler's name, whose dates will then be ascribed to his successor, and a few such omissions (or additions, if one double appellation is made into two different kings) would lead to the virtual scrambling of the original list. Such slips could even produce another phenomenon, visible in Chart B: that of dates being in some instances repeated backwards. Deliberate omissions should, moreover, not be ruled out. Cases often occur in lists of African kings of fairly recent memory when monarchs who fell into disfavor were simply left out of the record.

A further complication arises: the *tlacuilos,* or their masters, who tried to reconstruct lists from dates repeated orally, at times were at pains to lengthen these in order to increase the time-depth of their dynasties. The Culhua list of which we know different versions, seems to refer to a small number of reigns, but has been "stretched" by a process that works roughly as follows: the complete list of, say, Kings A,B,C,D,E, and F is first set down; then rulers

A,B,C,D,E, and F are given once more as Kings G,H,I,J,K, and L, using in some cases different names (of the several that each ruler possessed), plus a few faintly divergent dates; next, instead of repeating once more all six kings, rulers J,K, and L might be listed again, with a third set of names, and called this time over N,M, and O, and so on. Thereby a *tlacuilo,* starting with six rulers, from A to F, wittingly or unwittingly ends up with a magnificent list running from A to Z and comprising twenty-six reigns.

A Puzzling Pattern

Having discerned the presence in the Culhua lists of some kind of pattern, albeit rather a crazy one, it becomes necessary to set out again the dates given in the different sources for the rulers of Culhuacan, that were already listed in Appendix B to the first volume, though omitting this time those rulers of Tollan who are no longer relevant. This we will call Chart A.

CHART A

Anales de Cuauhtitlán

Rulers of Culhuacán		Accession	Death
1 A.	Nauhyotzin	1 Tecpatl ?	9 Tecpatl
2 A.	Cuauhtexpetlatzin	9 Tecpatl	1 Calli
3 A.	Huetzin	1 Calli	9 Tochtli
4 A.	Nonohualcatzin	9 Tochtli	4 Acatl
5 A.	Achitometl	4 Acatl	5 Calli
6 A.	Cuauhitonal	5 Calli	6 Acatl
7 A.	Mazatzin	6 Acatl	3 Tochtli
8 A.	Quetzaltzin	3 Tochtli	3 Acatl
9 A.	Chalchiuhtlatonac	3 Acatl	7 Tecpatl
	Cuauhtlixtli	7 Tecpatl	1 Acatl
	Yohuallatlatónac	1 Acatl	11 Calli
10 A.	Tziuhtecatzin	11 Calli	11 Tochtli
11 A.	Xihuiltemoctzin	11 Tochtli	3 Tecpatl
	Coxcoxteuctli	3 Tecpatl	1 Tecpatl

355

Chimalpain, *Memorial Breve*

Rulers of Culhuacán		Accession	Death
1 B.	Tepiltzin-Nauhyotzin (first ruler of Culhuacán)	5 Calli	3 Acatl
2 B.	Nonohualcatl	3 Acatl	3 Calli
	Yohuallatlatónac	3 Calli	10 Tecpatl
	Quetzalacxoyatzin	10 Tecpatl	7 Calli
	Chalchiuhtlatonac	7 Calli	13 Calli
3 B.	Totepeuh	13 Calli	2 Tochtli
4 B.	Nauhyotzin (called Nauhyotzin II)	2 Tochtli	9 Tecpatl
5 B.	Quauhtexpetlatzin	9 Tecpatl	1 Calli
6 B.	Nonohualcatl and Huetzin	2 Tochtli	9 Tochtli
7 B.	Achitometl	10 Acatl	4 Acatl
8 B.	Cuauhtlatonac	5 Tecpatl	5 Calli
9 B.	Mallatzin	6 Tochtli	7 Tecpatl
10 B.	Chalchiuhtlatonac	3 Acatl	13 Calli
11 B.	Quauhtlix	13 Calli	7 Tecpatl
12 B.	Yohuallatlatónac	7 Tecpatl	1 Tecpatl
	Tziuhtecatl	2 Tecpatl	?
	Xihuiltemoc	?	10 Calli
13 B.	Coxcox	10 Calli	?

Chimalpain, *Relaciones*

		Accession	Death
1 C.	Nauhyotzin	5 Calli or 11 Acatl	9 Tecpatl
2 C.	Cuauhtlix	?	7 Tecpatl
3 C.	Yohuallatónac	7 Tecpatl	1 Acatl
	Tziuhtecatl	?	11 Calli
	Xihuiltemoc	11 Calli or 7 Tecpatl	10 Calli or 11 Calli
4 C.	Coxcoxtli	9 Tecpatl or 10 Calli	10 Acatl

Relación de la Genealogía and *Origen de los Mexicanos*

Totepeuh
Nahuinci (Nauhyotzin)
Cuauhtexpetlatzin
Huetzin
Nonohualcatl
Achitometl
Cuauhtonal
Cuezan
Cuauhtlix
Yohualtonac
Xiuhtecatzin

The next step required is to classify these dates according to the principle stated above, treating a series of, say, 7 Tecpatl, 8 Calli, and 9 Tochtli, not as different dates but variations of the same one.

On re-examining the dates on this basis, it was found that most, but not all, of the seventy-five dates from the king-lists can be grouped into six such key date-groups, to which have been assigned the letters P to U; these may be specified as follows:

Group Designation	Different dates.	Median date.	Spread. (No. of years)
P	3 Acatl, 5 Calli, 6 Tochtli	5 Calli	4
Q	13 Calli	13 Calli	1
R	9 Tecpatl	9 Tecpatl	1
S	1 Calli, 2 Tochtli	1 Calli	2
T	6 Acatl, 7 Tecpatl, 9 Tochtli	7 Tecpatl	4
U	3 Tochtli, 4 Acatl, 5 Tecpatl	4 Acatl	3

(In naming the median, the most frequently used date of the middle years of the group has been taken).

357

To further the process of identification, the rulers of Chart A down to but excluding Coxcox have been lettered and numbered: the *Anales de Cuauhtitlán*'s Culhua kings from 1 A to 11 A: the *Memorial Breve* Culhua kings from 1 B to 13 B: those of Chimalpain's other *Relaciones* from 1 C to 4 C. However, in certain cases, where one or both dates of a ruler do not fall into the above-named groups, and therefore defy interpretation by the method so far proposed, their reigns have been bracketed with those of their successors or predecessors for the purpose of numbering, so that we are left only with reigns, single or composite, that *do* come within the above categories. For instance, in the early part of the *Memorial Breve* list of rulers, Nonohualcatl, Yohuallatónac [*sic*], Quetzalacxoyatzin, and Chalchiuhtlatonac are grouped together as 2B, in a reign from 3 Acatl (P) to 13 Calli (Q). The intermediate dates, say, for Yohuallatónac, have a most peculiar characteristic that may justify their temporary exclusion from the scheme—an ostensibly arbitrary step that will be justified at a later stage in the argument. The last rulers after Coxcox in the *Anales de Cuauhtitlan* and in Chimalpain's relaciones (Achitometl II, Huehue Acamapichtli and Nauhyotl II) have not been listed, as the post-Coxcox rulers follow a distinct pattern, that will be examined separately.

Having thus numbered the relevant rulers or reigns, they can now be set out in Chart B.

The pattern thus revealed may disconcert and even bewilder; but at least it exists. Twenty-eight identifiable reigns in all are listed in Chart B; if in some instances these had not been grouped as mentioned above, the total number of dated Culhua reigns given by the sources rises to thirty-nine, to which are assigned fourteen different rulers' names. Five of the thirty-nine reigns have only one date, not two, and of the total of seventy-three dates for rulers given by the *Anales de Cuauhtitlán,* Chimalpain's *Memorial Breve,* and his other *Relaciones,* including those to which I have not given a number, four dates fall in 13 Calli, six in 9 Tecpatl, seven in 7 Tecpatl, and four in 10 Calli. Thus twenty-one dates out of seventy-three, or nearly

30 per cent, fall in four out of fifty-two possible years, or 8 per cent of the total. Moreover, out of the seventy-three dates, fifty-three fall within the six date-groups P to U (i.e., those given in Chart B) that embrace a total of only fifteen of the fifty-two possible alternative years of the calendar—a coincidence too marked to be easily put down to pure chance.

The first puzzle concerns the twenty dates for reigns that do not fall within the narrow range of alternatives occupied by these fifty-three out of the seventy-three. At first sight they make no sense at all, since the dates of one list bear no relation to those of another; the same names crop up, but in a different order. Here also, however, a key to the riddle was found after other possibilities had been tried and discarded.

Since these twenty dates make so little sense if regarded as belonging to the same year-count as the other fifty-three, an eventual solution lay in treating them as belonging to another calendar. On this assumption, a more logical pattern emerged.

First, it was seen that when bracketing several rulers into one numbered reign—in seemingly arbitrary fashion—simply because they otherwise made no sense, these reigns invariably contained one Yohuallatónac, while the other names included in the series varied.

Second, if the *separate* dates of these bracketed rulers are listed, a peculiar phenomenon comes to light if one digit is added to each date—i.e., 1 Tecpatl is changed into 2 Tecpatl, or 8 Tochtli into 9 Tochtli, etc. The procedure itself is less arbitrary than it may appear, since a common tendency was observed both in this and in *The Toltecs* for sources to give two dates for an event, differing only from one another by one digit. Thus the usual date for the death of Topiltzin is 1 Acatl, but 2 Acatl also occurs. Xolotl dies in 12 Tecpatl in one account and in 13 Tecpatl in another.

The intermediate death dates may now be listed of rulers in bracketed reigns, 10A, 11A, 2B, and 3C, that do not conform to the PQRSTU groups of Chart B.

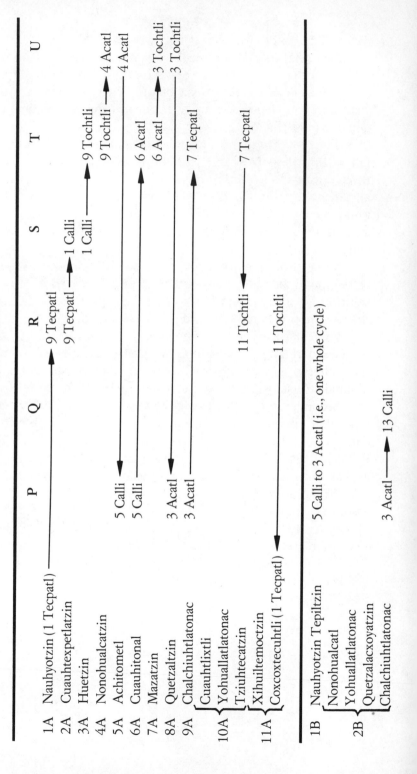

CHART B
RULERS OF CULHUACÁN

	P	Q	R	S	T	U
1A Nauhyotzin (1 Tecpatl)		9 Tecpatl →				
2A Cuauhtexpetlatzin			9 Tecpatl → 1 Calli			
3A Huetzin				1 Calli → 9 Tochtli		
4A Nonohualcatzin				9 Tochtli → 4 Acatl		
5A Achitometl	5 Calli					4 Acatl
6A Cuauhitonal	5 Calli				6 Acatl	
7A Mazatzin					6 Acatl → 3 Tochtli	
8A Quetzaltzin	3 Acatl					3 Tochtli
9A Chalchiuhtlatonac	3 Acatl			7 Tecpatl		
10A { Cuauhtlixtli / Yohuallatlatonac / Tziuhtecatzin			11 Tochtli	7 Tecpatl		
11A { Xihuiltemoctzin / Coxcoxtecuhtli (1 Tecpatl)			11 Tochtli			

1B Nauhyotzin Tepiltzin	5 Calli to 3 Acatl (i.e., one whole cycle)
2B { Nonohualcatl / Yohuallatlatonac / Quetzalacxoyatzin / Chalchiuhtlatonac	3 Acatl → 13 Calli

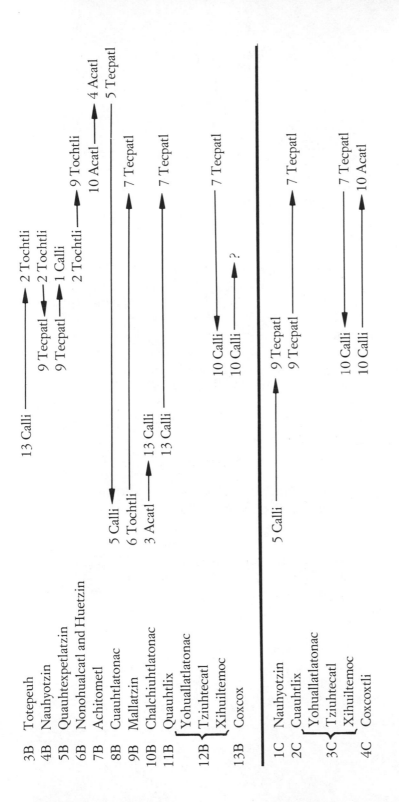

3B Totepeuh 13 Calli ⟶ 2 Tochtli
4B Nauhyotzin 9 Tecpatl ⟶ 2 Tochtli
5B Quauhtexpetlatzin 9 Tecpatl ⟶ 1 Calli
6B Nonohualcatl and Huetzin 2 Tochtli ⟶ 9 Tochtli
7B Achitometl 10 Acatl ⟶ 4 Acatl
   5 Tecpatl
8B Cuauhtlatonac 5 Calli ⟶
9B Mallatzin 6 Tochtli ⟶ 7 Tecpatl
10B Chalchiuhtlatonac 3 Acatl ⟶ 13 Calli
11B Quauhtlix 13 Calli ⟶ 7 Tecpatl
12B Yohuallatlatonac
3B Tziuhtecatl 10 Calli ⟶ 7 Tecpatl
    Xihuiltemoc 10 Calli ⟶ ?
13B Coxcox

1C Nauhyotzin 5 Calli ⟶ 9 Tecpatl
2C Cuauhtlix 9 Tecpatl ⟶ 7 Tecpatl
    Yohuallatlatonac
3C Tziuhtecatl 10 Calli ⟶ 7 Tecpatl
    Xihuiltemoc 10 Calli ⟶ 10 Acatl
4C Coxcoxtli

	Ruler	Death Date given in source.	Same Date, after adding one digit.
Reign 10A	Cuauhtlixtli	1 Acatl	2 Acatl
	Yohuallatlatonac	11 Calli	12 Calli
Reign 11A	Xihuiltemoctzin	3 Tecpatl	4 Tecpatl
Reign 2B	Nonohualcatl	3 Calli	4 Calli
	Yohuallatlatonic	10 Tecpatl	11 Tecpatl
	Quetzalacxoyatzin	7 Calli	8 Calli
Reign 12B	Yohuallatlatonic	1 Acatl	2 Acatl
Reign 3C	Yohuallatlatonic	1 Acatl	2 Acatl
	Tziuhtecatl	11 Calli	12 Calli

The above list accounts for eighteen of the additional twenty dates not included in Chart B, since each is repeated twice over, once for the end of a reign, and once for the beginning of the next. (The remaining two dates are both 1 Tecpatl, that will be accounted for below in a different manner.) After converting the eighteen dates to another calendar, that was demonstrably often used, by the addition of one digit, seventeen of them now fit into our established pattern. The one exception is Xihuiltemoctzin (11A); his dates, without adjustment, at a pinch conform to the pattern of Chart B as a reign running from 11 Tochtli (R) to 3 Tecpatl; 3 Tecpatl can be hitched on to the 7 Tecpatl group of dates (T), though it considerably widens the spread of that group.

The other dates given above have a major point in common: *once adjusted,* they are all clustered round the 7 Tecpatl date, though admittedly the cluster is fairly extended, from 2 Acatl (7 Tecpatl minus five years) to 12 Calli (7 Tecpatl plus five years). Therefore the intermediate kings in any bracketed reign in effect rule from 7 Tecpatl to 7 Tecpatl, plus or minus a maximum of five years; for instance, the adjusted dates of the two intermediate kings of the four bracketed together in reign 2B, would be from 4 Calli (7 Tecpatl minus three) to 11 Tecpatl (7 Tecpatl plus four) and from 11 Tecpatl to 8 Calli (7 Tecpatl plus one). It is surely significant that Ixtlil-xóchitl gives such ritual reigns of fifty-two years or thereabouts for the rulers of Tollan (or Culhuacán, as the case may be); however, his dates seem to belong to yet another calendar or to possess another significance, since they run from approximately 7 Acatl to 7 Acatl, not 7 Tecpatl to 7 Tecpatl. However, the principle remains the same: for instance, Nacazxoch [*sic*] reigns from 5 Calli (7 Acatl minus two) to 5 Calli; his successor, Tlacomihua, from 5 Calli to 11 Acatl (7 Acatl plus four).

Therefore we now discover that of the seventy-three dates in the Culhua king-lists of Chimalpain and the *Anales de Cuauhtitlán,* fifty-five can be classified as falling into the six groups P to U; the remainder (with the exception of two 1 Tecpatl dates) form another group more widely dispersed around the equivalent of 7 Tecpatl, but expressed in terms of a different but known year-count, differing by one digit. Accordingly, I view the lists as an odd mixture of historical dates interspersed with a sprinkling of ritual dates or reigns of approximately one fifty-two-year cycle from 7 Tecpatl to 7 Tecpatl, presumably taken from another list, of the kind that Ixtlilxóchitl used for the rulers of Tollan.

The special significance of 7 Tecpatl will be explained below, with reference to Coxcox and his successor. Leaving aside for the moment this category, the oddest feature of those other dates given in Chart B, centering on the six groups P to U, is that they do not follow in consecutive order, but go round in circles. The first Nauh-yotl of Culhuacán in the *Anales de Cuauhtitlán* begins his reign in 1 Tecpatl—the favorite ritual date for the start of a dynasty, used also for the first rulers of Tollan, Cuauhtitlán, and Cuitlahuac, as given by the same source. From 1 Tecpatl, Nauhyotzin reigns until R (9 Tecpatl); the sequence is then as follows: R (death of Nauh-yotzin) to S, S to T (death of Cuauhtexpetlatzin), T to U, U back to P, P to T, T to U, U back to P, P to T, T to R, and from R back to the ritual 1 Tecpatl. The phenomenon of dates going in reverse, e.g., T to R, is puzzling, but not out of keeping with such an odd pattern that seems to follow a circular, rather than a straight, course; more-over, the only way to make a long king-list out of a short one is to return from time to time to the point of departure, and start again.

The *Memorial Breve* list for Culhua rulers starts in peculiar fashion, with a reign that falls short of a ritual fifty-two-year cycle by only two years and thus runs from P to P. After this it goes as follows: P to Q, Q to S, S to R, R to S, S to T, T to U, U back to P, P to T, P to Q, Q to T, T to R.

363

An Exact Coincidence

A modicum of sense can be made of such a medley only by following the method used in Appendix B of *The Toltecs,* and where those parts of each list with the closest parallels were set side by side. Perplexing as these sequences may seem, if taken in toto, a near identity between certain sections can be recognized: for instance, the first ruler of Culhuacán in the *Anales de Cuauhtitlán* and the seventh ruler in the *Memorial Breve* are both called Nauhyotzin, and both die in 9 Tecpatl. In Chart C below the process was carried a stage further: the five rulers after these two Nauhyotzins, as given by the two sources, are also set out in the first two columns; and in the third column, three additional rulers of the *Anales de Cuauhtitlán* list are placed, for reasons that will also be made clear. The reign numbers (taken from Chart A) are placed in brackets beside the names.

CHART C

Anales de Cuauhtitlán	*Memorial Breve*	*Anales de Cuauhtitlán*
Nauhyotzin (Reign 1A) died 9 Tecpatl	Nauhyotzin (4B) died 9 Tecpatl	
Cuauhtexpetlatzin (2A) 9 Tecpatl to 1 Calli	Cuauhtexpetlatzin (5B) 9 Tecpatl to 1 Calli	
Huetzin (3A) 1 Calli to 9 Tochtli	Nonoalcatl and Huetzin (6B) 2 Tochtli to 9 Tochtli	
Nonoalcatzin (4A) 9 Tochtli to 4 Acatl	Achitometl (7B) 10 Acatl to 4 Acatl	Mazatzin (7A) 6 Acatl to 3 Tochtli
Achitometl (5A) 4 Acatl to 5 Calli	Cuauhtlatonac (8B) 5 Tecpatl to 5 Calli	Quetzaltzin (8A) 3 Tochtli to 3 Acatl
Cuauhitonal (6A) 5 Calli to 6 Acatl	Mallatzin (9B) 6 Tochtli 7 Tecpatl	Chalchiuhtlatonac (9A) 3 Acatl to 7 Tecpatl

These comparisons are striking and informative, since certain facts emerge. Numbers 2A to 6A *(Anales de Cuauhtitlán)* have dates, but not names, virtually identical with 5B to 9B *(Memorial Breve).* Moreover, if, as in the right-hand column, 7A to 9A are placed alongside the last three reigns in the other columns, the coincidence is also close. The dates for the continuous series given in the first two columns are the same to within one year. The names differ widely, and the process by which they jump a rung in the ladder can be clearly seen in column 2. The *Anales de Cuauhtitlán* list Nonoalcatl as successor to Huetzin, whereas the *Memorial Breve* gives them as joint rulers. As a result, in the *Memorial Breve,* the names that follow Nonoalcatl-Huetzin, i.e., Achitometl, Cuauhtlatonac, and Mallatzin, are given dates that repeat exactly those listed by the *Anales de Cuauhtitlán,* not for their namesakes, but for their namesakes' successors. Thus Achitometl of column 2 has the dates of Nonoalcatl of column 1, Cuauhtlatonac of column 2 those of Achitometl of column 1, etc. Incidentally, just as Cuauhtlatonac of column 2 is succeeded by Mallatzin, Cuauhitonal of column 1 is followed by a Mazatzin, though his dates differ.

The other main characteristic of these lists, the repetition of the same names or reigns, stands out clearly. In the *Anales de Cuauhtitlán* list, 7–9 A are a near repetition of 4–6 A, as can be seen in the third column of Chart C. The identity between 2A to 6A, as compared with 5B to 9B from the *Memorial Breve,* is so close that they certainly derive from a common source, though the names changed places. Moreover, as already explained, 1–6 A are the first six kings of Culhuacán in the *Anales de Cuauhtitlán,* but 4–9 B are the seventh to twelfth kings in the *Memorial Breve!*

After 9A and 9B, the same pattern of identity no longer applies: the *Anales de Cuauhtitlán* list proceeds in haphazard fashion from 7 Tecpatl (Cuauhtlixtli's accession) to 1 Tecpatl, given as the date of the end of Coxcox' reign. After Mallatzin (9B) in the *Memorial Breve,* a break occurs, and the following reign begins in 3 Acatl.

Six Reigns

From the above comparisons, it has already been seen that an identity in dates of *reigns* for a whole series of consecutive rulers can be traced in the two main sources, but that *names* can slip one or more places in the list, or in other cases change their order.

By comparing Charts B and C, it also becomes apparent that striking as are the parallels of Chart C, they omit the beginning and the end of the story. Stages P–Q and Q–R of Chart B are not represented in the reigns of Chart C; equally Chart B gives a wider range

365

of choice for the death of Coxcox, to be discussed later. This ruler has in effect also "slipped" a rung on the ladder, and in one list his reign begins in 10 Calli while in the other it ends in 11 Tochtli (10 Calli plus one). For reasons to be stated below, the date of 10 Acatl (or perhaps 7 Tecpatl, i.e. 10 Acatl minus three) is more likely to be the right one for the end of the reign of Coxcox, as given in Chimalpain's seventh *Relación.*

A logical list of Culhua rulers may thus be made by taking the five identical reigns of Chart C as a common basis, shared by the two main sources. But these reigns, beginning only in 1248, do not seem to go back to the start of the story, and the list may be completed by the insertion of two more reigns at the beginning, based on the clearly identifiable P to Q (5 Calli to 13 Calli) and Q to R (13 Calli to 9 Tecpatl) of Chart B. For reasons set out in Chapter II, the native dates are believed to correspond to the Culhua-Texcoco, not to the Tenochca count (i.e., 1 Acatl equals 1539, not 1519).

We are thus left with the following reigns:

Reign I	5 Calli to 13 Calli	A. D. 1205–13	?
Reign II	13 Calli to 9 Tecpatl	1213–48	Nauhyotzin
Reign III	9 Tecpatl to 1 Calli	1248–53	Cuauhtexpetlatzin
Reign IV	1 Calli to 7 Tecpatl	1248–72	Huetzin
Reign V	7 Tecpatl to 4 Acatl	1272–95	Nonoalcatl
Reign VI	4 Acatl to 5 Calli	1295–1309	Xihuiltemoc
Reign VII	5 Calli to 10 Acatl	1295–1327	Coxcox

Concerning the names of rulers given above, it is hard to be precise. Nauhyotzin according to all sources reigned until 9 Tecpatl, and the king most frequently named for the short reign of 9 Tecpatl to 1 Calli is Cuauhtexpetlatzin, succeeded by Huetzin, or Huetzin and Nonoalcatl, though a joint reign seems less likely. The naming of Xihuiltemoc for reign VI is very tentative, but several sources do name him as Coxcox' predecessor; Chimalpain states that they were brothers.

Coxcox and Achitometl

Somewhat arbitrarily perhaps, I have named Coxcox as the leading ruler in the last reign listed above, coinciding with the Mexica captivity. The sources contradict each other on this point. The

Anales de Tlatelolco list no less than four señores who reigned at that moment: Acxoquauhtli, Coxcox, Chalchiuhtlatonac, and Achitometl; the *Memorial Breve* also gives four simultaneous rulers: Coxcox, Huehue Acamapichtli, Achitometl II, and Chalchiuhtlatonac; this source names Coxcox as principal ruler, and refers to the others as his "señores" *(itlatocayohuan)*. The Codex Azcatitlan illustrates three rulers: Tillitl, Chalchiuhtlatonac, and Coxcox.

Other documents write of the presence of two rulers. Durán says that Culhuacán was then ruled by two señores, Coxcox and Achitometl; the *Historia de los Mexicanos* qualifies this by saying that, at the time of the Mexica captivity, Achitometl was señor and Chalchiuhtlatonac was his "principal"—perhaps a kind of *cihuacoatl,* or assistant ruler.

On the other hand, several sources write of Culhuacán as if it had one single dynasty, just as Tenochtitlán or Texcoco. The *Anales de Cuauhtitlán* simply state that Chalchiuhtlatonac was ruler when the Mexicas came, and give an unbroken succession of kings that followed him as sole ruler; the *Relación de la Genealogía,* the *Origen de los Mexicanos,* and Torquemada also give single lists. Ixtlilxóchitl writes of conflict between Coxcox and his son Huehue Acamapichtli, as if there was only one throne in dispute; like Torquemada, the *Relación de la Genealogía* mentions Chalchiuhtlatonac as single ruler during the Mexica stay in Tizapan.

An easy way out of this imbroglio would be found if previous suspicions that Coxcox is Chalchiuhtlatonac, or that Coxcox and Achitometl are one and the same person, could be placed on a firmer footing. But since the names in the lists have become so jumbled, a common identity can only be fixed to two names, if their bearers always have the same dates of accession and death in the king-lists. This has now proved impossible because rulers tend to slip a place on the king-list ladder—as already explained—so that a named ruler in one list will have the same dates as his successor in another.

Chalchiuhtlatonac seems to be a generic title, and this name may occupy almost any rung on the ladder, while Achitometl more often applies to later rulers, and Nauhyotzin (with one exception) to earlier ones. Therefore, to judge by their dates, it cannot be said categorically that Chalchiuhtlatonac is just another name for Achitometl or Coxcox, as I had previously suspected.

Evidence, by no means unanimous, favors Coxcox as the *principal* ruler at the start of the Mexica captivity; several sources state that he was grandson of Huetzin and son of Acolmiztli (who either ruled in Coatlichán rather than in Culhuacán, or was known by another name in this city). Equally, several accounts treat Huehue Acamapichtli (Coxcox' successor) as his son; that Coxcox was therefore at least one of the Culhuacán rulers in 1319 becomes reasonably clear.

The question remains: were there other rulers as well? Whereas the presence of two or four dynasties was previously moot, I now incline to wonder whether such reports involve a confusion between true *tlatoanis* and other leaders, more strictly comparable to the *cihuacoatl* of Tenochtitlán or even to the offices of *tlacochcalcatl* and *tlacateccatl.* The name Chalchiuhtlatonac might conceivably have pertained to such an office, since it crops up so regularly; thus, both Coxcox and Achitometl could at one time have also been called Chalchiuhtlatonac before becoming *tlatoani,* while at other times neither would have been thus called. This conforms to the accounts of the *Memorial Breve* and the *Anales de Tlatelolco,* that name Chalchiuhtlatonac as distinct from Achitometl or Coxcox. In addition, Cuauhitonal and/or Cuauhtlatonac probably applied to people who also possessed other appellations.

The presence of both a Coxcox and of an Achitometl in Culhuacán at the time of the Mexica captivity is mentioned fairly frequently. When the *Historia de los Mexicanos* says that Achitometl was the leading ruler and Chalchiuhtlatonac his "principal," it may be implying the same thing; conceivably Achitometl was then senior ruler, and Chalchiuhtlatonac at that time was a name or a title born by Coxcox, who only later became chief ruler on the death of this Achitometl. In point of fact, however, the reverse is far more likely to be true, since Achitometl, or Achitometl II, was Coxcox' successor-but-one as chief ruler. Any previous Achitometl, who ruled jointly with Coxcox or before him, is very hard to place chronologically. Achitometl seems to be as much a title as Chalchiuhtlatonac or Cuauhitonal, and the earliest mention of an Achitometl of Culhuacán is in connection with Nopaltzin, son of Xolotl. The *Anales de Cuauhtitlán,* Chimalpain, and Torquemada name Xihuiltemoc as preceding Coxcox. The tentative suggestion was therefore made that reign VI (1295–1309) belongs to Xihuiltemoc, and that reign VII applies to Coxcox (1295 to 1327, or thereabouts, since different versions of his death date vary by a few years).

Later Rulers

Following the death of Coxcox, matters become less complicated, since reports concur in naming Coxcox' successors as first Huehue Acamapichtli, second Achitometl II, and third another Nauhyotzin. Certain discrepancies arise over dates.

The *Crónica Mexicayotl* states that Huehue Acamapichtli was the second son of Coxcox; the *Anales de Cuauhtitlán* and Chimalpain's seventh *Relación* both say that Huehue Acamapichtli succeeded Coxcox in 1 Tecpatl. Ixtlilxóchitl even insists that a conflict arose between the two; Coxcox was defeated and retired to Coatlichán.

The only date we have for the accession of Huehue Acamapichtli, 1 Tecpatl, if attributed, like the prededing dates, to the Culhua count, is the equivalent of 1344. Now Chimalpain, without being aware of the possible use of several native calendars, did note the evident gap between his 10 Calli for the death of Coxcox and the 1 Tecpatl which he gives for Huehue Acamapichtli's accession. He accounts for this interval by saying that no king ruled in Culhuacán but only a military government *(çan ocuauhtlatolloc)* during sixteen years—i.e., the approximate gap between 10 Acatl and 1 Tecpatl, if both belong to the same year-count.

This is purely a deduction on the chronicler's part, in order to explain an *apparent* anomaly, as he saw it. But a better explanation can be put forward if the dates from Huehue Acamapichtli onwards are treated as coming from another list, based not on the Culhua but on the Tenochca count; 1 Tecpatl then becomes 1324, not 1344. Now, as stressed above, a spread of three years for one event is common, even in the case of the dates of the last Tenochca monarchs; for a period of two hundred years before the Conquest, three years rank as a rather minor discrepancy, and 1 Tecpatl Tenochca (= 1324) may reasonably be taken as forming part of the same date group as 10 Acatl, Culhua (= 1327).

Quite apart from the 10 Acatl date given for Coxcox' death,

other rulers with other names in the *Anales de Cuauhtitlán* and the Chimalpain lists—that may well be the same as Coxcox—end their reigns in 7 Tecpatl, that is the exact equivalent of 1 Tecpatl Tenochca. More significant still, the *Anales de Cuauhtitlán* actually name 1 Tecpatl as the year of Coxcox' death.

It is not so surprising that the dates for Huehue Acamapichtli and his successor should be given in the Tenochca count, and Jiménez Moreno has suggested that the change-over came at this time, after the defeat of Azcapotzalco. Acamapichtli's successor, Achitometl II, probably died about when Tezozómoc of Azcapotzalco mounted his throne; Huehue Acamapichtli's dates therefore merge into those of a period when the Tenochca count was brought into current use. Moreover, certain sources tend to confuse Huehue Acamapichtli with Acamapichtli of Tenochtitlán, sometimes described as his nephew. In a sense, therefore, Huehue Acamapichtli is part of Tenochca history and of its chronology.

I have always been puzzled by the story of military rule in Culhuacán at this juncture; no clear reason exists why the Culhua dynasty should have collapsed so early, in face of disasters that left an empty throne in their wake. Any change from Culhua to Tenochca count automatically presents the unwary chronicler with an apparent gap of twenty years; e.g., 1 Acatl Tenochca is 1519, while 1 Acatl Culhua is 1539, 2 Tecpatl 1540, etc. The adjustment from one calendar to another offers a simple explanation of the so-called interval between the reigns of Coxcox and Huehue Acamapichtli noted by Chimalpain. Whether a conflict occurred between the two, as Ixtlilxóchitl maintains, is uncertain; let it be sufficient to say that Coxcox died in 1327, or two or three years before or after that date, and was then succeeded by Huehue Acamapichtli.

This identification of a possible changeover from one count to another is significant. The hypothesis is strengthened, as explained in Chapter IX, by signs of an identical switch in both Cuauhtitlán and Toltitlan. Xaltemoctzin of Cuauhtitlán was killed in precisely 7 Tecpatl, and the first mention of his successor comes only in 3 Tochtli (1 Tecpatl plus two); this time it is the turn of the *Anales de Cuauhtitlán* to insist on a long gap in the Cuauhtitlán king-list. Exactly the same thing happened in Toltitlan (also described in the *Anales de Cuauhtitlán);* one ruler is liquidated in 7 Tecpatl and another ascends the throne after an apparent interlude of twenty years. One Tecpatl is a date of special significance, and it is noteworthy that in three different cases, involving three places and three dynasties, a reign ends in 7 Tecpatl or thereabouts, and the new reign starts in 1 Tecpatl—after a reported interregnum with no ruler. But a change-over from Culhua to Tenochca count, in view of the twenty year difference between the two, disposes of the interregnum; moreover, it is typical of Mesoamerican chronology that the change should come in such a way that the new calendar or new king-list begins to operate in 1 Tecpatl, a favorite year for the commencement of a dynasty.

According to the *Anales de Cuauhtitlán,* Achitometl (usually called Achitometl II) killed Huehue Acamapichtli in 13 Tecpatl, and usurped the Culhua throne. Chimalpain's seventh *Relación* gives the same date. The *Relación de la Genealogía* states that Huehue Acamapichtli reigned twelve years, and was the last "legitimate" señor, thereby also implying that his successor was a usurper, if not an assassin. Assuming that the accession date of Huehue Acamapichtli belongs to the Tenochca count, no reason exists to question the statement that he reigned twelve years or to suppose that his death date does not also belong to this calendar, in which it is the equivalent of 1336.

Chimalpain's seventh *Relación* states that Achitometl reigned until 11 Acatl, a figure also given by the *Anales de Cuauhtitlán,* and no other dates for his death exist. The *Anales de Cuauhtitlán* state that after Achitometl's death the Culhua polity disintegrated, through internal strife rather than any outside invasion. The source implies another gap in the king-list, since it states that Achitometl's successor was a Nauhyotzin, imposed by the Mexicas in 2 Calli, when they dispatched an expedition to Culhuacán. Now 2 Calli is 1377 in the Tenochca count, and follows one year after the 1 Tecpatl date that the source gives for the beginning of the Tepanec-Mexica war against Chalco; on the other hand, 11 Acatl would be 1347. Such a long interregnum between Achitometl and Nauhyotzin is unlikely, and no known reason exists why Culhuacán should have collapsed as early as 1347, only two years after the probable date of foundation of Tenochtitlán and before the era of the Tepanec-Mexica attacks on Culhuacán. Moreover, if Nauhyotl had become king immediately after the death of Achitometl in 1347, his reign becomes unrealistically long.

Another explanation exists: Chimalpain in his seventh *Relación* as well as the *Anales de Cuauhtitlán,* gives 11 Acatl as the year of the death of Achitometl; but, unlike the *Anales,* Chimalpain says that Nauhyotl succeeded in the same year; he adds that, also in 11 Acatl, the Chalcas saw smoke come from Popocatépetl (the mountain previously known as Xalliquehuac) and states that this was the first occurrence of its kind for a long time. But in the sixth *Relación,* Chimalpain inserts under 9, not 11 Acatl, information to the effect that in that year smoke rose from Popocatépetl, repeating that the mountain was previously known as Xalliquehuac and using almost identical words to those of the seventh *Relación;* plainly we are concerned with a single item of information repeated twice over.

The question still arises: when did the event really occur? It has been shown that Chimalpain's Julian calendar equivalents need careful interpretation, and his insistence in giving 1347 as the date for the death of Achitometl is therefore not necessarily reliable; his native dates are what matter. Now 9 Acatl, Tenochca count, is 1371, and the more likely solution is that Achitometl's death occurred in 9 Acatl Tenochca, that is 11 Acatl in another count; this accords with Chimalpain's sixth *Relación,* and with the statement of the *Anales de Cuauhtitlán* that total collapse ensued (known to have occurred about this time, not in 1347). A short gap then followed before the Tepanec-Mexicas installed their nominee in 1377. The *Anales de Cuauhtitlán* also state that Tezozómoc came to the throne in the same year that Huehue Acamapichtli was killed, but it seems probable that the source is in this instance confusing Acamapichtli with his successor, Achitometl.

The situation regarding subsequent rulers of Culhuacán is simpler: Nauhyotzin was killed in 12 Calli (Tenochca 1413) by Tezozómoc. His successor was killed by Nezahualcoyotl in 3 Tochtli (1430). It is therefore proposed that the sequence of the rulers of Culhuacán from Coxcox until the fall of Azcapotzalco was as follows:

Coxcox	1309–27.
Huehue Acamapichtli	1324–36.
Achitometl II	1336–71.
Nauhyotzin II	1377–1413.
Acoltzin	1413–30.

Notes & References

Chapter I. The Claim to Be a Toltec

1. Sahagún, *Florentine Codex,* Book III, chapters 13 and 14.
2. Davies, *The Toltecs,* 22–23.
3. *Ibid.,* Appendix B.
4. Sahagún, *Florentine Codex,* Book X, chapter 29, p. 191.
5. *Anales de Tlatelolco,* 35.
6. Swadesh, "Algunas fechas . . . ."
7. Ixtlilxóchitl, *Obras,* I, 472.
8. Davies, *The Toltecs,* 231
9. *Ibid.,* 233.
10. Davies, *Los Mexicas,* Appendix A, and Davies, *The Toltecs,* Appendix B.
11. Nicholson, "Western Mesoamerican Native Historical Traditions."
12. Davies, *Los Mexicas,* Appendix A.
13. Thompson, *Maya History and Religion,* xiii.
14. Davies, *The Toltecs,* Appendix A.
15. Johnson, *The Offshore Islanders,* 20–21.
16. Sahagún, *Florentine Codex,* Book IX.
17. *Anales Mexicanos,* 50.
18. Murra, *Formaciones,* 279–80.
19. Zuidema, "Reseña de Brundage, 1963," 231–32.

Chapter II. Favorite Sons

1. Chimalpain, *Memorial Breve,* 20.
2. *Ibid.,* 149.
3. *Relación de la Genealogía,* 241.
4. Davies, *The Toltecs,* chapter V.
5. *Historia de los Mexicanos,* 223.
6. Chimalpain, *Memorial Breve,* 113.
7. *Ibid.,* 37.
8. Ixtlilxóchitl, *Obras,* I, 67.
9. Davies, *The Toltecs,* Chapter VII.
10. Davies, *Los Mexicas,* 19–20.
11. Griffin and Espejo, "Alfarería," 128; Noguera, *La Cerámica,* 112.
12. Noguera and Piña Chan, "Estratigrafía de Teopanzolco," 152.
13. Ixtlilxóchitl, *Obras,* I, 59.
14. Torquemada, *Monarquía indiana,* 260.

15. *Relación de la Genealogía,* 247.
16. Chimalpain, *Memorial Breve,* 38.
17. Davies, *The Toltecs,* Appendix B, Table A.
18. Davies, *Los Señoríos,* Table B.
19. Davies, *Los Mexicas,* Appendix A.
20. *Anales de Cuauhtitlán,* 36.

21. Davies, *Los Mexicas,* 44–45.
22. Ixtlilxóchitl, *Obras,* I, 114.
23. Durán, *Historia,* II, 39; *Historia de los Mexicanos,* 226.
24. *Anales de Cuauhtitlán,* 29.
25. Ixtlilxóchitl, *Obras,* I, 120.
26. *Anales de Cuauhtitlán,* 29.

Chapter III. Back to Methuselah

1. Caso, "La época," 147–53.
2. Vetancurt, *Teatro mexicano,* 235.
3. Torquemada, *Monarquía indiana,* I, 39.
4. *Anónimo Mexicano,* 118.
5. Muñoz Camargo, *Historia,* 63.
6. *Ibid.,* 37.
7. Chimalpain, *Memorial Breve,* 7.
8. Davies, *The Toltecs,* chapter VIII.
9. *Ibid.,* Appendix A.
10. Chimalpain, *Memorial Breve,* 10.
11. Torquemada, *Monarquía indiana,* I, 58.
12. *Anales de Cuauhtitlán,* 42.
13. *Anales de Tlatelolco,* 21–22.
14. Ixtlilxóchitl, *Obras,* I, 96, 104.
15. Torquemada, *Monarquía indiana,* I, 62–63.

16. Chimalpain, *Relaciones,* 170.
17. Torquemada, *Monarquía indiana.* I, 58.
18. *Anales de Cuauhtitlán,* 23.
19. *Ibid.,* 23.
20. Davies, *Los Mexicas,* Appendix A.
21. *Anales de Cuauhtitlán,* 40.
22. Davies, *The Toltecs,* Appendix A.
23. Durán, *Historia,* II, 51–52.
24. Chimalpain, *Memorial Breve,* 104.
25. *Anales de Cuauhtitlán,* 17–18.
26. *Ibid.,* 17; Chimalpain, *Memorial Breve,* 37–38.
27. Chimalpain, *Memorial Breve,* 37–38.
28. Caso, "La época."
29. Monzón and Espejo.
30. Davies, *Los Mexicas,* Appendix A.

Chapter IV. Chichimecs and Ex–Chichimecs

1. Davies, *The Toltecs,* 398–99.
2. Armillas, "Condiciones ambientales."
3. Davies, *The Toltecs,* 399–400.
4. Carrasco, *Los otomíes.*
5. *Ibid.,* 60.
6. Jiménez Moreno, "La Colonización," 17.
7. Kirchhoff, "Dos tipos," 256.
8. Soustelle, *La famille Otomi-Pame,* 408.
9. Armillas, "Condiciones."
10. *Historia de los Mexicanos,* 216.
11. Jiménez Moreno, "Síntesis," 1068.
12. Ixtlilxóchitl, *Obras,* I, 106.
13. *Ibid.*
14. Kirchhoff, "Civilizing the Chichimecs."
15. Ixtlilxóchitl, *Obras,* II, 41.

16. Ixtlilxóchitl, *Obras,* I, 93–95.
17. Sahagún, *Florentine Codex,* Book X, chapter 29.
18. Davies, "Tula, reality, myth, and symbol."
19. Kirchhoff, "Civilizing the Chichimecs."
20. Sahagún, *Florentine Codex,* Book X, chapter 29.
21. *Ibid.*
22. Carrasco, "Los otomíes," 265.
23. Soustelle, *La famille,* 480, 489, 491–96.
24. Las Casas, *Tratados,* 28–40.
25. Motolinía, *Historia,* 270.
26. Ixtlilxóchitl, *Obras,* II, 59.
27. Kirchhoff, "Civilizing the Chichimecs."
28. Muñoz Camargo, *Historia,* 31.

29. Armillas, "Condiciones ambientales."
30. Saravia, "La Nueva Vizcaya."
31. *Historia Tolteca-Chichimeca*, 93.
32. Davies, *Los Mexicas*, 20–21.

Chapter V. The Early Acolhuas

1. Pomar, *Relaciones*, 6.
2. Thelma Sullivan, personal communication.
3. *Anales de Cuauhtitlán*, 63.
4. Chimalpain, *Relaciones*, 63.
5. Chimalpain, *Memorial Breve*, 37.
6. Tezozómoc, *Crónica Mexicayotl*, 38.
7. Torquemada, *Monarquía indiana*, I, 260.
8. Pomar, *Relaciones*, 6.
9. *Historia Tolteca-Chichimeca*, 97.
10. *Ibid.*, III.
11. Torquemada, *Monarquía indiana*, I, 97.
12. Pomar, *Relaciones*, 6.
13. Muñoz Camargo, *Historia*, 36.
14. *Historia Tolteca-Chichimeca*, 93.
15. Ixtlilxóchitl, *Obras*, I, 107.
16. Clavijero, *Historia antigua*, 15.
17. Ixtlilxóchitl, *Obras*, I, 94.
18. *Ibid.*, I, 183–84; II, 103–104.
19. *Ibid.*, I, 95.
20. Muñoz Camargo, *Historia*, 25.
21. *Histoyre du Mechique*, 18.
22. Ixtlilxóchitl, *Obras*, I, 303.
23. *Ibid.*, I, 124–5.

24. Torquemada, *Monarquía indiana*, I, 55.
25. *Ibid.*, 58.
26. Ixtlilxóchitl, *Obras*, II, 62.
27. Davies, *Los Mexicas*, Appendix A, Table A.
28. Ixtlilxóchitl, *Obras*, II, 62–63.
29. *Ibid.*, I, 135.
30. *Ibid.*, II, 78.
31. *Ibid.*, I, 131; II, 70.
32. *Ibid.*, I, 131.
33. *Ibid.*, I, 119.
34. *Ibid.*, II, 74.
35. *Ibid.*, I, 139.
36. *Ibid.*, I, 139.
37. *Anales de Cuauhtitlán*, 29.
38. Vetancurt, *Teatro mexicano*, II, 253; Tezozómoc, *Crónica Mexicayotl*, 112.
39. Ixtlilxóchitl, *Obras*, I, 178; II, 169.
40. *Anales de Cuauhtitlán*, 39.
41. *Ibid.*, 18–19.
42. Chimalpain, *Memorial Breve*, 104.
43. García Granados, *Diccionario*, II, 108–109.
44. Davies, *Los Mexicas*, Appendix A, Table A.

Chapter VI. The Dark Secret

1. Seler, *Gesammelte*, II, 1043.
2. *Anales de Tlatelolco*, 55.
3. Muñoz Camargo, *Historia*, 42–43.
4. Durán, *Historia*, II, 99.
5. *Relación de la Genealogía*, 247.
6. *Ibid.*, 252.
7. Durán, *Historia*, II, 21.
8. Chimalpain, *Relaciones*, 65.
9. *Anales de Tlatelolco*, 31.
10. Sahagún, *Florentine Codex*, Book X, chapter 29.
11. Ixtlilxóchitl, *Obras*, II, 41.

12. Sahagún, *Florentine Codex*, Book X, chapter 29.
13. Chimalpain, *Relaciones*, 59.
14. *Historia de los Mexicanos*, 219.
15. *Ibid.*, 228.
16. Torquemada, *Monarquía indiana*, I, 260.
17. Muñoz Camargo, *Historia*, 26.
18. *Historia de los Mexicanos*, 219.
19. Davies, *Los Mexicas*, 27.
20. Martínez Marín, "La migración acolhua," 378.

21. *Relación de Temazcaltepec,* 15–29.
22. Tezozómoc, *Crónica Mexicana,* 41.
23. *Historia de los Mexicanos,* 219.
24. Seler, *Gesammelte,* II, 1052.
25. Davies, *The Toltecs,* Appendix A.
26. Soustelle, *La famille,* 404.
27. Davies, *Los Mexicas,* 17–18.
28. Davies, *The Toltecs,* chapter VII.
29. Davies, *Los Mexicas,* 20.
30. *Anales de Cuauhtitlán,* 25.
31. Sahagún, *Florentine Codex,* Book X, chapter 29.
32. Ixtlilixóchitl, *Obras,* I, 105.
33. Davies, *Los señoríos,* 24.
34. Ixtlilxóchitl, *Obras,* 11, 129.
35. *Anales de Tlatelolco,* 21–22.
36. *Ibid.,* 28.
37. Torquemada, *Monarquía indiana,* I, 252.
38. Veytia, *Historia,* I, 275, 332.
39. *Anales Mexicanos,* 49.
40. Ixtlilxóchitl, *Obras,* II, 127.
41. *Historia de los Mexicanos,* 228.
42. *Anales de Tlatelolco,* 37.
43. Chimalpain, *Memorial Breve,* 39.
44. Sahagún, *Florentine Codex,* Book VIII, chapter 4.
45. *Anales de Tlatelolco,* 52.
46. Torquemada, *Monarquía indiana,* I, 83.
47. Davies, *Los Mexicas,* 96.
48. Ixtlilxóchitl, *Obras,* I, 115.
49. Davies, *Los Mexicas,* 96.
50. *Anales de Cuauhtitlán,* 46.
51. *Relación de Tecpatepec,* 34–35.
52. Davies, *Los Mexicas,* 97–100.
53. *Anales de Cuauhtitlán,* 32.
54. *Relación de la Genealogía,* 250.

Chapter VII. Friends and Neighbors

1. Noguera and Piña Chan, "Estratigrafía de Teopanzolco," 152.
2. Davies, *Los Mexicas,* 110.
3. Mendieta, *Historia,* I, 99.
4. Davies, *The Toltecs,* chapter III.
5. *Ibid.,* chapter VIII.
6. Kirchhoff, *Prologue,* chapter 2.
7. Schmidt, "El Postclásico."
8. Davies, *The Toltecs,* Appendix A.
9. Muñoz Camargo, *Historia,* 45–55.
10. García Cook, "Una secuencia."
11. García Cook, "Las fases."
12. Torquemada, *Monarquía indiana,* I, 283.
13. *Anales de Cuauhtitlán,* 12.
14. Muñoz Camargo, *Historia,* 67.
15. Torquemada, *Monarquía indiana,* I, 265.
16. Muñoz Camargo, Historia, 41.
17. Kirchhoff, *Prologue,* xxxi.
18. Davies, *Los Mexicas,* 93.
19. Pomar, *Relaciones,* 10.
20. Durán, *Historia,* II, 463.
21. Jiménez Moreno, "Calendarios."
22. Muñoz Camargo, *Historia,* 73–76.
23. *Anales de Cuauhtitlán,* 22.
24. Torquemada, *Monarquía indiana,* I, 138.
25. *Anales de Cuauhtitlán,* 24.
26. Muñoz Camargo, *Historia,* 127.
27. Davies, *Los señoríos,* 108–50.
28. *Anales de Cuauhtitlán,* 57.
29. Ixtlilxóchitl, *Obras,* II, 41.
30. *Anales de Cuauhtitlán,* 38.
31. Torquemada, *Monarquía indiana,* I, 134.
32. Ixtlilxóchitl, *Obras,* II, 275.

Chapter VIII. Toltzalan Acatzalan

1. Davies, *Los señoríos,* 24.
2. *Tira de la Peregrinación,* Plate II.
3. Durán, *Historia,* II, 25–26.
4. Radin, *Sources and authenticity.*
5. Tezozómoc, *Crónica Mexicana,* 15.
6. Davies, *Los Mexicas,* chapter II.
7. *Anales de Cuauhtitlán,* 16.
8. *Anales Mexicanos,* 117.
9. Ixtlilxóchitl, *Obras,* II, 83.
10. *Anales de Cuauhtitlán,* 13.
11. Chimalpain, *Relaciones,* 67.
12. Durán, *Historia,* 55.

13. *Ibid.*
14. Tezozómoc, *Crónica Mexicayotl,* 15.
15. Codex Vaticano Ríos, 67.
16. Cristóbal del Castillo, *Fragmentos,* 83.
17. Tezozómoc, Crónica Mexicayotl, 36.
18. *Origen de los Mexicanos,* 264.
19. Davies, *Los Mexicas,* 41.
20. Ibid.
21. Ibid.
22. Tezozómoc, *Crónica Mexicana,* 16–17.
23. *Ibid.,* 39.
24. *Historia de los Mexicanos,* 224.
25. *Anales de Cuauhtitlán,* 18.
26. Davies, *Los Mexicas,* 39–40.
27. Torquemada, *Monarquía indiana,* I, 83; Tezozómoc, *Crónica Mexicana,* 16; Veytia, *Historia antigua,* I, 260.
28. *Anales de Tlatelolco,* 35.
29. van Zantwijk, "La organización," 201.
30. Barlow, "El códice Azcatitlan," 113.
31. Torquemada, *Monarquía indiana,* I, 83.
32. Durán, *Historia,* II, 39.
33. *Anales de Tlatelolco,* 36.
34. Bernal, *Tenochtitlán,* 109.
35. Armillas, "Condiciones," 20–21.
36. Radin, *Sources and Authenticity.*
37. Tezozómoc, *Crónica Mexicayotl,* 70, 77.
38. Torquemada, *Monarquía indiana,* I, 29.
39. van Zantwijk, "La organización," 201.
40. Tezozómoc, *Crónica Mexicayotl,*

75; Torquemada, *Monarquía indiana,* I, 93; *Anales de Tlatelolco,* 45.
41. Veytia, *Historia antigua,* I, 317.
42. Torquemada, *Monarquía indiana,* I, 291.
43. Durán, *Historia,* II, 49.
44. Vetancurt, *Teatro mexicano,* I, 269; Mendieta, *Historia,* I, 163.
45. Ixtlilxóchitl, *Obras,* I, 118–9, 274.
46. Tezozómoc, *Crónica Mexicana,* 19.
47. Torquemada, *Monarquía indiana,* I, 98.
48. *Anales de Tlatelolco,* 51.
49. Ixtlilxóchitl, *Obras,* I, 119.
50. Motolinía, *Memoriales,* 6.
51. *Relación de la Genealogía,* 249–50.
52. *Historia de los Mexicanos,* 228.
53. Tezozómoc, *Crónica Mexicayotl,* 84.
54. *Relación de la Genealogía,* 251.
55. van Zantwijk, personal communication.
56. Tezozómoc, *Crónica Mexicayotl,* 85.
57. Chimalpain, *Relaciones,* 81; Torquemada, *Monarquía indiana,* I, 96; Vetancurt, *Teatro mexicano,* I, 269.
58. *Relación de la Genealogía,* 251.
59. Davies, *Los Mexicas,* Appendix A.
60. *Ibid.,* 73–89.
61. Dyckerhoff and Prem, "La estratificación social."
62. *Anales de Cuauhtitlán,* 27.
63. Kirchhoff, "Dos tipos de relaciones," 256.
64. van Zantwijk, "La organización," 201.
65. Davies, *Los Mexicas,* 50.

Chapter IX. *The Will to Conquer*

1. *Historia de los Mexicanos,* 228.
2. *Anales de Tlatelolco,* 51.
3. Tezozómoc, *Crónica Mexicayotl,* 78.
4. Ixtlilxóchitl, *Obras,* I, 115–6.
5. Sahagún, *Florentine Codex,* Book VIII, chapter 2.
6. *Anales de Tlatelolco,* 52.

7. Ixtlilxóchitl, *Obras,* I, 103.
8. *Ibid.,* I, 120–21.
9. Codex Mexicanus, 440.
10. Davies, *Los Mexicas,* 108.
11. *Anales de Cuauhtitlán,* 33.
12. Tezozómoc, *Crónica Mexicayotl,* 94–95.

13. *Historia de los Mexicanos,* 229.
14. *Anales de Tlatelolco,* 57.
15. *Historia Tolteca-Chichimeca,* 114.
16. *Anales de Cuauhtitlan,* 34; *Anales de Tula,* 4.
17. *Anales de Tlatelolco,* 52–53.
18. Davies, *Los Mexicas,* 116.
19. *Anales de Tlatelolco,* 54.
20. *Anales de Cuauhtitlán,* 18.
21. *Ibid.,* 6.
22. Ixtlilxóchitl, *Obras,* II, 77–78.
23. Veytia, *Historia antigua,* I, 353; Clavijero, *Historia antigua,* 78.
24. Trautmann, "Untersuchungen," 43.

25. Chimalpain, *Memorial Breve,* 118.
26. Carrasco, *Los otomíes,* 259.
27. Torquemada, *Monarquía indiana,* I, 185.
28. Jiménez Moreno, "Síntesis," 230.
29. Trautmann, *Untersuchungen,* 58–60.
30. Ixtlilxóchitl, *Obras,* I, 491.
31. *Descripción de Hueypochtla,* 44.
32. Ixtlilxóchitl, *Obras,* I, 158.
33. Trautmann, *Untersuchungen,* 48.
34. *Relación de Iguala,* 222.
35. Ixtlilxóchitl, *Obras,* I, 491.

Chapter X. The Third Claimant

1. O'Neill, "Preliminary report," 48–50.
2. Muñoz Camargo, *Historia,* 19.
3. Chimalpain, *Memorial Breve,* 84.
4. *Ibid.,* 92.
5. *Ibid.,* 48.
6. Ixtlilxóchitl, *Obras,* II, 57.
7. *Anales de Cuauhtitlán,* 36.
8. Chimalpain, *Relaciones,* 23.
9. *Anales de Cuauhtitlán,* 23.
10. Ixtlilxóchitl, *Obras,* II, 70.
11. Trautmann, *Untersuchungen,* 29.
12. *Anales de Cuauhtitlán,* 16.
13. *Ibid.,* 19.
14. Ixtlilxóchitl, *Obras,* II, 70.
15. *Anales de Tlatelolco,* 35.
16. *Relación de Coatepec Chalco,* 55–56.
17. Trautmann, *Untersuchungen,* 44.
18. Chimalpain, *Relaciones,* 187.
19. *Ibid.,* 139.

20. Davies, *Los Mexicas,* Appendix A, Table A.
21. Chimalpain, *Relaciones,* 160.
22. *Ibid.,* 136.
23. Durand Forest, "Los Grupos Nahuas."
24. *Anales de Cuauhtitlán,* 32.
25. Trautmann, *Untersuchungen,* 43.
26. *Anales de Cuauhtitlán,* 25.
27. *Ibid.,* 32.
28. Davies, *Los Mexicas,* Appendix A.
29. Tezozómoc, *Crónica Mexicayotl,* 148.
30. *Anales de Cuauhtitlán,* 36.
31. *Historia de los Mexicanos,* 229.
32. *Anales de Tlatelolco,* 53.
33. Chimalpain, *Die Relationen,* 80.
34. *Anales de Tlatelolco,* 16.
35. Codex Mexicanus, 448.
36. *Anales de Cuauhtitlán,* 33.

Chapter XI. The Disputed Heritage

1. Davies, *Los Mexicas,* chapter VIII.
2. Tezozómoc, *Crónica Mexicana,* 23.
3. Clavijero, *Historia antigua,* 78.
4. *Anales de Cuauhtitlán,* 184–85.
5. Ixtlilxóchitl, *Obras,* II, 104.
6. Torquemada, *Monarquía indiana,* I, 114.
7. Davies, *Los Mexicas,* chapter VII.
8. Chimalpain, *Relaciones,* 187.

9. Lehmann, *Die Geschichte,* 189.
10. *Anales de Cuauhtitlán,* 48.
11. Davies, *Los Mexicas,* Table A.
12. Codex en Cruz, 23–24.
13. *Anales de Tlatelolco,* 4.
14. Clavijero, *Historia antigua,* 78.
15. *Anales de Cuauhtitlán,* 36.
16. Ixtlilxóchitl, *Obras,* II, 67.
17. *Ibid.,* I, 146; II, 81.

18. Veytia, *Historia antigua,* I, 383.
19. Ixtlilxóchitl, *Obras,* I, 148–49.
20. Torquemada, *Monarquía indiana,* I, 108.
21. Ixtlilxóchitl, *Obras,* I, 153.
22. *Ibid.,* I, 158.
23. *Ibid.,* I, 158.
24. *Ibid.,* I, 159.
25. *Ibid.,* II, 88.
26. Davies, *Los Mexicas,* 135–37.
27. Ixtlilxóchitl, *Obras,* I, 185, 195.
28. Vetancurt, *Teatro mexicano,* I, 281.
29. Torquemada, *Monarquía indiana,* I, 114.
30. Davies, "The military organization."
31. *Anales de Cuauhtitlán,* 39–42.
32. Ixtlilxóchitl, *Obras,* II, 104–21.
33. *Ibid.,* I, 181.

34. Durán, *Historia,* II, 71.
35. Barlow, "Conquistas," 215.
36. Ixtlilxóchitl, *Obras,* I, 201.
37. Torquemada, *Monarquía indiana,* I, 119.
38. *Anales Mexicanos,* 50.
39. Tezozómoc, *Crónica Mexicayotl,* 104.
40. Ixtlilxóchitl, *Obras,* II, III.
41. Durán, *Historia,* II, 73.
42. Torquemada, *Monarquía indiana,* I, 131–32.
43. Durán, *Historia,* II, 79–80.
44. Ixtlilxóchitl, *Obras,* II, 145.
45. *Ibid.,* I, 201.
46. *Anales de Cuauhtitlán,* 45.
47. Veytia, *Historia antigua,* II, 126–27.
48. Davies, *Los Mexicas,* chapter VII.

Chapter XII. Civilization and Savagery

1. Lévi-Strauss, *Anthropologie Structurale,* 282.
2. Davies, *Voyagers to the New World,* chapter XI.
3. Broda, "Los estamentos."
4. Harner, "The enigma."
5. Davies, *The Aztecs,* 168–73.
6. Armillas, "Condiciones ambientales," 63.
7. *Ibid.,* 63.
8. Adams, *Evolution,* 158.
9. Roux, *Ancient Iraq,* 147.
10. Métraux, "The ethnography," 199.
11. Kirchhoff, "Civilizing the Chichimecs," 84.
12. Armillas, "Condiciones ambientales," 78–9.
13. McNetting, "The ecological approach."

14. Adams, *Evolution,* 60.
15. *Ibid.,* 58.
16. *Ibid.,* 58.
17. Needham, *Science and Civilization,* I, 100.
18. Brain, *"The last,"* 45.
19. Turnbull, *The Forest People.*
20. Davies, *The Aztecs,* 235.
21. Torquemada, *Monarquía indiana,* I, 185.
22. Carrasco and Broda, "Los estamentos".
23. Dyckerhoff and Prem, "La estratificación social," 27.
24. Carrasco, "Los Linajes," 27.
25. Carrasco, "La estratificación social."
26. Davies, "The military organization."
27. Adams, *Evolution,* 174–75.

Bibliography

Acosta Saignes, Miguel
1946 "Migraciones de los mexicas", *Memorias de la Academia Mexicana de la Historia,* Vol. V, No. 2, pp. 177–87. Mexico.

Adams, Robert McC.
1966 *The Evolution of Urban Society.* Aldine Publishing Company, Chicago.

Anales de Cuauhtitlán
1945 In *Códice Chimalpopoca.* Edited and translated by Primo F. Velásquez. Imprenta Universitaria, Mexico. *See also* Walter Lehmann, 1938.

Anales Mexicanos
1903 Mexico-Azcapotzalco (1426–1589), in *Anales del Museo Nacional de México, época* I, Vol. 7, Mexico, pp. 49–74.

Anales de Tlatelolco
1948 Edited and translated by Heinrich Berlin. Antigua Librería Robredo, Mexico.

Anales de Tula (1361–1521)
1949 In *Tlalocan,* Vol. III, No. I., pp. 2–14.

Anónimo Mexicano
1903 In *Anales del Museo Nacional de México, época* I, Vol. 7, pp. 115–32. Mexico.

Armillas, Pedro
1951 "Tecnología, formación socio-económica y religión in Mesoamérica," *Selected Papers of the XXIX International Congress of Americanists.* University of Chicago.
1964 "Condiciones ambientales y movimientos de pueblos en la frontera septen-

trional de Mesoamérica", in *Homenaje a Fernando Márquez Miranda.* Madrid.

Barlow, R.H.
1947 "Conquistas de los antiguos mexicanos," *Journal de la Société des Américanistes de Paris,* Vol. 36, pp. 215–222. Paris.
1948 "Un problema cronológico: la conquista de Cuauhtinchan por Tlatelolco," Memorias de la Academia Mexicana de la Historia, Vol. VII, No. 2, pp. 147–50. Mexico.
1949 "La fundación de la Triple Alianza", *Anales del Instituto Nacional de Antropología e Historia,* Vol. III, pp. 147–57. Mexico.
1949 "El códice Azcatitlan," in the *Journal de la Société des Américanistes de Paris,* Vol. XXXVIII, pp. 101–35. Paris.

Bernal, Ignacio
1959 *Tenochtitlán en una isla.* Mexico, Instituto Nacional de Antropología e Historia.

Brain, Robert
1976 *The Last Primitive Peoples.* Crown, New York.

Brinton, Daniel
1887 *Were the Toltecs an Historic Nationality?* McCatten, Philadelphia.

Broda, Johanna
1976 "Los estamentos en el ceremonial mexica," in *Estratificación social en la Mesoamérica prehispánica,* pp. 37–66. I.N.A.H., Mexico.

Carrasco Pizana, Pedro
1950 *Los otomíes. Publications* of the Institute of History, National University of Mexico, Mexico.
1976 "Los Linajes Nobles del México Antiguo," in *Estratificación social en la Mesoamérica prehispánica,* pp. 19–36. I.N.A.H., Mexico.

Caso, Alfonso
1966 "La época de los señoríos independientes," *Revista Mexicana de Estudios Antropológicos,* Vol. XX, pp. 147–53. Mexico.
1977 *Los calendarios prehispánicos.* Instituto de Investigaciones Históricas, U.N.A.M., Mexico.

Chimalpain
1958 *Das Memorial Breve acerca de la fundación de la ciudad de Culhuacán.* Translated by Walter Lehmann and Gerdt Kutscher. W. Kohlhammer Verlag, Stuttgart.
1963 *Die Relationen Chimalpains zur Geschichte Mexicos,* Teil I, *die Zeit bis zur Conquista.* Edited by Günter Zimmermann. Hamburg University, Hamburg.
1965 *Relaciones originales de Chalco-Amaquemecan.* Translated by Silvia Rendon. Fondo de Cultura Económica, Mexico.

Clavijero, Francisco Xavier
1964 *Historia antigua de México.* Editorial Porrua, Mexico.

Codex Aubin
1902 Oficina Tipológica de la Secretaría de Fomento, Mexico.
Codex Azcatitlan
1949 Société des Américanistes de Paris, Paris.
Codex Boturini, *see* Tira de la Peregrinación.
Codex en Cruz
1942 Edited by Charles E. Dibble. Mexico.
Codex Mexicanus 23–24.
1952 Commentary by Ernest Mengin, in *Société des Américanistes de Paris,* Vol. XLI, pp. 387–498. Paris.
Codex Telleriano-Remensis
1899 Edited by Le Duc de Lubat. Imprimeries Burdin, Paris.
Codex Vaticano-Ríos
1964 Edited by Viscount Kingsborough. Secretaría de Hacienda y Credito Público, Mexico.
Codex Xolotl
1951 Edited by Charles Dibble, Instituto de Historia, U.N.A.M., Mexico.
Crónica Mexicayotl
  See Tezozómoc, Hernando Alvarado.

Davies, Nigel
1968 *Los señoríos independientes del imperio azteca.* I.N.A.H., Mexico.
1972 "The military organization of the Aztec Empire," *Proceedings of the XL Congress of Americanists,* Vol IV, pp. 212–22. Rome.
1973 *Los mexicas: primeros pasos hacia el imperio.* Instituto de Investigaciones Historicas, U.N.A.M., Mexico.
1973 *The Aztecs.* Macmillan, London.
1974 "Tula, Reality, Myth, and Symbol," in *Proyecto,* Tula. No. 15, *Collección Científica,* I.N.A.H., Mexico.
1979 *Voyagers to the New World: Fact and Fantasy,* Morrow, New York.
1977 *The Toltecs: until the fall of Tula.* University of Oklahoma Press, Norman.
1976 "Mixcoatl, Man and God," *Proceedings of XLII Congress of Americanists,* Paris.
Del Castillo, Cristóbal.
1908 *Fragmentos sobre la obra general sobre historia de los Mexicanos.* S. Landi, Florence.
Descripción de Hueypochtla
1905–1906 In *Papeles de Nueva España,* Vol. III, pp. 47–49.
Durand Forest, Jaqueline de
1971 "Cambios económicos y moneda entre los Aztecas," *Estudios de Cultura Nahuatl,* Vol. 9, pp. 105–24. U.N.A.M., Mexico.
1974 "Los Grupos Nahuas y sus Divinidades Según Chimalpain," *Estudios de Cultura Nahuatl,* Vol XI, pp. 37–44. U.N.A.M., Mexico.

BIBLIOGRAPHY

Dykerhoff, Ursula, and Hanns Prem
1976 "La Estratificación social en Huexotzinco," In *Estratificación social en la Mesoamérica prehispánica,* pp. 157–77. I.N.A.H., Mexico.

Espejo, Antonieta
1944 "Algunas semejanzas entre Tenayuca y Tlatelolco," *Memorias de la Academia Mexicana de la Historia,* Vol. III, No. 4.
1947 *See under* J.B. Griffin.

Florentine Codex
See Fray Bernardino Sahagún, 1950–63.

Gamio, Manuel
1912 "Arqueología de Azcapotzalco," *Cuadernos Americanos,* Vol. XIII, pp. 180–87.
García Cook, Angel
1974 "Una Secuencia natural para Tlaxcala," in *Comunicaciones,* No. 10, pp. 5–22. Fundación Alemana para la Investigación Científica, Puebla.
1975 "Las fases Texcalac y Tlaxcala o Postclásico de Tlaxcala," in *XIII Round Table Conference,* Sociedad Mexicana de Antropología, Vol. I, pp. 127–70.
García Granados, Rafael
1952 *Diccionario Biográfico de Historia Antigua de México.* 3 vols. Instituto de Historia, Mexico.
Griffin, James B., and Antonieta Espejo
1947 "Alfarería correspondiente al último período de ocupación nahua del Valle de México," *Memorias de la Academia Mexicana de la Historia,* Vol. VI, pp. 131–47.

Harner, Michael
1977 "The Enigma of Aztec Sacrifice," *Natural History,* April 1977.
Historia de los Mexicanos por sus Pinturas
1941 In *Relaciones de Texcoco y de la Nueva España,* pp. 209–40. Editorial Chávez Hayhoe, Mexico.
Historia Tolteca-Chichimeca
1947 and 1952 Translated from Nahuatl into Spanish by Heinrich Berlin and Silvia Rendon. Prologue by Paul Kirchhoff. Antigue Librería Robredo, Mexico. New edition published by I.N.A.H., Mexico, 1976. References in the text are taken from the 1952 edition.
Histoyre du Mechique
1905 Edited by Eduard Yonghue. *Journal de la Société des Américanistes de Paris,* Vol. II, pp. 1–41.

Ixtlilxóchitl, Fernando de Alva
1952 *Obras históricas.* 2 vols. Editora Nacional, Mexico. (References in the

text are taken from the 1952 edition, in conformity with Vol. I of this work.)
1975 *Obras Históricas.* 2 vols. Edited by Edmundo O'Gorman. Universidad Nacional Autónoma de México.

Jiménez Moreno, Wigberto
1943 "La Colonización y evangelización de Guanajuato en el siglo XVL," in *El Norte de México y el Sur de Estados Unidos.* III Round Table Conference of the Sociedad Mexicana de Antropología, pp. 17–39.
1943 "Tribus e idiomas del Norte de México," in *El Norte de México y el Sur de Estados Unidos.* III Round Table Conference of the Sociedad Mexicana de Antropología, pp. 17–39.
1954–55 "Síntesis de la historia precolonial del Valle de México," R.M.E.A., Vol. XIV, No. 1, pp. 219–36.
1961 "Diferentes principios del año entre diversos pueblos y sus consecuencias para la cronología prehispánica," *México Antiguo,* Vol. IX, pp. 81–85.
Johnson, Paul
1972 *The Offshore Islanders.* Penguin, London.

Kirchhoff, Paul
1947 "Prologue to the Historia Tolteca-Chichimeca," in *Historia Tolteca-Chichimeca,* pp. XIX-LXIV. Antigua Librería Robredo, Mexico.
1955–56 "Calendarios tenochca, tlatelolca y otros," *R.M.E.A.,* Vol. XIV, No. 2, pp. 257–67.
1956–57 "Composición étnica y organización política de Chalco según las *Relaciones* de Chimalpain," *R.M.E.A.,* Vol. XIV, No. 2, pp. 297–99.
1963 "Dos tipos de relaciones entre pueblos en el México antiguo," *Homenaje a Pedro Bosch Gimpera.* Instituto Nacional de Antropología e Historia pp. 255–61. Mexico.
n.d. "Civilizing the Chichimecs: A Chapter in the Culture History of Ancient Mexico," *Latin American Studies* No. 5. University of Texas, Austin.

Las Casas, Bartolomé de
1965 *Tratados.* 2 vols. Fondo de Cultura Económica, Mexico.
Lehmann, Walter
1938 *Die Geschichte der Königreiche von Culhuacan und Mexico.* W. Kohlhammer Verlag, Stuttgart.
León-Portilla, Miguel
1967 "Los chichimecas de Xolotl y su proceso de aculturación," lecture No. 6 in the series *Historia Prehispánica.* Museo Nacional de Antropología, Mexico.
Lévi-Strauss, Claude
1958 *Anthropologie Structurale.* Paris.

McNetting, Robert
1971 *The Ecological Approach in Cultural Study.* Addison-Wesley Modular Publications, Module 6.

BIBLIOGRAPHY

Mapa Quinatzin
1886 In Anales del Museo Nacional de México, época I, vol. III, México, pp. 345–368.
Mapa Tlotzin
1886 In *Anales del Museo Nacional de México, Epoca* I, vol. III, pp. 304–320. Mexico.
Martínez Marín, Carlos
1954–55 "La migración acolhua del siglo XIII," *R.M.E.A.,* Vol. XIV, part I, pp. 377–79.
Mendieta, Fray Gerónimo de
1945 *Historia eclesiástica indiana.* 4 vols., Editorial Chávez Hayhoe, Mexico.
Métraux, Alfred
1944 "The Ethnography of the Chaco," in *Handbook of the South American Indians,* Vol. I, pp. 197–371. Smithsonian Institution, Washington D.C.
Motolinía, fray Toribio de Benavente
1941 *Historia de los indios de la Nueva España.* Editorial Chávez Hayhoe, Mexico.
1967 *Memoriales.* Published by Luis García Pimentel, reproduced in facsimile edition by Edmundo Aviña Levy, Guadalajara.
Muñoz Camargo, Diego
1947 *Historia de Tlaxcala.* Publicaciones del Ateneo de Ciencias y Artes de México.
Murra, John
1975 *Formaciones económicas y políticas del mundo Andino.* Instituto de Estudios Peruanos, Lima.

Needham, Sir Joseph
1954–74 *Science and Civilization in China.* 5 vols. Cambridge University Press.
Nicholson, Henry B.
1978 "Western Mesoamerican Native Historical Traditions and the Chronology of the Postclassic." Ed. by R. E. Taylor and Clement W. Meighan, *Chronologies in New World Archaeology,* Seminar Press, New York.
Noguera, Eduardo
1963 *La cerámica arqueológica de Mesoamérica.* Universidad Nacional Autónoma de México.
Noguera, Eduardo and Ramón Piña Chan
1956–57 "Estratigrafía de Teopanzolco," *R.M.E.A.,* Vol. XIV, No. 2, pp. 167–91.

O'Neill, George
1956–57 "Preliminary Report on Stratigraphic Excavation in the Southern Valley of Mexico: Chalco-Xico," *R.M.E.A.,* Vol. XIV, No. 2, pp. 45–51.
Origen de los Mexicanos
1941 In *Relaciones de Texcoco y de la Nueva España,* pp. 256–80. Editorial Salvador Chávez Hayhoe, Mexico.

Orozco y Berra, Manuel
1960 Historia antigua y de la conquista de México. 4 vols. Editorial Porrúa, Mexico.

Papeles de Nueva España
1905-1906 Edited by Francisco del Paso y Troncoso. Second series, 9 vols. Sucesores de Rivadeneyra, Madrid.
Piña Chan, Román
See Eduardo Noguera.
Pomar, Juan Batista
1941 Relaciones de Texcoco y de la Nueva España. Editorial Chávez Hayhoe, Mexico.
Prem, Hanns
See under Dyckerhoff and Prem.

Radin, Paul
1920 The Sources and Authenticity of the Ancient Mexicans. University of California Publications, Vol. 17, No. 1.
Relación de Coatepec Chalco
1905-1906 In Papeles de Nueva España, Vol. VI, pp. 41-55.
Relación de Iguala
1938 In M. Toussaint, Taxco. Mexico.
Relación de la Genealogíade los señores que han señoreado esta tierra de la Nueva España.
1941 in Relaciones de Texcoco y de la Nueva España, pp. 240-56. Editorial Chávez Hayhoe, Mexico.
Relación de Tecpatepec
1905-1906 In Papeles de Nueva España, vol. VI, pp. 34-38.
Relación de Temazcaltepec
1905-1906 In Papeles de Nueva España, Vol. VII, pp. 15-29.

Sahagún, Fray Bernardino de
1956 Historia general de las cosas de Nueva España. 4 vols. Editorial Porrua, Mexico.
1950-63 Florentine Codex. General History of the Things of New Spain. Translated from Nahuatl into English by Charles E. Dibble and Arthur J. O. Anderson. 11 vols. The school of American Research and the University of Utah, Santa Fe, New Mexico.
Saravia, Anastasio G.
1944 "La Nueva Vizcaya, Durango Oriental," in El Norte de México y el Sur de Estados Unidos, III Round Table Conference of the Sociedad Mexicana de Antropología, pp. 52-82.
Schmidt, Peter J.
1975 "El Postclásico en la Región de Huejotzingo, Puebla," in Comunicaciones No. 12. Fundación Alemana para la Investigación Científica, Puebla.

BIBLIOGRAPHY

Seler, Eduard
1960 *Gesammelte Abhandlungen zur Amerikanischen Sprach-und Altertums-kunde.* 5 vols. Akademische Druckanstalt, Graz.
1963 *Codex Borgia,* with commentary by Eduard Seler. 3 vols. Fondo de Cultura Económica, Mexico.
Soustelle, Jacques
1937 *La famille Otomí-Pame du Mexique Central.* Institut d'Ethnologie, Paris.
Swadesh, M.
1954–55 "Algunas fechas glotocronológicas importantes para la prehistoria nahua," 55 *R.M.E.A.,* Vol. XIV, No. I, pp. 173–92.

Tezozómoc, Hernando Alvarado
1944 *Crónica mexicana.* Editorial Leyenda, Mexico
1949 *Crónica Mexicayotl.* Instituto de Historia, U.N.A.M., Mexico.
Thompson, J. Eric S.
1970 *Maya History and Religion.* University of Oklahoma Press, Norman.
Tira de la Peregrinación
1944 (Codex Boturini), Librería Anticuaria, Mexico.
Torquemada, fray Juan de
1943–44 *Monarquía indiana.* 3 vols. Editorial S. Chávez Hayhoe, Mexico.
Trautmann, Wolfgang
1968 *Untersuchungen zur Indianischen Siedlungs-und-Teritorialgeschichte im Becken von Mexico biz zur Frühen Kolonialzeit.* Selbstverlag des Hamburgischen Museum für Völkerkunde und Vorgeschischte, Hamburg.
Turnbull, Colin
1976 *The Forest People.* Pan Books, London.

Vetancurt, Agustín de
1780 *Teatro mexicano,* 4 vols. Imprenta de I. Escalante y Compañía, Mexico.
Veytia, Mariano
1944 *Historia antigua de México.* 2 vols. Editorial Leyenda, Mexico.

Zantwijk, Rudolf van
1966 "Los seis barrios sirvientes de Huitzilopochtli", *Estudios de Cultura Nahuatl,* Vol. VI, pp. 177–87.
1975 "La organización social de la México-Tenochtitlán naciente," *XLI International Congress of Americanists,* vol. 2, pp. 188–208. Mexico.
Zaragoza Ocaña, Diana
1977 *Procesos de desarollo en el area de Cuauhtinchan-Tepeaca.* Escuela Nacional de Antropología e Historia, Mexico.
Zuidema, R. Tom
1965 "Reseña de Brundage 1963," *American Anthropologist,* Vol. 68, pp. 231–32.

Index

389

"Cucutliqueci": 184
Cuechteca-Ichocayan: 43
Cuecuex: 139ff., 148
Cuernavaca: 27
Cuetlachcihuatl: 93
Cuetlachcihuatzin: 94, 154; see also Cuetlachxochitl
Cuetlachxochitl: 65, 94; see also Cuetlachcihuatzin
Cuetlachxochitzin: 45, 51, 60, 93, 147
Cuexconpixque (Cuezconpiaia): 280 ff.
Cuextecatl Ichocayan: 179
Cuextecatl Ixocayan: 179
Cuicateca: 7
Cuitlachtepec: 64, 66, 147
Cuitlahuac (Cuitlahuacas): 23, 27, 117, 122, 127, 136f., 145, 175, 189f., 225f., 251ff., 261, 271, 277, 296
Cuitlahua calendar: 267, 279, 300ff.
Cuitlatelco: 257
Cuitlatetelco: 271
Cuixtecatlycaca: 179
Culhua: 9, 23f., 30f., 41f., 86
Culhuacán: 11, 70, 87, 89, 92f., 116, 130f., 141ff., 151ff., 158, 162, 178, 184, 187f., 196, 206, 208, 227, 252, 294, 296, 345; history of, 23–41; rulers of, 31–41, 44, 53, 62–68 passim, 120–29 passim, 132, 183, 190, 199, 205, 207, 232, 315, 347–72; fall of, 218–25 passim, 245; and Cuauhtitlán, 238ff.; pottery in, 249; importance of, 338–39; chart of rulers of, 360–61; see also Teoculhuacán
Culhuas: 25, 38f., 95, 129f., 136ff., 142f., 150, 169, 178, 188f., 206f., 337
Culhuatecuhtlicuanex: 167
Culhua-Texcoco (year count): 35ff., 235–37, 255, 265ff., 279, 282ff., 292, 339, 350f., 366, 369ff.

Eagle: 192–93
Ecatepec: 115, 178, 243
Epcoatl: 37, 198, 234ff., 292
Eztloquencatzin: 238

Florentíne Codex: 3, 75

Guachilcos: 83
Guamares: 75, 83ff., 325
Guanajuato: 24, 74, 79, 83
Guatemala (Guatemalans): 7, 77
Guerrero: 241, 243f.
Gulf Coast: 7, 9, 78f., 159, 165

Hill of Culiacán: 24
Historia de los Mexicanos: 25, 38, 76, 92, 137f., 140, 149, 152, 165, 179, 184, 198, 201, 221, 225ff., 280, 367f.
Historia Tolteca-Chichimeca: 4, 6, 50, 69, 76, 90ff., 116f., 135, 160–74 passim, 228, 272
Histoyre du Mechique: 7, 119
Huactli: 231
Huactzin: 205, 231ff., 238f., 278
Hualteomama: 272
Huaquechula: 7
Huaxtecs (Huaxteca): 5, 45, 77f., 169, 254
Huaxtepec: 127, 255
Huehue Acamapichtli: 35f., 38f., 198, 221, 367–71 passim, see also Acamapichtli
Huehue Ixtlilxóchitl: 67f., 96, 123, 131, 133, 172, 244f., 282, 292ff., 304, 352; see also Ixtlilxóchitl
Huehuequauhquechollan: 170
Huehue Quinatzin: 230f., 233, 238; see also Quinatzin
Huehuetecos: 171
Huehuetocan: 172, 234, 236
Huehuetzin: 175
Huemac: 4, 135
Huepoxtla: 243
Huetlapallan: 272, 274
Huetlapalli: 165
Huetzin: 28ff., 38, 40, 45–66 passim, 86, 95f., 120ff., 144, 152, 154f., 159, 205, 293, 315, 338, 351, 365f.
Huetzintecuhtli: 148
Huexotla: 43, 46, 49, 51, 64, 66, 94, 96, 115–30 passim, 143, 155, 288f., 295, 297, 303
Huexotzincas: 136f.
Huexotzingo (Huexotzingans): 45, 117, 121, 153, 159, 162ff., 178, 249f., 282f., 285, 289, 313ff.

INDEX

Meconetl: 54; *see also* Topiltzin Quetzalcoatl

Memorial Breve: 23–38 *passim,* 50–64 *passim,* 93, 116, 119, 126, 132, 135, 143–48 *passim,* 249ff., 262–73 *passim,* 315, 347–58 *passim,* 363ff.; *see also* Chimalpain

Memorial de los Pueblos sujetos a Tlacopan: 139, 241f.

Metztitlán: 46f., 96, 121, 124, 131, 144, 146, 155, 159, 234, 340

Mexi: 181

Mexicaltzingo: 254

Mexicas: 7, 12, 15, 19, 24, 70, 86, 97, 129, 143, 145, 177, 181, 192f., 227, 252, 274f.; and Tepanecs, 10f., 28, 31, 38, 41, 119, 123, 128, 130f., 137f., 142, 150, 152f., 175, 201, 220, 226, 229, 234, 245, 248f., 256, 277, 281f., 287–316; in Chapultepec, 11, 39, 54, 151, 182f., 186–89, 236, 265, 347; migration of, 20, 25–26, 43, 115, 142, 177ff., 190, 254; in Culhuacán, 28, 31, 38, 41, 122, 125, 130ff., 151f., 183, 189–90, 218–24 *passim,* 265; founders of Tenochtitlán, 31, 127, 191f.; "Chichimecs," 76–77, 79, 137, 337; and Chalco, 128, 152, 176, 239, 248ff., 256, 277f., 280ff., 340; founders of Tlatelolco, 194ff.; dynasties of, 196–201; origins of, 202–209; and Cuauhtitlán, 230f., 237; and Xaltocán, 234f., 240; and Texcocans, 311–16

Mexicanization: 130f.

Mexitin: 206

Mexitli: 193

Mezquital valley: 241

Miahuaxochtzin, Doña María: 8

Miahyatotocihuatzin: 51

Miccacalcatl: 171

Michoaca-Chichimecs: 44–45

Michoacán: 44, 84, 88, 95, 117, 119, 137, 244, 323

Michoaque: 137

Michuacán: 77, 263

Michuaques (Mihuaques): 77, 95, 137, 263, 269, 271, 273, 276

Mimich: 179

Mimixcoas: 180

Mitl: 50, 154; *see also* Iztacmitl

Mitliztac: 43

Mixcoamazatzin: 116

Mixcoatl (Camaxtli, Citecatl, Cuacuapitzahuac, Iztaccaltzin, Iztacmixcoatl, Mazatzin, Mecitin, Totepeuh): 27, 30, 54, 76, 87, 91–95, 97, 116, 119, 139–41, 154, 161, 165, 168, 177, 179f., 188, 198, 239, 272, 339

Mixteca (Mixtecs): 7f., 77, 129, 137, 159, 169

Mizquiahuala: 43

Mizquic (Mizquicas): 23, 27, 122, 127f., 136, 189f., 225, 252f., 277, 296

Moceloquichtli: 49, 93

Moctezuma: 181, 313f.

Moctezuma, Don Pedro: 8

Moctezuma I (Moctezuma Ilhuicamina): 21, 25, 67, 128, 172, 176, 282, 285, 309; *see also* Ilhuicamina

Moctezuma II: 8, 33, 352

Mollanco (Molango): 271

Moquihuix: 90f., 162

Morelos: 10, 157, 243, 245, 254f.; *see also* Valley of Morelos

Motezumatzin: 61

Mozxomatzin: 125ff.

Muñoz Camargo: 272

Nacaxoch: 54; *see also* Topiltzin Quetzalcoatl

Nacxitl: 54; *see also* Topiltzin Quetzalcoatl

Nahuas: 5, 137, 155f., 205f., 209

Nahuatecuhtli: 271

Nahuatization: 124, 129f., 143

Nahuatl (language): 7ff., 47, 74, 78, 95f., 115, 138, 168

Nahuatlato: 162

Nauhyotecuhtli: 251, 271

Nauhyotl: 28f., 44, 52, 62f., 89, 205, 372

Nauhyotzin: 28f., 40f., 44, 48, 62, 116, 198, 224, 364–72 *passim*

Nazareo, Don Pablo: 225, 227, 231, 240ff.